Virginia Woolf and Trauma

EMBODIED TEXTS

Also Published by Pace University Press

Woolf Across Cultures
Ed. Natalya Reinhold

Woolf Studies Annual
Ed. Mark Hussey

Virginia Woolf and Communities
Ed. Jeanette McVicker and Laura Davis

Virginia Woolf: Turning the Centuries
Ed. Ann Ardis and Bonnie Kime Scott

Virginia Woolf: Out Of Bounds
Ed. Jessica Berman and Jane Goldman

Virginia Woolf and Trauma

EMBODIED TEXTS

Edited By

Suzette Henke and David Eberly

with the assistance of Jane Lilienfeld

PACE UNIVERSITY PRESS • NEW YORK

ISBN 0-944473-79-2

Library of Congress Cataloging-in-Publication Data

Virginia Woolf and trauma : embodied texts / edited by Suzette
Henke and David Eberly.
   p. cm.
Includes bibliographical references and index.
ISBN 0-944473-79-2
1. Woolf, Virginia, 1882-1941--Psychology. 2. Psychic trauma in
literature. I. Henke, Suzette A. II. Eberly, David.
PR6045.O72Z89243 2007
823'.912--dc22
             2006038012

CONTENTS

vi

ABBREVIATIONS OF WORKS BY VIRGINIA WOOLF

AROO	*A Room of One's Own*
BA	*Between the Acts*
CDB	*The Captain's Death Bed and Other Essays*
CE	*Collected Essays (4 vols.)*
CR1	*The Common Reader*
CSF	*The Complete Shorter Fiction*
D	*The Diary of Virginia Woolf (5 vols.)*
DM	*The Death of the Moth and Other Essays*
GR	*Granite & Rainbow: Essays*
JR	*Jacob's Room*
L	*The Letters of Virginia Woolf (6 vols.)*
M	*The Moment and Other Essays*
MOB	*Moments of Being*
MD	*Mrs. Dalloway*
P	*The Pargiters*
PA	*A Passionate Apprentice*
TG	*Three Guineas*
TTL	*To the Lighthouse*
TYH	*The Years* Holograph
VO	*The Voyage Out*
W	*The Waves*
WD	*A Writer's Diary*
WH	*The Waves: The Two Holograph Drafts*
Y	*The Years*

ACKNOWLEDGMENTS

This collection would not have appeared without the inspiration and assistance of Jane Lilienfeld. Encouraged by the renewed vigor of scholarship about the effects of trauma on the life and work of Virginia Woolf that characterized the 1999 International Woolf Conference at the University of Delaware, Jane, together with David Eberly, issued a call for essays. Toni McNaron responded with an updated version of her now classic essay, "The Uneasy Solace of Art," originally published in *Women's Studies: An International Forum* 15.2 (1992). Patricia Cramer offered her astute support, together with a promise to write a chapter, as did Patricia Moran. Suzette Henke submitted a nascent version of her essay on *The Waves*. When, in the spring of 2003, Jane felt it necessary to withdraw as editor, Suzette stepped forward in the role of new co-editor.

Reconfiguring the anthology, we invited a number of Woolf scholars to contribute to the volume. Karen DeMeester built on her provocative piece, "Trauma and Recovery in Virginia Woolf's *Mrs. Dalloway*," which had first appeared in *Modern Fiction Studies* 44.3 (1998). Claire Kahane, Holly Laird, and Clifford Wulfman all submitted critical essays original to the project. Since its inception at the millennium, this collection on Woolf and trauma has been substantially revised and expanded. The co-editors wish sincerely to thank our contributors for their enduring patience and commitment throughout this long, sometimes arduous, process.

We are both enormously grateful to Mark Hussey for his unflagging support and superb editorial recommendations. His expertise and efficiency have been invaluable at every stage. Many thanks to Karen Alexander, Linda Torok, and Mark Fasano for their help with research and copyediting. Suzette Henke would like to acknowledge the Thruston B. Morton, Sr. Endowment at the University of Louisville and to thank Professor Blaine Hudson, Dean of the College of Arts and Sciences, and Dr. Susan Griffin, Chair of the English Department, for a 2004-05 sabbatical leave. As always, Suzette owes a debt of gratitude to her husband, James Francis Rooney, whose patience and gentle humor add joy to the journey. David Eberly would like to express his appreciation to the many "Woolfians" who so warmly welcomed him as he set out on what has become a lengthening path of independent scholarship. We both trust that this collaborative effort will help reshape the critical understanding of Woolf's work, while honoring her genius and her art.

INTRODUCTION
David Eberly and Suzette Henke

Writing more than a decade after Virginia Woolf's suicide in 1941, Leonard Woolf contended that his wife's selected diary entries would offer her readers "an unusual psychological picture of artistic production from within" (*WD* ix). Ever since the appearance of *A Writer's Diary* in 1954, the public reception of Woolf's writing has been characterized by a dual discourse of interpretive analysis in response to the challenges presented by her work. Discussion of her contribution to the modernist canon has been accompanied by critical speculation about her mental health, mingling scholarly assessment of Woolf's literary achievement with intense scrutiny of her psychological stability. Her readers—both common and academic—have continued to inquire about polarized possibilities of madness or sanity. Critics struggle to resurrect an intact biographical subject from Woolf's letters, diaries, notebooks, novels, and polemical prose, even as they consider the aesthetic impact of private experience transformed into fiction.

The contributors to this volume collectively propose that a haunting, if sometimes repressed trauma narrative can be found embodied throughout Woolf's texts, which repeat and reflect her traumatic experiences over a lifetime of literary production. These experiences encompass a daunting catalogue of traumas, including the deaths of her mother, her half-sister Stella, and her elder brother Thoby; the disturbing mental illness of her half-sister Laura; and sexual abuse by Gerald and George Duckworth, her two half-brothers. Far from being the stereotypical haven of nurturance that the Victorian household has been presumed to be, the Stephen family was, in the words of Louise DeSalvo, "a family in nearly a perpetual state of crisis and instability" (*Impact* 19). To these traumatic experiences should be added repeated episodes of psychological affliction, which would haunt Woolf until her suicide; the impact of medical regimens that she endured as a powerless adolescent and young woman; and the national trauma of two world wars, unprecedented in their carnage.

All the authors in this collection take Woolf at her word and refer to the specificity of the descriptions of sexual abuse found in her memoirs, grounding their interpretations in the context of her autobiographical testimony. In "A Sketch of the Past," Woolf records a graphic instance of abuse when she was five or six years old: her half-brother Gerald lifted her onto a "slab outside the dining room door" and "began to explore [her] body." "I can remember," she writes, "the feel of his hand going under my clothes. . . how I stiffened and wriggled as his hand approached my private parts. . . . [W]hat is the word for so dumb and mixed a feeling?" (*MOB* 69). Shortly thereafter, she describes what might be considered post-traumatic flashbacks in the form of nocturnal hauntings by the face of a savage animal leering at her from a looking-glass. Examining this traumatic memory, Woolf rationalizes its impact and hypothesizes that it was her acute sensitivity, and her "shock-receiving" capacity, that spurred her to become a writer. "I feel that I have had a blow . . . and I make it real by putting it into words" (*MOB* 72). Reformulating traumatic memories by virtue of what now might be called *scriptotherapy*, she can exorcise their debilitating intrusions. "It is only by putting it [trauma] into words that I make it whole," she proclaims, concluding that in the act of writing, the psychological wound "has lost its power to hurt me" (*MOB* 72).[1]

Woolf's half-brother George Duckworth continued the pattern of abuse during what she would later describe as the "Greek slave years" of her adolescence (*MOB* 106). In her memoir "22 Hyde Park Gate," which preceded the "Sketch" by twenty years, Woolf reveals how she and her sister Vanessa were coerced by George into attending high society balls and tedious parties. After returning home, Virginia would suffer his repeated assaults. Invading her bedroom like a lover, George would subject his half-sister to a volley of kisses, cuddlings, and other inappropriate expressions of affection. Like any perpetrator, he would admonish her "not to be frightened" before he "flung himself on [her] bed, and took [her] in his arms" (*MOB* 177). "Everything," Woolf writes, "was drowned in kisses," giving poignant voice to the feelings of a fragile adolescent girl overwhelmed by the adult emotional and sexual demands of an incestuous relative. "One felt like an unfortunate minnow shut up with an unwieldy and turbulent whale" (*MOB* 169). At the conclusion of "22 Hyde Park Gate," Virginia remarks acerbically that "the old ladies of Kensington and Belgravia never knew that George Duckworth was not only father and mother, brother and sister to those poor Stephen girls; he was their lover also" (*MOB* 177).

Although Woolf herself was quite specific in describing incidents of sexual abuse in both memoirs, her testimony about incest trauma has not gone unquestioned by some literary critics and biographers. Mitchell Leaska, for instance, casts doubt on Woolf's memory of her molestation in "Sketch" and suggests in his introduction to *A Passionate Apprentice* that "her perception of the Duckworth brothers in 1939, when she began writing her memoir, does not seem to coincide with her record of them in this earliest of her journals" (*PA* xxxv). Speculating that Rose Pargiter's sexual trauma in *The Years* was the result not of the flashing she witnessed but of the "strong attachment" she had for her father Abel, Leaska concludes: "It is not only possible but highly probable that a similar transformation took hold in Virginia's *adult* imagination" (*PA* xxxv). He comes perilously close to declaring Woolf's memoir, which contains her most specific charges against her half-brothers, to be a projection of sexual fantasy. In arguing that the "Sketch" is a work of fiction, Leaska denies its status as Woolf's truthful account of her abuse, written with care and craft.

Because of its dual nature as both literary text and factual testimony, "A Sketch of the Past" has become a locus for the same controversy and denial that has characterized many contemporary accounts of childhood sexual abuse. As Sue Campbell notes, "Undermining survivor testimonio has been made easier by the vulnerable position of such narrative in the first place" (63). Many of the vulnerabilities that Campbell enumerates are familiar to those who have sought to increase public awareness of childhood sexual abuse. The harms done to its (generally) female narrators are inflicted in private, and therefore unverifiable. White, middle-class, and privileged, these speakers are often held to be susceptible to false memories and described as self-indulgent, with "little moral sense of what constitutes real suffering" (63). Hermione Lee, in a complex assessment of Woolf's relationship to her half-brothers, writes that "*whatever the facts* [italics ours], they were turned into jokes," thus questioning the explicit account offered by Woolf in her memoir. To suggest, as Lee does, that the evidence is both "strong" and "ambiguous" and that "what matters most in this story is what Virginia Woolf made out of what happened" is to minimize Woolf's testimony as an abuse survivor and to challenge her insistence in "Sketch" that Gerald's abuse in the "incident of the looking-glass . . . happened to me personally; and I have no motive for lying about it" (*MOB* 69). Describing a feeling of physical

3

dissociation indicative of post-traumatic stress disorder, Woolf explains that the looking-glass aversion "did not prevent me from feeling ecstasies and raptures spontaneously and intensely and without any shame or the least sense of guilt, so long as they were disconnected with my own body. . . . I must have been ashamed or afraid of my own body" (*MOB* 68).

Added to Woolf's sexual molestations was a series of personal losses that a highly sensitive adolescent must surely have experienced as unendurable. How can one calculate the impact of a mother's death on an impressionable girl of thirteen? Consider Virginia's account, in "A Sketch of the Past," of the shock experienced on the morning of May 5, 1895, when the Stephen children were invited to view the still-warm corpse of their deceased mother Julia. "I remember very clearly," she tells us, "how even as I was taken to the bedside I noticed that one nurse was sobbing, and a desire to laugh came over me, and I said to myself, . . . 'I feel nothing whatever.' Then I stooped and kissed my mother's face" (*MOB* 92). The young Virginia, suffering from the profound shock of parental loss, may well be exhibiting symptoms of the kind of psychic numbing and emotional anesthesia now associated with post-traumatic stress disorder (PTSD). Other defining moments of bereavement would further disrupt Virginia's adolescence and early adulthood: the death of her half-sister Stella Duckworth after Stella's marriage to Jack Hills; the death of her father, Leslie Stephen, from cancer in 1904; and two years later, the precipitous loss, from typhoid, of her beloved brother Thoby, the model for Jacob Flanders in *Jacob's Room* and for Percival in *The Waves*.

In his 1978 path-breaking study, *The Unknown Virginia Woolf*, Roger Poole interpreted these traumatic episodes of Woolf's life through phenomenological insights gleaned from Merleau-Ponty's notion of the "embodied subject," as well as from R. D. Laing's theories about ontological insecurity.[2] Poole challenges the use of terms like "madness" and "lunacy" scattered throughout Leonard Woolf's *Autobiography*, Quentin Bell's biography, and the diaries and letters edited by Nigel Nicolson, Joanne Trautmann, and Anne Olivier Bell. Writing against the grain of received opinion, he perspicaciously attributes the "crude and offensive" language of lunacy to Stephen family lore. Applying an empathic phenomenological method of perspectival re-creation to understanding the traumatic episodes that so affected Woolf's creative consciousness, Poole concludes that Virginia's experience of mental distress and her so-called breakdowns, as well as their psychological impact, should be interpreted in the context of what would now be identified as post-traumatic stress disorder. Her major novels, he insists, "were written to master people and states of mind and states of embodiment that [had] previously mastered her" (3). Like the contributors to this volume, Poole takes for granted a phenomenological integration of Woolf's life experience and her artistic development. He suggests that her identity as a writer is inflected with her emotional responses to memories of pain, bereavement, shock, and sexual abuse. Although he does not invoke trauma theory as such, Poole implies that Woolf, throughout her life, made use of fiction as a means of re-scripting and mastering traumatic experiences by means of a therapeutic process of narrative reformulation.

In 1989, Louise DeSalvo's publication of *Virginia Woolf: The Impact of Childhood Sexual Abuse on Her Life and Work* dramatically shifted critical characterizations of Woolf as an historical subject. DeSalvo, drawing extensively on the work of psychologists like Judith Herman and Alice Miller, argues that the symptoms of Woolf's illness and mental distress can best be explained by the incestuous abuse perpetrated by her half-brothers. According to DeSalvo, Woolf "wrote about her sexual abuse in order to understand why it happened and how it affected her. She wrote about it in her fiction, in her essays; she wrote about it in her memoirs and in her letters. . . . She left, at her death, diaries, memoirs, letters, notebooks, notes, which document the trauma she endured as a child and how she coped with it, reacted to it, and understood it" (13). Like DeSalvo and Poole, contributors to this volume ground their literary interpretations in the premise that Woolf's artistic oeuvre was profoundly affected and shaped by the consequences of the trauma she endured.[3]

Critical awareness of the impact of multiple traumas on Virginia Woolf's art has continued to gain clearer focus in the last two decades. One of the most important of these areas to receive greater scrutiny has been the impact of World War I on Woolf and her generation.[4] (Here we might be reminded that Woolf's two most extreme mental breakdowns occurred in 1915 and in 1941 in the midst of two world wars.) Physicians in the early twentieth century were well acquainted with the symptoms of hysteria whose etiology, as Elaine Showalter has illustrated in *The Female Malady,* seemed at the time mysteriously allied with the influence of the womb and ovaries on woman's mental stability. Only with the eruption of similar symptoms in males fighting on the front during World War I were nerve specialists like Charles S. Myers and W. H. R. Rivers able to diagnose the effects of combat neurosis or "shell shock" on a ravaged military population. As Showalter points out, "shell shock" was an implicitly gendered concept, "related to social expectations of the masculine role in war." Men who chose "alternatives to combat—pacifism, conscientious objection, desertion, even suicide—were viewed as unmanly . . . and forced, like women, to express their conflicts through the body" (171). It is not surprising, then, that the *DSM-IV* includes both the effects of military combat and the repercussions of sexual assault in its recent definition of post-traumatic stress disorder, and that "developmentally inappropriate sexual experience" is categorized as a trauma similar, in potential harm, to the shock of witnessing "the serious injury or unnatural death of another" (*DSM-IV* 464). Several authors in this collection focus on the aesthetic and psychological ramifications of Woolf's dual position as a (female) survivor of incest and a vulnerable noncombatant in a nation at war. As Claire Kahane observes in her essay on "Snakes, Toads, and Duckweed," for Woolf, the perils of war clearly commingled with memories of traumatic sexual violation.

Hermione Lee tells us that once the Hogarth Press agreed to publish Sigmund Freud's papers in the early 1920's, his theories "became one of the dominant topics of Bloomsbury. . . . In her letters to Jacques Raverat, psychoanalysis featured as something Virginia was holding at bay, though the language of her confessions to him was influenced by what she was hearing of Freud" (*Virginia* 465). With a psychologically informed awareness of postwar trauma, Woolf sought to depict, in the character of Septimus Smith, a World War I veteran suffering the effects of post-traumatic stress disorder. Like Freud, Woolf "linked her personal history to world history, as she linked Septimus's madness to the 'cataclysms' of war" (Lee, *Virginia* 459). According to Lee, Smith's figure combines Woolf's own autobiographical trauma with her observations of the postwar malaise suffered by friends like Ralph Partridge and Gerald Brenan. "[T]ogether, these young men out of the war, with their disturbingly intense emotional lives and their uncertainty about the future, seemed to her to represent the postwar trauma of a whole generation" (Lee, *Virginia* 459).[5]

Freud's association of traumatic symptoms with female hysteria and male combat neurosis paved the way for later psychiatric acknowledgements of post-traumatic stress disorder as a real illness affecting countless men and women in quotidian situations. Judith Herman observes in *Trauma and Recovery* that it was only in the 1970's, with the dawn of the women's movement, that therapists "recognized that the most common post-traumatic disorders are those not of men in war but of women in civilian life" (28). As several contributors to this volume argue, Woolf seems intuitively to have grasped a connection between her own experience of mental anguish and the post-traumatic stress disorder associated with combat neurosis. The effects of heightened mental and emotional states evinced by her periodic "breakdowns" enabled her to create an astonishingly accurate portrait of the shellshocked Septimus Smith in *Mrs. Dalloway.*

Echoing Herman's comment on the growing understanding of the pervasive presence of trauma in the lives of women, Bessel van der Kolk has noted that "[t]he rediscovery of trauma as an etiological factor in mental disorders is only about 20 years old" (*Healing Trauma* 189). During these last two decades, our knowledge of the nature and impact of trauma has continued to grow. First, the biology of post-traumatic stress disorder is better understood and its complex impact on the victim more deeply comprehended. "Modern research," writes van der Kolk, "has come to elucidate the degree to which PTSD is, indeed, a 'physioneurosis,' a mental disorder based on the persistence of biological emergency responses" (*Healing Trauma* 177). Trauma, he continues, "seems to affect people over a wide range of biological functioning, involving a large variety of brain structures and neurotransmitter systems" (*Healing Trauma* 178). In response to the shock of trauma, the brain's ability to integrate experience falls apart. The consequences of this breakdown are physical as well as mental, affecting not only basic biological responses, but also the psychological processes upon which our sense of personal identity is established. As with other mental illnesses, the impact of PTSD on the brain is now more fully comprehended through a technology that facilitates the imaging of brain activity, as well as through chemical studies of neuro-hormonal levels. Recently developed techniques have enabled psychiatrists to chart the biology of PTSD symptoms, narrowing the gap in trauma studies between physical and psychological etiologies.

The American Psychiatric Association, in the fourth edition of its *Diagnostic and Statistical Manual of Mental Disorders*, delineates the following symptoms characteristic of post-traumatic stress disorder: "recurrent and intrusive recollections of the [traumatic] event, . . .

7

'psychic numbing' or 'emotional anesthesia,'" and a sense of alienation characterized by a "markedly reduced ability to feel emotions" (*DSM-IV* 424-25). Further effects associated with interpersonal stress disorders include "self-destructive and impulsive behavior; dissociative symptoms; somatic complaints; feelings of ineffectiveness, shame, despair, or hopelessness; . . . hostility; social withdrawal" (425). As Judith Herman explains, traumatic events "shatter the construction of the self that is formed and sustained in relation to others" and "cast the victim into a state of existential crisis" (51). This kind of ontological anxiety is clearly evident throughout Woolf's literary canon, as is the melancholic response that Kay Redfield Jamison, in *Touched with Fire*, associates with metaphysical inquiry in the face of human mortality. A lifelong atheist, Woolf once confided to E. M. Forster that her so-called bouts of madness had served in lieu of religious belief to provide her with creative inspiration through semi-mystical visions of transcendence (*L2*: 499). Woolf evidently ascribed a positive, visionary, and redemptive value to the periods of psychic dissociation that defied accurate or conclusive diagnosis during her lifetime, and that might have provided a major inspiration for her desire to reformulate auto/biographical trauma into healing and integrated narratives.

The essays collected in this volume display a wide range of theoretical, clinical, and social directions in the field of trauma studies that bring together knowledge of the kind of medical and clinical diagnosis of trauma found in the *DSM-IV* with wider psychological and social concerns. Building on the foundational theories of Sigmund Freud and Sandor Ferenczi, the contributors also make use of publications by a number of more recent theorists and clinicians. Far from speaking with a single voice, they sometimes reach different conclusions about the implications of contemporary research in the field of trauma studies. Yet all share similar convictions about the influence of trauma on Woolf's creative production and posit a phenomenological link between her life experience and artistic oeuvre. These essays are grounded in the understanding that literary texts reflect, in some way, the author's own historically embodied consciousness. The writer's experiential horizons may be directly represented, sublimated, parodied, or inverted in a work of art. But whatever the history of an authorial subject, residues of personal biography subtly inform the fictional texts that the writer imagines and artistically (re)constructs. All literary production replicates, in the form

8

of textual embodiment, historical experiences annealed on the psyche, memory, and imagination of the writer who often reformulates personal trauma, either consciously or inadvertently, into narratives of life writing or fiction.

As Daniel Ferrer insists in *Virginia Woolf and the Madness of Language*, "there *is* a link between printed words and their writer's life and death"—a connection that Woolf herself corroborates in an essay on "Craftsmanship" (Ferrer 4). Setting herself in opposition to the "new criticism" configured in Percy Lubbock's formalist treatise on *The Craft of Fiction*, Woolf "reintroduces the writer and thereby the unconscious which the whole system was set up to deny. What appeared to be an impregnable position of control is gently circumvented; beyond the suture, the [traumatic] wound is reopened" (Ferrer 3). According to Ferrer, Woolf "refuses to separate the product from the producer. 'It is the custom to draw a distinction between a man and his works and, . . . although the world has a claim to read every line of his writing, it must not ask questions about the author' (*CE3*:86), she says, but maintains that such a distinction has no basis. . . . And how could it be possible, in Virginia Woolf's case, to separate the text and what is outside it, the writing and the life?" (6).

In her essay "Trauma and Lesbian Returns in Virginia Woolf's *The Voyage Out* and *The Years*," Patricia Cramer combines current trauma theory, especially work verifying the responses of incest survivors, with Woolf's own experience of childhood sexual abuse and its later incorporation into her fiction. Enlarging on Woolf's detailed and nuanced account of the abuse perpetrated by her two half-brothers, Cramer establishes the foundation for a close reading of Woolf's fiction as a therapeutic reformulation of sexual trauma. Cramer traces a clear trajectory from early trauma-inflected scenes depicted in *The Voyage Out* to more mature representations of healing and recovery in *The Years*. She analyzes *The Voyage Out* as a text marked by graphic traces of Woolf's abuse and identifies scenes of traumatic re-enactment that Woolf would later reconfigure and resolve. Reworking those scenes in *The Years* in light of the emotional force of her adult lesbian experience with Vita Sackville-West, as well as with the heightened clarity of an emerging radical feminist perspective, Woolf offers a healthier and more successful reformulation of traumatic abuse. Cramer contrasts Kitty Malone's "more steadfast" lesbian vision in *The Years*—a perspective which allows her to overcome the life-threatening consequences of abuse—with Rachel's trauma-dominated reaction to the possibility of a relationship with a woman. Cramer concludes that Woolf, as she matured, perceived in her own lesbian experience an alternative to the repetition of the childhood sexual trauma she had suffered.

In "The Uneasy Solace of Art," Toni McNaron shows that early trauma experiences of incest abuse continued to haunt Woolf and virtually to construct the parameters of a modernist aesthetic that simultaneously asserted the power of art to evoke an alternative microcosm and the precarious fragility of the artistic universe created. Throughout her life, Woolf felt psychologically impaired by a negative self-image and susceptible to unanticipated emotional calamities. As an essayist writing in the tradition of Montaigne, she could fabricate picture-stories of nostalgic pastoral settings that were nonetheless prone to the intrusion of unexpected disaster. Woolf, argues McNaron, rarely took comfort in the fictive worlds she so elegantly created. The shadow of incest trauma haunted her imagination and made the creative act a test of courage, threatened by the revelation of a monstrous presence reflecting the repressed fear and guilt of an incest victim. According to McNaron, images of melancholia were translated by Woolf into watery worlds of potential destruction. Affected by her memories of sexual violation, the mature author envisaged the human subject as a leaky craft afloat on turbulent ocean waves—a sealed vessel, whose psychological cracks admitted the perilous flow of historical events destined to burst the boundaries of a vulnerable ego.

In "Trauma, Post-Traumatic Stress Disorder, and Obstacles to Postwar Recovery in *Mrs. Dalloway*," Karen DeMeester delineates the crucial need for survivors of military combat to give meaning to their suffering in order to recover from post-traumatic stress disorder. As Sue Thomas reminds us, "Woolf's development and treatment of Septimus Smith" might reflect "her angry response to the *Report of the War Office Committee of Enquiry into 'Shell-shock*,'" presented to the British Parliament in August 1922, and to the publicity given the *Report* in *The Times* in August and September, 1922" (49). DeMeester argues that Smith's suicide is a direct result of his inability to inflict his war experiences with a sense of political purpose or spiritual value. By bearing witness to the physical and psychological torment of soldiers in battle, Septimus attempts to reveal the truth about war to the British populace and to expose the treachery of social and political institutions that condone imperial conquest. Unable to project a heroic and redemptive value into the senseless sacrifice of millions of young men in World War I, the shell-shocked veteran takes refuge in post-traumatic repetition and in hallucinations that connect his shattered psyche with a beloved war hero whom he continues, unsuccessfully, to mourn through encrypted sentiments of melancholy and regret.

How does one disclose abuse? That is the question Jane Lilienfeld explores in her essay, "Could They Tell What They Knew: Modes of Disclosure in *To the Lighthouse.*" Lilienfeld argues that in order to depict the patriarchal system that fostered her abuse, Woolf employed such strategies as polyvocal narration, free indirect discourse, and image plot. These allowed her to draw an acutely personal and politically contextualized portrait of her family members. But if Woolf describes the Ramsay household with an accurate narrative eye, vision as presented in the novel remains obstructed and obscure. As the observing artist, Lily Briscoe embodies Woolf's nuanced awareness of how sight and comprehension are formed and distorted within the abusive family pattern. In Woolf's subtle inscription of a destabilized and unreliable field of perception, one can descry the residue of trauma. Woolf's strategies trouble the reader's expectation of narrative transparency and dramatize denial as a significant aspect of abuse. Lilienfeld focuses her interpretation on two familiar scenes from *To the Lighthouse*—the Ramsays' argument about the weather and James's response to his father's emotional demands on his mother. Lifting "the thin veil of civilization" from the Victorian household, Lilienfeld demonstrates the power of violations that silenced its female members and terrorized its young at home as effectively as Britain's leaders exploited its colonial populations abroad. At the same time, she adroitly links male political aggression with the patriarchal assertion of masculine (sexual) rights. By positioning James as a surrogate observer to the emotional abuse that she herself experienced at his age, Woolf was able safely to explore in her novel the memories that would emerge more explicitly in "A Sketch of the Past."

In "*The Waves* As Ontological Trauma Narrative," Suzette Henke interprets Woolf's experimental play-poem as a modern psychological allegory contingent on subtle evocations of an original traumatic moment that remains undefined and amorphous throughout the text. At the heart of Woolf's lyrical novel is the accidental death of Percival, a young Cambridge athlete sacrificed on the altar of British imperialism. Modeled on Woolf's brother, Thoby Stephen, who died prematurely of typhoid, Percival functions as the mythic center of Woolf's elegiac tribute—a mysterious, unknowable, godlike figure, fascinating in his spectral inscrutability. Behind the trauma of Percival's death, Woolf incorporates into the palimpsestic text of *The Waves* subtle evocations of an existential trauma experienced as undefined and inexplicable—a Lacanian lack-in-being (*manque-à-être*) analogous to the Catholic doctrine of original sin, but all the more threatening in its utter uncanniness. Her aesthetic preoccupations shift from the representation of trauma as a specific mental wound to more pervasive psychological anxieties precipitated by parturition and abjection, by neonatal separation from the maternal body, and by subsequent intimations of mortality. Percival's death, Henke argues, serves as a pre-text or cover story for Woolf's own meditation on ontological crisis, precipitated by a haunting but inarticulate awareness of the threat of personal extinction. Percival's uncanny accident gives shape to the specter of mortality and allows Woolf's novel to function as a protracted experiment in the therapeutic reformulation of bereavement evoked by the impotence of the speaking subject in an implicitly godless universe.

"The task of fiction is fundamentally a traumatic response," Clifford Wulfman writes. In "Woolf and the Discourse of Trauma," he argues that as Woolf became increasingly aware of the effects of trauma on her life and art, she sought fictionally to reproduce in *The Waves* the pattern of those traumatic shocks to consciousness described in *Moments of Being*. Characterized by two radically different concepts of time and marked by tropes of closure, entrapment, interruption, and the failure to connect, Woolf's novel intentionally reenacts the breakdown of traditional narrative. This breakdown represents, in turn, a trauma of language, which becomes in *The Waves* a language of trauma. Wulfman argues that in showing how a character like Bernard ties himself up in linguistic knots, Woolf suggests that narrative structures collapse when they become self-consciously solipsistic. The resulting rupture is a traumatic one, behind which lurks the fear of a self that will not (or cannot) emerge when called. Faced with this lack of self-connection, Bernard also gives voice to Woolf's groundbreaking attempt to forge a new kind of language in her lyrical fiction. In probing the nature of avant-garde narrative in *The Waves*, Wulfman attempts to demonstrate how Woolf sought to create a "little language" made of broken words and phrases, whose linguistic impact is tantamount to the shock of trauma on human consciousness.

In her essay "Gunpowder Plots: Sexuality and Censorship in Woolf's Later Works," Patricia Moran illustrates ways in which Woolf's mature fiction is imbued with a sense of post-traumatic shame and corporeal disgust, as the silenced survivor of incest struggles to communicate the subterranean resonance of a sexual shock so deeply hidden and pathologically repressed that it defies iterability and remains an unspoken source of pain and self-disgust at the heart of adult identity. Can trauma pass from one generation to the next? Moran believes that it can, and that Woolf set forth an "evolutionary model of traumatic affect" in *The Pargiters* and *The Years*. Examining the sexual life of women in both these manuscripts, Woolf developed an aesthetics of sexual trauma whereby she incorporated unresolved models of trauma, nonverbal and iconic in form, into the bodily memories of women unable to articulate private anguish. In *The Years,* secret experiences of corporeal shame evoked by Rose's childhood traumatic encounter with an exhibitionist permanently scar her consciousness and defy confessional iteration. In the sprawling Victorian/Edwardian family epic set forth in *The Years*, Woolf introduces an evolutionary concept of sexual restraint to expose a Darwinian process of emotional atrophy restricting middle-class females at the dawn of the twentieth century. She "situates rape as the foundational moment of women's sexual/textual experience" and mimetically replicates the corporeal shock of sexual trauma that evades language and iterability.

David Eberly turns his attention to *Between the Acts*, arguing that Woolf's last novel records her search for an audience to listen and respond to her underlying trauma, which she was exploring with increasing urgency as the second World War threatened to engulf her. Building upon the concept of the "face-of-the-other" found in the work of the philosopher Emmanuel Levinas, Eberly explores the dense allusion to facial encounter among the characters of the novel. Referring to Levinas' detailed expositions of the "face," Eberly pays particular attention to the role skin plays in defining the boundary of the selfhood between ourselves and others, a boundary which can be severely damaged by trauma. He then examines these "fragile encounters" with the face of the other, ranging from the most intimate interactions in the marriage between Isa and Giles Oliver to the most public performance of Miss La

Trobe's play. Pivotal to Eberly's discussion of the "face-to-face" encounter is the understanding of the need for an audience of others to witness and validate the narrative of the trauma survivor. It is in "the circumstance of audience" that Woolf seeks to find a community which will offer respite, if not recovery, from the effects of trauma.

Claire Kahane, in a psychoanalytic study "Of Snakes, Toads and Duckweed" in *Between the Acts*, shows Woolf amalgamating her integrated responses to personal trauma with a political reaction to the global catastrophe of World War II. Kahane analyzes the pivotal intersection between traumatic flashbacks of early incestuous abuse and Woolf's justifiable anxieties about the threat of Nazi invasion in 1940-41. As a subversive British author married to a Jew, Woolf had good reason to fear Hitler's death squads. Her last novel presents what Kahane describes as an uncanny vision of "ontological dis-integration," lyrically embodied in a shocking metaphor of violence and aggression when Giles Oliver kills a snake whose entrails are fatally engorged with the remains of a toad. This greedy reptile is a figure of evil literally caught "between the acts" in a drama of self-destruction. The novel's simulacrum of an Aesopian fable captures the primal scene being enacted by fascist powers on a world historical stage, in a tableau of helpless paralysis provoking reactive rage and global tragedy. In *Between the Acts*, Woolf brilliantly captures the mood of England's political paralysis in the face of impending invasion and links it, through subtle textual allusions to rape and patriarchal aggression, to her own traumatic psychohistory of corporeal invasion and childhood sexual abuse.

In a culminating essay devoted to "Reading 'Virginia's Death,'" Holly Laird focuses a sharp critical eye on Leonard Woolf's testimony in the last volume of his autobiography, *The Journey Not the Arrival Matters* (1969). As Laird shrewdly observes, Leonard's memoir of "Virginia's Death" functions as a separate, framed narrative that emphasizes a sense of the "catastrophic," which follows a seemingly endless, dreary waiting, in contrast to the journey or the arrival to which the title ostensibly refers. Offering a close textual analysis of the opening chapter of *Journey*, Laird concludes that this complex, sometimes contradictory autobiographical essay needs to be read as a partly self-absolving, partly self-indicting record of Leonard's own traumatic past, rather than as a transparent vessel of factual information about the implicit cause of Virginia's suicide.

In a brief "Afterword," Suzette Henke discusses Virginia's three suicide notes housed in the archives of the British Library. Two of these letters were left by Virginia in the sitting-room at Monk's House on 28 March, 1941, the morning of her suicide. One is addressed to Leonard and the second to Vanessa. Both documents have been carefully identified by Leonard in a handwritten annotation to the British Library archive. But what about the third letter? Leonard explains that he discovered this document, also addressed to him, later that afternoon on Virginia's desk in the writing lodge at the back of Monk's House garden (a renovated shed separate from the house). Considering contradictory interpretations of this enigmatic archival evidence by Woolf's recent biographers, Henke concludes that an exact dating of Virginia's three suicide notes might, in fact, be irrelevant. Whatever the sequence of composition, the duplication of the letter to Leonard proves that Woolf intentionally authored two different versions of her epistolary farewell. A writer to the end, Virginia would almost certainly have composed more than one text of her final communication to those who most loved her and would forever mourn her passing. It would seem all the more crucial, then, for twenty-first century readers to define Woolf's heritage in terms neither of "madness" nor of suicide, but through acts of writing, which sustained her and bequeathed so many literary gifts to her readers.

Notes

1. For further discussion of *scriptotherapy*, or writing as healing through the aegis of traumatic reformulation, see Henke, *Shattered Subjects*. As Judith Herman observes in *Trauma and Recovery*, traumatic memories tend to be "wordless and static" (175), imprinted on the brain in "the form of vivid sensations and images" (38). The purpose of scriptotherapy, like that of psychoanalysis, is to "reassemble an organized, detailed, verbal account, oriented in time and historical context" out of "fragmented components of frozen imagery and sensation" (177). In other words, the reformulation of traumatic memory as verbal narrative, either in talk therapy or through creative writing, seems to effect an abreaction or catharsis that restores to the trauma survivor a sense of agency and control. What scriptotherapy implements is a shift in the mind's fixation on pathological melancholia to a healthier abreaction consigning traumatic experience to a register of mourning, whereby disturbing life events can successfully be "worked through."

2. In his preface to the fourth edition of *The Unknown Virginia Woolf*, Poole reminds us that his book was "regarded as radical, heretical and iconoclastic" when it was first

published in 1978 (vii). Although he blames the historical intersection of his study with the emergence of feminist theories of difference for the relative neglect of his book, he fails to note that this critical text appeared prior to many of the theoretical and clinical studies on trauma and its intersection with the lives of women. Nonetheless, Poole's work has had a strong, if sometimes unacknowledged, effect on the evolution of Woolf studies.

3. DeSalvo's model was quickly countered by Thomas Caramagno's 1992 study, *The Flight of the* Mind, which contended that Woolf suffered from manic depression. Caramagno contrasted his biological version of Woolf's illness to what he saw as a psychoanalytically constituted one. In the decade following the publication of his book, the account of Woolf as manic-depressive has come to dominate the biographical assessment of Woolf's symptoms. Raising the issue of Woolf's "madness" in her 1997 biography, Hermione Lee stated that Woolf's illness "conforms to the profile of what is called manic-depressive" (*Virginia* 172). Recent biographies have been less nuanced. Katherine Dalsimer confidently argues that "[f]rom the vantage point of the present it is clear that Virginia Woolf suffered from manic-depressive illness" (177), which becomes for Sybil Oldfield, writing in 2005, "acute bipolar affective disorder" (xxi).

4. In their 1991 essay, "Virginia Woolf's Keen Sensitivity to War," Nancy Topping Bazin and Jane Hamovitt Lauter explore Woolf's "early and persistent preoccupation with the consequences of war," linking it to patriarchal attitudes and, more explicitly, to rape as well as to her personal experience with death. Karen Levenback's later book-length study greatly expands our understanding of Woolf as a war novelist throughout her career. In *The Great War and the Language of Modernism,* Vincent Sherry explores the tension between the "unspeakability" of the war and the modernist language that Woolf sought to develop. Sherry argues for Woolf's keen awareness that the "intrusiveness of war" may be smoothed over, and its outrage assimilated by the conventions of a plot that reflects a wider cultural denial (275).

5. In *Psychoanalysis, Psychiatry and Modernist Literature*, Kylie Valentine explores the bifurcated approach to mental illness in England between the two world wars. The increasing visibility of Freudian thought in Britain, abetted in large part by the publication of the English translation of Freud's collected work by the Hogarth Press and by the public advocacy of psychiatrists like Ernest Jones and David Eder, was countered by a growing knowledge of the visible impact of brain injury on personality and the newly discovered effects of electroshock therapy on affective states. "These two approaches," Valentine writes, "were interdependent and mutually influential, but were finally constituted by differences in their visions of madness and the mad" (91). Continuing a debate inaugurated in the Enlightenment when Mesmer's displays of the power of hypnosis and

early attempts to cure disease with the newly discovered effects of electricity challenged notions of soul and will, this division still persists today.

TRAUMA AND LESBIAN RETURNS IN VIRGINIA WOOLF'S *THE VOYAGE OUT* AND *THE YEARS*

Patricia Morgne Cramer

Woolf critics have long been familiar with the extent to which Woolf's fiction is preoccupied with key figures and experiences from her own life—or, as Avrom Fleishman notes, "how much of her art turns on a few central facts subtly varied in a series of imaginative transformations" (606). Recently, Suzanne Raitt has reiterated how important "returning" is to Woolf's work. To illustrate, Raitt cites Woolf's multiple and painstaking revisions of her major texts as well as Woolf's recurrent returns to her past in her fiction "either . . . to re-envision or to change it" (11). George and Gerald Duckworth's sexual violations of Virginia Woolf are among those "central autobiographical facts" that Woolf revisits again and again in her essays, her letters and diaries, and her fiction. As other Woolf critics have already identified—most notably Louise DeSalvo, David Eberly, Suzette Henke, Jane Lilienfeld, Toni McNaron, Roger Poole, Rebecca Sutcliffe, Diana Swanson, and Lisa Tyler—Woolf revisits her trauma history in her novels in order "to re-envision or to change it."

Working within trauma studies, Woolf critics have primarily focused on *The Voyage Out* and *The Years* because it is in these two novels that Woolf specifically revisits the scene of George Duckworth's sexual violation: in Rachel's nightmare reactions to Richard Dalloway's kiss, and in Rose's terrified reaction to the male sexual predator she encounters on her way to Lamley's. Building on this scholarly tradition, I claim that in *The Years* (1931-1937) Woolf "returns to and revises" her first novel, *The Voyage Out* (1904/08-15), in order to rewrite scenes that refer to childhood sexual trauma.[1] By the 1930s, Woolf was a mature, successful writer—no longer the novice who first wrote about her incest memories in *The Voyage Out*. She was also an experienced lesbian recovering from the end of her love affair with Vita Sackville-West. In *The Years* Woolf returns to memories of lesbian love as well as memories of childhood sexual abuse and loss, and she celebrates lesbian love with a confidence missing in her first novel. As indicated in her autobiographical essays and *The Years*, Woolf's incest legacy is inseparable from her lesbian history:

she identifies male sexual abuse as the "block" to (*not cause of*) her lesbian desire and lesbian love as the "passageway out" of a life stuck in what Harvey Schwartz aptly names the "nonredeemable suffering of unbridled [trauma] reenactments" (162).

Furthermore, by comparing Woolf's later resolutions to the sexual dilemmas first delineated in *The Voyage Out,* we can better identify Woolf's mature reevaluation of the enormous influence of sexuality on her political acumen, her literary innovations, and her revisionary idealism. As Woolf's essays and fiction attest, her sexual evolution and creative development are concomitant phenomena. By tracing the transformations recorded in these novels, I isolate not only Woolf's progressive resistance to the aftereffects of childhood sexual abuse but also the teleology of her creative process.

Woolf composed *The Years* during a spell of unprecedented self-confidence and urgency for articulating her own "point of view, as writer, as being" (*D5*: 65)—more fully, more clearly than ever before. For example, in 1932, Woolf declared herself "free to define my attitude with a vigour & certainty I have never known before" (*D4*: 135). This well-earned self-confidence inspired Woolf's grandiose plans for *The Years* to be a "terrific affair," "a summing up of all [she knew]" (*D4*: 151-52). It also provided the impetus and courage for Woolf's return to sexual dilemmas she left unresolved in her first novel, *The Voyage Out.*

Woolf wrote both *The Voyage Out* and *The Years* during turning points in her love life, and both novels are preoccupied with romantic love and marriage. During the composition of *The Voyage Out*, Virginia was courted by Hilton Young, Walter Lamb, and Sydney Waterlow; conducted her painful flirtation with Clive Bell; received a marriage proposal from Lytton Strachey; and married Leonard Woolf (DeSalvo, *First Voyage* 11). As Mark Hussey notes, as early as 1906 Vanessa's jokes in her letters about Virginia's sapphism suggest that Woolf's lesbian predilections were already a familiar topic between them ("Refractions of Desire" 143; see also Barrett, "Introduction" 4-5). Thus, both heterosexual and lesbian romance were much on Woolf's mind as she composed *The Voyage Out.* Among Woolf's novels, *The Voyage Out* and *The Years* took the longest to complete and were the most difficult for her to write (*D5*: 24; *D5*: 17). Given the focus on sexuality in both novels, it is likely that these difficulties had something to do with the sexual themes central to both: the aftereffects of her incest trauma, the predatory nature of male sexual practices, and her lesbian sexual preferences.

Both *The Voyage Out* and *The Years* return to childhood traumas Woolf depicts in her autobiographical essays from *Moments of Being*: "Reminiscences" (1907), "22 Hyde Park" (1920), and "A Sketch of the Past" (1939). I begin, therefore, with these essays in order to isolate the trauma patterns Woolf reconfigures in less obvious forms in the novels. At the same time, I examine Woolf's incest autobiography within the context of contemporary trauma theory in order to place the female incest survivor in Woolf's essays and fiction in dialogue with contemporary communities of incest survivors and trauma experts. However, I do not apply trauma theory as the authority over Woolf's text. Rather, I model the relationship in this essay between Woolf's and contemporary sexual trauma testimonies on feminist consciousness-raising practices as well as speak outs and support groups for victims of sexual assault. In keeping with this tradition, I highlight the areas of consensus between Woolf's incest story and the testimonies of survivor communities not available in her lifetime in order to support the authenticity of Woolf's trauma testimony in her life writing and the contemporary relevance of her insights into the effects of childhood trauma.

In these essays from *Moments of Being*, Woolf's descriptions of her family structure, George's perpetrator strategies, and the emotional effects of incest trauma at the time of the violations and afterwards depict what are now recognized as typical trauma schemas. For example, the family of Leslie and Julia Stephen closely matches the family constellation identified as at high risk for incest (Tyler, "Atrocities" 30-31; Lilienfeld, "[Critic]"). Families in which incest has occurred tend to be conventional to an extreme, with authoritarian fathers and mothers who are withdrawn or absent. Like Leslie Stephen, the fathers are "perfect patriarchs," feared by family members but admired by outsiders. Like Julia Stephen, these mothers support men's rights to dominate the lives of the women in the family (Browning and Boatman 69; Herman, *Incest* 71-78). Studies have shown that fathers in these families expect daughters, usually the oldest, to assume an absent mother's nurturant and, at times, sexual duties. Recall how Leslie emotionally exploited first Stella, and then Vanessa and Virginia after Julia's death (Herman, *Incest* 46). Perhaps one of the most salient features of families in which incest occurs is the "painful estrangement between the mother and her victimized daughter."

This mother-daughter estrangement appears in such families as both cause and effect of incest violation (Butler [1978] 109).

The conditions trauma experts have discovered to be specific to brother-sister incest were also present in Woolf's family. For example, in brother-sister incest situations, the brother has usually taken on the parental role because both parents are unable to do so (Jacobs 107). Shortly after Woolf's mother's death, George "for all practical purposes . . . [became] the head of the family. . . . he was father and mother, and sister and brother in one" (*MOB* 168). A strong mother-daughter bond can guarantee against incest (Herman, *Incest* 48-49): "When [Virginia's mother] died. . . , some restraint seemed to burst" so that George began giving full rein to those "profuse, voluble affections which during his mother's lifetime were kept in check" (*MOB* 57). In her memoir, Woolf identifies how the power imbalance between George and herself, typical of incest relationships, contributed to her acquiescence: "George was thir-ty-six when I was twenty. And had [a] thousand pounds [a] year whereas I had fifty" (*MOB* 131).[2]

Trauma studies recognize not only Woolf's family dynamics as consistent with families in which incest has occurred, but also her descriptions of her half-brothers' violations. Anyone familiar with contemporary trauma studies can readily recognize George's behaviors as typical perpetrator strategies. It is surprising, then, to find some recent biographers of Virginia Woolf questioning the credibility of Woolf's incest testimony. For example, both Mitchell Leaska and Hermione Lee describe George as, in Lee's words, such a "worthy gentleman— landowner, family man, Christian, public citizen, knight" (148), thus making it unlikely that he would have perpetrated such an outrage. According to Lee, "[George] makes an unlikely villain. In later years he was always anxious to help his half-sisters, and is remembered by all who knew him well as kind-hearted, benign, and a pillar of the establishment" (119).[3]

Contrary to Lee's profile of a "man least likely to perpetrate child-hood sexual abuse," trauma research and victim testimonies indicate that child molesters typically lead a "double life" as outstanding citizens in public and sexual abusers in their private lives. Judith Herman notes, for example, that "the most consistent feature" among perpetrators is their "apparent normality": "[their] demeanor provides an excellent camou-flage, for few people believe that extraordinary crimes can be committed by men of such conventional appearance" (*Trauma* 75; see also Forward and Buck [1988] 32; Salter, *Trauma* 29-33). Perpetrators tend to be "exquisitely sensitive to the realities of power and to social norms" (Herman, *Trauma* 75). George "believed in society," and he was adept at "going through the hoops; doing the required acts" (*MOB* 153).

Thus, the fact that outsiders to the Stephen family admired Gerald and George is not credible evidence of their innocence. Within trauma research, there is an overwhelming consensus that incest perpetrators tend to deliberately cultivate public respect as a defense against possible disclosure of their sexual crimes. Childhood sexual abuse is rarely the result of random impulse: it is "cultivated. . . . systematic . . . possess[ing] both purpose and method" (Nachmani, "Discussion" 195). As Anna Salter notes, most child molesters deliberately construct lives of public virtue in order to cultivate the trust of the victim's family and community. Salter calls this the "grooming" stage in the cycle of pedophile deviancy and finds it "nearly universal" (*Trauma* 74) among child molesters. Perpetrators will carefully groom the potential victim, family, and extended community so that the victim, were she to ever accuse the perpetrator, would not be believed. One pedophile explains this grooming process in an interview with Anna Salter: "The more I got into my deviancy, the more I would try to do what was good in the eyes of everyone else" ("Truth"). It appears that during his sexual abuse of Virginia and her sister Vanessa, George was "grooming" not only his chosen victims but their extended family, as well: "he was always shutting doors and opening windows; . . . remembered the birthdays of aunts, and sent turtle soup to the invalids" (*MOB* 166).

Woolf's description of George's actions indicates that he manifested another behavior identified by Salter as typical of child molesters: "SUDS" (seemingly unimportant decisions). These "thinking errors" are "internal lies" the offender tells himself to justify his sexual abuse of children. For example, an abuser will convince himself that his daily trips to the playground have nothing to do with his sexual intentions or that the child's acquiescence means consent (Salter, *Trauma* 97-101). Woolf implies that George had convinced even himself that he was doing nothing wrong when he forced himself upon her: "under the name of unselfishness he allowed himself to commit acts which a cleverer man would have called tyrannical; and, profoundly believing in the purity of his love, he behaved little better than a brute" (*MOB* 58). Coincident with "thinking errors" is the "trademark" of sexual perpetrators—what psychologists Susan Forward and Craig Buck call their "incomprehensible lack of compassion or empathy for victims" ([1988] 32). We might recall that when Dr. Savage confronted George about his sexual assault, George claimed he was just trying to comfort Virginia at the time of Leslie Stephen's death. Apparently, the fact that Dr. Savage and Vanessa seem to have linked Virginia's breakdown at the time to George's molestation meant nothing to George (*MOB* 182).

By ignoring the last thirty years of trauma research, biographers fail to recognize the authenticity of Woolf's emotional responses to Gerald and George. Many of them, in fact, when discussing Woolf's incest testimonies, adopt the same predictable victim-blaming clichés perpetrators use to confuse and silence their victims. As Herman notes, perpetrators and their colluders typically defend abuse by claiming "it never happened; the victim lies; the victim exaggerates; the victim brought it upon herself; and in any case it is time to forget the past and move on" (*Trauma* 8). Leaska and Lee, for instance, emphasize the fact that Woolf sometimes recorded positive memories of George in her diaries and letters. If she had really been molested, they argue, she would never have described him affectionately. After all, Lee reminds us: "the relations [with the Duckworths] were not entirely broken off" (*Virginia* 155). Leaska notes that when she was fifteen, "Virginia recorded impressions of him that were bright and intimate, impressions that did not support the claims she would make of him in 1939" (*Granite* 355). Both also make much of the fact that in 1934, when Woolf heard of George's death, she remembered him fondly, rather than reiterating the caricatures with which she usually described him (see, for example, *D*4:211). Leaska claims that such "affectionate memories of George Duckworth are so different from the monster she would make of him later when she was writing her memoir. . . . one would have expected his death to come as a relief, that she was at last free of that nasty pedophilic sex offender" (355; see also Lee 155).[4]

In fact, Woolf's ambivalent emotions toward her perpetrators, George and Gerald, are normal victim reactions to childhood sexual abuse. Woolf's infrequent expressions of gratitude toward her molesters were due in part to the kindnesses she received, especially from George, as well as her childhood and adult memories of her own emotional dependence after Julia's death. A child victim is understandably unsure: is this family member so trusted by others hurting her, or is this muddle of pain and kindness love? Relationships between adult perpetrators and juvenile victims are rarely overtly abusive—they are usually "relationship[s] of persuasive warmth" (Salter, *Trauma* 81). Typically, "the offender seduces her into a relationship with him; he tells her he loves her, gives her presents, makes her feel special, all the while preparing her for silence and abuse" (Veldhuis and Freyd 268). It is clear from Woolf's narrative that George adopted these strategies: Woolf writes that he lavished jewels; a "Jews' Harp" for Virginia, a "blue enamel butterfly" for Vanessa (*MOB* 172;170). Perpetrators' cynically contrived gift-giving further marginalizes the child by constructing a "special relationship" between them that excludes others in the child's environment who might have offered help (Nachmani, "Discussion" 195). George's manipulative attempts to seduce first Vanessa and then Virginia to their evenings out may have been an unsuccessful ploy to set up competition between the two sisters.

Perpetrator gifts and acts of intermittent kindness not only co-opt the child's trust but confuse the child and undermine her trust in her own perceptions. As Schwartz notes, "In many forms of childhood sexual abuse, the negative impact comes more from the depth of betrayal than the severity of the violence itself" (11; see also Salter 88-89; Freyd, *Betrayal Trauma*). The following excerpt from a narrative by a woman raped by her brother is typical: "My mother was depressed for the first year after I was born and John and I were really kind of symbiotic. We liked each other. . . . [W]e were kind to each other in a way that no one in the family really was . . . I didn't understand why he was doing what he was doing because it made me so uncomfortable. . . . I felt sorry for him a lot" (qtd. in Jacobs 107). Victims typically vacillate between "feelings of rage for the perpetrator and feelings of sympathy" (Jacobs 138).

Furthermore, perpetrators frequently combine gift-giving with "appeals to loyalty and compassion" (Herman, *Trauma* 79). The perpetrator typically exploits the emotional vulnerability of the victim, so that the perpetrator appears to be the one in need of caretaking. As Janet Liebman Jacobs notes, "the self pity of the perpetrator defines the emotional climate around which the incest occurs" (64). George's blackmail tactics are familiar to Woolf's readers. Woolf's memoir recalls how he "quivered" with repressed tears when he wanted to get Virginia to accompany him to the evenings out which preceded his sexual aggression against her, and how he threatened that the "chaste, the immaculate George

Duckworth would be forced into the arms of whores" if Virginia did not comply (*MOB* 172). Victims often speak of being "*disarmed by their feelings for the perpetrator*" (Russell 131); after recalling George's manipulations, Woolf tells us that "The end of it was that he begged me, and I agreed, to go" (*MOB* 173).

Therefore, Woolf's few positive comments about her half-brothers are not at all surprising. What is surprising is the consistency with which she was usually able to sustain her contempt for Gerald and George. It is more common that through forced sexual intimacy the perpetrator instills a victim-perpetrator alliance so that the victim adopts the perpetrator's point of view (Jacobs 65). As a survival strategy, the victim "forgets" her own pain; she learns to love those who hurt her, desperately seeking approval from those who seek to destroy her (Schwartz 35; Alice Miller *Banished* 163).

This "identification with the perpetrator" is exacerbated in family environments which mirror the perpetrator's point of view (Schwartz 33). This was, clearly, Woolf's family situation: her father was entirely self-absorbed and, like George, saw his daughters as domestic servants. Even after their deaths, Woolf felt the "ghosts of Stella and [her] Mother" pressuring her to give in to George. As for the other adults around her, "the voices of all women cried aloud in his praise, and men were touched by his modest virtues"; "How could we resist his wishes . . . ?" (*MOB* 57; 157). Quentin Bell's letter to Panthea Reid indicates how completely Vanessa and Virginia's social environment mirrored George and Gerald's world views. Bell contends that if they had complained about the sexual abuse, everyone around them "would either have called it a wicked lie or made an appalling scandal in which the sufferers, as always in Victorian scandals, would have been the victims" (qtd. in Lee, *Virginia* 63).

It is essential that victims break from childhood habits of loyalty to the perpetrator, his allies, and his point of view (Schwartz 35; Jacobs 33-54). Therefore, Woolf's shift in attitude from revering George as "hero" to condemning George as a "brute" (*MOB* 57; 58) is a commendable sign of Woolf's success in achieving this necessary separation. Her humorous caricatures of George and Gerald deflate the exaggerated idealization of perpetrators that is one of the most damaging effects of childhood sexual abuse. Such strategic use of humor, gleaned at least in part from the hard lessons of her childhood, flourishes in her mockeries of perpetrator-like patriarchs in her essays and fiction: most notably Professor Von X in *A*

Room of One's Own and the "fuhrer" figure who is the "quintessence of virility" in *Three Guineas* (*TG* 142). When in *The Years* Maggie caricatures the "fat old patriarch" (*Y* 382; 389) in her drawing, Woolf encourages her readers to laugh their way out of the network of alliances that protect perpetrators like Gerald and George. Woolf's ability to laugh at George and Gerald's charades coincides with the "indifference" toward dictators at home and abroad Woolf requires for membership in the "outsider's society" envisioned in *Three Guineas*. Most contemporary trauma experts would say that such "freedom from unreal loyalties" (*TG* 113) to betraying caretakers is, in fact, a precondition for freedom in the public sphere.

Woolf's descriptions of the emotional impact of incest are remarkably similar to many contemporary accounts by incest victims. Trauma experts generally agree with Bessel van der Kolk's definition of trauma "as an inescapably stressful event that overwhelms people's existing coping mechanisms" ("Trauma and Memory" 279). Trauma is, as Gilead Nachmani describes it, "the moment of breakdown, the sudden confusion of impact, of being overwhelmed by the stunning shock where everything adaptive fails, except for the obliteration of knowledge" ("Trauma and Ignorance" 423). The victim's immediate responses are, typically, "terror, loss of control, and intense fear of annihilation" (Brison "Trauma Narratives" 40). These "trauma markers"—shock, breakdown, numbing, speechlessness, terror, and annihilation—appear in Woolf's accounts of Gerald and George's sexual violations. For example, in Woolf's description of her little-girl acquiescence to Gerald's enforced exploration of her "private parts," we find the same numbing paralysis and helplessness in the face of an overwhelming force characteristic of victim reactions. Woolf recalls trying to "wriggle" away from his violating hand, "But it did not stop" (*MOB* 69). As Jody Messler Davies notes, what is typically missing in a victim's traumatic memories—particularly when the trauma occurs in early childhood—"are the words [to] . . . describe and name that which has occurred but has yet to be thought about" (59). Woolf remembers only that her feelings then were "dumb and mixed" (69). Since Gerald had already groomed her in sexual submission at such an early age, it is not surprising that in early adolescence Woolf reacted to George's sexual demands with the same stunned acquiescence.

Woolf's recollections of her "looking-glass dream" and her inexplicable terror when crossing a puddle are consistent with what is now recognized as "state-dependent trauma recall." Trauma experts generally agree that traumatic memories are not encoded in the same way as other memories. As van der Kolk notes, "in contrast with the way people process ordinary information, traumatic experiences are initially imprinted as sensations or feeling states, and are not collated and transcribed into personal narratives" ("Trauma and Memory" 296). This dissociation of trauma emotions from originating event can occur because people are capable of storing sensory experiences without understanding their cause (van der Kolk, "Black Hole" 10). In other words, because traumatic memories are consciously disavowed, they are stored as "discrete personality states" outside conscious awareness and control (van der Kolk et al. "Dissociation" 306).

As long as the trauma memories remain split off from conscious narrative, "they will continue to intrude as terrifying perceptions, obsessional preoccupations, and somatic reexperiences" (van der Kolk *et. al.*, "Dissociation" 309). Recurrences are "state dependent" because they are most likely to occur in response to life events reminiscent of the early trauma (Rothschild 35). When dissociated memories reemerge, they usually intrude just as they were stored during the trauma: "Unverbalized, unsymbolized, fragmented, and undigested" (Gartner 18). Therefore, they are most likely to return as intense visual, auditory, or somatic disturbances seemingly unconnected to any reasonable source. They may return as "a rush of terror seemingly unattached" (Rivera 19); as flashbacks and nightmares (Herman, *Trauma* 37); "as visual images; olfactory, auditory, or kinesthetic sensations" (van der Kolk "Trauma and Memory" 287); "as a swift, strong perception or a dream" (Terr, *Unchained* 12). When traumatic memories break suddenly into consciousness, the survivor may suffer as if the trauma were occurring all over again (Rothschild 6; Herman, *Trauma* 37; Schacter 52-70).

Woolf's "looking-glass" dream and memory of her emotional paralysis when crossing a puddle have all the markings of what contemporary trauma experts recognize as "state-dependent recall": a trivial event in a survivor's current life that triggers an intense emotional response that the survivor cannot explain because the trauma-induced emotions were never consciously connected with the traumatic event. For example, both of these events elicited the feelings of paralysis, terror, and helplessness characteristic of trauma but without any apparent connection to their traumatic origins. Woolf's looking-glass memory seems to have appeared to her as that "strong perception or dream" identified by Lenore Terr as typical of traumatic intrusions. In fact, Woolf says she remained uncertain if this recurring perception were a dream or an actual memory. In retrospect, Woolf reconnects her "looking-glass" memory with Gerald's sexual molestation of her when she was a little girl. Characteristically, the memory contains only a few fragments the looking-glass and the "horrible face . . . of an animal . . . over [her] shoulder" (*MOB* 69), but her emotional fright, seemingly out of proportion to the content of the fragments themselves, is consistent with trauma reactions. The feeling of frozen terror evinced by the puddle is consistent with Woolf's description of her response to Gerald's molestation: "dumb horror," helplessness in the face of adult force ("passive under the sledge-hammer blow"), isolation ("unprotected"), powerlessness ("nothing to ward it off"), and paralysis ("huddled up at my end of the bath, motionless") (*MOB* 78).

Among the most detrimental effects of childhood sexual abuse is its ability to freeze a victim's "capacity for critical thinking and psychological reflection" (Schwartz 306). As Nachmani notes, "Confusion and doubt are not only the experimental scar tissue of trauma, they are also the cunning goals and purpose of the traumatizer" ("Discussion" 202). Alice K. Miller similarly finds that perpetrators consistently attempt to destroy their victim's confidence in their own perceptions, as the victim is subtly "conditioned not to be aware of what is really being done to him or her" (*Good* 9). In typical incest situations, the perpetrator and (as in Woolf's case) often other family members name reality in ways that do not match the victim's emotions and point of view. The perpetrator's word for what is occurring—cuddling, tickling, or purported "comfort"— overrides the victim's experience of terror, shame, and helplessness (Veldhuis and Freyd 268). As a result, survivors of incest may enter adulthood lacking confidence in their own voice and their own perceptions.

Similarly, in "Reminiscences," Woolf recalls the confusion she and Vanessa confronted at home: she says that she and Vanessa were "simply credulous" of their half-brothers for a long period of time. In their "blindfold state," they mistrusted their own perceptions and tried to join those around them in judging George the family hero. But George's contradictory behaviors were "for ever confusing [them], deceiving [them] and leading [them] alternately to trust and suspect him" (*MOB* 58). As Nachmani notes, perpetrators systematically undermine the victim's ability to distinguish right from wrong, safe from dangerous, friend from foe"

("Discussion" 199). After describing her confused responses to George's behaviors, Woolf concludes: "But who again can distinguish the good from the bad, the feeling from the sentiment, the truth from the pose?" (*MOB* 58).

Trauma-induced chaos can also leave a victim in a confused relationship with her own desires and ambitions. Because a victim first experiences sexual arousal in association with violation, she may continue to experience all types of sexual feeling as dangerous or degrading. In fact, trauma may inhibit not only sexual desire but all forms of desire inconsistent with internalized perpetrator edicts (Ehrenberg 593-94; van der Kolk, "Body" 219). In other words, the "footprints on the soul" of the victim/survivor left by the perpetrator (Salter, *Trauma* xvii) may create an "internal backlash" any time a survivor "steps out of the domination systems" (Schwartz 33). Survivors often live constricted and constricting lives, unless they are able to connect with others outside the trauma schema and with emotional resources not entirely colonized by the sexual assault.

In *Moments of Being*, Woolf's "voyage out" of the nightmare of a life reduced to trauma reenactments is to recover other memories not entirely destroyed by George and Gerald's predation: the "purest ecstasy" she felt as a small child in her mother's presence, and the political acumen developed in her childhood's "continuous romance" and "close conspiracy" with Vanessa (*MOB* 65; 28; 143). In Woolf's memories of her mother and Vanessa, we find "in embryo" the imagery Woolf later attaches to lesbian memories to form the metaphoric pathways back to that "purest ecstasy" she first experienced in proximity to her mother as well as the outsider's "enhanced perception" (Nachmani, "Trauma" 427) first developed in alliance with Vanessa. Fragments from St. Ives memories reappear throughout the novels as metaphors for lesbian-based ecstasies pointing the way out of trauma-controlled sexual desires: "the red and purple flowers" on her mother's dress; the sound of the "waves breaking — one two one two—"; "the long train journey"; the "yellow blind . . . draw[ing] its little acorns across the floor"; "rooks falling from a great height rooks cawing"; "The buzz, the croon, the smell"; and "the murmur of bees." Her access to these woman-centered ecstasies, Woolf writes, was checked by George and Gerald's sexual violations and "that world of many men coming and going" (*MOB* 143) in which her half-brothers reigned.

Once again, Woolf's self-analysis is consistent with what trauma survivors and experts tell us when they try to name the "essence" of what abusers aim to destroy. Alice K. Miller finds that perpetrators require "the suppression of vitality, creativity, and feeling" in their victims, and she identifies a core aftereffect of childhood sexual betrayal as the victim's "loss of capacity for spontaneous feeling" (*Good* 58; 24). Eve Ensler, speaking as a woman who survived incest, explains what is lost to incest in similar ways: "it shut[s] down. . . . the best of us. . . . The part that has inherent faith, that allows us to take chances and initiate love and move towards intimacy. The part that is gentle and craves light and has great imagination. . . . our life force" (11).

Woolf is quite specific about what Gerald and George's sexual viola-tions nearly destroyed: her access to sexual and spiritual ecstasy and intellectual autonomy. She suggests, for example, that Gerald's sexual molestation may explain why her "natural love for beauty was checked" at an early age and why she was so often "ashamed or afraid of [her] own body" (*MOB* 68; 69). George's unwelcome nighttime visitations to her bed also interrupted her bedtime musings on her intellectual ambitions and joyfully anticipated classes with her beloved tutor, Janet Case. In her memoir, Woolf recalls that George's nocturnal violations terminated her bedtime intellectual fantasies: "I felt I knew much more about the dialogues of Plato than Miss Case could ever do" (*MOB* 177). By juxta-posing her adolescent self-confidence with George's nightly visits, Woolf reveals that she experienced George's sexual invasion as an attack on her intellectual as well as sexual self-confidence and, further, that Woolf conceived sexual and intellectual freedom as interdependent.

The trauma-induced confusions Woolf describes in her autobiograph-ical essays were compounded by the death of her mother when she was thirteen. Woolf describes her emotional landscape at the time of her moth-er's death ("the greatest disaster that could happen") in images that recall the same fear of annihilation, paralysis, and terror associated with Gerald's molestation: "the racing clouds . . . stood still . . . the wind flagged, and all the creatures on the earth moaned or wandered seeking aimlessly" (*MOB* 40). Therefore, following Suzette Henke's lead, I iden-tify Woolf's sexual abuse and the sudden death of her mother as concurrent traumatic events. Thus, the effects of George's sexual viola-tions which began shortly after her mother's death were exacerbated by her mother's death and the residual effects of Gerald's prior sexual violations ("Post-Traumatic Subjectivity" 148). Woolf's ambivalence toward women—most prominent in *The Voyage Out*—was further compounded by her recognition that neither her mother nor Stella would have protected her.

In her autobiographical essays on the incest theme, especially "A Sketch of the Past," Woolf alternates joyful memories associated with her mother or sister with painful memories of George and Gerald's sexual assaults, as well as with troubled reminders of her mother and Stella's betrayals. By writing these memories side by side, Woolf suggests that in her emotional landscape these three events were, at least early in her life, confusingly merged. Therefore, Woolf's mature clarity about her mother's complicity within the family system that protected George and Gerald—evidenced in *The Years*—meant that her lesbian returns to emotional currents first experienced in proximity to her mother could not depend on any illusory return to a pre-Oedipal mother who would protect her. The woman-centered ecstasies Woolf depicts in *The Years* are reminiscent but not merely imitative of her pre-incest idyllic maternal/sororal memories. The adult lesbian Woolf differentiates female colluders from feminist allies and reconnects female-to-female love with feminist aims and loyalties.

Although George and Gerald's family narratives dominated her childhood, in both *The Voyage Out* and *The Years*, Woolf "reestablishes order" by exposing what conventional family relations look like from the victimized daughter's point of view. As Bessel A. van der Kolk and Onno van der Hart note, because "Traumatic memories are the unassimilated scraps of overwhelming experiences, [they] need to be integrated within existing mental schemas and . . . transformed into narrative language" ("Intrusive Past" 176). Thus, because "[c]oherent narrative events and trauma are antithetical" (Nachmani, "Discussion" 193), Woolf's "returns" to the scenes of trauma in her autobiographical essays and fiction shatter the charisma of the perpetrator's traumatizing versions of reality by resurrecting the narrating, judging voice her half-brothers and her collaborating extended family nearly obliterated.[5] In both *The Voyage Out* and *The Years* Woolf recreates the family structure, perpetrator strategies, and victim response she describes in *Moments of Being* and typical of incest situations.

For example, the case for reading Rachel as a victim of paternal incest is well-established. Louise DeSalvo interprets Helen's comment about Willoughby's "nameless atrocities" (24) against Rachel as a reference to his sexual abuse, and she identifies Rachel's incest symptomology (*Impact* 162-69; see also Swanson 291-92; and Tyler, "Nameless Atrocities" 28-32). Building on DeSalvo's work, Diana Swanson identifies aspects of Willoughby's behavior that are typical of fathers who sexually violate their daughters: his bullying, emotional dishonesty, disrespect for his daughter's physical boundaries (e.g. his shoulder punches), and his treatment of Rachel as a substitute wife. Swanson further notes that Woolf displaces characteristic paternal abuse patterns on other father figures in the novel, such as Richard Dalloway and Ridley Ambrose, who inflict various types of abuse and neglect on Rachel (290; see also Tyler, "Atrocities" 30-31).

As Lisa Tyler illustrates, in *The Voyage Out*, Willoughby Vinrace (like Gerald and George) pursues that "extreme conventionality" typical of incest perpetrators. He aggressively perfects his public image as a successful businessman, loyal to the empire; he insists on his daughter's sexual ignorance; he enforces conventional gender roles in the home; and he uses emotional manipulation to guarantee his daughter's obedience ("Atrocities" 30-31). Similarly, Colonel Pargiter is a well-respected citizen who leads a "double-life" with his mistress, Myra. He exerts minute control over the lives of his daughters and forces Eleanor to fulfill the roles of his dead wife. Like George, he is self-pitying and utterly indifferent to the pain of those around him. Additionally, in both the Vinrace and Pargiter families, maternal deaths give these bullying fathers full control over their daughters—a situation conducive to child abuse.

Rachel and Rose's extreme emotional responses to their first sexual experiences closely replicate Woolf's emotional responses to incest recalled in *Moments of Being*. Richard Dalloway is much like George and Gerald in his pursuit of social acceptability. He is further linked with George when he pontificates on duckweed and admits: "Sisters particularly are delightful" (*VO* 56). In Rachel's response to Richard Dalloway's kiss, we find the same shock ("tremendous beats of the heart" and "black waves across her eyes"), numbing ("chill of body and mind"), and feelings of entrapment ("tunnel . . . [that] became a vault") that Woolf felt during Gerald's molestation. Like Woolf's looking-glass nightmare, Rachel's dream following Dalloway's kiss presents confusing fragments—the deformed man and woman (*VO* 76; 77)—that refer back to Dalloway but perhaps also to an earlier experience of sexual trauma. In Rachel's trauma-induced nightmare after Dalloway's kiss, Woolf describes again the power of trauma to "freeze" a victim's thinking and creative faculties: "Still and cold as death [Rachel] lay, not daring to move" (*VO* 77). The "barbarian men . . . scuffling down the passages . . . snuffl[ing] at her door" (*VO* 77), recall George outside her bedroom door, about to enter.

As DeSalvo and Tyler note, Terence's reading of the rape narrative in *Comus* is a probable trigger for Rachel's illness ("Virginia" 181; "Atrocities" 37).[6] This scene, which juxtaposes a rape story and a man (Hewet) who expects sexual gratification from her in the name of love, is enough like the conditions of childhood sexual trauma to cause Rachel to return to dissociative defenses which, in childhood, saved her. In her trance-state, Rachel recognizes that Terence's invitation to sexual love could force her to prematurely abandon her dissociative defenses and to "remember something. . . . She did not wish to remember." Because trauma "splits affect and cognition" (Schwartz 140), Rachel does not want to "join mind to body" (*VO* 347). Thus, Rachel's retreat can be read as her inability to endure adult sexuality, including her unresolved lesbian emotions. Like many survivors of incest, Rachel retreats from intimacy rather than relive the agony of reintegrating dissociated memories.

Rachel's death scene is resonant with the types of "trauma echoes" (Schwartz 313) typical of state-dependent trauma reenactments. Here, Rachel reenacts the speechlessness, isolation, and passivity Woolf describes as her own childhood response to sexual violation. Rachel is "unable to communicate" and "completely cut off" (*VO* 330). Just as the child Virginia felt helpless against Gerald's inexorable hands, Rachel lies in numbed acquiescence to the hands that "every now and then . . . turn her over at the bottom of the sea" (341). In this death scene, Woolf provides a window not only on her own traumatized imagination, but on the inner life of fellow victims of incest. Contemporary trauma theorists and incest survivors generally agree that "Childhood sexual abuse is as much an invasion of mind and spirit as it is a violent invasion of the body" (Davies 59). In other words, sexual violation colonizes not only the body but the inner life of the victim, as well. Woolf's depiction of the distorted imagination of a woman who has been sexually violated is consistent with contemporary survivor testimonies. Cathy Winkler, a woman who survived rape, explains that "Rapists' threats extend beyond superficial retorts and mentally and psychologically invade victims' being and self-definition" (12). Nancy Venable Raine, who also survived rape, describes her traumatized imagination: "[the rape] was no longer an event in the past. It was my present emotional landscape, the jungles of the island upon which many survivors . . . of overwhelming terror find themselves stranded, sometimes forever" (57). Marcia Cameron, a victim of childhood abuse, explains the inner life of a trauma survivor in a similar way: "but I was folded into the black place that lies at the back of my brain beyond the space of logic. In that black void there flashed the jumble of images that aroused the terror" (3).

To Rachel's colonized imagination, the "jumble of images" that terrorize her—among them the man with "hairy hands" and an "old woman slicing a man's head off" (*VO* 329; 339)—are incomprehensible, but to savvy readers they are recognizable metaphors for actual violations. The saddest of Rachel's hallucinations merges memory fragments from St. Ives—memories associated with sensual ecstasy and girlish vulnerability—with memory fragments associated with both Gerald and George's violations. Rachel sees "the movement of the blind . . . drawing the cord with a little trailing sound along the floor . . . as if it were the movement of an animal in the room" (*VO* 328). The blind recalls a happy childhood memory of sleeping safely while the "yellow blind . . . dr[e]w its little acorn across the floor" at St. Ives. The animal refers back to the animal-face at her shoulder in the looking-glass nightmare linked with Gerald's sexual violation, and the "movement in the room" recalls George's terrifying late night approaches to her bed (see also DeSalvo, *Impact* 102; 325). Here, Woolf depicts how trauma terrors can contaminate even pleasant memories because a victim cannot discriminate love from betrayal, or joy from pain: in other words, if trust and ecstasy can be so violated and betrayed, why risk joy again?

Rachel's nightmare "dead-end tunnels" are similar to what trauma specialist Harvey Schwartz calls the "dissociative labyrinth" of trauma survivors stuck in trauma reenactments: "Existing inside a dissociative labyrinth with its oblique and unarticulated grief and continuous intrapsychic pressures (e.g., cacophony of voices) is like living in a permanent state of exile from the human community" (10). In response to intolerable perpetrator demands, "the [victim's] true self'—her will, vitality, voice, and cognition—"may go into hiding and hold the pain, the grief"

(Whitfield 34; see also Laub and Auerhahn 291). Rachel's inner life is so thoroughly colonized that she cannot imagine a future different from her past and present. Therefore, her impression that "she is not dead, but curled up at the bottom of the sea" (*VO* 341) may be analogous to "what living in a permanent state of exile" feels like to a survivor of sexual trauma.

The following section traces a trajectory in Woolf's fiction from the confused loyalties and unremitting sexual terrors of *The Voyage Out* to the separatist clarity and lesbian epiphanies of *The Years,* a movement evidenced in Woolf's mature narrative resolutions of her own sexual dilemmas, as well as her evolving ideas about the impact of male sexual violence on female subjectivity and ambitions. At the conclusion of *The Years,* when Eleanor asks, "Does everything come over again a little differently?" (*Y* 369), Woolf subtly exposes the central aim of this novel: to rewrite scenes from her first novel that depicted themes about sexuality and romance with greater boldness and clarity. For example, in *The Years,* Edward's idealized worship of Kitty revisits Willoughby's worship of his dead wife as "ideal beloved" (*VO* 85), but with Edward, Woolf more overtly exposes the homoerotic misogyny underlying men's romanticized objectifications of women as "virgin beloveds." In both novels, we find a woman of ambiguous sexual orientation "in love" with a homosexual man. However, in *The Years* the "romance" between Sara and Nicholas is delineated more overtly than that between Helen and Hirst. In *The Years,* Woolf rewrites Hewet and Hirst's undressing scene so that the homoerotic flirtation between closeted gay men is more obvious. In *The Voyage Out,* Hewet "paid no attention to the undressing of Mr. Hirst," and we hear nothing of what Hirst is feeling (106). In *The Years,* Woolf depicts Ashley openly admiring Edward's body as Edward self-consciously flirts with Ashley.

The most important revisions, however, occur in those scenes that are trauma-related. In *The Voyage Out* and *The Years,* Rachel and Rose, respectively, are depicted as survivors of childhood sexual trauma. Both Rachel and Rose learn early to associate sensuality with vulnerability and debasement. The "infinite possibilities" (*VO* 76) Rachel momentarily feels after Dalloway's kiss are instantly destroyed by Dalloway's crude intentions and, as DeSalvo, Swanson, and Tyler convincingly argue, dissociated memories of prior incest violation by her father. The exhibitionist whom Rose meets on her way to Lamley's teaches her to associate her exuberant rebelliousness with male sexual retaliation. Roger Poole and David Eberly have noted the references to Woolf's childhood sexual trauma in this scene. Poole, for example, traces the "horrid face" (*Y* 28; *MOB* 69) that haunts Rose's nightmares to Woolf's descriptions of George's face, and both Poole and Eberly note that the "shuffling in the passage" (*Y* 40) outside Rose's door that evening recalls George's night-time visits to Virginia's bedroom. Furthermore, Rose's feelings of terror and isolation—"She was quite alone" with "[s]omething horrible" (40; 42)—repeat Woolf's own feelings at the time of Gerald and George's sexual violations (Poole 36-38; Eberly, "Incest" 148-49).

Rachel, like Virginia in her childhood, is alone with memories and insights no one in her environment is willing to share (Swanson 303). Although Rose's response to the exhibitionist repeats the same traumatic patterns as Rachel's response to Dalloway's kiss, Rose's fate is less trag-ic because she is not left entirely alone with her pain. Dori Laub and Nanette C. Auerhahn emphasize that in childhood sexual abuse, the "essential experience of trauma was an unraveling of the relationship between self and nurturing other, the very fabric of psychic life" (286); therefore, reinstating trustworthy people is essential to recovery. This is the function of what Alice K. Miller calls the "enlightened witness": a person near to the child who can attest to versions of reality outside the perpetrator's worldview (*Banished* 7).

As Rose lies in bed terrified, expecting the exhibitionist to break in at any moment, the door opens and—instead—Eleanor steps in. Here, and many times in *The Years*, Woolf revisits and defuses this trauma marker based on George's nighttime sexual assaults: the scuffling outside the door of the sleeping female just before a door opens. Through her volun-teer work with the poor, Eleanor already has connections with points of view outside those of her own, self-enclosed family. Eleanor enjoys rela-tive freedom because, unlike Rachel, she refuses heterosexual love and marriage. Unlike Helen, who trivializes Rachel's sexual terrors, Eleanor responds to Rose's fright with empathy and compassion. Eleanor accepts that she has seen "[s]omething horrible, something hidden. . . . behind [Rose's] strained eyes" (*Y* 42-43). Unlike Helen, who stays loyal to her Bluebeard-husband Ridley, Eleanor reenacts the disobedient wife's forbidden descent into her husband's basement, a journey to the under-world of family secrets (*Y* 43).

Rachel cannot move out from "the weight of the entire world" of "Lies! lies! lies!" (*VO* 258; 29) that surround her. When Eleanor begins to move out, she, too, is checked by "a weight [that] seemed to descend on her"; but Eleanor bravely "straighten[s] her candle and walk[s] down the stair" (*Y* 43). Although Eleanor does not speak to Rose, she shares Rose's burden—significantly, in her imagination. Rachel's deathbed scene depicts the horrifying colonization of the female imagination. However, by stepping outside the family system, even momentarily, Eleanor begins the process of reclaiming ownership of her inner life. By her unspoken identification with Rose's pain, Eleanor begins the heroic reclamation of a female collective imaginary that is a central aim of this novel. Later in the novel, in Eleanor and Kitty's lesbian-based imaginative ecstasies, Woolf reclaims what, as Christine Froula notes, Rachel (and Woolf at that earlier time) lacks: "the words for the life of the female imagination" ("Out Of" 88).

Sara, another woman who resists compulsory heterosexuality, imaginatively shares Rose's burden, as well. Like Rachel, Rose responds to sexual terror by withdrawing. However, Woolf transforms Rose's (and Rachel's) trauma response from self-destructive to self-protective withdrawal by having Sara share it. During Sara's dialogue about courtship and marriage with her mother and sister, Sara, like Rose earlier in the novel, wraps herself up in blankets: "she looked like a chrysalis wrapped round in the sharp white folds of the sheet" (*Y* 144). The chrysalis comparison changes trauma withdrawal from a lifetime sentence to an opportunity for self-transformation.

In *The Voyage Out*, Woolf inserts references to someone touching Rachel's shoulder to mark how trauma-induced habits of constriction and terror can be reactivated whenever intimacy becomes possible. As already discussed, for many incest survivors, love and betrayal are so violently merged that even potentially joyful human relationships seem threatening. In *The Voyage Out*, Rachel's father "enforc[es] his words as he often did, when he spoke to his daughter, by a smart blow upon the shoulder." Rachel responds automatically by laughing at her father's jokes although she does not really find them funny (*VO* 28). In Rachel's automatic willingness to shape her will in accordance with her father's demands, Woolf encapsulates what Alice K. Miller aptly identifies as "the unconscious pain of the little child who had to disown [her] keen observation for the sake of the conformity required of [her]" (*Thou Shalt Not* 82). In fact, not only her perpetrator but everyone in Rachel's environment expects her to bury her own voice and point of view, even the women she most relies on, Helen and her aunts. The heterosexual sacrifice of one's own vitality, intelligence, and point of view demanded by the incest perpetrator in childhood is reenacted for Rachel in the seemingly universal expectation that she acquiesce to traditional British marriage.

This trauma marker reappears whenever women attempt to become intimate with Rachel. Mrs. Flushing (like the animal-face in the looking-glass nightmare) approaches Rachel from behind—"Rachel felt a hand drop upon her shoulder"—when she invites Rachel to lunch. Similarly, Miss Allan "put[s] one hand upon Rachel's shoulder" as they leave Miss Allan's room. And most importantly, Helen initiates the much-discussed lesbian seduction scene when she rolls Rachel in the grass, with a "hand dropped abrupt as iron on Rachel's shoulder" (232; 257; 283). Bessel van der Kolk and Alexander C. McFarlane observe that in trauma "the memory of one particular [traumatic] event comes to taint all other experience, spoiling appreciation of the present. This tyranny of the past interferes with the ability to pay attention to both new and familiar situations" ("Black Hole" 4). Like Rachel's hallucination, which merges incest and maternal memories, these scenes dramatize Woolf's sense, even in this early work, that her childhood sexual trauma held her back from the kind of intimacies with women that she most desired.

In *The Years*, when Woolf returns to the "shoulder" as incest marker, she demarcates her mature capacity to bypass trauma-related restraints on her lesbian attachments and enthusiasms. In the holograph, Woolf more overtly links Sara's deformed shoulder to adult sexual crimes against her. Elvira (Sara's name in the draft) declares "the god of love forced me out of his arms down the kitchen stairs"—which, she explains, means the nursemaid dropped her when she was an infant to greet her lover as he appeared at the bottom of the kitchen stairs. Elsewhere in the draft, Woolf similarly links Rose's unbalanced psychological development with childhood crimes against her: Elvira observes that Rose's "powers of expression have obviously been atrophied by some early and painful I should venture to say hideous experiences. which she doesn't want to talk about. Just as a tree . . . if you put a ring round its wood all the apples on one side are small, wrinkled—bitter about the size of a half penny. . . . but on the other side dipped in golden lustre" (*TYH* 4: 51-52)

The holograph suggests that Woolf originally intended to trace Sara's eventual freedom from the effects of her physical/psychological trauma. In the draft Woolf depicts Sara's progressive shift from trauma victim to survivor in terms of her shoulder deformity which eventually nearly heals. Woolf's declaration in the holograph that "As a child she [Elvira] had looked queer; now she was scarcely crooked" (*TYH* 5: 75) reappears more subtly in the published version as the progressively liberated response of the female characters to shoulder touches. Willoughby's violating contact with Rachel's shoulder reappears in Colonel Pargiter's "hand that had lost two fingers . . . [fumbling] rather lower down where the neck joins the shoulder. Mira . . . leant her back against his knee" (*Y* 8). However, as the daughters begin to shed the effects of the family legacy of male sexual exploitation, they gradually reclaim the trauma-contaminated gestures of intimacy for themselves. For example, Sara playfully strikes Rose on the shoulder and says "Don't be such an ass!" and they walk off laughing, carrying violets. Woolf's favorite jokes about Vita during her 1930s retreat to her garden and tower are of Vita alone, writing in her tower, surrounded by pigeons (*L5*: 266). This trauma replay is so successful that when Sara recounts it to Maggie, the pigeons, a lesbian signature, begin crooning approval and Kitty, the character closest to Vita in the novel, walks triumphantly in, "clothed in starlight." What a grand transformation of Willoughby's shoulder-punch version of love! Similarly, when Nicholas "take[s] [Sara] by the shoulder" his gesture is loving and protective, as is Eleanor's "hand on [North's] shoulder" at the family reunion (*Y* 174; 187; 298; 307).[7]

The Years traces the Pargiter offsprings' progressive development toward freedom from the tyranny of the past. For the women, at least, this freedom from past influences is limited but nonetheless significant. In the culminating chapter of *The Years*, shoulder contacts inspire ecstasy rather than the trauma-induced revulsion Rachel experiences. Delia, "laying a hand on [Peggy's] shoulder," tells Peggy that her teacher had praised her. When, at the family reunion, Eleanor "tap[s] [Peggy] on the shoulder," Peggy's ecstasies are more fully embodied. This scene where Peggy sits at Eleanor's feet rewrites the predatory exchange between the Colonel and Mira sitting at his feet in the first chapter. In the final chapter, non-exploitative intimacy between two women reinvents past erotic habits and inspires both to dream about "Enjoy[ing] the moment" unfettered from the constricting habits of the past (*Y* 362; 384).

In both *The Voyage Out* and *The Years*, Woolf depicts the same range of lesbian "types": the spinster scholars (Miss Allan and Lucy Craddock), feminist marriage resisters (Evelyn Murgatroyd and Rose Pargiter), and artist/visionaries (Rachel Vinrace, Kitty Malone and Eleanor Pargiter). However, lesbian figures that Rachel perceives demonically, such as Miss Allan and Evelyn, return as heroes and visionaries in *The Years*, and Rachel's buried alienation from marriage norms, feminist rage, and visionary dreams is more successfully resurrected in Kitty's companionate marriage, Eleanor's spinsterhood, and Rose's feminist activism. Predictably, therefore, the "lesbian difference" in *The Years* is most clearly demarcated in Woolf's revision of Rachel's three-part journey into women-centered spaces. Rachel's visits to the rooms of Mrs. Flushing, Evelyn Murgatroyd, and Miss Allan are revised in Kitty's encounter with Mrs. Fripp, Nell Robson and Lucy Craddock, respectively. Patricia Smith has fully documented the lesbian seductions governing these scenes. Inspired by Hewet's reading of Sappho, Mrs. Flushing insists that Rachel lunch with her. Rachel goes, but is repelled by Mrs. Flushing's greed, all her "treasures" having been stolen from indigenous peoples. Rachel's meeting with Evelyn is at first "exciting" but soon becomes "disagreeable." Miss Allan seems the character most likely to have something worthwhile to tell Rachel, but Rachel flees her sphere of erotic and intellectual influence. Significantly, Rachel laments the repression of her body, "the source of all the life in the world," at the end of her disappointing lesbian escapade (*VO* 237; 249; 258). Rachel's perception is so trauma-dominated that it is unclear whether these women are as disappointing as she finds them, or whether they could, in fact, offer Rachel hope of a freedom she cannot acknowledge.

In Kitty's encounter with Mrs. Fripp, Woolf revises not only Rachel's visit with Mrs. Flushing but the scene of a young woman's "first kiss." Rachel's kiss by Dalloway evokes emotional confusion and panic. Rather than Kitty's "open window" and "garden" (*Y* 60), Rachel sees her life a "hedged-in thing" (*VO* 82). Kitty's "warm glow on her cheek" (*Y* 60) from Mrs. Fripp's kiss revises Rachel's "chill" (*VO* 76). Like Rachel, Kitty's sexual arousal is quickly checked by trauma-related terrors—the omnipresent St. Ives "muslin blind, blowing out [recalling St. Ives joy]. . . almost touch[es] the flame" (*Y* 60-61). Startled, Kitty interrupts her joyful reveries. She is next checked by an internalized maternal voice warning her not to stand by open windows. Kitty's maternal checks hark back to Mrs. Paley "blocking up [Rachel's] passage" (*VO* 258), and to Woolf's childhood memories of maternal betrayal.

However, unlike Rachel, Kitty stays true to her lesbian inclinations and does not let the past dictate present or future possibilities. She returns to the memory of Mrs. Fripp's kiss, "feeling again the glow on her cheek." Access to lesbian emotion boosts her confidence in her own perceptions: she admits she finds Oxford "obsolete" and undergraduates "silly" and she decides to leave Oxford as soon as she can. When Kitty also thinks excitedly about her next day's lessons with Miss Craddock, Woolf rewrites her own bedtime anticipation of lessons with Janet Case; but this time, neither the perpetrator nor his internalized edicts disrupt the sleepy adolescent's intellectual dreams. Instead, Kitty's clarity and self-assertion are "blessed" by lesbian metaphors—"walloping like a slow porpoise through the drizzling air"(*Y* 60-62). The porpoise is a favorite metaphor for Woolf's beloved Vita, and Vita's presence here underlines the importance of their love affair to Woolf's transformed relationship to traumatized desires (see *L5*; 370; *L6*; 195).

In this scene, Kitty unravels two key trauma-induced disabilities: the loss of faith in one's own perceptions, and the "confusion and doubt" perpetrators instill in victims. Rachel's emotional confusion mixes the "acorn and the blind" with the "animal in the room": she experiences all intense emotions, especially sexual joys, as dangers that must be avoided. She cannot tell the difference between Clarissa Dalloway and Miss Allan, or Richard and Evelyn. But Kitty's lesbian eye achieves that ability to "distinguish" and "discriminate" (Nachmani, "Trauma" 428) recommended by trauma experts as essential to recovery. To borrow Schwartz's words, Kitty knows "what to be afraid of"—Oxford—and "what not to be afraid of"—Miss Craddock (162). Unlike Rachel, who is immobilized by the "persecutory theater of [her violated] mind" (Schwartz 10), Kitty bypasses the internalized voices of perpetrator ideologies in favor of her own. By her steadfast adherence to her own desires and point of view, as well as her visionary expectations outside her family's values, Kitty marks the teleology of Woolf's own creative process: that "move . . . from being a victim of [her] mind (and of control by the perverse mind of the perpetrator) to authentic ownership of that mind and body and spirit" (Schwartz 149).

In Kitty's visit to Miss Craddock's room, Woolf returns to Rachel's failed interchange with the spinster-scholar, Miss Allan. Both women engage in lesbian-coded dialogues with their students; but whereas Rachel is repelled by Miss Allan's gingered offerings, Kitty is thrilled to "touch . . . [Miss Craddock's] little flowers tenderly." Although Kitty's "excitement" in Miss Craddock's presence is at first "mixed with fear," Kitty's "eyes [remain] full of love and admiration" for her teacher. Kitty's "heart beat[ing] faster" (*Y* 64-66) as she approaches Miss Craddock's room replaces Rachel's "tremendous beats of the heart" (*VO* 76) following Dalloway's kiss, just as Kitty's lesbian sexual ecstasy replaces Rachel's heterosexual terror and revulsion.

Kitty finishes her day's lesbian adventures by a visit to her working class friend Nell Robson's home. Here, Kitty meets a family where women are respected, and more importantly, she finds in the portrait of Nell's grandmother—not the vacant, colluding eyes of her own and the Pargiters' mother—but the "sturdy look" and "piercing eye" of the woman who knows what has been done to her and is still being done to other women (*Y* 72). Nachmani describes what other trauma experts similarly recognize as a "signature of trauma": a "form of memory: *not knowing*" ("Trauma" 423). This self-protective ignorance in the presence of sexual violation afflicts witnesses as well as victims. So Kitty's imaginative identification with a maternal figure whose perception is confident, clear, and "on her side" is important in the bolstering of her own outsider point of view. Note, however, that Kitty's lesbian fantasies of Eleanor and Miss Craddock precede this identification with a transformed maternal figure: for Woolf it is the lesbian lover, not the literal or symbolic mother, who is a catalyst for the liberating epiphanies in her novels.[8]

At the end of her day's three-part lesbian quest, Rachel concludes that life is "intolerable!" (*VO* 258). But in Woolf's revision of this quest in *The Years*, Kitty finds life full of exciting possibilities. Inspired partly by Dalloway's kiss, Rachel shares her inarticulate desires with Clarissa Dalloway. "I want—" Rachel begins, but tragically, Clarissa redirects Rachel's unformulated desires back to the perpetrator by responding: "When I was your age I wanted too. . . . [until Richard] gave me all I wanted" (*VO* 60). Kitty repeats Rachel's words "I want," but her desires slip easily to thoughts of her beloved Eleanor. Kitty's lesbian fantasies are accompanied by St. Ives metaphors: "the garden . . . full of murmurings and cooings." Then the trajectory of Kitty's lesbian desire is momentarily checked by rape-associated memory fragments: "he had wood shavings in his head." In the context of the narrative, "wood shavings" reflect back on Nell's brother, but autobiographically they are linked with Vita's adolescent encounter with a farmer's son, Jackie, who nearly raped her (Glendinning 22).[9] Nevertheless, Kitty's lesbian will bypasses this trauma checkpoint and her maverick desires are bolstered—this time by Woolf's adult lesbian as well as childhood St. Ives memory fragments: "pigeons . . . cooing. Take two coos, . . Take two coos" (*Y* 73-76). The pigeons, as noted earlier, recall Woolf's beloved, Vita, and the pigeons' cooing recalls the sound of the "waves breaking — one two one two—" at St. Ives.

All Rachel's experiences of the "unreasonable exaltations" that make creative life possible are abruptly truncated by trauma echoes. For example, when the word "love" momentarily "unveil[s] the skies for Rachel," she is checked by violent imagery and incest memory fragments—warships and Richard's incest incantation—"By George!" (*VO* 68-69; see also 173-74). Thus Rachel's sexual yearnings are repeatedly tunneled back on those "railway lines of convention" (*D2*: 177-78) which lead women to "enjoy" sexual submission in exchange for love. In contrast, Kitty's more steadfast lesbian vision provides the ecstasy and insight which enables her to see through and reject trauma-related barriers within and around her. Whereas Rachel disappears beneath the weight of trauma memories, by midlife Kitty's managing/observing "I" is fully supported by imaginative alliances with women she has loved, as well as a plethora of St. Ives and adult lesbian memories.

Kitty's mature, woman-centered imagination triumphs during her hilltop epiphany which culminates her train ride escape from family life. Just as Rachel's death scene exposes the chaos of the traumatized imagination, Kitty's revelation reclaims a female, lesbian-based imagination. Kitty makes her "escape" in May (*Y* 276), the month Rachel dies. In "22 Hyde Park Gate," Woolf associates "May Week at Cambridge" with her party dates with George (*MOB* 173). In both novels, May is linked with disaster and pain. Rachel's nurse warns "Things seem to go wrong in May" (*VO* 344). Kitty muses "Spring was sad always, . . . it brought back memories" (*Y* 277).

The train ride itself reenacts the "long train journey" (*MOB* 65) Woolf took as a girl to St. Ives each summer. This childhood theme opens the scene, when Woolf compares Kitty fleeing London to "a little girl who had run away from her nurse and escaped." Other St. Ives memory fragments pervading this scene include the St. Ives "blind" (*Y* 270; *MOB* 66), the "bee buzz," and the "pigeons' croon" (*Y* 275; *MOB* 66); the "land that went rising and falling" (*Y* 278) merges with the St. Ives rhythm of rooks and waves—"The rooks cawing [being] part of the waves breaking" (*MOB* 98). In "A Sketch of the Past," Woolf writes that "the present when backed by the past is a thousand times deeper than the present when it presses so close that you can feel nothing else" (*MOB* 98). By "attaching" lesbian and maternal/sororal memories, Woolf is able to retrace and access a sensual optimism violated by Gerald and George's sexual betrayals. These erotic combinations of maternal/sororal and lesbian metaphors provide depth for her adult lesbian life and longevity for her childhood female-inspired joys.

As Kitty warns, eventually "One's not a child . . . any longer" (*Y* 271), and by 1937, Woolf's version of an adult female imagination requires adult ecstatic experiences as well as keen insight. Thus, one cannot underestimate Vita's contribution to Woolf's revisions of the female imagination and, subsequently, to Woolf's trajectories of lesbian will and desire. Memory fragments associated with Vita imbue virtually every culminating "moment" of epiphany in Woolf's novels, including this one. For example, Kitty's overnight train ride revisits not just the childhood train ride to St. Ives, but a journey Virginia took with Vita to view an eclipse on June 29, 1927.[10] As Woolf describes in "The Sun and the Fish," her train ride with Vita, like Kitty's, began in London late at night and ended in Yorkshire at dawn at approximately the same time of year: May (Kitty) and June (Virginia and Vita). In the "cold raw air" (*Y* 272) and "chill early morning" (*CDB* 212), Virginia, Vita, and Kitty find themselves on high ground overlooking the moors (*CDB* 213; *Y* 277). In "The Sun and the Fish," Woolf recalls her train ride with Vita as a journey outside familiar time and space: "we were no longer in the same relation to people, houses and trees" (*CDB* 213). Similarly, Kitty feels as though she is "passing from one world to another" (*Y* 267). The lesbian resonances in this scene reach back to earlier times in the novel as well as in Woolf's life. The "blue and white flowers, trembling on the cushions of green moss" Kitty finds on the hilltop, recall the "wild flowers, blue and white, stuck into a cushion of wet green moss" (*Y* 65) Miss Craddock had given to her. Furthermore, Vita once gave Virginia a miniature garden similar to the garden Miss Craddock gave to Kitty: "an earthenware pan containing several rocks and small alpine plants" (*L3*: 210).

Fueled by this armory of lesbian emotional triggers, Kitty's train ride completes Rachel's aborted "voyage out" of patriarchally defined perceptions, desires, and life narrative. Tunnels and train tracks are among Woolf's favorite sexual metaphors (*D2*: 177-78). Kitty's train ride, therefore, "rush[es] with a roar through [Rachel's] tunnels," motivated by erotic aims outside heterosexual conventions (*Y* 270). At the end of the novel, Eleanor reenacts Kitty's train ride in her imagination, briefly revisiting Rachel's deadend tunnel before moving quickly on: "[Eleanor] looked ahead of her as though she saw opening in front of her a very long dark tunnel. But thinking of the dark, something baffled her; in fact it was growing light. The blinds were white" (428). Freedom from the effects of past sexual trauma means learning to live in a present no longer hostage to the past. It is significant, therefore, that Kitty experiences her first rush through a tunnel as an "amputation" cutting her off from London, configured here as the city of the damned ("the eternally burning city") (*Y* 129; 270); and during her second rush through a tunnel Kitty demarcates her elegy to the past with an incantation to "*Now . . . Now . . . Now.*" Analogously, Eleanor's train ride epiphany ends in the "Present Day" (*Y* 271; 428).

Woolf's radical fiction aims to take readers out of those familiar emotional and cognitive tracks that keep perpetrator ideologies in place. One of those "convenient railway lines of convention" I'd like to avoid "returns us to" the Stephen family myth that Virginia was mentally ill. In this regard, Hermione Lee's insistence that Woolf was a "sane woman. . . . of exceptional courage, intelligence, and stoicism . . . who . . . came to the deepest understanding possible to her, of her own condition" (171) is a welcome corrective to lingering caricatures of Woolf as depressive, fragile, and/or damaged. My intention is that, like myself, Woolf scholars engaged in trauma studies align our reading of Woolf with Lee's impressive tribute to Woolf's strengths, but without sacrificing, as she does, our own "critically discerning eye" on the reality and severity of the childhood sexual abuse Woolf suffered.

Most contemporary trauma experts seem to agree with van der Kolk's assessment that: "There is no evidence to support Freud's idea that repetition eventually leads to mastery and resolution. In fact, reliving the trauma repeatedly in psychotherapy may serve to re-enforce the preoccupation and fixation" ("Compulsion" 399; see also Herman, *Incest* 229). In the 1930's Sandor Ferenczi found that just reproducing trauma "produced no better results than the original trauma." However, when Ferenczi deliberately admitted his own mistakes to his clients, he broke away from the Freudian model of the therapist-client relationship. By encouraging his clients' critical thinking rather than imposing his own point of view, he saw dramatic improvements in his clients' abilities to detach from traumatic reenactments. Ferenczi isolates the *"setting free of his [or her] critical feelings"* as the key to freedom for adults still suffering from the aftereffects of childhood sexual trauma (199-200; emphasis added).[11]

Ferenczi's insight into the importance of rationality for attaining detachment from the aftereffects of incest can help highlight the enormous differences between Woolf's depictions of incest themes in *The Voyage Out* and *The Years*. In *The Years*, Woolf's trauma-related scenes suggest that critical discernment and feminist decision-making, not emotional instability, are the motives for her trauma re-enactments.[12] For example, throughout *The Years*, Woolf's narrative eye (like Kitty's and Eleanor's) distinguishes between people and emotions that are "like" the perpetrator, and hence to be rejected, and those that are woman-centered. Trauma markers like the "sucking noise" Rose's exhibitionist makes, the lamppost he leans against, or the semen-like stain on Rose's pinafore reappear throughout the novel attached to people or incidents that evidence that same "Soul Murder" (Shengold) perpetrators aim for. However, the lesbian-St. Ives metaphors suggest not only ecstasy but clarity and decision-making for Woolf's closeted lesbian characters. As already discussed, Kitty's reveries following her encounters with Mrs. Fripp, Nell Robson, and Miss Craddock depict the pattern for defeating trauma echoes that Woolf devised: lesbian erotic ecstasy, followed by trauma-related checks, countered by lesbian fantasy inspiring feminist clarity and decision-making.[13] In *The Years*, Woolf posits lesbian desire as the motor "setting free" the critical faculties capable of discrediting family and cultural deceptions.

This same intermingling of woman-centered ecstasy and political discernment reappears throughout the novel. The culmination of all those (lesbian) pigeons cooing over the suffragette meeting is Kitty's clear-headed outburst to Eleanor that "Force is always wrong." Eleanor's delight in her work with the poor (inspired, in part, by her admiration for Mrs. Levy's daughter [*Y* 31]) is accompanied by St. Ives echoes —"rooks swooping in a field, rising and falling"—and she ends her happy musings on her spinster life by rejecting Miriam's self-sacrificing approach to work and by giving a "very definite opinion" when asked by Major Porter. Even Martin, possibly inspired by the St. Ives "gulls screaming as they rose and sank over a lady who was feeding them" achieves momentary clarity when he bursts out, "Possessiveness is the devil" (*Y* 179; 94-96; 244-45).

As Jennifer Freyd notes, adults who were molested in childhood are especially prone to what she calls "betrayal blindness": "the systematic filtering of reality in order to maintain human relationships" (193). Alice K. Miller adds that "only the painful journey to the facts, to the relinquishing of blindness, illusions, and the useless prosthesis of self-delusion and confusion" (*Banished* 162) can undo the moral and cognitive confusion Freyd describes. Woolf's 1930s returns to incest themes are motivated not by masochism, emotional obsession, or repetition compulsion, but rather by that passion for truth-telling that trauma specialists Freyd and Miller, like so many who have survived sexual trauma, prescribe. Thus, reading Woolf's fiction from the perspective of her incest themes need not, as Lee fears, "reduce[ ] it to a coded expression of neurotic symptoms" (156). Rather, trauma theory reveals yet another terrain in which Woolf's disciplined intellect took her "to the deepest understanding possible to her, [not only] of her own condition" (Lee 171), but of conditions widespread in her own and our culture conducive to child abuse and its lasting repercussions.

Furthermore, while Rachel's impasse depicts Woolf's own uncertainties at this early time in her career, in *The Years* Woolf reveals a discerning narrative eye fully cognizant of perpetrator strategies in her past and "Present Day." It is important, therefore, for those of us engaged in trauma studies to differentiate the early Woolf, overwhelmed by her incest experiences, from the mature writer of *The Years,* who delineates not only the life-destroying impasse of trauma but a lesbian "voyage out" of the "rut of feeling the old rut. . . so cheap, so banal"(*TYH7*: 72) of endless trauma reenactments.

Notes

1. See Hussey, *A to Z* (332-36) on dates for *The Voyage Out.*

2. Russell rates sexual abuse by brothers as second only to paternal abuse in its traumatic effects. Yet women sexually abused by brothers suffer most from the stereotype of

mutuality. Where the victim felt positive feelings toward the brother, the trauma was greatest (149; 271; 388). On mothers in incest families, see Jacobs 12-31 and Herman, *Incest* 67-95.

3. "Pillar of the Community" is such a catchword for perpetrators, it is a title of a moving essay by a brother and sister (David and Sara) raped throughout childhood by their father. David's description of their rapist/father is familiar: "And my dad was a "life of the party type person. Always doing for other people" (206). For a brilliant (and hilarious) "play on" perpetrator respectability, see *Thanatron*, available at http://www.carolyngage.com/. In his eloquent preface to Ariel Jordan's incest story, Mark Hussey offers a far more astute model for approaching incest testimonies. He writes, "the choice of who[m] we listen to and who[m] we believe is an ethical one," and he adds, "For those of us who are not survivors, it will take a new courage to believe these stories with our bodies, to make them part of our own reality" ("Violent Hunger" 69).

4. I focus on Leaska and Lee because they are recent biographers and typify misconceptions about incest that also reappear in email discussions, in published essays, and at conferences. For example, Panthea Reid also claims that Woolf's positive statements written during George's violations are "hard to square with her subsequent attacks" (62). Both Reid and Lee seem to think it important to emphasize that, in Reid's words, George "did not rape them [Vanessa and Virginia]" (62). Similarly, Lee defends her belittling of Woolf's credibility by concluding: "There is no way of knowing whether the teenage Virginia Stephen was fucked or forced to have oral sex or buggered" (156)—strange criteria for what constitutes childhood sexual trauma when experts and survivors tell us that unwanted fondling by a trusted family member, of the sort inflicted on Virginia by both Gerald and George—is more than enough to cause serious childhood trauma.

5. See Henke, *Shattered Subjects,* on Woolf's use of narrative to undo the aftereffects of trauma (xxii). This important work shows that other twentieth-century women writers, including Colette, H.D., Anais Nin, Janet Frame, Audre Lorde, and Sylvia Fraser, share Woolf's preoccupation with trauma. See Jen Shelton on incest structure as "narrative contests" between perpetrator and victim's "competing and mutually exclusive stories" (224).

6. For discussion of additional literary allusions that point toward Rachel's incest history see DeSalvo, "Virginia, Virginius, Virginity"; Tyler, "Nameless Atrocities"; and Swanson.

7. For a full tracing of the lesbian codes in *The Years,* including the "pigeons," "porpoises" and Kitty's train ride discussed here, see Cramer, "Pearls" and "*Vita Nuova.*"

8. I disagree, therefore, with Tyler's argument that Rachel dies because she lacks a mother to protect her ("Mother-Daughter Passion" 78). The role of maternal memory in

49

Woolf's lesbian imagination is too complex for full explication here. However, I do urge Woolf readers to finally move beyond lesbophobic clichés about lesbian love as motivated by a search for mother substitutes. For example, Leaska writes about Virginia and Vita: "Could [Vita] give all the things Julia never gave, could never give? This was to become the bond joining Virginia to Vita." Leaska even equates Vita's affair with Mary Campbell with mother-daughter love (230; 270). However, Lee is equally absurd when she insists that we cannot call Woolf a lesbian because in her work "there are no romances between Byronic heroes and languid girls, no sadomasochistic erotic scenes, no gloomy doomed transvestites" (485). Both Leaska and Lee are stuck on early twentieth-century stereotypes of lesbians as oedipal failures (Freud) and exotic sex and gender transgressors (the sexologists)—the very stereotypes Woolf herself deliberately revised. See Barrett, "Inverted World," on Woolf's revision of these lesbian stereotypes. For more complex, psychoanalytic readings of Rachel's death as retreat to a maternal terrain which are closer to my own, see Henke, "De/Colonizing the Subject" and Claire Kahane, *Passions of the Voice*. Woolf's strategy for preserving lesbian memories by joining them to other memories is comparable to Freyd's notion of "shareability," which states that memories that are shared undergo a mental coding that enables them to remain consistent and accessible over time (108-111). See Annette Oxindine "Sexing," and Patricia Cramer, "Notes from Underground" and "Introduction" on the lesbian content in Woolf's epiphanies.

9. Vita recalls that when she was eleven, the local farmer's son, Jackie, "put his hand on her thigh." Vita writes, "But because of his inborn respect, his sense of class, he didn't rape me." Vita adds ". . . I think that there was nothing wrong about what Jackie and I did" (Glendinning 22). Toni McNaron suggests that Vita may have been an "enlightened witness" to Woolf's incest story when Woolf confided in Vita about her childhood molestation when they were alone in France (253).

10. On this train ride see "The Sun and the Fish" *Time and Tide*, February 3, 1928. On February 8, 1928, Vita wrote to Virginia, "I can't tell you how much I like the Sun and the Fish (all the more because it is all about things we did together)" (*Sackville-West* 255).

11. On Ferenczi's pioneering role in trauma studies, see van der Kolk et al. "History of Trauma in Psychiatry."

12. See Shelton, who also rejects reading Woolf's incest narratives as symptomology.

13. Eberly traces this same sexual "dynamic of impulse and restraint" in Woolf's short stories. I agree with Eberly that the "penetrating finger" ("Safety Pins" 136; 139) of the perpetrator intrudes quickly in Woolf's fiction whenever lesbian sexual arousal occurs.

THE UNEASY SOLACE OF ART: THE EFFECT OF SEXUAL ABUSE ON VIRGINIA WOOLF'S AESTHETIC

Toni A. H. McNaron

In her germinal study, *Virginia Woolf: The Impact of Childhood Sexual Abuse on her Life and Work,* Louise DeSalvo closely documented the lasting effects of Virginia Stephen Woolf's molestation by her two half-brothers, George and Gerald Duckworth. She also set off a veritable fire-storm within the community of Woolf scholars, embers of which still surface at conferences and on electronic bulletin boards. DeSalvo's basic tenet is quite simple: the nightmare experiences from Virginia Stephen's childhood and early adulthood are replayed not only in Virginia Woolf's adult psyche but in her writing. DeSalvo sees Woolf's fiction—both her *juvenilia* and adult productions—as a laboratory in which to observe the writer's brave, if halting, efforts to name her experience and to resolve it as best she could with the limited resources available. This articulation of Woolf's psychological context lends greater significance to the quantity and quality of her writing than previously assigned it on purely literary grounds. While DeSalvo's critics insist that she stretches the data or that she interprets them too broadly, her heavy reliance on primary documents from the Stephen family and from the culture surrounding it offers tangible evidence of Woolf's own awareness of what happened in her childhood and of its permanent coloring of her adult reality.

I will argue that Woolf continues to cope with her early abuse in her essays. At the heart of her aesthetic lie her valiant attempts to create a world in which men do not violate women relatives as a matter of patriarchal inheritance. By envisioning such a world, Woolf is enlarging on a life-saving strategy familiar to contemporary students of incest. Several studies (Fraser, 1988; Danica, 1988; Bass and Davis, 1988; Courtois, 1988; Armstrong, 1994; Gilmartin, 1994; Johnston, 1997) show that victims of incest often make up a second self or imaginary friend to whom terrible things happen in the night. Simultaneously, they retain a daytime persona that continues to function more or less successfully because she stands (dangerously) separate from the receiver of the abuse. As DeSalvo points out, during 1897 when Virginia Stephen was recovering from the devastating death of her mother and experiencing the trauma of George's first sexual molestations, Woolf's writing speaks often of a character called "Jan" onto whom she projected emotional responses deemed inappropriate by her immediate family or culture. DeSalvo traces the process of Virginia's splitting in this way: "Woolf, knowing that *her* authentic feelings will not be heeded, knowing that a display of her real feelings is dangerous, reacts, appropriately, with anger: 'I have been in a dreadful temper all day long.' But as soon as she describes her rage, she dissociates herself from it—'I have been in a dreadful temper all day, poor creature.' She stops being Virginia when she has these feelings and she becomes a poor creature, [a] self whom she allows to express her feelings" (*Impact* 241-242). While such a need to divide the self may serve a protective purpose, it also further fractures the violated individual, usually inhibiting if not preventing self-knowledge.

Many women today report having created fantasy realms in order to endure the annihilating nature of their sexual abuse. In the words of one such survivor, "When I was smaller and alone a lot, I used to pretend a world of my own in which I was the only real human being. I played with my dolls way up into high school, and it was *my* world. It was *beautiful* and *complete*, and it was *clean*. And most of all it was *safe*. No one could get to me when I was in my world" (Butler [1979], 167. Emphasis on "my" is the author's; subsequent emphases are mine.)

The emphasized words set forth an (albeit unarticulated) aesthetic in which the world of the imagination is preferable to the world of daily life precisely because it is the opposite of the material world the victim is forced to continue to inhabit. Just as this late twentieth-century woman did, Virginia Woolf constructed a parallel universe intended to help her forget parts of her life. She then extended this psychological strategy into her formulations about the nature of art. Ironically, however, she was not always successful in maintaining a protective distance; someone or something could "get" Woolf even in her most elaborately made-up fictions. That someone or something lived deep within memories which seemed inevitably to shatter her safe, beautiful, complete, clean world. The explosion of her safe world is often expressed in images stemming from her experience of abuse, and establishing an unmistakable correlation between these shatterings and her own fearful memories.

In his comprehensive study of memory and trauma, Richard J. McNally speaks about "involuntary explicit memory" in ways that correspond closely with Woolf's complex process:

People with posttraumatic stress disorder suffer from involuntary explicit memory as exemplified by unbidden intrusive
recollection of horrific events from their past. Involuntary
explicit memory deserves more attention from psychologists
interested in how people remember trauma (34-35).

McNally also asserts that the opposite, implicit memory, involves "unin-
tentionality and unconsciousness. That is, words come to mind without
any deliberate search" (35). Not only would Woolf have understood this
argument, but her essays often demonstrate it, as I show in this study.

When Woolf's aesthetic has been considered seriously, it has usually
been framed within the tenets of modernism. Like her male cohorts, she
is seen as having installed a kingdom of art on the throne vacated by a
God who, if not dead, had become too capricious or lame to warrant
belief. Her abandonment of linear structure within her narratives further
aligns her with such modernists as Forster, Ford, Joyce, and Lawrence. A
preference for multiple narrators confirms the modernist position of
increasing authorial detachment from the unfolding narrative. This exercise in placement has resulted in critics and readers having too easily
dismissed Woolf's aesthetic by using a label whose meaning is automatically assumed.

Careful examination of her own comments on the powers and limitations of art, on the other hand, will reveal an idiosyncratic and complex
attitude influenced by the peculiar shape of her life as much as by prevailing fashions within Bloomsbury and other artistic circles. The following
study began while I was teaching a graduate seminar on Woolf as critic.
As we worked through her essays on virtually every aspect of society and
culture, I was struck by her repeated recountings of having her fictional
imaginings ("making ups" as she would name them) punctured by some
aspect of daily life. In "The New Biography," written in 1929, she coined
a phrase which aptly describes this juxtaposition: speaking of the new
biographer's wish to mesh a heady realm of abstraction with the world of
mundane details, she wonders how to combine "granite and rainbow." In
her system, the "rainbow" is largely the product of artistic imagining; the
"granite," contrarily, is provided by life itself. This essay reference cannot
fail to remind readers of a crucial scene in *Mrs. Dalloway*, when Peter
trivializes Sally's kissing Clarissa by asking if they are "star-gazing." The
narrator remarks: "It was like running one's face against a granite wall in
the darkness! It was shocking; it was horrible!" (*MD* 36).

Certainly there is nothing unique to Woolf in this observation. Many of her contemporaries in the 1920s were painfully aware that the center was no longer holding, and that if there had ever been any illusion that it could, World War I had destroyed that permanently, making the job of being an artist, a philosopher, or even a citizen, considerably more difficult. What is unique to Woolf's case is the manner in which she expresses her sense of life as an interruption of the safety and wholeness possible in the world of art. In "A Sketch of the Past," written in 1939 to break the intensity involved in her work on Roger Fry's biography, Woolf offers a trenchant commentary on her own artistic process:

> we are sealed vessels afloat on what it is convenient to call reality; and at some moments, the sealing matter cracks; in floods reality; that is, these scenes—for why do they survive undamaged year after year unless they are made of something comparatively permanent? (*MOB* [1976] 122)

Two important threads are present here: Woolf clearly differentiates between what society labels "reality" and something quite different, for which she uses the same term; she employs a pervasive image of water to describe that societally defined world in which we go about in "sealed vessels." But these vessels do not offer reliable protection and when their glue cracks, a flood occurs which obviously threatens to drown the person inside.

This latter conceit of a shell which promises to hold off chaos and danger is strikingly similar to Woolf's view of art itself. That her vessel in this passage is actually permeable and destructible points to a fragility or illusion at the base of her metaphor and its larger analogue, the constructed world of art. What is surely idiosyncratic to Woolf's own psychology and history is her final position that not even a constructed world of art is violence-proof if childhood and youth have been betrayed at so fundamental a level as hers had been. Sexual abuse seems to have cracked the "sealing matter" beyond any hope of permanent repair or restoration, even (and at times especially) through her extraordinary capacity for "scene making" (*MOB* [1976] 122).

Until recently, most people have tended to discount childhood trauma, mouthing shibboleths such as "well, children are so resilient, you know," or using any sign of minimal adult functioning as proof of the absence of lasting effects. Fortunately, it is no longer possible to deny or to trivialize abuse in this manner without being challenged. Alice Miller has stated in the clearest terms a list of "Newly Recognized, Shattering Effects of Child Abuse." Among her points is this one: "The normal reactions to such injury should be anger and pain; since children in this hurtful kind of environment, however, are forbidden to express their anger and since it would be unbearable to experience their pain all alone, they are compelled to suppress their feelings, repress all memory of the trauma, and idealize those guilty of the abuse. Later they will have *no memory of what was done to them*." Miller also notes that: "If mistreated children are not to become criminals or mentally ill, it is essential that *at least once in their life* they come in contact with a person who knows without any doubt that the environment, not the helpless, battered child, is at fault" (*Untouched* 168-169, emphasis is the author's). From all evidence, it would seem that Vita Sackville-West performed this crucial function in Virginia Woolf's case. DeSalvo points out that during a trip to France with Vita in 1928, Virginia told her of the molestation by her half brother and read her the relevant memoir. As DeSalvo says, "On the trip, Virginia bought herself an antique mirror, an extremely significant act, given her 'looking glass complex,' which suggests that telling Vita provided temporary comfort" (*Impact* 123). The fact, however, that this moment of support came so late in relation to the traumatic events argues against even its power to offset entirely Woolf's already firmly entrenched suppression of the horror.

In remembering the atmosphere in her house after her mother's death, Woolf makes this explicit statement: "A finger seemed laid on one's lips" (*MOB* [1976] 94). Her frequent remarks about how much could not be spoken within the culture of 22 Hyde Park Gate, together with her persistent attempts to paint even her abusers, George and Gerald Duckworth, as having a good side, must be reexamined in light of Miller's thesis that abuse victims tend to romanticize or glorify their abusers. Similarly, her injunction to her audience of young women in *A Room of One's Own* not to write their anger for fear it will mar their composition deserves closer scrutiny. Generally frowned upon in middle-class Victorian households, anger and truthful speaking became particularly dangerous in cases where the speaker was also being subjected to incestuous assaults by other members of those households.

Though she is fearfully mirrored in Miller's statement, Woolf practiced an art that worked against a permanent blotting out of memory both by allowing her to encode certain aspects of her past and by forcing her further and further into her unconscious, where the suppressed feelings were stored. Her writing then served a deeply ambivalent function. On the one hand, as DeSalvo asserts in her analysis of one of Woolf's juvenile stories, "The traumatic experience of incest, or of sexual assault is being detoxified, as it were, so that it will not become a pernicious memory. I believe that we are seeing Virginia . . . taking something terrifying and denying its potentially lethal nature by turning it into something innocuous" (*Impact* 145). Through her writing, she could gain a certain mastery over the ugly details of her past. On the other hand, she turned to art as a refuge only to find that it could, without warning, become a window onto her suffering. The same process that allowed her to escape could trigger memories of the horrors of her childhood and young adulthood. At times, even as she was making up innocuous or soothing scenes, some detail from the outside world could reverse her fantasy, propelling her back into the shame and terror felt during her sexual assaults. Thus the stream of her consciousness could carry her back to moments of trauma.

One of the clearest examples of my thesis occurs in Woolf's essay "Three Pictures." (I refer to this piece as an "essay" partly because it was originally published in her collection *The Death of the Moth and Other Essays.* It has subsequently also been included in the collection *Virginia Woolf: The Complete Shorter Fiction,* edited by Susan Dick. If we consider current understanding of such genres as the personal essay and creative non-fiction, there should be little worry over my viewing the piece as an essay rather than a short story.) Spying a "fine young sailor carrying a bundle; a girl with her hand on his arm," she immediately begins "making up" a story about them: he is back from China with a present for his wife, who is carrying their first child. Scenes within their simple cottage are ringed with domestic tenderness as witnessed in this passage:

> The imagination supplied other pictures springing from that first one, a picture of the sailor cutting firewood, drawing water; and they talked about China; and the girl set his present on the chimney-piece where everyone who came could see it; and she sewed at her baby clothes, and all the doors and windows were open into the garden so that the birds were flittering and the bees humming, and Rogers—that was his name—could not say how much to his liking all this was after the China seas. As he smoked his pipe, with his foot in the garden (*DM* 13).

Significantly enough, this artistic construction portrays a perfect hetero-sexual family. References to the man's pipe and foot in the garden, however, set up certain imagistic tensions. Since Woolf's prose is full of explicitly sexual imagery deriving from her psychoanalytic understand-ings, I take the phallic references seriously. Furthermore, the garden, replete with its ancient overtones of woman's sexuality, is in danger of being crushed under foot. This otherwise pacific scene is threatened, just as the parallelism of Woolf's syntax is broken by her placing the threat-ening content into a sentence fragment. Ominous disruption of the fantasy world exists even within the fantasy itself. Contemporary scholars of incest tend to believe that women who have not worked through their early experiences remain haunted by them and that frozen memories may flare up at totally inappropriate or unexpected moments. So Woolf's escapist construction of an ideal family contains the subversive potential to awaken scenes from her own family life.

Immediately following the scene with flittering birds and pipe smoke, "The Second Picture" opens with this Spartan sentence: "In the middle of the night a loud cry rang through the village" (*DM* 13). In contrast to the previous rosy picture created by Woolf, what follows is full of absence and dark mystery. She comments that "The cry made everything seem ominous" and goes on to declare that it was a woman's voice "made by some extremity of feeling almost sexless, almost expressionless. It was as if human nature had cried out against some iniquity, some inexpressible horror" (*DM* 14). What follows is a catalogue of lacks: someone should be running down the road (to get help?); a light should be moving about (searching for the woman who cried out?); nearby cottages should be alight (from geographical sympathy or fear?); a second cry should be heard, but only if it is "less sexless, less wordless, comforted, appeased" (*DM* 14). Such absences are often the stuff of Woolf's fiction, as she herself avows at the beginning of this essay: "It is impossible that one should not see pictures" (*DM* 11). The woman's lone cry interrupts Woolf's creation of her string of details chosen to strike the desired tone. Her own silence becomes the final missing element in this text.

Part of what keeps her awake is the inability to connect the voice with any pictures, pictures which would, as she puts it, "interpret it [the cry], make it more intelligible to the mind" (*DM* 14). Here she affirms a central doctrine of her aesthetic, i.e. that the "making up" faculty shapes random sensory perceptions which bombard us into something comprehensible and manageable. The act of artistic creation, then, holds out the illusion of control for the artist. In the absence of such constructions, perceptions remain "guilty, convicted, ominous" (*DM* 14). Here again Woolf is borrowing modernist theories of the power of the artist to remake a fragmented world; simultaneously, however, she is admitting that there are certain literal facts which preempt this capacity, leaving the artist undefended against the crashing force of violence and loss.

Woolf concludes this central section of her verbal triptych by saying: "But as the dark arose at last all one saw was an obscure human form, almost without shape, raising a gigantic arm in vain against some overwhelming iniquity" (*DM* 14). Her words belie her statement about not being able to have pictures, but the pictures which emerge are not the aesthetically consoling kind she needs so desperately, and which she could so easily compose before hearing the night-rending cry.

This fragmenting section, which destroys the aura of domestic bliss, may easily be understood in light of the body of current research on incest and childhood sexual abuse and of Woolf's own experiences. From such a perspective, it becomes a symbolic scene, perhaps reflecting on her own feelings experienced during nocturnal visits from George Duckworth. In her descriptions of these assaults, she never mentions being able to say anything, much less scream or protect herself from his advances. So this woman who cries so chillingly in the night may well tap into Woolf's own smothered self. The paralytic nature of one's surroundings is an element often found in contemporary women's reports of how they remember feeling during or immediately following their abuse. Many victims of childhood sexual abuse comment on their need to achieve a degree of numbness in order to continue functioning. Woolf's own choice of the words "sexless" and "expressionless" reflects contemporary understanding of the true nature of the incest experience for its victims. Such children are robbed of their essential selves and left without words or pictures, since nowhere in their environment are they likely to find any clear depictions or warnings about incesters within their families.

At the end of this second section of the essay, Woolf describes the emerging human form, "almost without shape," attempting to resist what has happened but being finally impotent because of the magnitude of the "iniquity." This metaphoric moment mirrors autobiographical accounts by incest victims in which they compare their small and essentially helpless natures to the consuming horror inflicted so often by an adult who is destroying a system of fundamental trust. The experience of incest effectively erases necessary personality boundaries by violating them at such a fundamental level, leaving the child or young person no more than an "obscure human form" struggling unsuccessfully against the "overwhelming" force of abuse.

Woolf begins the third and final section of her essay by describing the world as it lies before her on the morning following the scream. Everything seen by the light of day is reminiscent of the created world of the previous day—external nature seems to confirm aesthetic making up. But the accompanying sense of hazy well-being is irrevocably lost: "Wherever one went, . . . something seemed to turn uneasily beneath the surface, making the peace, the stability all round one seem a little unreal" (*DM* 15). Incest victims often report a sense of living in perpetual fear of something lurking behind the scenes of daily life. To cope with this terrifying palimpsest, many people stop looking, becoming less and less reachable by visual stimuli or human scenarios. For Woolf, as a writer, such looking away or loss of focus would of necessity have thwarted the very means she devised to help her endure and thrive.

Woolf summarizes the beautiful morning by saying: "All was as quiet, as safe as could be" (*DM* 15). Here is the triumph of art over life, of daytime over darkness. But her next sentence argues against the power of such an aesthetic to sustain her once she has heard the scream: "Yet, one kept thinking, a cry had rent it; all this beauty had been an accomplice that night; had consented; to remain calm, to be still beautiful; at any moment it might be sundered again. This goodness, this safety were only on the surface" (*DM* 15). Here Woolf acknowledges the inability of art to exclude forces which can destroy smooth surfaces shaped by the artist. Her suggestion that beauty has been an "accomplice" to something evil and frightening cannot fail to remind those familiar with her biography of the much-reputed beauty of her mother, Julia Duckworth Stephen. As DeSalvo has shown, Virginia (and her siblings) would have felt the absence of their mother during bad times or, worse, her silent consent to various frightening aspects of their childhood. So Woolf may have experienced profound dismay at her mother's "part" in what happened to her within the family, echoing current theories of incest survivor psychology. Not to be protected from domestic harm by one's mother often elicits more profound emotional responses from the victim than those attached to the physical abuser.

To free herself from this morass, Woolf returns to her created cottage, sailor and wife, quite conscious that she does so "to cheer oneself out of this apprehensive mood" (*DM* 15). Many embellishments are added, suggesting the depth of disturbance caused by the night cry. In what seems an extraordinary instance of self-knowledge, as well as knowledge about the essence of art, Woolf says: "And so one turned back home, with one's mind *fixed* on the sailor and his wife, making up picture after picture of them so that one picture after another of happiness and satis-faction might be *laid over* that unrest, that hideous cry, until it was *crushed and silenced* by their pressure out of existence" (*DM* 15-16, emphases mine).

The effort involved in this cover-up is apparent from such verbs as "fixed" and "laid over," accompanied by the violence implied in "crushed and silenced." The scream has forcefully deconstructed the crafted scene, and Woolf comprehends the concentration needed to put the pieces back together again. Clearly, this renewed act of making up is strenuous and determined, utterly changed from the day before when images floated up unbidden and with ease. If her artistic process on the day before the fate-ful cry could be characterized as stream of consciousness, the process presented on the day following is more nearly agonistic labor conducted in full consciousness and with explicit purpose. Her language suggests even a degree of desperation in the face of so rending a reminder of lived life. The making up before the cry was for her pleasure; now it is for sheer sanity in the lingering face of that sexless, wordless night sound.

The final paragraph of the piece shows Woolf now in the village, coming upon a grave-digger at work. She immediately starts collecting pictures as if to stave off the reality of death: "As the shovels of yellow earth were thrown up, the children were sprawling about eating bread and jam and drinking milk out of large mugs. The gravedigger's wife, a fat fair woman, had propped herself against a tombstone and spread her apron on the grass by the open grave to serve as a tea-table" (*DM* 16). Woolf attempts to tame death in this scene, weaving an aura of folksy domesticity around one of life's starkest realities, perhaps reminding herself of Shakespeare's use of humor in a comparable scene from *Hamlet*.

When she asks if "old Mr. Dodson" has died, the pieces of her puzzle suddenly come together with frightening clarity. She learns that it was "young Rogers, the sailor," who had died in the night of "some foreign fever." The "fat fair woman" is surprised that the walker does not know: "Didn't you hear his wife? She rushed into the road and cried out. . ." (*DM* 16). The narrator steps back sharply, concluding with an oblique exclamation: "What a picture it made!" Given life's constant threat to her constructed world, this final comment remains ironic at best.

This compact essay is prototypical of others in which Woolf attempts to build up positive, safe images only to have them collapse or be fractured by some unexpected but persistent interruption/intrusion from daily life. Her making up becomes an attempt to cloak the horrors of lived experience, and a means through which she can safely retell the story of her trauma in order to continue to live with it. But a danger lurks in the night which can instantly shatter her artistic visions of bliss or control, revealing the fragility of the self behind the story. This clarity also positions Woolf as someone able to see through the consoling scrim modernism tried to create for its founders.

Woolf is candid in her discussions of her belief in the potential solace of art. Simultaneously, she recognizes the limitations of the very art which offers partial safety. A pivotal example of this recognition comes in her essay "The Moment: Summer's Night." After her opening comments about how all-important the slant of light is to what any of us sees or feels, she asserts that at the center of the moment is "consciousness." The process of arriving at knowing about that center begins when something upsets the surface around us. So in this instance, the sound of a sneeze breaks into the smooth reverie. Then someone lights a match and the narrator hears, "He beats her every Saturday; from boredom, I should say; not drink; there's nothing else to do" (*M* 12).

From the instant "beats her" enters Woolf's consciousness, the previous reverie is lost and all she can do is to envision the violence. She is experiencing Richard McNally's theory of "involuntary explicit memory" most assuredly. When she can bear no more, she pleads, as it were, with her own imagination: "let us [here Woolf engages in a characteristic splitting of her "self" into multiple voices] do something then, something to end this horrible moment, this plausible glistening moment that reflects in its smooth sides this intolerable kitchen, this squalor; this woman moaning; and the rattle of the toy on the flags, and the man munching. Let us smash it by breaking a match. There—snap" (*M* 12). That Woolf uses a violent verb to counter her vivid makings-up about the wife-beating

61

marks the degree of her internal agitation, even if what is demolished is only a simple match.

Her eye then falls upon a group of cows going home and she hopes for a more romantic view of the life around her, but as dusk falls, things lose their shape and distinction, engendering a fundamental ambivalence in the narrative voice. She writes of the shapes and sounds at this moment: "they come from no bodies; they are cries to the left and to the right. Nothing can be seen. Then comes the terror, the exultation; the power to rush out unnoticed, alone; to be consumed; to be swept away to become a rider on the random wind" (*M* 12). On one level, Woolf yearns to become one with the great amorphous force she feels all around her. But within this diction lurks fear and an attendant desire to lose individuality and to vanish—"to be consumed." Contemporary theorists and clinicians writing about women surviving incest speak often of victims' framing a wish to be invisible or to become absolutely nothing in their need to escape the abuse (McNaron & Morgan; DeSalvo, *Impact*, 10-12; Forward and Buck 22-24). Such women also speak eloquently about feeling as if they were being completely engulfed in the destructiveness of that experience.

At the very end of this essay, just as the author is losing touch with her surroundings, a second human being—Leonard, most likely—enters. He speaks in welcome monotones about mundane facts: "Everything's sopping wet. It's the dew off the grass. Time to go in" (*M* 13). This plain speech brings the narrator back into a boundaried world, allowing her to conclude what has been a harrowing mental journey by saying, "we pass, trailing coats, down the path toward the lighted windows, the dim glow behind the branches, and so enter the door, and the square draws its lines round us, and here is a chair, a table, glasses, knives, and thus we are boxed and housed, and will soon require a draught of soda-water and to find something to read in bed" (*M* 13).

Her meticulous naming of familiar objects recalls incest victims who write about having to ground themselves in their surroundings to avoid losing all sense of self because of the essentially disembodying nature of the abuse. Women speaking about their experiences of childhood incest/sexual abuse often describe directly the process of becoming disembodied: "It's as if inside, from my neck down, it's hollow, and there's this ladder, and depending on how things are going, I'm climbing up the ladder, and this little person that is me is sitting in my head, looking out through my eyes"; "It's like I'd actually rise up out of my body. I could feel myself sitting in a chair, and I could feel myself floating up out of my body. That's exactly what it is, like being suspended in mid-air. I know that my body is in the chair, but the rest of me is out of my body" (Bass and Davis 210). Incest is at base an attack on selfhood in the child or young person, making the logical impulse to escape ironically destructive. Escaping the experience means escaping the self and the body in particular. Trying to live in such a detached and abstracted state often causes a loosening of sanity and a dangerous distancing from the self needed to function as a person. Consequently, modernism held out to Woolf a peculiarly seductive justification for placing aesthetic distance between herself and her life experiences. Following the trend within her literary milieu might well have silenced this author so determined to remain open to what she conceived of as her "unconscious." So in this essay that began innocently enough with a discussion of the centrality inherent in the slant of light on one's environment, Woolf has found herself immersed in an atmosphere fraught with terror, even as it is tinged by exultation. By skirting the safety of modernist theory, she has found that her creative powers are insufficient to combat the shapeless memories unleashed by hearing a chance remark about physical violence done to a woman by a man because he is bored.

Virginia Woolf is grappling in "The Moment: Summer's Night" with contradictory feelings similar to those in "Three Pictures." If we couple passages like this one, in which she makes repeated references to feeling as if she were drowning, with the incestuous implications of such images, a picture emerges once again in which this powerful writer understands that her making-up capacity can turn on her if her artistic or aesthetic stimulus is too similar to her own lived reality. But without that capacity, she would be at the total mercy of the power of random events to propel her back into the maelstrom of her own incestuous nightmare. DeSalvo has argued convincingly that Woolf's references to feeling as if she were sinking into or existing under water are incest metaphors (*Impact* 254-261). Current statements from incest survivors substantiate such a reading, since these women often speak of feeling as if they could drown in their shame or sorrow, that their emotions feel like a great body of water in which they will lose themselves, and that they usually feel as if they look at life through a watery film which distorts everything.

In one of her many flashes of insight into her psychological make-up, Woolf writes in her journal for Sunday, June 23, 1929, while correcting proofs for *A Room of One's Own*, "And so I pitched into my great lake of melancholy. Lord how deep it is! What a born melancholiac I am! The only way I keep afloat is by working. A note for the summer—I must take more work than I can possibly get done. —no, I don't know what it comes from. Directly I stop working I feel that I am sinking down, down. And as usual, I feel that if I sink further I shall reach the truth. That is the only mitigation; a kind of nobility. Solemnity. I shall make myself face the fact that there is nothing—nothing for any of us. Work, reading, writing are all disguises; & relations with people. Yes, even having children would be useless" (*D3*: 235). Though Woolf sees her "melancholy" as a matter of birth, most contemporary scholars would shun such deterministic pronouncements in favor of an argument based on the influence of environmental forces most likely occurring in infancy or early childhood. Since generalized depression is a primary symptom in adults who have been sexually abused as children or adolescents, I would attribute Woolf's melancholy to her shameful, suppressed feelings about her body brought on or exacerbated by her abuse. We know from her own writing that she felt such shame, since she comments on how difficult it is for her to look at herself in a mirror, to feel attractive in her clothes, or not to feel stared at and made fun of by passersby on the streets of London.

When Woolf asserts that nothing has any meaning, that all our engagements are in fact "disguises" or falsities, which we will see as such if we stop moving and acting, she may be articulating a major incest credo rather than espousing modernist doctrines based on loss of shared or reliable cultural meanings. Because it robs children of their childhood and forces them to detach from their own bodies in order to endure what is going on in the present moment, incest tends to erase vast fields of meaning. Survivors often speak of having sensations of rising out of their bodies to watch the abuse, or of becoming tinier and tinier inside themselves so that some core will remain out of reach of the horror. Indeed, the experience of incest can erase a belief in meaning altogether, leaving adult women with a sense of exactly the state of flatness and emptiness described and implied in Woolf's journal entry.

Within Woolf's aesthetic, night and darkness occupy a distinctly ambivalent position, constituting that moment in each day during which precision and control are lost. Such loss results from the fact that external shapes are distorted or obliterated altogether, while the inner "self" is merged in sleep, dreams, and fearful imaginings. To this generic reality, Woolf would have to add the fact that George invaded her bedroom to make his inappropriate and traumatic visits, saying to her "Don't turn on the light." Darkness thereby came to be connected in her psyche with sexual ugliness and pain, tainting or subsuming any previously positive associations. So in "The Moment: Summer's Night," on one level she exhibits an erotically charged excitement about this inevitable blurring of line and form, while simultaneously seeming peculiarly vulnerable to a certain kind of intrusion from the outside world or from her own memory.

Examples from but a few of her essays will indicate the extent of this pattern as an operative force in Woolf's imagination. In "Reading," for instance (exact date unknown, with some scholars, e.g. Ted Bishop, placing it shortly before she took her own life, and others believing it to be much earlier, circa 1919, based on internal textual evidence), the speaker sets out to catch a particularly precious species of moth. This search follows pages of discussion of such familiar and comforting subjects as her family's house; the long tradition of English writers, with which she was entirely familiar; and Queen Elizabeth I's imagination, which she figures as "still lusting for the strange tales. . . still young in its wrinkled and fantastic casket" (*CDB* 158). Only after indulging in this leisurely fantasy, elicited by her reading of one of the books at hand, does she detail how a group of her associates sets off in search of a specimen moth reputed to be in the nearby woods. To lure the giant moths, "several pieces of flannel soaked in rum and sugar had been pinned to a number of trees" (*CDB* 165)

After much vain pursuit by the little band of moth hunters, Woolf comes upon the prize, captures it, and sets off to return home bathed in feelings of triumph and well-being. Unexpectedly, her sense of conquest is destroyed by a violent interruption: "And then, standing there with the moth safely in our hands, suddenly a volley of shot rang out, a hollow rattle of sound in the deep silence of the wood which had I know not what of mournful and ominous about it" (*CDB* 168-169). This scene in the late personal essay is a reworking of a similar moment in her third novel, *Jacob's Room,* wherein several characters are walking in a damp woods when Rebecca catches a death's-head moth (23). The innocence of this scene is violently interrupted by both a tree's falling and a pistol shot coming from deep within the woods. Woolf's fiction is replete with moments when similarly unexpected and mood-shattering events or behaviors destroy whatever peace or pleasure is being experienced by characters. Scholars within the field of incest studies would see such repetitions as further evidence of the writer's awareness of the precariousness, not only of lived life, but of created universes.

Woolf's instant response within the essay of moth-hunting surely resonates if we consider her late night intrusions by her half-brother: "What is it that happens between the hour of midnight and dawn, the little shock, the queer, uneasy moment, as of eyes half open to the light, after which sleep is never so sound again? Is it experience, perhaps—repeated shocks, each unfelt at the time, suddenly loosening the fabric? breaking something away?" (*CDB* 169) Rather than continue in this vein, Woolf abruptly shifts to the glories of morning when "a rod of light" brings order to tumult, spreading "form upon chaos" (*CDB* 169).

This wrenching of mood by the essayist seems to restore her earlier calm, and she indulges in cool discussion of English poets, in particular Sir Thomas Browne, noted both for his meditational bent and for his strange fixation on death. For the remainder of the essay, Woolf engages in one of her spiraling intellectual journeys into the mind of a sympathetic author, attributing to Browne all sorts of profound understandings of the human mind and spirit. Though she makes no further reference to the frightening possibilities for loss of control and one's very self during nighttime hours, the moment lies at the heart of this essay, hovering near the surface of the text and its author's mind, a kind of negative jack-in-the-box, capable of intruding into the cool regions of speculative analysis imposed upon the ominous possibilities of darkness.

Similarly, in "Flying over London" (exact date unknown but generally taken to be a late work), Woolf describes a moment when the light in the plane goes out and she imagines the pilot to be Charon, that fateful transporter of souls across the River Styx. The passage begins quite positively, full of erotic language about her desire to become one with all her surroundings: "carry me on; thrust me deep, deep; till every glimmer of light in me, of heat of knowledge, even the tingling I feel in my toes is dulled; after all this living, all this scratching and tingling of sensation, that too—darkness, dullness, the black wet—will be also a sensation . . . a consummation" (*CDB* 206). That the word "consummation" may refer to either an act of sexual union or to a process of being devoured suggests the inherent ambivalence Woolf felt about her own impulses. (Since the Hogarth Press published Freud, we may assume Woolf was familiar with his major work on dreams in which he says that flying is a classical metaphor for an erection of the male organ or of sexual intercourse; further, Freud also concludes that an airplane, because it is able to elevate itself in defiance of gravity, becomes an appropriate phallic symbol in dreams.) And, even as she makes use of flying in this erotic sense, the scene is marred by another, quite different impulse: "Then Charon turned his head with its fringe of fur and laughed at us. It was an ugly face, with high cheek bones, and little deep sunk eyes, and all down one cheek was a crease where he had been cut and stitched together" (*CDB* 206). Representations of Charon, whether in reference works or paintings, while revealing a variety of grimaces and other signs of evil, yield no evidence of facial scarring.

To name her pilot after the ferryman who rows the damned across the River Styx surely bespeaks some profound aversion amidst her excitement. Images of an ugly male face appear repeatedly in Woolf's fiction: he may be seen at the bottom of a deep well or at the end of a long tunnel; he may jump out of the dark unexpectedly from a bush in a park to ruin all else going on at the time; his visage may seem to emerge from the depths of a mirror into which a female character is peering. One of Woolf's own clearest comments on this incest trope comes in a letter to Ethel Smyth during a period late in life when she was attempting to make sense out of what had happened to her in her youth: "suddenly. . . . I approach madness and that end of a drainpipe with a gibbering old man" (*L3*: 297-98). As DeSalvo points out, Woolf viewed this as part of her "suicide dream," first described in "A Sketch of the Past": "I dreamt that I was looking in a glass when a horrible face—the face of an animal— suddenly showed over my shoulder. I cannot be sure if this was a dream, or if it happened" (*MOB* [1976] 69).

Woolf associated this dream not only with her abuse but with her terror and avoidance of looking at herself in a mirror, since she could never be sure that she would not see a bestial image in addition to her own. At some level, she feared a fusion of the two images. This confusion of a monster who stands as the abuser and oneself as the abused occurs often in contemporary women's accounts of their experience: "Since I didn't know what or whom I truly feared, I feared the house we shared, which by guilty association became the house that knew. In my imagination, monsters prowled its cubbyholes—my monstrous secret, my monstrous other self, turned into something outside me that I could fear" (Fraser 15-16).

In her memoir detailing Gerald's fondling her at a much earlier age than she was when George molested her, Virginia stipulates that he began this unforgivable behavior outside the family dining room. "There was a slab outside the dining room door for standing dishes upon. Once when I was very small Gerald Duckworth lifted me onto this, and as I sat there he began to explore my body. I can remember the feel of his hand going under my clothes. . . . His hand explored my private parts too. I remember resenting, disliking it—what is the word for so dumb and mixed a feeling? It must have been strong, since I still recall it" (*MOB* [1976] 69). Woolf's supposition is borne out by McNally's research that found that stress "does not impair memory; it strengthens it" (62). Just before her candid account of this violation, Woolf has told us that there was a "small looking glass in the hall" which "had, I remember, a ledge with a brush on it. By standing on tiptoe I could see my face in the glass. When I was six or seven perhaps, I got into the habit of looking at my face in the glass. But I only did this if I was sure that I was alone. I was ashamed of it. A strong feeling of guilt seemed naturally attached to it. But why was this so?" (*MOB* [1976] 68). That "guilt" clearly was not shared by Gerald, since the fact that he positioned the young Virginia so that he could see both her and his own image suggests that he enjoyed watching himself molesting his half-sister as much as he did scrutinizing her.

The proximity of the looking glass ledge and the slab onto which Gerald sat her makes clear that the young Virginia saw not only herself but also the face of her abuser reflected in its primal ugliness. This would more logically explain the shame which she already felt at age six or seven than her proffered explanations, e.g. that she and Vanessa were tomboys, or that her grandfather once smoked a cigar. Given what we now understand about monstrosity as a metaphoric construction used by many incest victims to describe those who assault them, these repeated scenes may be read as a way for Woolf to express the nightmare vision embedded in her psyche. Her imagination, then, enlisted to take her away from the world of every day, could without warning fling her back into it with a vengeance, thereby destroying any illusion she might harbor about the healing, controlling powers of art.

Current incest literature emphasizes victims' fear of the dark, and Virginia's own documentation of her particular ordeal describes awful nights when George would come into her bedroom to press himself upon her literally and figuratively. She speaks most directly about this molestation in her personal account presented to the Memoir Club some time around 1920. All through this sketch, Woolf presents George as someone unable to contain certain emotional excesses toward his mother and half-sisters. He emerges as someone distinctly unpleasant, combining sexual aberration with a self-conscious observance of social decorum. At the end of this revealing piece, Woolf writes of returning from one of the endless late-night parties to which George dragged her against her will. Alone in her room at last, she sheds the uncomfortable party dress and begins to contemplate having her Greek lesson next morning with her teacher, Janet Case. Finally ready for bed, she says:

> Many different things were whirling round in my mind—
> diamonds and countesses, copulations, the dialogues of Plato,
> Mad Dick Popham and "The Light of the World." Ah, how
> pleasant it would be to stretch out in bed, fall asleep and forget
> them all! Sleep had almost come to me. The room was dark.
> The house silent. Then, creaking stealthily, the door opened;
> treading gingerly, someone entered. "Who?" I cried. "Don't be
> frightened," George whispered. "And don't turn on the light,
> oh beloved. Beloved—" and he flung himself on my bed, and
> took me in his arms (*MOB* [1976] 155).

Given this unequivocal report, it should not come as a surprise to find Woolf's powerful description of witnessing an eclipse of the sun in her essay, "The Sun and the Fish." Following her narrative habit, she begins by describing her excitement over witnessing the phenomenon, her willingness to travel to exactly the right place in England from which to see it to best advantage, and her thrill as the darkening begins. But in that instant in which the sun is fully extinguished, Woolf's rhetoric changes utterly and she speaks of the "defeat" of the sun as if it were in mortal combat with some gigantic enemy: "The flesh and blood of the world was dead; only the skeleton was left" (*CDB* 215). Woolf's metaphors suggest a feeling of extreme apprehensiveness during the momentary darkness, followed by a palpable happiness at the return of the light: "Lightly, on the other side of the world, up it [the sun] rose; it sprang up as if the one movement, after a second's tremendous pause, completed the other, and the light which had died here rose again elsewhere. Never was there such a sense of rejuvenescence and recovery" (*CDB* 215-216). Not only does this language convey excitement and relief, but her phrase "died here rose again" places the reappearance of the lost light into a religious context, recalling as it does Jesus's burial and brief descent, followed by his reportedly miraculous resurrection. Since she seldom utilized religious imagery, the appearance here may signal either a wish for a similar release from George's deadening assaults or a realization that no such blissful release exists for her. Whatever the case, her diction speaks to a subject far deeper and more consequential than the apparent one of driving out into the country to see a brilliant display of nature's mutability. I believe her extra emotional investment stems from her early and protracted dread of night, that smaller eclipsing time, when the ugly face from the mirror came so distressingly close to her own, shutting out for a time all potential light from her eyes.

Continuing her reflection about the return of the light, Woolf writes,

> Yet, at first, . . . it seemed as if the earth could never live decked out in such frail tints. It hung beneath us, like a cage, like a hoop, like a globe of glass. It might be blown out; it might be stove in. But steadily and surely our relief broadened and our confidence established itself as *the great paint-brush* washed in woods dark on the valley, and massed hills blue above them. The world became more and more solid; it became populous; it became a place where an infinite number of farmhouses, of villages, of railway lines have lodgement; until *the whole fabric* of civilization was *modelled* and *moulded*. But still the memory endured that the earth we stand on is made of colour; colour can be blown out; and then we stand on a dead leaf; and we who tread the earth securely now have seen it dead (*CDB* 216, emphases mine).

Woolf's consistent use of metaphors of artistic creation supports my premise that she depended upon the world of art to give shape and color (literally, in this instance) where life too often exposes bleakness. On one level, then, she conceives of the artist as a world-maker, able to frame a reality amidst and apart from the larger chaos, and, in so doing subscribes to one of the fundamental beliefs of high modernism. Her final cautionary note, however, in which memory stands as a potentially frightening faculty for those who have experienced the death of light, immediately undercuts the ability of that world of art to do more than momentarily stave off life's traumas. The overwhelming sense of an underside or palimpsest of terror parallels Woolf's phobic attitude toward looking at herself in a mirror. Having once seen the distorted, monstrous face of Gerald in one mirror, traumatically close to her own face, Woolf was forever vulnerable to its reappearance if she looked at herself in any other mirror. Indeed, perhaps it is no accident that she chooses, as one of her similes for the earth in danger from cosmic darkness, "a globe of glass." Such globes allow illumination but remain fundamentally vulnerable to forces that can, in an instant, smash them to smithereens.

If darkness was fearful because of its associations with George's nocturnal violations, it also represented a fixed time when a rational individual might lose all sense of proper boundaries. This loss, in turn, was fraught with anxiety because it so often meant becoming engulfed by something or someone invisible and overpowering. The pattern for this complex emotional theme is articulated in the essay, "The Moment: Summer's Night," referred to earlier. In the essay, Woolf traces her experience of a downward progression as she becomes one with the night. In her landscape, the two forces or conditions are not equivalent. Rather, she imagines the light as sinking back into darkness, suggesting that it is the smaller, temporary element subsumed into a permanent and massive context of darkness. Once the source of light in her day has sunk, other reassuring signposts of order follow suit in unnervingly rapid succession: legs of chairs sink, the sky loses its color, the lamp sinks down, as the amorphous "we" of the essay act as "passive participants in a pageant" (*M* 4). This passage is strikingly similar to some of the early paragraphs in the middle section of *To the Lighthouse*: "So with the lamps all put out, the moon sunk, and a thin rain drumming on the roof a downpouring of immense darkness began. Nothing, it seemed, could survive the flood" (*TTL* 125).

Once her world has lost its usual anchors, Woolf begins to imagine the moment's quivering with "malice and amusement" (*M* 5), surely a macabre combination of qualities carrying both predatory and sadistic overtones. The description also has a certain disembodiedness about it which may bespeak the beginning of a recurrent incest memory which haunted Woolf throughout her life. To assert some power and agency over this increasingly ominous time, she proposes being able to fly, an idea which on first blush excites her: she speaks of being "one wing; all embracing, all gathering." However, there are limits to the flight, as she

71

makes clear in the very next phrase, "and these boundaries, these pryings over hedge into hidden compartments. . ." (*M* 5). The positive reverie breaks off suddenly with the mention of "pryings" and "hidden compart- ments," both carrying negative sexual connotations to anyone abused as a child or adolescent. Woolf is unable to allow her sensuality free rein, at least in part because beginning to speak of it sets off a frightening train of memories capable of altering the accumulation of pleasant images beyond repair. So her aesthetic formulations which stress the free flow of memories are foiled by the dysfunctional sexual experiences in her early years. Her stream of consciousness demands a degree of watchfulness in order to keep it from drowning her in the duckweed, associated with George and Gerald Duckworth, about which she wrote so often and so fearfully.

What follows in the essay surely might be read as a mirroring of what happened to Woolf herself at George's hands so many evenings in her own bedroom. "Here the body is gripped; and shaken;. . . and the whole universe is shaken" (*M* 5). The metaphors here are familiar in the writings of incest victims. The invasion of a person's sexual boundaries by inap- propriate family members is so primal as to alter the entire structure of that individual's universe. Her image of a body's being "gripped" and "shaken" seems to remind Woolf of her own nightmare world of abusive sexual contact. After such an experience, nothing seen is ever quite the same as it was before one's "body is gripped" by the monster/abuser.

The idea of sinking down into an element much larger than the indi- vidual self reappears in enough of Woolf's essays to suggest a psychological pattern. Long before she literally sank her body in the River Ouse, she contemplated what such an experience might feel like. Her conclusions are almost always full of a terror born of loss of control, yet that very loss is something she gravitates towards both as an author and a passionately sentient being.

Given Woolf's understanding of a common source for sexuality and creativity, her partially fearful responses to fantasies of flying and of sink- ing into darkness are particularly painful to consider. She would have comprehended that letting herself get in touch with her deeper reaches of metaphoric and emotional knowing was necessary to the composition of the kind of fiction she set out to write. Yet her damaged psyche, which had endured her half-brothers' sexual abuse, fled from such reaches because she had pushed into the horrifying memories of their actions. Her

72

success at writing novels assumes even more amazing proportions when considered in this light, since many a lesser combatant would simply have settled for more conventional narrative strategies. Like the oceans depicted by early cartographers, Woolf's stream of consciousness was inhabited by dangerous monsters, yet she repeatedly placed herself in its midst, risking inevitable confrontation with the granite wall of masculine abuse.

Woolf phrased the process in almost exactly such terms in her essay, "On Being Ill," first published in 1930. In the opening paragraphs, she comments, perhaps facetiously, on how strange it is that literature has not placed illness in the same illustrious light as "love and battle and jealousy." Rather, it seems that literature has insisted that "the body is a sheet of plain glass through which the soul looks straight and clear, and, save for one or two passions such as desire and greed, is null, and negligible and non-existent" (*M* 14). For Woolf, however, everything is filtered through the body; her conviction about the unavoidable connection between it and the mind is expressed in sharp images: "it [the mind] cannot separate off from the body like the sheath of a knife or the pod of a pea for a single instant; it must go through the whole unending procession of changes . . . until there comes the inevitable catastrophe; the body smashes itself to smithereens, and the soul (it is said) escapes" (*M* 15). The progress of her language suggests that more is going on than an attempt to describe what it feels like to be ill. While many of us who have suffered from influenza-like conditions may recognize her description of how our heads feel, Woolf's language is extreme: "the waters of annihilation close above our heads" (*M* 9).

Her sense of losing touch with mundane reality because of her illness, of ceasing "to be [a soldier] in the army of the upright," (*M* 18) clearly flings Woolf into the same fiercely ambiguous state as her fantasy of flying over London or her witnessing the solar eclipse. What all these have in common is a potential for engulfment; therefore, they all can remind her, quite against her will, of a history of incest and sexual abuse about which she spoke, often using such coded images as the "cottonwool." Her fears of being lost in darkness, of perceiving things and people through a lingering fog or emotional haze, as well as her sense of vulnerability to drowning, all indicate the depth and intensity of trauma.

Contemporary studies of women with similar histories of childhood and/or adolescent sexual abuse record a sense of meaninglessness in the victims brought on by their correct perception of the fundamental unfairness and betrayal lying at the heart of sexual abuse by family members. While Woolf seldom speaks of her views on "God" or even something as vague as universal justice, in "On Being Ill" she does project a vision of nature, an examination of which will further clarify just how tenuous her house of art proved to be.

Having sunk into her bed pillows, she begins a contemplation of the sky above—another much neglected subject owing to the "soldiers'" need to keep their eyes fixed on the ground before them. What she finds shocks her:

> This then has been going on all the time without our knowing it!—this incessant making up of shapes and casting them down, this buffeting of clouds together, and drawing vast trains of ships and waggons from North to South, this incessant ringing up and down of curtains of light and shade, this interminable experiment with gold shafts and blue shadows, with veiling the sun and unveiling it, with making rock ramparts and wafting them away— this endless activity, with the waste of Heaven knows how many million horse power of energy, has been left to work its will year in year out." (*M* 18)

Though there is a marked similarity between what nature has been doing and what Woolf called her own creation—making up—their purposes seem quite different. Whereas nature seems to do it all "for some purpose which has nothing to do with human pleasure or human profit" (*M* 18), Woolf's motives are most often to secure the world around her in an effort to hold back some darker inner world.

Her idle musings about how there needs to be an audience for all this are abruptly interrupted by her next awareness: "Divinely beautiful it is also divinely heartless" (*M* 18). Finding this idea frightening, she breaks away from the sky to find "something very small and close and familiar" in order to regain a sense of sympathy from nature. She focuses first upon a rose and then upon all the flowers in her garden, but finds them equally "indifferent" to human vagaries. In fact, Woolf asserts that it is their very indifference, their stillness and self-sufficiency, that humans traditionally have found comforting.

Woolf is unable to maintain this anthropomorphic attitude, however, and as she becomes once again "recumbent," she reaches her conclusion about the essence of nature: "she in the end will conquer; heat will leave the world; stiff with frost we shall cease to drag ourselves about the fields; ice will lie thick upon factory and engine; the sun will go out" (*M* 19). Again the extremity of language impresses me, as does the sense of combat reminiscent of her impression of the sun's "defeat" by an eclipse in the essay discussed earlier. Her loss of innocence and childhood had robbed her of a light and warmth without which she sometimes saw herself as a creature of this cold apocalypse. In *Mrs. Dalloway*, Woolf has Clarissa voice a similarly intense and lingering shame over being incapable of loving her husband. Speaking with heroic candor, she names a certain lack of warmth, a certain coldness which she cannot lose even through childbirth. This quality is also found within the wedge-shaped core of darkness about which Mrs. Ramsay has so much to say in her midnight reveries. It is reflected, furthermore, in the chill bitterness between Isa and Giles Oliver in *Between the Acts*. Woolf articulates the brutal aftershock of incest as felt by thousands of contemporary women who struggle to "warm" themselves, even as they recoil, from the very contacts which might hasten that process because an early trauma carried with it such utter devastation of self.

Virginia Woolf presents a careful reader with a fascinating and disturbing matrix within which art is certainly central, the human enterprise most likely to bring order to a world increasingly devoid of permanence or beauty. In this regard, she aligns herself with her modernist colleagues, asserting the value of creative expression against the onslaught of personal and cultural destructiveness. Her own words make her allegiance to her writing absolutely clear. Over and over, Woolf will affirm her indebtedness to it, not only for aesthetic pleasure but for her very existence. In her diary of 1929, she admits, "The only way I keep afloat is by working." Any swimmer knows that staying afloat in the water is tantamount to staying alive. To not do so is to sink to the bottom, risking temporary or permanent loss of breath and sensation.

Within this simple metaphoric adjective "afloat" resides potential danger, however, since Woolf uses this same word to describe the human condition susceptible to sudden and devastating floods from a reality outside the control of artistic making-up: "We are sealed vessels afloat on what it is convenient to call reality" (*MOB* [1976] 142). I find it significant that the same term can offer her solace and lead her into chaos. This verbal ambiguity reflects a more far-reaching level of simultaneity: Woolf is actively engaged in technical experimentation even as she maps an older landscape of the human psyche. She both is and is not a disciple of modernism, and her separation from this early twentieth-century ideology stems, in large measure, from her inability finally to distance herself from her subject matter. Yet this very inability meant that at any moment in her "making-up" process, she could be catapulted back into the nightmarish memories of her devastating sexual treatment at the hands of her half-brothers.

Woolf claimed art as the best sealing wax available to protect human beings as the vulnerable vessels she imagined them to be. But memory, the stuff from which her particular fictional "dreams" were made, shatters the made-up images, leaving their maker to confront the image in the mirror from which she tried to flee through her art. That face was sometimes her own, reflecting a permanent shame about her body, stemming in large part from her incestuous assault at age six, and reinforced by her persistent abuse during her late teens. When it was not her own visage she saw, it was often that of her abuser, imaged as monstrous because anyone capable of inflicting such atrocities on a child or young person is perforce monstrous. In her historical overview of incest in western culture, Florence Rush notes that "Depressed women who were raped in childhood are said to have turned their anger resulting from violation against themselves" (182). Art quite forsook Woolf when she saw the horrid or shameful faces in her inner mirror. Indeed, if my reading is correct, it was her special kind of art which, as often as not, roused the memories which started the unsealing process. That process allowed the flooding which resulted in her feelings of drowning in memories long before she carefully pocketed rocks to increase her weight and walked into the River Ouse. But it also produced an amazing series of novels and essays which delve into the psycho-sexual world opening so rapidly around her. And it contributed to her complicated aesthetic, in which art both warded off and revealed anew the terrible scenes and scars inflicted when she was forming her sense of her self.

TRAUMA, POST-TRAUMATIC STRESS DISORDER, AND OBSTACLES TO POSTWAR RECOVERY IN *MRS. DALLOWAY*

Karen DeMeester

Modernist literature is a literature of trauma. In the 1920s, it gave form and representation to a psychological condition that psychiatrists would not understand for another fifty years. Virginia Woolf's characterization of Septimus Smith in *Mrs. Dalloway* illustrates not only the psychological injuries suffered by victims of severe trauma, such as those endured by soldiers in combat, but also the need for survivors to give meaning to their suffering in order to recover from post-traumatic stress disorder. In the following essay, I argue that Septimus's suicide is a direct result of his inability to communicate his experiences to others and thereby give those experiences meaning and purpose. By bearing witness to the trauma of combat, Septimus could attempt to reveal the truth about war, and the beguiling yet dubious jingoism of political institutions that emerge from and reflect the darker side of human nature. Septimus's war trauma, however, is perpetuated and its psychological damage aggravated by a culturally sanctioned process of postwar reintegration that silences and marginalizes war veterans. To comprehend fully Septimus Smith's tragedy, one must understand the psychological effects of trauma and the process of recovery.

The modernist narrative form of Woolf's novel brilliantly mirrors the mind of a trauma survivor like Septimus. In fact, a number of modernist literary works written in the decade after the First World War constitute a literature of trauma: their forms often replicate the damaged psyche of a trauma survivor and their contents portray his characteristic disorientation and despair. Imagist poetry and the experimental novels of the postwar decade, for example, reflect the fragmentation of consciousness and the disorder and confusion that a victim experiences in the wake of a traumatic event. Trauma inevitably damages the victim's faith in the assumptions he has held in the past about himself and the world and leaves him struggling to find new, more reliable ideologies to give order and meaning to his post-traumatic life. Like trauma survivors, modernist writers suffered a similar loss of faith in the ideologies of the past and particularly in the literary forms that emerged from those ideologies.

Their works depict in both form and content a modern age severed from the traditions and values of the past—first, by new discoveries in such fields as psychology, anthropology, physics, and biology; and later, by the First World War's unprecedented destruction, the magnitude of which revealed the pernicious potential of technological developments originally intended to improve and extend life.

The modernists were attempting to cope with and create a language to represent what Kirby Farrell refers to as the "shock of radical historical change" (2). Such a shock is registered as an injury, a trauma that sabotages faith in traditional value systems and the cultural order, undermines our sense of safety and stability, erodes identity and self-esteem, challenges interpretation, and often defies or destroys meaning. According to Farrell, trauma functions as a trope, "a strategic fiction that a complex, stressful society is using to account for a world that seems threateningly out of control" (2). When change occurs in our lives or our culture, we experience trauma and fantasies about trauma in an effort to cope with change and to mitigate our fears of disorder and cosmic chaos or indeterminacy.

In *Mrs. Dalloway*, Virginia Woolf demonstrates the power of the modernist literary form to delineate the psyche of a trauma survivor and the shock of radical change. Her narrative preserves the psychological chaos caused by trauma instead of reordering it, as more traditional narratives do. In *Achilles in Vietnam: Combat Trauma and the Undoing of Character*, psychiatrist Jonathan Shay describes how traditional narratives restructure the survivor's fragmented consciousness: "Severe trauma explodes the cohesion of consciousness. When a survivor creates [a] fully realized narrative that brings together the shattered knowledge of what happened, the emotions that were aroused by the meanings of the events, and the bodily sensations that the physical events created, the survivor pieces back together the fragmentation of consciousness that trauma has caused" (188). The trauma story, before the survivor has structured it into a "fully realized narrative," is a "prenarrative" that "does not develop or progress in time" (Herman, *Trauma* 174). By drawing her narratives from characters' prespeech levels of consciousness (Humphrey 2-3), Woolf created such a prenarrative in many of her novels and preserved the fragmentation of consciousness that occurs in the aftermath of trauma. At the prespeech level of consciousness, the protagonist has not yet attempted to order his fragmented thoughts into a sequentially arranged, communicable narrative.

Woolf's stream of consciousness narrative form also mimics the trauma survivor's perception of time. The survivor's traumatized mind apprehends the traumatic event as ever-present, and his memories of the event often exist in present consciousness as encapsulated images and fragments of thought that are juxtaposed with other nontraumatic memories but do not meaningfully relate to them sequentially or chronologically. The survivor cannot think of the traumatic event in chronological terms such as: "This was my life before. . . . This is what happened. . . . This is what I became." He struggles to describe his traumatic experience "in a language that insists on 'was' and 'will be' [when] [t]he trauma world knows only *is*" (Shay 191). He is consequently unable to integrate the traumatic event into his personal life history and ultimately to re-envision the event as a critical moment in his life, but not one that must inevitably define his identity. Woolf similarly contracts time, intermingling the past and future with the present in a continuous flow of narrative temporality. Woolf's readers, like the survivor contemplating the meaning of the traumatic event, cannot apprehend the text chronologically because, as Joseph Frank observes, the meaning of the text does not emerge from temporal relationships but rather from spatial ones (10).

One technique Woolf uses to structure her narratives spatially is repetition. She often repeats entire sentences or resonant phrases. For example, in *To the Lighthouse*, when readers encounter Mr. Ramsay's refrain "Some one had blundered" from "The Charge of the Light Brigade," they can locate the moment within the story's chronology, which the many shifting consciousnesses and their lengthy wanderings often interrupt. Woolf also creates set pieces by beginning and ending a section of narrative with the same sentence. These set pieces and refrains suggest a lack of advancement in understanding because the character, despite his intervening speculations, does not revise the original thought but merely reiterates it. The repetition establishes a rhythm of futility in which thoughts fail to lead to new understandings and conclusions.

The trauma survivor similarly tends to structure his life around a single traumatic event that he constantly relives and reconsiders in the closed system of his private, subjective consciousness. Consequently, all other events derive meaning from their relationship to and association with the traumatic event. The survivor is unable to escape the entropy created by continuous repetition; caught in his own set piece, he is unable to create forward movement toward recovery. Although Woolf's form brilliantly depicts trauma and deftly manifests in art a psychological condition that science failed to understand until half a century and several wars later, it less reliably depicts a trauma survivor's recovery.

Meaningful recovery from the "madness" suffered by a trauma survivor requires an escape from the private, self-reflexive view of the traumatic event because the traumatic event and the shards of emotionally charged images and sensations associated with it retain their power when they remain encapsulated and dissociated from the social discourse of the time, the reality of experience, and the social function the suffering may serve. To recover, the survivor must escape the debilitating repetition and the isolation of his own consciousness and reestablish a connection between his pre- and post-traumatic worlds. The survivor must successfully reclaim the past "in order to 'recreate the flow' of ... life and restore a sense of continuity" (Herman, *Trauma* 176). Such an exploration of the past "provides a context within which the particular meaning of the trauma can be understood" (176). The victim must escape the prespeech chaos of his traumatized psyche and reformulate his fragmentary thoughts into a coherent, communicable narrative.

The ultimate paradigm of the trauma survivor and modernist man emerged in the aftermath of the First World War—the shell-shocked war veteran. The severely traumatized war veteran, whom Septimus Smith epitomizes, embodies the essential characteristics of the fragmented, modernist subject. The discoveries the World War I veteran made during the war alienated him from his past by undermining his prewar assumptions about himself and the world that had previously given order and meaning to his life. His traumatic war experiences shattered the cohesion of his consciousness and left it fragmented, a stream of incongruous and disconnected images and bits of memory devoid of the connections and relationships necessary to give meaning to those experiences. Septimus Smith suffers not from a psychological pathology but from a psychological injury, one inflicted by his culture through war and made septic by that same culture's treatment of its veterans.[1]

Since the publication of *Mrs. Dalloway*, substantial advances have been made in our understanding of war neurosis and the psychological effects of trauma. It was previously assumed, for example, that veterans experiencing symptoms six months after service ended suffered from the traumatic effects of a childhood trauma rather than from combat neurosis. Septimus defies conventional notions of shell shock because he suffers from a delayed stress response. He does not experience a breakdown until four years after the Armistice and nine months before the novel opens (Knox-Shaw 100). His wife Rezia, remembering Septimus before his breakdown, thinks, "Only last autumn she and Septimus had stood on the Embankment wrapped in the same cloak and Septimus reading a paper instead of talking" (*MD* 16). Contrary to the opinion expressed in the *Report of the War Office Committee of Enquiry into 'Shell-Shock,'* published in 1922, the etiology of severe and persistent war neurosis, like that suffered by Septimus, is not a crisis of will or courage as a result of "sudden or prolonged fear" (Thomas 52). Persistent and delayed responses to combat stress occur because traumatic events, especially war, damage the foundations of the victim's identity. According to psychologist Erik Erikson, combat experience damages the soldier's ego identity, which is "[a] sense of identity [that] produces the ability to experience oneself as something that has continuity and sameness." In the absence of such continuity, the soldiers' lives "no longer hung together and never would again" (qtd. in Leed 3-4). War neurosis is the result of a shattered sense of identity, the inability to integrate the veteran's identity as a warrior into his pre- and postwar civilian identities.

Woolf's characterization of Septimus Smith illustrates the disillusionment and confusion that result from this postwar identity crisis. Septimus could no longer be the man he was before the war or have faith in his prewar beliefs and values: "The War had taught him. It was sublime. He had gone through the whole show, friendship, European War, death, had won promotion" (*MD* 86). But after the war, the conventions of British life that defined his assumptions and expectations about himself and his world had lost their meaning. Even his reading of the literature— Shakespeare, Dante, and Aeschylus (translated)—revealed a different message after the war. No longer blinded by "that boy's business of the intoxication of language" (*MD* 88), Septimus felt that war invalidated the fundamental beliefs that had given his prewar life meaning.[2] Septimus projects "loathing, hatred, despair" (*MD* 88) into the texts he reads. The beauty of the words belied the sordid, inglorious aspects of human nature that Septimus witnessed during combat.

During the war, Septimus saw humanity stripped of the trappings of civilization and witnessed its primitive nature and its potential for evil and destruction, which is merely constrained—not eradicated—by civilized order. Continuous combat experience erodes the layers of socially prescribed beliefs and identities that distance us from our basic and often more stimulating nature. In such a void, socially defined distinctions, even between good and evil, are rendered meaningless. Soldiers' testimonies often reveal the vulnerability, weakness, and depravity of men confronted with the prospect of death under conditions of extreme deprivation. Septimus claimed to be condemned to death by human nature, and Dr. Holmes was his executioner: "Human nature, in short, was on him—the repulsive brute, with the blood red nostrils. Holmes was on him" (*MD* 92). Art or polite society could no longer shield him from the truth: "Scientifically speaking, the flesh was melted off the world. His body was macerated until only the nerve fibres were left" (*MD* 68).[3] Unlike Clarissa Dalloway, he fears the heat of the sun.

Paradoxically, Septimus Smith claims that despite his raw, exposed nerve fibers, he is unable to feel pain any longer or to empathize with the suffering of loved ones like Rezia and Evans. Woolf's characterization of Septimus's sensual and emotional paralysis illustrates the numbing effect so characteristic of traumatic injury and the obstruction of grief that contemporary psychologists recognize in their combat-veteran clients.[4] During combat, indifference is a survival tool that protects the psyche from being overwhelmed by war's horrifying assault upon the senses—the sight of mutilated comrades, the smell of their blood and bowels, the incessant sound of their cries and moans heard through the noise of machine guns and exploding shells, and even the taste of death.[5] Though Septimus's anhedonia or inability to feel begins before the end of the war, it is perpetuated and exacerbated by his inability to find meaning either in his war experiences or in his suffering during and after those experiences. Friedrich Nietzsche claimed that it isn't the horror of pain but rather the realization that one's suffering is meaningless and serves no purpose that proves unbearable to the sufferer. As Septimus illustrates, the traumatized veteran faces an existential vacuum and feels that nothing has meaning. Septimus's "brain was perfect; it must be the fault of the world then—that he could not feel. . . . It might be possible, Septimus thought, looking at England from the train window, as they left Newhaven; it might be possible that the world itself is without meaning" (*MD* 88).

Psychiatrist and neurologist Viktor Frankl, the founder of what has come to be called the Third Viennese School of Psychotherapy (after Freud's psychoanalysis and Adler's individual psychology)—the school of logotherapy—claims that "[m]an's search for meaning is the primary motivation in his life and not a 'secondary rationalization' of instinctual drives" (Frankl 121).[6] The principles of logotherapy reveal much about how victims of trauma survive and recover from their ordeals because Frankl developed his concepts while a prisoner in German concentration camps during World War II.

According to Frankl, the ability to give meaning to suffering is an essential element for survival and recovery. When man's will to meaning is frustrated—what Frankl refers to as "existential frustration"—neurosis occurs. In order to fill this "existential vacuum," the victim must "bring repressed meanings and meaning opportunities to the conscious level of awareness. . . . [T]he awareness and discovery of meaning occur in response to the self-transcendent relationship. Self-transcendence occurs in a relationship with another person, a useful and important cause, or in a relationship with nature" (Lantz 487). Frankl's approach reveals that, for trauma victims like Septimus, "the pain of the trauma experience can be transformed into meaning awareness, as opposed to being repressed and/or acted out" (Lantz 487). Septimus struggles to "discover and make use of unique personal meaning opportunities for self-transcendent giving to the world which can be found within the memories of trauma and terror" (Lantz 487).

Although the belief that one has knowledge or truths to give to the world suggests a delusional sense of megalomania, Septimus wants to offer the truth revealed to him during the war as a gift, however unwelcome, to the British populace. As a trauma survivor and war veteran, Septimus potentially has power, through his story, to criticize the actions of those politicians who sent him and his compatriots to war. Septimus's position as a survivor gives him power, as well as the burden to assert that power, and Evans and the ghosts of other dead soldiers haunt him to remind him of his obligation as a survivor to educate those who can prevent such a cataclysm from happening again. The unseen bade him— "the greatest of mankind, Septimus, lately taken from life to death, the lord who had come to renew society"—to justify his survival and validate their deaths (*MD* 25). "Septimus, was alonecalled forth in advance of the mass of men to hear the truth, to learn the meaning, which now, at last

. . . was to be given whole to. . . . 'To whom?' he asked aloud. 'To the Prime Minster,' the voices which rustled above his head replied. The supreme secret must be told to the Cabinet" (*MD* 67). He reluctantly carries the burden of the dead's eternal suffering and loneliness and the message that could change the world entirely. To discharge his burden and fulfill the unique prophetic role the war so brutally prepared him for, he must communicate and share the secret, the guilty knowledge, that the brute, human nature, that frightens and excites us, is not restrained within our souls but called forth by the very institutions struggling to repress it. By telling his story, he performs "a personally reconstitutive act and expresses the hope that it will also be a socially reconstitutive act—changing the order of things as they are and working to prevent the enactment of similar horrors in the future" (Tal, "Speaking" 230).

Septimus senses that his own potential for recovery lies in telling his story: "Communication is health, communication is happiness" (*MD* 93). Communication creates the possibility for him to form a self-transcendent relationship, to give his knowledge to others, to inspire positive change, and to become the standard bearer Evans' ghost exhorts him to become. Septimus, however, struggles with the central dialectic of trauma—"the conflict between the will to deny horrible events and the will to proclaim them aloud" (Herman, *Trauma* 1)—and is silenced and marginalized when he does attempt to communicate with bourgeois authoritarian figures, represented by Dr. Holmes and Sir William Bradshaw, physicians who are unwilling to engage in such a relationship with him. Confronted with the shocking revelations in veterans' testimonies, it is not surprising that a community may wish to avoid or deny their truth because the testimonies may create a sense of instability and confusion in the community and, consequently, cause it to suffer the same feelings of disorientation the veteran himself suffers. The typical reactions to trauma—"[d]enial, repression, and dissociation[—]operate on a social as well as an individual level" (Herman, *Trauma* 2).

Trauma and recovery, particularly in the case of war, are simultaneously individual and communal experiences. The community that places the soldier in combat, like the soldier himself, can either change and create a new identity that reflects the experiences of war, or stagnate in an attempt to reestablish a prewar identity that gave rise to the conflict in the first place. Ancient warrior cultures acknowledged the social, communal aspect of war by performing reintegration ceremonies in which the community metaphorically took blood from the returning soldiers' hands, accepting responsibility for the military deaths they had inflicted on its behalf.[7]

In contemporary society, the process of communalization—"being able safely to tell the story [of the trauma] to someone who is listening and who can be trusted to retell it truthfully to others in the community" (Shay 4)—replaces the blood of the ancient ritual with the trauma story or testimonial narrative. Communalization functions as a means of self-transcendent giving and a conduit through which meaning and purpose can emerge from the trauma. The soldier asks the community, through the telling and retelling of his stories, "to engage with . . . [him] in the lacer-ating moral complexities" he experienced in combat. From those who hear the story, the soldier "seeks not absolution but fairness, compassion, and the willingness to share the guilty knowledge of what happens to people in extremity" (Herman, *Trauma* 69). War stories describe the extremities of combat—the soldier's capacity for violence, the ferocious instinct to survive, and the vulnerability of the human body—and the guilty truth that, despite the suffering, soldiers experience exhilaration and freedom when focused solely on survival. In battle, combatants aban-don the struggle to hold back the power of Clarissa's "brutal monster"—its "hooves planted down in the depth of that leaf-encumbered forest, the soul" (*MD* 12)—and no longer share her worry and fear of the brute stirring, but give rein to its power and relish the thrill of what Pat Barker calls "pure naked self assertion" (Barker 170).

The safety of the social order depends, however, on that brutal monster remaining quiet and is inevitably threatened by stories extolling its virtues. Powerful forces in the community, defenders of the social order like Sir William Bradshaw, fight to repress the story and appropri-ate or codify it to affirm rather than challenge the established order and the beliefs and conventions that secure it. A struggle for control over the interpretation of the trauma, in this instance war, may develop between the community and the survivor: "If survivors retain control over the interpretation of their trauma, they can sometimes force a shift in the social and political structure. If the dominant culture manages to appro-priate the trauma and can codify it in its own terms, the status quo will remain unchanged" (Tal, *Worlds* 7). The outcome of this struggle influ-ences the progress toward recovery because the acceptance of change is a fundamental aspect of meaningful recovery. In its effort to protect and preserve itself, the community jeopardizes the veteran's recovery from his own trauma by forcing him to deny or repress what he learned in war and to resurrect his prewar identity rather than to establish a new one that incorporates his experiences as a warrior. Because the soldier had escaped the "restraints, inhibitions, and controls upon 'primitive' asocial instincts . . . [he] was a threat to the society of his origins . . . [and] had to be reintegrated, reacculturated, and reeducated" (Leed 196). The community wants him to be the man he was before the war—the man who was willing to die to preserve the community's social order, a man who "went to France to save an England which consisted entirely of Shakespeare's plays and Miss Isabel Pole in a green dress walking in a square" (*MD 86*) —and to affirm its belief in that order or to bear the burden of his knowledge in silence.

Communalization is not only necessary for the individual soldier's postwar recovery. From a cultural perspective, it is a necessary deconstructive and revolutionary force that encourages change by first undermining the status quo—the political, social, and economic stasis from which the conflict, along with its traumatic consequences, originally emerged. As Kalí Tal explains,

> Bearing witness is an aggressive act. It is born out of a refusal to bow to outside pressure to revise or to repress experience, a decision to embrace conflict rather than conformity, to endure a lifetime of anger and pain rather than to submit to the seductive pull of revision and repression. Its goal is change. The battle over the meaning of a traumatic experience is fought in the arena of political discourse, popular culture, and scholarly debate. The outcome of this battle shapes the rhetoric of the dominant culture and influences future political action. (*Worlds* 7)

Sir William Bradshaw is well versed in the rhetoric of the dominant culture and is deeply invested in preserving it because it affirms his identity and the organizing principles by which he gives meaning to his life. "Proportion" is the rhetoric of the dominant culture, and Bradshaw silences or converts those who threaten Proportion or an England prospering under its auspices. Sir William "secluded her lunatics, forbade childbirth, penalised despair, made it impossible for the unfit to propagate their views until they, too, shared his sense of proportion" (*MD* 99). His rest cure ensures that Septimus and others who threaten the status quo will never share their revelations with others in the community, especially not with the Prime Minister. Moreover, the isolation it imposes encourages conversion by weakening the resolve of incarcerated patients so that they will deny what they know to be true in order to be permitted to return to conventional society. Despite its designation as a cure, this conversion therapy prevents recovery because, although it removes sources of agitation or stress that might aggravate individual symptoms, it fails to address the origin of the disorder—the patient's frustrated search for meaning.

In addition to isolating those whose stories may criticize the status quo, the proponents of "conversion" may gain control of the interpretation of those stories by codifying them to affirm rather than condemn the status quo. The paradigm of the hero is one example of how military experiences are codified to protect Proportion. The hero, with his heritage of mythic and chivalric traditions, serves as a paradigm of social and moral excellence, so that by stereotyping all soldiers in that role, the community can view them as champions of the prevailing social order rather than dissenters. Bradshaw reminds Septimus that he had served with great distinction, but Septimus thinks, "in the War itself he had failed" (*MD* 96). By celebrating heroism, valor, and victory as collective achievements, while ignoring the demoralizing and dehumanizing tasks required of the soldier and his less than heroic feelings of fear, guilt, and shock at his own brutality, defenders of the dominant culture corrupt the concept of communalization.

As Dr. Holmes and Sir William Bradshaw champion Proportion, they also champion her alter ego, Conversion, who "feasts on the wills of the weakly, loving to impress, to impose, adoring her own features stamped on the face of the populace" (*MD* 100). Holmes's advice to Rezia to get Septimus to look at "real things, go to a music hall, play cricket" (*MD* 25) suggests that such conventional activities are more representative of reality and truth than what Septimus experienced and learned in the war. Holmes and Bradshaw encourage Septimus to repress the understanding and knowledge he obtained during the war. They want him to accept and confirm rather than to question the jingoist rhetoric predicated on British public-school ideals of sportsmanship, etiquette, and ceremony. Septimus acerbically refers to the Great War as that "little shindy of schoolboys with gunpowder" (*MD* 96), despite the public's naïve subscription to delusions of patriotic ardor and futile self-sacrifice. Bradshaw's cure would deprive Septimus of the opportunity to achieve self-transcendence and satisfy his will to meaning by rendering him unable publicly to communicate the truths he discovered in the war and to expose the lies of imperialism.

The result of Holmes and Bradshaw's effort to silence Septimus is twofold: they destroy Septimus's chance to recover by robbing him of the possibility of giving meaning to his war experiences, and they destroy his own culture's meaningful recovery from the war by perpetuating a social, political, and economic structure that sacrificed an entire generation of young men to the First World War. Septimus' choice to end his life might be interpreted as a revolutionary act whereby he defies his doctors' attempts to codify his experience. His suicide is a desperate attempt to communicate and constitutes his final "refusal to bow to outside pressure to revise or to repress experience, a decision to embrace conflict rather than conformity" (Tal, *Worlds* 7). It is not Septimus's psychological pain that causes his tragic self-destruction, but rather his inability to give meaning to that pain: "He did not want to die. Life was good. The sun hot. Only human beings—what did *they* want?" (*MD* 149).

Septimus's death, if not the truths he has to share, comes to Clarissa's party uninvited but not wholly unexpected. According to Christine Froula, "death comes to Clarissa's party, of all the parties in London, because she can admit it; because she lets it in. . . . Death comes to her party because she (the perfect hostess) can entertain it, a guest, and a familiar" (Froula, "Mrs. Dalloway's" 18). Clarissa is uniquely able to receive Septimus's message because she senses the brutal monster—the vulnerability, the frailty, the evil—stirring about in her and her social and political circles where it is "wreathed about with chatter, defaced, obscured . . . let drop every day in corruption, lies, chatter" (*MD* 184). She admires Septimus and envies him the embrace of death—the solitude achieved as "closeness drew apart"—and contact with "the centre," as all the layers of daily rituals and vacuous concerns fall away (*MD* 184). Clarissa does not, however, proclaim aloud in the middle of her party that this young man had killed himself to protest the twin evils of proportion and conversion. Instead, the process of communalization breaks down as she reframes Smith's message in the context of her own life and experiences it as a personal moment of insight and affirmation rather than an opportunity for collective insight. Septimus's message can only have meaning if it is shared with others in a larger community and has the potential to inspire change. Trapped in Clarissa's consciousness, Septimus's message cannot effect social or political change unless

Clarissa herself, through her own actions or testimony, channels it to those in the community who need to hear it. Apparently, Clarissa does not have sufficient vision to aspire to the communalization of trauma—her own, Septimus's, or England's.

Clarissa has instead developed an alternative approach to recovery. She creates moments of beauty, harmony, and unity that offer sanctuary from trauma and mitigate its destructive power. She developed this philosophy as she struggled to give meaning to her own shattering experiences. For Clarissa is a trauma survivor herself, as Peter Walsh recalls: "To see your own sister killed by a falling tree . . . before your very eyes, a girl too on the verge of life, the most gifted of them, Clarissa always said, was enough to turn one bitter" (*MD* 78). After the death of her sister Sylvia, Clarissa struggled to find a way to rebel against the cruelty of the gods and concluded that "[t]hose ruffians, the Gods . . . who never lost a chance of hurting, thwarting, and spoiling human lives were seriously put out if, all the same, you behaved like a lady. . . . Later she wasn't so positive perhaps; she thought there were no Gods; no one was to blame; and so she evolved this atheist's religion of doing good for the sake of goodness" (*MD* 77-78).

Doing good for the sake of goodness sounds a bit like the aesthetic philosophy of art for art's sake, and Clarissa is one of Virginia Woolf's social artists of everyday life. Her attempt to organize post-traumatic chaos is elegiac in nature (Froula "Mrs. Dalloway's" 129). Clarissa "embodies the elegy's very principle: the necessity of relinquishing the dead and of forming new attachments in order to carry on with life" (129), and her parties "mediate the mourner's arduous journey from loss, grief, and rage to renewed life and hope" (126). Clarissa's party is an artistic moment of unity and order, a scene "that wrenches her guests from the dullness of habitual activity and serves as a stage for moments of heightened consciousness" (Henke, "Communion" 142). Clarissa's art is modernist in form, insofar as it remains personal, internal, and private. One gets the sense that the order, the pattern that emerges at her party is not organic but cultivated. Clarissa envisions the components—the people, the flowers, the china—converging, crystallizing into an intricate pattern of perfect balance and symmetry. As her guests scatter across the surface of her design, moving from room to room, from conversation to conversation, she holds her breath, waiting for the moment when they all settle into their appropriate places and the pattern emerges. Her art, her gift, resides in the ability to configure that aesthetic pattern, and thus to create transcendent moments of unity and beauty.

Clarissa's art masks the truth and shields her like a parasol—"a sacred weapon which a Goddess, having acquitted herself honorably in the field of battle, sheds, and place[s] . . . in the umbrella stand. . . . Fear no more, said Clarissa. Fear no more the heat o' the sun" (*MD* 30). As she chose flowers for her party, "she said to herself, more and more gently, as if this beauty, this scent, this colour, and Miss Pym liking her, trusting her, were a wave which she let flow over her and surmount that hatred, that monster, surmount it all; and it lifted her up and up" (*MD* 13). As soldiers know, freeing that monster is exhilarating, and the price she pays for its captivity is "The death of the soul" (89). In her effort to avoid the heat of the sun, Clarissa has denied herself its warmth; and in her effort to quiet the beast in her soul, she has denied herself the better part of its nature—passion, inspiration, and vitality. "Her ideals have been tempered, her beliefs eroded in the gradual process of adaptation and compromise" (Henke, "Communion" 143). Clarissa remains on the fringes of life, walking on the porch at Bourton, watching the woman from her window, standing at the edge of the Serpentine, and even dying vicariously through another. She ultimately is able "to hate Conversion and convert, to be both Septimus and part of the world that sacrifices him, to die and continue her life unchanged" (Guth 22-23). According to Deborah Guth,

> It is this standing at the window, on the edge of the Serpentine of life, that constitutes her major problem: the incapacity to commit herself fully. . . . [B]y the end of the novel, as she watches the old woman opposite closing the blinds, she is poised . . . outside the loop of time. This, it would appear, is the condition of her visionary freedom, and this is what invalidates it. (25)

Clarissa accepts the choices she has made and the world that she inhabits and, to a degree, that she herself has created. She does not try to change or influence the vicissitudes of fate and the high jinks of those ruffian gods, but rather looks for emotional and communal consolation, and through her parties, seeks to offer gifts of sympathy and comprehension to others.

Although Clarissa's art provides a much needed respite from chaos and reminds us that beauty is still possible, it is too ephemeral to instigate real change or to effect the kind of change Septimus's message demands. Unity and harmony sustain the status quo; chaos is the harbinger of change. Change is heralded by defiance, aggression, and ultimately, for Septimus, violent destruction. "'I'll give it you!' he cried, and flung himself vigorously, violently down on to Mrs. Filmer's area railings" (*MD* 149). Clarissa's approach to recovery seems better suited to the inevitable, private and individual traumas that the gods fling at us, rather than a communal trauma like war that human beings instigate and engineer. Christine Froula concludes that, at the moment of insight the novel journeys towards, "Clarissa reflects on her conversion, acknowledges loss, and affirms the consolations that reward the elegist's bowing to reality" ("Mrs. Dalloway's" 151).

The First World War, like subsequent wars, forced art to bow to reality and called into question the purpose, role, and function of artistic creation. Does art for art's sake, like "doing good for the sake of goodness," really reflect a world so mired in reality? Should art be a means to pull us out of the mud, or should it shove our faces deeper until we emerge gasping and willing to change drastically and violently, if necessary? Modernist forms reflect trauma on the most personal level, and meaning lies in the internal and private, the subjective, and the consciousness of the individual. But war is a particularly communal trauma and demands a collective response. For a soldier like Septimus to find meaning in his combat experiences, his story must not only be heard but also understood by those in power. Trying to communicate the reality of war to those who have never experienced it is a struggle against the confines of language and the inadequacy of myth and metaphor, but attempting to communicate it via a narrative formed in the prespeech consciousness of the soldier is even more daunting. The fragmentation and incongruity of Septimus's message, while artistically stunning, would prevent successful communalization outside the fictional world of Woolf's text. The next generation of writers, some of whom would be veterans of another war, felt the strain of the outside world bearing down on the esoteric aesthetics of art and attempted to create a literature that would inspire action and change. They bowed not just to reality, but to history as well. Discussing the work of the writers of the 1930s, Jean-Paul Sartre attributes the change in the new generation to its realization of the gap between "literary myth and historical reality" (Sartre 174). Ironically, the new generation discovered that its art, like the Modernist art it rejected, failed to bring about tangible social change, and Europe embarked on a second World War, having never truly recovered from the first.

Notes

1. Septimus Smith's disorder has been diagnosed as schizophrenia. See articles by Ban Wang and So Hee Lee. Both schizophrenia and post-traumatic stress disorder involve a loss of ego identity; however, as Victor J. DeFazio claims, men suffering from traumatic war neurosis are often misdiagnosed because "[t]he contraction of ego functioning often resembles schizophrenic deterioration while the phobic elaboration that the world is a hostile enemy-infested place is often mistaken for a psychotic persecutory delusion" (38). In "Virginia Woolf and Post-traumatic Subjectivity," Suzette Henke, referring to a 1985 article in which she described Septimus' illness in terms of schizophrenia, alters this implicit diagnosis to suggest that Woolf's characterization of Septimus offers, in the light of trauma theory, a "particularly striking figure of the shellshocked soldier" who has survived the carnage of World War I (149). In an essay on "Woolf's *Prime Minister*" Henke argues that Woolf's initial delineation of Septimus offered a more manic and mentally disturbed portrait of a young man determined to assassinate the British prime minister, then to commit suicide and to offer his body as a Eucharistic communion to feed the hordes of refugees from eastern Europe. See also Henke, "Modernism."

2. Kalí Tal explains this process as follows: "Psychologist Daniel Goleman suggests that personal myths take the form of schemas—unconscious assumptions about experience and the way the world works. The schemas operating in a particular situation determine the actual information an individual absorbs and interprets. Such operations inevitably skew perceptions of events; in fact, that is their purpose. . . . Grand revision of a personal myth must always spring from a traumatic experience, for the mechanism which maintains those foundational schemas will automatically distort or revise all but the most shattering revelations. (Tal, "Speaking" 225.) See also Daniel Goleman.

3. John Del Vecchio in his novel about the postwar adjustment of Vietnam veterans, *Carry Me Home*, echoes Woolf's reference to the war's stripping away of the soldier's skin. Del Vecchio's veteran Robert Wapinski says, "[S]ometimes I feel like I've been shaved by a razor that was set too high. . . . It's like it's taken off my outer layer of skin. It's like my nerves are exposed. Like everything rubs the raw ends" (80).

4. Herman explains that the trauma victim's "[p]erceptions may be numbed or distorted, with partial anesthesia or the loss of particular sensations. . . . These perceptual changes combine with a feeling of indifference, emotional detachment, and profound passivity in which the person relinquishes all initiative and struggle" (*Trauma* 43). In addition, Shay observed in working with Vietnam veterans that the "long-term obstruction of grief and failure to communalize grief can imprison a person in endless swinging between rage and emotional deadness as a permanent way of being in the world" (40).

5. Pat Barker in her novel *Regeneration* describes an incident in which a World War I soldier named Burns tastes death: "He'd been thrown into the air by the explosion of a shell and had landed, head-first, on a German corpse, whose gas-filled belly had ruptured

on impact. Before Burns lost consciousness, he'd had time to realize that what filled his nose and mouth was decomposing human flesh" (19).

6. Jim Lantz claims, "In Frankl's system of treatment, the human will to meaning is more powerful than the motivational factors of sex, safety, pleasure, achievement, security, comfort, or power" (486). Frankl offers an alternative to a strictly Freudian reading of Septimus. The history of hysteria, a disorder consistently associated with war neurosis, suggests a shift in Freud's view of experience as the catalyst of neurosis. In 1896, Freud, in a report entitled *The Aetiology of Hysteria*, claimed that hysteria was caused by "one or more occurrences of premature sexual experience" (203), the trauma experienced as a result of childhood sexual molestation. However, within a year of publishing this report, Freud repudiated this theory because of its disturbing social implications. According to Judith Herman,

> His correspondence makes clear that he was increasingly troubled by the radical social implications of his hypothesis. Hysteria was so common among women that if his patients' stories were true, and if his theory were correct, he would be forced to conclude that what he called "perverted acts against children" were endemic, not only among the proletariat of Paris, . . . but also among the respectable bourgeois families of Vienna, where he had established his practice. (*Trauma* 14)

Consequently, "[p]sychoanalysis became a study of the internal vicissitudes of fantasy and desire, dissociated from the reality of experience" (14). Herman cites Jeffrey Moussaieff Masson's seminal work *The Assault on Truth: Freud's Suppression of the Seduction Theory*. In addition to revealing the change in Freud's belief about the origin of his female patients' seduction memories, Masson also suggests the power of the trauma story to challenge and destabilize the social status quo and the associated need to control that story. Attributing violent sexual crimes to the victims' imagination, "was a comforting view for society, for Freud's interpretation, that the sexual violence that so affected the lives of his women patients was nothing but fantasy, posed no threat to the existing social order (xxii).

7 Jonathan Shay points out that most warrior societies had some type of communal purification ritual for soldiers returning from battle. He contends that the Athenian tragic theater provided Greek soldiers the communal space for such a ritual (see *Achilles in Vietnam*, p. 230, note 14), and there is evidence that early Roman soldiers participated in such purification ceremonies as well. Shay cites French scholar Georges Dumézil's description of annual ceremonies that "marked the end of the military season" (Shay 153).

"COULD THEY TELL ONE WHAT THEY KNEW?": MODES OF DISCLOSURE IN *TO THE LIGHTHOUSE*

Jane Lilienfeld

Juxtaposing diverse theoretical discourses, this essay interrogates the representation of familial abuse in Virginia Woolf's *To the Lighthouse*. The postmodern destabilization of the binary oppositions that sustain Western philosophical discourse challenges the truth-claims of psychological research, but also the rigid boundaries separating genres such as autobiographical fiction and memoir. The facts of familial incest and the seriousness of its impact have generated controversy among the fields of psychoanalysis, psychological theory, and the psychological practice of woman-centered therapeutic work. In turn, these divergences have affected the theoretical paradigms underpinning the psychological treatment of trauma survivors. Such divergence is not new, nor is its politicization new, as Judith Lewis Herman (*Trauma* 7-9), and Bessel van der Kolk (*Traumatic Stress* 37-39) argue.[1] Nevertheless, the clashes among methodologies, therapeutic practices, and research studies have affected the biographical study of Virginia Woolf's life, an impact further exacerbated by the divergence of interpretation between American and British literary critics about the life and works of Virginia Woolf (Silver 152-175, Marcus, "Wrapped"). Not proposing to solve these controversies, this essay will situate its argument within them, thus emphasizing the ambiguity of that which is represented and the interpretation of it, both in *To the Lighthouse* itself and within critical discourses about the novel.

Emily Dalgarno challenges Louise DeSalvo's reading of the now iconic paragraph in "A Sketch of the Past" in which Woolf reviews Gerald's digital rape of her on a ledge in the hallway (Woolf, *MOB* 69): "DeSalvo assumes that what took place with Gerald was visible in the mirror. . . . But in a passage otherwise devoted to reflection, Woolf presented this experience as a tactile image" (Dalgarno 141). To Louise DeSalvo, Virginia Woolf not only experienced her own victimization but was forced to witness it: "I strongly suspect that what intensified the horror of the experience was the fact that Virginia Woolf was able to see herself in the mirror: she was watching herself be assaulted" (*Impact*

105). Dalgarno, however, questions what Woolf saw and from what angle she observed her own violation: "Perhaps she was denied a visual perspective. Seated on a slab she faced a larger person, so that if the mirror were opposite she saw the reflection of Gerald's back, or if it were the shelf over which she peered into the mirror, she had her own back to the reflection" (Dalgarno 141).[2]

"Although she had written and spoken of George Duckworth's 'male-factions,' as she phrased it, and although she spoke of both the Duckworths in conjunction with her abuse, this is the first recorded instance in which she directly implicates Gerald. And this is the first time I believe that she remembers how far back the history of her abuse went [,]" argues Louise DeSalvo (*Impact* 100). DeSalvo places Gerald's digital rape of the young Virginia Stephen as having occurred at St. Ives when the child was six (*Impact* 100). At this time, Virginia Woolf was recovering from a severe attack of whooping cough, as were all her siblings; all the children were nursed by their mother, whose own mother was ill. Simultaneously, Leslie Stephen suffered from "one of his several breakdowns" (DeSalvo, *Impact* 113). Hence, "[t]he first episode of her abuse coincided with serious family emergencies" (DeSalvo, *Impact* 113).[3]

The seriousness of traumatic after-effects may be inextricably tied to how people near the survivor respond to his or her report of abuse (Herman, *Trauma* 61-7, Jacobs 6-7). If the attacker is a family member, the negative after-shocks are exacerbated. Contemporary abuse survivors like those working with therapist Janet Liebman Jacobs attest to their rage and despair at not being heard, supported, or believed (22-23). What could a child of six years old in a late-Victorian family as destabilized as that of the Stephens have hoped for,[4] could she even have found the words to tell of such an event? (Bell 1: 43). DeSalvo speculates that the little girl would have blamed herself (*Impact* 104) and argues that, given her consistent preference for sons over daughters, Julia Stephen would have refused to honor such stories, had she heard them (*Impact* 113). On the other hand, Quentin Bell reported that Vanessa Bell had intervened during the time of her sister's 1904 breakdown to report George's incestuous advances: "Vanessa told [Dr.] Savage of what had been happening and Savage, it seems, taxed George with his conduct" (1: 95-6).

Nor was Vanessa Bell alone in bringing the attacks on the adolescent sisters to the attention of some members of the male establishment. "Sometime between March 1920 and May 25 1921," states Jeanne

Schulkind (*MOB* 140), Virginia Woolf read a sketch of her earlier life entitled "22 Hyde Park Gate" to the Memoir Club, which included members of what came to be known as the Bloombsury Group (Hussey, *A-Z* 158). Although much has been written that presents its members as unusually liberated for their era, this was not, in fact, a group supportive of women. Jane Marcus argues that what made their misogyny particularly harmful was their power:

> These men had class and cultural power, an old-boy network with connections in government, diplomacy, education, publishing, and the literary journals. They were not, like homosexuals of more vulnerable classes, the natural allies of women, fellow outsiders. (*Languages* 76)

Perhaps because presentations to the members of the Memoir Club were expected to be "completely honest" (Hussey, *A-Z* 158) it was to that audience that Virginia Woolf read "22 Hyde Park Gate." The memoir culminates in a paragraph describing her half-brothers' attacks on herself and Vanessa when they were adolescents (*MOB* 155).[5] John Maynard Keynes dismissed the material as an exaggerated fiction (*MOB* 140).[6] Viewed in light of Marcus' analysis, Keynes' response is understandable and suggests that disclosure to a male used to occupying positions of power, even in the 1920s, did not result in belief of or support for the female survivor. How unlikely, then, that a little girl's revelation in 1890 would have been taken seriously. Questions thus remain: does any child have the language with which to report abuse like Gerald's digital rape (McNaron 254-255)? If so, to whom might it have been reported, and what might have been their reaction? This question reverberates throughout *To the Lighthouse*, a novel in which the recognition, naming, and disclosure of abuse are problematized.

To say that the line between creative nonfiction and autobiographical fiction is porous becomes especially problematic now that there has been a resurgence of attacks on the truth-claims of incest survivors. Nor is this the first time that the political needs of a group of women conflict with the theoretical assumptions that buttress some of the more useful modes of literary theory. Currently, the credibility of women trauma survivors is being undercut in the U.S. court system (Pitman et al. 386-388, van der Kolk 566-568, McNally 256-259). This is a situation somewhat similar to that which occurred when, just as erased and silenced groups became able to valorize their subjectivity as the underpinning to renewed political activism, literary theory posited that subject positions were specious categories (Wolfe and Penelope 8) and "essentialism" was categorized as a political transgression (Fuss). That creative nonfiction is in some sense "fictional" points to the fact that autobiography may be read as an inherently mendacious formal category. Feminist theorists, however, have problematized that very point, for theoretically, women's autobiography has never had the authority of that written by men (Gilmore 25-28). Shari Benstock created the term "life-writing" in order to trouble rigid generic categories, encompassing in the term "memoirs, diaries, letters, and journals, as well as the *bildungsroman* and other personally inflected texts" (Henke, *Shattered* xiii, italics mine; see also DeSalvo, *Writing* 208-216). Women's therapeutic "life writing" becomes suspect too, not just because some may not consider the product as "art," but because it is written by those who are perceived to be excluded from positions of power (Gilmore 26, 80). To move Virginia Woolf's *To the Lighthouse* into this theoretical maelstrom challenges the book's recently established status as an icon of high modernist art. Nevertheless, I will argue that the novel, crafted to create a non-permeable boundary against less artful literary forms, may have served as a precursor to the author's more candid "life writing."

Virginia Woolf, like contemporary theorists, troubled and was troubled by the permeable boundary between fiction and "life writing". By the time Woolf wrote *To the Lighthouse*, she had become convinced that autobiographical self-referentiality ruined fictional narratives: "I suppose the danger is the damned egotistical self; which ruins Joyce & [Dorothy] Richardson to my mind: is one pliant and rich enough to provide a wall for the book from oneself without its becoming, as in Joyce & Richardson, narrowing and constricting?" (*D2*: 14) That art must be neither propaganda nor biographically self-serving, however, did not mean that art should evade the hard truths of human life, as Woolf argued eloquently in her posthumously published essay "The Leaning Tower" (*M* 140-54). In fact, Woolf sought to find the mode by which, in all her novels, she could "tell all the truth/but tell it slant," as Emily Dickinson had advised. Further, as the tone *of A Room of One's Own* indicates—to the aggravation of numerous feminist critics—during the 1920s Woolf rejected direct expression of anger, preferring to disguise her rage as wit (Radin 3-7, Restuccia). Keynes's response to her memoir might have been one origin for what Virginia Woolf later termed male fear of women's frankness about the female body ("Professions for Women,"

DM 240). Hence, in the 1920s, Woolf seems to have been persuaded that only oblique challenges to social norms might most effectively prevent resistance from novel readers. In composing *To the Lighthouse*, exactly which familial experiences was Woolf willing to represent, and stylistically how might such material be narrated? If family systems that sustained abuse were to be depicted, how were these to be characterized? How much did Woolf's conception of the artifice of the novel, her recognition of the constraints imposed by gender, and her fear of public censure dictate the narrative method and content of *To the Lighthouse*?

Virginia Woolf told two different stories of origin when describing the composition of the novel. At the time of its inception, Woolf four times declared that she wished to avoid what she terms "sentimentality" (*D3*: 36, 106-7, 110, 134). Even so, asserts Mark Spilka, "she remained diffusely afraid of being charged with Victorianism, or sentimentality, in dealing with all the emotions of family life and childhood" (76). Perhaps by the words "Victorianism" and "sentimentality" Virginia Woolf meant something other than the excessively maudlin? As I have noted, Woolf was aware that circumspection rather than overt declaration might be a strategic literary necessity. Woolf said at first that she wanted to recreate her parents' characters. "This is going to be fairly short: to have father's character done complete in it; & mother's. . . . But the centre is father's character, sitting in a boat, reciting We perished, each alone, while he crushes a dying mackerel" (*D3*: 18-19). On the other hand, as the work progressed, Virginia Woolf expanded her focus to the family as a whole, which she characterized as "father & mother & child in the garden" (*D3*: 36).

However, in "A Sketch of the Past," (the same narrative in which Woolf reported her violation as a six year old), Woolf differentiated the inception of the novel from the later stages of its composition. In the "Sketch," she stated that in writing *To the Lighthouse,* "I suppose that I did for myself what psycho-analysts do for their patients. I expressed some very long felt and deeply felt emotion. And in expressing it I explained it and laid it to rest" (*MOB* 81). *To the Lighthouse* burst into Woolf's mind as a visual and verbal narrative, for as she noted about her earliest memories, "sight was always then so much mixed with sound that picture is not the right word" (*MOB* 67). "Blowing bubbles out of a pipe gives the feeling of the rapid crowd of ideas and scenes which blew out of my mind. . . . What blew the bubbles? Why then? I have no notion"

(*MOB* 81). Elizabeth Abel characterizes this experience "as if a curtain had been lifted and a prior image of origin had been revealed. *To the Lighthouse* appears increasingly to articulate an obsession emerging into consciousness" (46). Conscious of the artifice of shaping her novel at the time she composed it, in retrospect Woolf acknowledged that the narrative represented more inchoate material than she had at first admitted.

Virginia Woolf argued that families are systems[7] which replicate the patriarchal state, not only in *Three Guineas* and in *The Years*, but asserting in *A Room of One's Own* that "England is under the rule of a Patriarchy" (33). This she explicitly defines as an interlocking nexus composed of the judiciary, corporations, the educational establishment, the media, the military and competitive school and professional sports. These, she asserts, are run by "the fathers" for their own benefit, in a system that results in the economic, emotional, and social oppression of women, children, and people of color (*AROO* 34, Black 64). This political interpretation of the family system underpins Woolf's depiction of family life in *To the Lighthouse*.

In order to depict the family as a patriarchal system, Virginia Woolf implemented two specific narrative techniques in *To the Lighthouse*. She replaced omniscient narration by polyvocality, arising from the use of free indirect discourse and the use of image plots. A narrative of imagery takes the place of what would be the story-telling function of an omniscient voice. Harvena Richter names these "symbol clusters," which accrue increasing meaning at each appearance (Richter 201).

Writing in her diary on September 3, 1926, Woolf stated: "[*To the Lighthouse*] is all in oratio obliqua. Not quite all; for I have a few direct sentences" (*D3*: 106). According to the *New Latin Grammar* published in New York in 1888 by Ginn and Company, the literal translation for the term is "indirect discourse." Different readers experience different degrees of narratorial control in Woolf's use of what is now called "free indirect discourse," but most agree that the technique creates polyvocality, dispersing "the unitary authorial voice, by attributing discourse to many different voices and undermining distinctions between them . . ." (Mezei 85; Prince 34-5). This technique disguises the originating point of the narrative voice, thus effectively nullifying a reader's sense that an omniscient authority controls all textual discourse (Rimmon-Kenan 113).

Susan Lanser has argued that the characters share "a semantically common voice" with the constructed narrator of *To the Lighthouse* (114), and that "Woolf's [narrator] represents itself as feminist and bears its author's own name" (119). In contrast, Roger Poole asserts that numerous narrative voices with less than omniscient knowledge infiltrate this text, among them the voices of community gossip, the air itself, and Lily Briscoe (84, 86-90). I have argued elsewhere that Mrs. Ramsay's voice is presented via free indirect discourse in twelve of the nineteen sections of Book One of the novel, even though the narrative voice(s) insist that she cannot be known (*Reading* 196). Norman Friedman considered *To the Lighthouse* an example of "multiple selective omniscience" (1176), an argument that J. Hillis Miller effectively countered by demonstrating that the novel displays a mastery of dialogic such that the narrator functions as a kind of "ubiquitous bugging apparatus" (177).

Perhaps as effective a device in problematizing the reader's sense of authorial omniscience is the use of image plots. Feminist critics have proven that what Richter identified as "symbol clusters" may also be read as a series of allusions. Many North American feminist Woolf critics have traced these allusions to their sources and have discovered them to reveal more than a character's personal psychology or the cultural unconscious. They are, in fact, sustained cultural and political commentaries. These indirect commentaries reject violation, represent the interpenetration of social being by cultural ideologies, and convey an ongoing class and gender analysis. In its explication of simile, metaphor and allusion in Woolf's work, much North American feminist criticism from the mid-1970s to the present will substantiate this assertion.[8]

Male aggression throughout *To the Lighthouse* is rendered pictorially, where it vividly suggests, while containing, the incipient threat to women, children, and indigenous peoples of male power in the home, state and British Empire. Mrs. Ramsay's conviction that she was able to hide the secret of her husband's raging temper (*TTL* 196) is contradicted by repeated images of male brutality. For instance, while charming Minta Doyle at the dinner party, Mr. Ramsay is compared to a carnivore, about to devour the young girl with his "fangs" (*TTL* 102). The image of Mr. Ramsay as a beast combines images of British monarchy (the lion) with the hunted prey in the jungles of empire and is later made overt when Lily recognizes that in his pain in Book Three, Mr. Ramsay is "like a lion seeking whom he could devour" (*TTL* 156). But he is an animal armed, as for instance, when he becomes enraged that Mr. Carmichael delays the progress of the dinner party by requesting another plate of soup: "[His wife] saw his anger fly like a pack of hounds into his eyes, his brow, and she knew that in a moment something violent would explode, and then— thank goodness! she [sic] saw him clutch himself and clap a brake on the wheel, and the whole of his body seemed to emit sparks but not words" (TTL 95). Here Mr. Ramsay is seen as Mars, riding his golden chariot into the battlefield of a late Victorian family dinner party. Ridiculous and threatening simultaneously, Mr. Ramsay slammed things around in his rages, as, for instance, when he "whiz[zed] his plate through the window" at an earlier breakfast, because he had found an "earwig" in his milk (TTL 199). Mr. Ramsay's stamping his foot and swearing at his wife is part of the same pattern of aggressive behavior, not an aberration.

One might dismiss this pattern of imagery as just a means to expose the childishness at the heart of Mr. Ramsay's grandiose demands, but, in fact, images of explosions, fiery rages, and male violence are also used in the depiction of Paul Rayley, whose name is an aural echo of the older man's. Paul's passion for Minta is hardly benign, burning with what Lily sees as "the heat of love, its horror, its cruelty, it unscrupulosity . . ." (TTL 102). Much later, Lily imagines Paul as he clutches a fire poker, holding it aloft over the staircase, ostensibly to use against a thief, but perhaps really to threaten his late-returning wife with physical harm (TTL 173-4). For a moment at least Paul has indeed become what Lily's vision had presaged years before at the dinner party, "a bully with a crowbar (he was swaggering, he was insolent) in the Mile End Road" (TTL 103).

On her return in Book Three, Lily remembers the Rayleys' first love as an all-consuming fire, "[which] repelled her with fear and disgust, . . . [although] she saw its splendour and power . . ." (TTL 175). Lily Briscoe experiences this fire as celebratory, set by "savages on a distant beach" (TTL 175). This resonant image questions who are the "savages" and on what beach did they set the fire? The image might conflate the European colonizers of Imperial domains with the guests who had walked on the beach after the dinner party (TTL 125). These images coalesce in the aftermath of the fire power of World War One: "the silent apparition of an ashen-coloured ship, for instance, come, gone; there was a purplish stain upon the bland surface of the sea as if something had boiled and bled, invisibly, beneath" (TTL 134). The fire imagery and the figure of Mars, suggested by the image of Mr. Ramsay in his war chariot, are examples of what Richter terms "symbol clusters (201), pictorial narrative devices that subtly assert authorial interventions. Through such imagery, the narrative pictorially links Mr. Ramsay, Paul Rayley, and Andrew Ramsay's death in the war, with rapacious British colonialism and male brutalization of the citizens of empire, as well as of European women.

Few readers now disagree with the idea that the Ramsay family in its rigidly hierarchical/patriarchal structure is both destructive to its female members and the children and is emblematic of sites of Imperial domination beyond the private home.[9] The rights of the Victorian patriarch are indirectly but clearly manifested by the image plots in *To the Lighthouse*. The text is careful to ascribe his rapacity to unslaked emotional neediness, hence the insistence through imagery that Mr. Ramsay is always on the verge of explosion. Nor is Mr. Ramsay expected to maintain self-control. Mrs. Ramsay fears "perhaps it was her fault that it was necessary" (*TTL* 108) and holds herself always in readiness to meet his never-ending need for emotional tending. Not only does his wife think that doing so is her primary emotional responsibility, so does the culture in which the family is embedded, for common gossip opined, "[t]hen she was weak with her husband. She let him make those scenes" (*TTL* 195). Burdened with the strain of the enraged and self-indulgent patriarch, family members are expected to accede to the father's needs and demands without question, even as they repress this crucial aspect of their lives both in consciousness and speech. Thus the reverberating rages of Mr. Ramsay are perhaps one way to textualize a family system whose very structure, by privileging male dominance, encourages abuse and violence.

Image plots are but one form of the rejection of omniscience, which is simultaneously a narrative technique and a theme of *To the Lighthouse*. "Baring the device," *To the Lighthouse* problematizes the search for meaning, not just in Mr. Ramsay's quest for R (*TTL* 33-5), but through the narrative means by which information is blocked, questioned, or obfuscated. The refusal of omniscience permeates the novel, where knowledge is impossible to verify, emphasizing the impossibility of achieving epistemological certainty.

In fact, the novel has been interpreted as a feminist satire of those epistemological arguments central to the Western philosophical tradition (Hussey, *A-Z* 313, Nussbaum). Mr. Ramsay is an empiricist, believing that knowledge is best available through sensual apprehension, though he struggles with the Idealist position. Vision is inseparable from knowledge in *To the Lighthouse*, a "baring of the device" that comments both on epistemology and narratology, as for example, in the now iconic admonition of Andrew Ramsay to Lily Briscoe about Mr. Ramsay's philosophical investigations, "Think of a kitchen table then, he told her, when you're not there" (*TTL* 23). In ironic obedience, Lily dutifully visualizes Mr. Ramsay's endeavors: "So now she always saw, when she thought of Mr. Ramsay's work, a scrubbed kitchen table. It lodged now in the fork of a pear tree, for they had reached the orchard" (*TTL* 23). But not only does the painter Lily Briscoe "think" in pictures, so does almost everyone else whose consciousness is available to the reader. When Mr. Ramsay views himself as questing for R, he sees himself in the frozen wastes of the Arctic and climbing Mt. Everest (*TTL* 35). When Mr. Bankes thinks about the impediments to his friendship with Mr. Ramsay, he pictures chickens straggling along a road (*TTL* 21). When Mrs. Ramsay tries to stop herself from worrying about the children who scrambled around the rocks with Minta Doyle and Paul Rayley, she "summoned before her again the little group on the terrace in front of the hall door, standing looking up at the sky" (*TTL* 61). Because sight and that which is seen are so important in this text, occluded vision is itself significant. Vision in *To the Lighthouse* is often doubtful, obstructed, or denied.[10]

Imagery reiterates the cloudiness of so-called objective truth-claims. The idealism which the empiricist Mr. Ramsay rejects has some of its roots in the Platonic assertion that human vision is impeded, veiled. Lily Briscoe, for example, in trying to make sense of Mr. Ramsay's complex commingling of positive and negative traits, imagines her conflicting ideas "danc[ing] up and down, like a company of gnats . . . controlled in an invisible elastic net," a kind of veil that in this case holds but does not organize information (*TTL* 25). When putting her son and daughter to sleep, Mrs. Ramsay throws her shawl over the offending boar's head in the attic, presenting two mutually exclusive explanations for the resulting shadowy shape (*TTL* 114-5). "Truth" remains tantalizingly hinted at, yet obscured.[11]

Louise DeSalvo was the first critic to remark on Virginia Woolf's assertion of the obstructed vision of her childhood: "the more usual feeling for her, the 'normal' way that she experienced life as a child was 'the feeling . . . of lying in a grape and seeing through a film of semi-transparent yellow'" (*Impact* 102, ellipses in original). Indeed, Woolf's depiction of a "blue gummy veil" as the atmosphere in which she lived suggests that the film resulted not from the passage of time, but was itself the medium through which she as a child observed aspects of her experience (*MOB* 65-66). DeSalvo attributes Woolf's impeded vision to depression consequent to the powerlessness experienced by a child in a household such as that of the Stephens', " a sense that her life was being lived behind a screen, within an envelope that protects the child from trauma or neglect" (*Impact* 103).

Lily Briscoe, serving as "a surrogate daughter" to Mrs. Ramsay (Lilienfeld, "'Deceptiveness'" 348), is both an outsider, bearing witness to the story of the family, and an insider, a major perceptual focal point of the novel, though not the only one (Poole, "'We'" 84, 86-90). Gender is the lens through which Lily Briscoe interprets people, events and even her own painting techniques. She is highly critical of the double standard and is hypersensitive to the sacrifice of the female to the needs of the male. Never once does she seem ashamed of being a spinster, a "fate" that middle- and upper-class Victorians and Edwardians considered as social failure. She is empathic, restrained in speech, but aggressive in thought. She has been deliberately crafted as a specific kind of feminist whose political analysis is integral to the novel.[12] Her lesbian obsession with Mrs. Ramsay (Lilienfeld, "'Deceptiveness'" 349-51, Risolo 241, Smith, *Lesbian* 64-70) provides the rationale for her use as a narrative eye. Further, her observations are reiterated by the image-plots, and both counteract Mrs. Ramsay's persistent denial of the negative consequences of her marriage for her children and herself.

However, Lily witnesses some moments of her life with the Ramsay family through severe perceptual distortion, as if she, too, were "seeing through a film of semi-transparent yellow" (*MOB* 65). For example, viewing the Ramsays on the lawn with their children in the first part of the novel, Lily felt, "[d]irectly one looked up and saw them, what she called 'being in love' flooded them. They became part of that unreal but penetrating and exciting universe which is the world seen through the eyes of love. The sky stuck to them; the birds sang through them" (*TTL* 46-7). Who is the "They" who is flooded? Is it Lily or it is the Ramsay family? This unclear pronoun reference may be intended to suggest a merger of Lily into that which is viewed, a subtle absorption into the Ramsay family.

Several pages later, Lily's experience of visual flooding is elaborated further:

> [She and Mr. Bankes] turned and saw the Ramsays. So that is marriage, Lily thought, a man and a woman looking at a girl throwing a ball. That is what Mrs. Ramsay tried to tell me the other night, she thought. For Mrs. Ramsay was wearing a green shawl, and they were standing close together watching Prue and Jasper throwing catches. And suddenly the meaning which, for no reason at all, as perhaps they are stepping out of the Tube or ringing a doorbell, descends on people, making them symbolical, making them representative, came upon them, and made them in the dusk standing, looking the symbols of marriage, husband and wife. Then, after an instant, the symbolical outline which transcended the real figures sank down again, and they became, as they met them, Mr. and Mrs. Ramsay watching the children throwing catches (*TTL* 72).

Again, the lack of clarity of the pronoun reference may be significant. To what does the pronoun "that" refer? The physical closeness of Mr. and Mrs. Ramsay? The children's seemingly happy play? What is "the meaning" which "has descend[ed] on them"? Although the "real" Ramsays are "transcended" by "symbolical outline," what that outline means is deliberately left ambiguous. Its ambiguity is well represented by the presence of Mrs. Ramsay's "green shawl," which simultaneously turns the boar's head into a "fairy garden" for Cam, while fully revealing the skeleton to James (*TTL* 114-5). Seen through the veil of "love," the "meaning" of the Ramsay family is hazy, undecidable. Lily's vision enlarges and distorts the figures, who cease to be the limited human beings whom she knows in clearer moments.

Further, as Lily herself acknowledges, being enmeshed with the Ramsay family challenges her sense of identity. Frequently, all that summer while staying with the Ramsays, she "had much ado to control her impulse to fling herself (thank Heaven she had always resisted so far) at Mrs. Ramsay's knee and say to her—but what could one say to her? 'I'm in love with you?' No, that was not true. 'I'm in love with all this,' waving her hand at the hedge, at the house, at the children" (*TTL* 19). This longing for merger is intensified later in the text, when, laying her head on Mrs. Ramsay's knee, Lily wonders, "What art was there, known to love or cunning, by which one pressed through into those secret chambers? What device for becoming, like waters poured into one jar, inextricably the same, one with the object one adored?" (*TTL* 51). Sensing that the engaged couple will attempt to pattern their own union after the Ramsays' marriage, Lily longs to join Minta Doyle and Paul

Rayley, merging her identity with that of the sacrificial couple (*TTL* 102-3). Lily is thus aware that "being in love" is dangerous (*TTL* 154), but she is not always able to maintain consistent consciousness of selfhood when living in such close proximity to it, as for instance, when Lily rescues Charles Tansley from his tantrum at the dinner party. Doing so, she acknowledges to herself, is a sacrifice of her feminist principles to her need to assuage Mrs. Ramsay's pain (*TTL* 92-3). That Lily Briscoe, who strives for a precision of vision matched only by her fierce integrity, cannot always see clearly when in the presence of the Ramsays' family system and desires self-surrender, suggests the power of that system to overwhelm cognition.

On her return to the family after the passage of a decade and Mrs. Ramsay's death, however, Lily Briscoe recognizes that the Ramsays' family system is harmful. "[I]t struck her, this was tragedy—not palls, dust, and the shroud; but children coerced, their spirits subdued" (*TTL* 149). The veil is drawn aside to reveal oppression. Her view of James and Cam is accurate: "[t]hey looked, she thought, as if fate had devoted them to some stern enterprise, and they went to it, still young enough to be drawn acquiescent in their father's wake, obediently, but with a pallor in their eyes which made her feel that they suffered something beyond their years in silence" (*TTL* 155). Just as she understands how the Ramsay children have been impaired, she knows the cause of their mother's death. "Mrs. Ramsay had given. Giving, giving, giving, she had died—and left all this" (*TTL* 149). Having gained distance through the passage of time, Lily Briscoe can acknowledge the mechanisms of the family's life, and she understands that the system causes pain and the sacrifice of children and women to the Patriarchy.

Sigmund Freud analyzed denial in *An Outline of Psychoanalysis* as a "disavowal of external reality" (qtd. in Bean 72). Denial is a part of the mechanisms of defense, for, according to Freud, "the essence of repression lies simply in turning something away, and keeping it at a distance, from the conscious" (qtd. in Wolman 151, emphasis in original). Anna Freud classified denial as a defense against "situations of helplessness against painful reality from which the person cannot escape" (qtd. in Bean 72). That which cannot be fought, which cannot be changed, which cannot be evaded, may not be tolerated. Hence, denial may be a life-saving defense in some circumstances. It is an inadvertent, unconscious, unwilled experience in the face of overwhelming internal or external events. *To the Lighthouse* is a novel of "half dazed" observers (*TTL* 146) and witnesses who later repudiate their observations (*TTL* 203). It is a novel in which participants in intimate interchanges cannot themselves honestly evaluate harmful interactions in which they are at risk, who believe their choices are entirely voluntary (*TTL* 32-3). In its disclosure of varied discourses of denial, *To the Lighthouse* represents some aspects of the residue of traumatic experience.

The polyvocal sites of narration, the use of free indirect discourse, and the replacement of omniscient commentary with image-plots challenge a reader's expectations of narrative transparency in *To the Lighthouse*. With its refusal to use an omniscient narrator's voice to simplify the human mind, or to privilege one character's truths over another's, the novel is well positioned to represent the conflicting points of view in a family where women and children are silenced. Because it can represent varied aspects of a single consciousness, mingled with oblique commentary analyzing the contents of that consciousness, and can expand these suggestions through an extensive narrative of interconnected imagery, the narrative method can depict what I term "denied disclosure." Thus Woolf has constructed a way to tell the story of the Ramsays' marriage so that the husband and wife within it understand the marriage as a reasonably happy one (Nussbaum 69-71), while others might have a very different interpretation. Melding the information from the many focalized points of view, drawing conclusions from the implications of repeated patterns of imagery, the reader can grasp the abusive nature of certain incidents, even while characters remain in denial. In this way, the narrative method of *To the Lighthouse* dramatizes denial.

Consider, for example, two often-analyzed scenes in *To the Lighthouse*, the Ramsays' argument about the weather and James's response to Mr. Ramsay's use of his wife for emotional sustenance. Mrs. Ramsay challenges her husband's omniscience by reminding him that he does not control the shifting winds, although what they actually say to each other is unclear (*TTL* 31). Mr. Ramsay's unassuaged anxieties erupt into abusive rage. In his tantrum, Mr. Ramsay curses his wife. "He stamped his foot. . . . 'Damn you,' he said. But what had she said? Simply that it might be fine tomorrow. So it might" (*TTL* 31). Almost no direct, attributed dialogue occurs in *To the Lighthouse*. Yet this curse is placed in quotation marks. Attributed dialogue in a narrative almost wholly formed of free indirect discourse may be seen as a textual enactment of the actual curse. The quoted line stands out on the page, just as the curse does in the mind of some readers.

For a middle-class Victorian observer, the aftermath of the scene might be less noteworthy than the ungentlemanly act itself. Yet Mrs. Ramsay seems unaware that her husband has verbally assaulted her. That which is absent, the idea that might be phrased as "my husband cursed me," is moved from being silenced in the mind of the character to echoing loudly in the mind of a contemporary reader sensitive to the nature of verbal violence. Mrs. Ramsay's consciousness cannot acknowledge the remark because to do so would challenge the foundational beliefs on which her marriage is based. She thus cannot name Mr. Ramsay's insult to herself and argues back only in the terms he has set, the debate on the weather conditions. Although some readers might dismiss Mr. Ramsay's outburst as a childish tantrum, contained within emotional and verbal violence of this sort is the implicit threat of physical violence. Uncontrolled rage may suggest the physical force implicit behind the social control of women (Schechter 216-34), a conclusion certainly suggested, albeit indirectly, by the persistent imagery linking male violence to warfare.

In response to her husband's behavior, Mrs. Ramsay experiences self pity. Her husband's behavior "was to her so horrible an outrage of human decency that without replying, dazed and *blinded*, she bent her head as if to let the pelt of jagged hail, the drench of dirty water, bespatter her unrebuked. There was nothing to be said" (*TTL* 31, emphasis mine). As was Lily's, Mrs. Ramsay's vision is impeded. A "blinded" witness, Mrs. Ramsay is rendered silent because she cannot put into words the threat implicit within the tantrum. Hence, her *oratio obliqua* is cast in the language of white middle-class Victorian familial ideology, not the language of self-awareness. Where is the word "I" in this passage? Where is the recognition that "I" was the object of a curse uttered in passionate rage? Where is the recognition that a child witnessed the father cursing the mother and stamping his foot? As is clear to the reader, Mr. Ramsay is not pursuing truth. He is pursuing the advantage the powerful have over the powerless. Where is the "I's" recognition of this? Silenced.

Nevertheless, even though the absent "I" cannot name its own violation or that of the child, encoded in this passage is a recognition of "brutality" and an assault on "human decency." The unnamed thing is not called violence, but becomes a "lack of consideration" for "people's feelings." But it is given an equivalent: "wanton," "brutal," "outrage." For the phrase, "the thin veils of civilization," with its ironic contestation of Matthew Arnold's exhortations, encodes the implication that in "uncivilized" places like the empire, such behavior may be acceptable. In the white Victorian middle-class home, such behavior is not supposed to happen. Yet it has, even though the witness cannot name it. The "veils of civilization" part here to display the more violent implications of patriarchal privilege. That this is the case is apparent from "I's" body language. Mrs. Ramsay's response is to bend her head because "there was nothing to be said," acknowledging subservience to the out-of-control patriarch (*TTL* 31).

Why is there "nothing to be said"? As I have noted, Mrs. Ramsay, now fifty (*TTL* 6), in a narrative set in 1909, was thus born around 1860 and raised as an upper-middle-class Victorian woman. It is neither cowardice nor lack of intelligence that silences Mrs. Ramsay. According to middle-class Victorian mores, anger was unacceptable in women and children. Mrs. Ramsay's behaviors in her marriage and in her mothering suggest to me that in the process of being raised in a traditional Victorian middle-class family, she has been trained to self-suppression (Lilienfeld, "Spear"151-56). Instead of confrontation, Mrs. Ramsay manipulates her husband by what Patricia Laurence has called "strategic silence," maintaining her ladylike composure. Shaming him produces results, but often leaves her without any direct means of self-care.

Mr. Ramsay indirectly apologizes, or tries to, for what he may have said "at length" (*TTL* 32) is summarized in ten words. Mrs. Ramsay's immediate response is: "There was nobody whom she reverenced as she reverenced him" (*TTL* 32). To make it unmistakable, her response is set off in a paragraph to itself, and is later repeated almost exactly (*TTL* 32). Her husband's attempt at an apology elicits worship from her rather than emotions such as anger, acknowledgment of his limits, or worry that her son has been a vulnerable witness to their domestic conflict.

Idealizing her husband serves many purposes. It protects her from having to admit some of the problematic aspects of her marriage. Idealizing Mr. Ramsay protects him, too, and protecting him from negative emotions is one of her primary goals. Rather than raging, which is as unladylike as it is unimaginable to her, Mrs. Ramsay "veils" her anger under self-abnegation: "She was quite ready to take his word for it, she said. Only then they need not cut sandwiches—that was all. They came to her, naturally, since she was a woman . . . one wanting this, another that. . . . [S]he often felt she was nothing but a sponge sopped full of human emotions" (*TTL* 32). The key word here is "natural." Because she seems to see the innate female role as that which mops up after people, it is not surprising that Mrs. Ramsay may experience herself as a material whose sole purpose is to absorb others' unacceptable feelings and behavior.

What is revealed at this point in this passage is the voice of a woman whose conviction that she must give all and take nothing has reached the point of self-immolation. The paragraph continues with no indication of a break in thought from her definition of woman's "natural" role to "Then he said, Damn you. He said, It must rain. He said, It won't rain; and instantly a Heaven of security opened before her. There was nobody she reverenced more. She was not good enough to tie his shoe strings, she felt" (*TTL* 32). At no point in this passage of *oratio obliqua* is Mrs. Ramsay shown to acknowledge experiences the reader has witnessed. Reproduced in language is that which Mrs. Ramsay seems to choose as action: denial of her husband's violent outburst. Anger is absent. Idealization takes the place of any acknowledgment of how she might feel when confronted with verbal violence.

It is no accident that Mrs. Ramsay's idealization of her husband ends in her vision of herself as unfit to tie his shoes. The image reverses her daughters' comparison of her courtesy to that of "a Queen's raising from the mud to wash a beggar's dirty foot" (*TTL* 7), an image inextricable from her daughters' view of her as a symbol of the British empire with her "ringed fingers and lace" (*TTL* 7). Although it does not strip her entirely of elite class position to equate her with the kneeling beggar, the image of Mrs. Ramsay as unfit to tie Mr. Ramsay's shoes allies her with the myriads of servants—male and female—who scrubbed thousands of their employers' Victorian boots.[13] The "veils" ripped by Mr. Ramsay's curse here suggest the cloth rags used by the Victorian servant to clean up the detritus of class- and gender privilege. The narrative method reveals Mr. Ramsay's verbal violence and its negative impact on his wife. While Mrs. Ramsay cannot speak of it, nevertheless, the reader is aware of what the character cannot name. A verbal assault has been committed, and even though no one has spoken of it, its occurrence and its effects have been made clear.

III

To maintain the recognition that Mr. Ramsay's verbal violence is serious in spite of the fact that his wife can neither acknowledge it nor defend herself or her son against it, Mr. Ramsay must not be a sympathetic figure following the argument with his wife on the terrace. The narrative achieves this objective in a variety of ways. First, Mrs. Ramsay's effort to deny the implications of her husband's behavior has little obvious effect. Rather than satiating his need for dominance, her self-sacrifice has delayed, not prevented, her husband's attack of self-hatred and conviction of his failure as a philosopher (*TTL* 33-36). Mr. Ramsay thus returns to the wife whom he had just cursed, requiring "sympathy." Because James was silenced by being removed from his parents' consciousnesses during their argument, the fact that parts of chapter 7 are reported from James's free indirect discourse gives the reader a sense of almost exact repetition, as Mr. Ramsay draws emotional sustenance from Mrs. Ramsay's love for him.

If in this scene James is read as wishing to kill his father and marry his mother, then what he feels about what he witnesses may be read symbolically. But what if James is not mistaken? What if it is not an exaggeration to read Mr. Ramsay's need as a violent, phallic weapon? That this might be the case is suggested by the implications of the image plots, linking male aggression and male rights within the Victorian family and state. James experiences the interaction between his parents in chapter 7 as a brutal attack on his mother. James witnesses the exercise of male power over a female whose self is so erased that she experiences intrusion as a voluntary act of giving. During the transaction, his is the only consciousness in the scene able to verbalize that which, as is clear from chapter 6, Mrs. Ramsay is represented as unable to acknowledge to herself.

So rapacious is the father that James "felt all her strength flaring up to be drunk and quenched by" his father's "beak of brass," which James felt repeatedly "smote" his mother (*TTL* 38). The "beak of brass" is not just a symbolic pen or a penis, but "an arid scimitar," a weapon of hand-to-hand combat (*TTL* 38). Once ripped open by this curved blade, Mrs. Ramsay's strength, her very blood and being, are being drunk. James's metaphoric view of his father's insatiable need may seem childishly exaggerated, but perhaps that is the point, for a frightened and powerless child might need extravagant language to convey his feelings. The metaphor of "flar[ing]" blood hints at vampirism, for perhaps the "fangs" that Mr.

Ramsay wishes to sink into Minta Doyle signify a figure other than a lion (*TTL* 102)?[14]

Here, however, Mr. Ramsay receives milk, not blood: His wife becomes a "nurse" reassuring "a fractious child," not a grown man (*TTL* 38). Her efforts are successful. "[L]ike a child who drops off satisfied," he returns to his philosophical speculations "restored" (*TTL* 38).

At first Mrs. Ramsay is exhausted, almost completely emptied of self, but, even so, she "throbbed [with] the rapture of successful creation" (*TTL* 38). The narrative voice emanating from and surrounding Mrs. Ramsay dramatizes her denial of any point of view other than that which focuses on her husband's needs. In the moments of impact, she experiences as love the intrusions of what James interprets as a battering beak. If her husband needs, she must give; with each move he makes, she makes the move he wants. Even his insatiability is unremarked by her consciousness as a problem. Having seen her unable to acknowledge that her husband has cursed her, a reader may not be surprised that she has no language for that which James has more realistically defined as an intrusion into the wife by instruments of war.

But instead of woundedness, what Mrs. Ramsay experiences is orgasmic: "the rapture" of having totally given over her consciousness (*TTL* 38). She feels that the beings of husband and wife have merged (*TTL* 39). However, afterwards, Mrs. Ramsay is strong and courageous enough to acknowledge—though powerless to stop it except through death—the costs of her behavior (*TTL* 38-40).

Throughout this scene, James is standing between his mother's legs. Far from signifying a phallus or lighthouse, his stance suggests that he is as vulnerable as she is, for he stands encircled by a body under what he perceives as attack. Even though unacknowledged by either parent, is six-year-old James as violated as his mother? Traveling in the boat with his father to the lighthouse, an older James painfully forces himself to recall what he can of the origin of his desire to hack his father to pieces. The first thing he pictures is a repeated attack on himself: "something he remembered, stayed and darkened over him; would not move; something flourished up in the air, something arid and sharp descended even there, like a blade, like a scimitar" (*TTL* 186, see also Lilienfeld, *Reading* 196, 198, 202). As he continues forcing himself to recall his past, James experiences himself not so much as the recipient of his father's physical abuse, but rather as abandoned and shamed by his mother. "She had risen somehow and gone away and left him there, impotent, ridiculous, sitting on the floor grasping a pair of scissors" (*TTL* 187).

Clinicians note that some children who witness attacks on a parent often feel themselves as the violated party, as this scene would suggest (Gilligan 1-8, see also Dobash and Dobash 187). Further, although her work was with female survivors, Janet Liebman Jacobs attests that a majority of her clients blame the mother for their abuse, not the male perpetrator. Jacobs speculates that to focus on the mother as having been capable of warding off attacks is a way of denying the powerlessness of the mother in the face of the powers of the father and the patriarchal system on which his rule depends (22-27). According to Jacobs' analysis, James Ramsay would be a violated witness whose re-experienced memory is an emotionally astute, though not fully accurate, representation of his experience as a little boy. For his mother did abandon him emotionally in favor of the father whose beak battered them both. She had "gone away and left him there" (*TTL* 278).

James recalls in pictorial sequence the pain of his victimization as a result of the parental interchange, but memories of childhood trauma are neither verbal nor sequential (van der Kolk, *Traumatic*, 282-299).

> Stored in the brain during the adrenaline rush that accompanies the human biological response to danger, [traumatic memories] 'are not encoded like the ordinary memories of adults in a verbal, linear narrative.' Instead, they are imprinted on the brain like infantile recollections 'in the form of vivid sensations and images.' Iconic and visual in form, these images [may resemble] 'a series of still snapshots or a silent movie.' (Henke, *Shattered* xvii-xviii, quoting Herman, *Trauma*)

Theorists argue, thus, that reconstructing traumatic experience, occurs in "a language that defies, even as it claims, our understanding" (Caruth, *Unclaimed* 5). For many survivors, putting the experience into words, even to a sympathetic auditor, is not possible at first (Herman 177-78). However, "[w]hat cannot be uttered might at least be written—cloaked in the mask of fiction or sanctioned by the protective space of iteration that separates the author/narrator from the protagonist/character she or he creates and from the anonymous reader/auditor she or he envisages" (Henke, *Shattered* xix). As previously noted, Virginia Woolf had attributed psychological "catharsis" to her experience of writing the novel (Abel 46). Did the writing of James Ramsay's recovered memory create the verbal potential for the later reconstruction of Woolf's own experience? Is the unfurling of James's decade-long repressed memory a discursive precursor to Virginia Woolf's recovered memory of Gerald's abuse of her when she was James's age?

The use of James Ramsay as a fictionalized surrogate figure for the six-year-old Virginia Stephen would have provided the verbal "wall" that Woolf declared was necessary to stave off self-indulgent deployment of the biographical self that marred the fictions of Joyce and Richardson (D2: 14). Further, if James is modeled on Adrian Stephen, as numerous critics argue, then the boy's use as a "wall" might provide a certain emotional gratification. Adrian Stephen was his mother's favorite, reported Virginia Woolf: "Him she cherished separately; she called him 'My joy'" (MOB 83). To represent such a child as physically unsafe might make him seem less of a threat to the other children in the family. Denying a fictionalized Adrian Stephen status and punishing him emotionally might have been deeply satisfying. The gender privileges that a little boy would enjoy in such a family as that of the Ramsays are hence troubled by the use of the boy as an auxiliary recipient of verbal abuse.[15]

Musing as she wrote "A Sketch of the Past," Virginia Woolf acknowledged that the act of writing about memory performed an ambiguous intervention among creation, intention, and remembrance. "At times I can go back to St. Ives . . . I can reach a state where I seem to be watching things happen as if I were there. That is, I suppose, that my memory supplies what I had forgotten, so that it seems as if it were happening independently, though I am really making it happen" (MOB 67). Contemporary theorists such as Leigh Gilmore question, just as Woolf did, the nature of authorial control and representational "truth" in writing the reconstructed figure: is "autobiography . . . any experientially truer than other representations of the self" (Gilmore 25)? Does autobiography "offer an identity any less constructed than that produced by other forms of representation simply because the autobiographer intends the subject to correspond to herself or himself" (Gilmore 25)?

With these questions in mind, the reader may not be surprised that imagery which Virginia Woolf had used in To the Lighthouse to describe the setting of some of James's earliest memories, she would later use in "A Sketch of the Past" to describe her own. Compare, for instance,

James's visualization of what things had looked like to him when he was a little boy in the Ramsays' summer home:

> Everything tended to set itself in a garden . . . and the blinds were sucked in and out by the breeze; all was blowing; all was growing; and over all these plates and bowls and tall brandishing red and yellow flowers a very thin yellow veil would be drawn, like a vine leaf, at night. (*TTL* 185)

to that of Virginia Woolf in "A Sketch of the Past":

> the impression of the waves and the acorn on the blind; the feeling, . . . of lying in a grape and seeing through a film of semi-transparent yellow . . . There was the pale yellow blind; the green sea; and the silver of the passion flowers . . . sounds would come through this petal or leaf—sounds indistinguishable from sights. (*MOB* 66)

The synesthesia of these passages, the colors, sights, sounds and textures of very early childhood memories of character and writer are strikingly similar. For both character and author, the moving "blind" veils objects, temporality and textures, suggesting the shape-altering perspective supplied by sense memories. Both James Ramsay and Virginia Stephen hear, feel, and see things vividly and sensually. Both acknowledge the threatening as well as comforting sense of the "veil" separating while enclosing them. The veil that James remembers could signify the shawl that his mother had thrown over the boar's head in the attic, but it also suggests the occluding haze that had distorted Lily Briscoe's clear perception, as well as the problematized nature of philosophical truth-claims in the novel.

As James follows his memory of his mother throughout the summer house after what he interprets as her abandonment of him, he finds her again in the kitchen of the fictionalized Talland House. "And at last they came to a room where in a blue light, as if the reflection came from many china dishes, she talked to somebody" (*TTL* 187). In following her memories while writing "A Sketch of the Past," Virginia Woolf came to a hallway of the Stephens' summer home, where she found not her mother among the dishes, but Gerald Duckworth: "There was a slab outside the dining room door for standing dishes upon. Once when I was very small Gerald Duckworth lifted me onto this, and as I sat there he began to explore my body" (*MOB* 69).[16]

As I noted above, the obscure interconnection between malleable memory and the discursive indeterminacy of a series of selves constructed in language were equally problematic for Virginia Woolf (*MOB* 67). Such questions destabilizing socially acceptable definitions of "truth" and "reality" permeate the novel itself, where indeterminacy rather than sentimental closure serves as its signature narrative method. Contemporary criticism authorizes readers to continue to ask the very questions raised by Virginia Woolf. "Feminist theories of self-representation and subjectivity offer more shaded and internally differential interpretations as a way to explore what happens formally when the category 'women' and the instabilities in genre manifest in the category 'autobiography' converge," argues Leigh Gilmore (26, see also 44). Might the idea that Woolf may have prepared the ground work for her recovered memory of childhood sexual abuse by first writing from the perspective of a little six-year-old boy, observing and sustaining what he experienced as a brutal attack on himself and his mother, negate the truth-claim of the author's memory of early sexual abuse? Far more likely is the fact that Virginia Woolf's continued exploration of painful materials through writing might demonstrate her courageous determination to seek that which she could know in the way she could most comfortably know it, through language. The porous boundary between autobiographical fiction and "life-writing" is permeable, facilitating negotiation (Henke xiii-xix, Gilmore 44).

Writing *To the Lighthouse*, with its implicit analysis of familial abuse embedded in a fictionalized father-centered household, Woolf created a verbal construct of that fraught setting. That represented world could be controlled and manipulated through language; it could be renegotiated verbally. Perhaps because she had written *To the Lighthouse*, Virginia Woolf could subsequently write "A Sketch of the Past"? This question might be indirectly answered through an assertion generated by the "Personal Narratives Group," that "[t]he story of survival in the face of . . . psychosexual adversity . . . serves as its own testimony [and enables the survivor to mount] meaningful resistance to received ideologies [and develop] effective agency in the world" (qtd. in Henke, *Shattered* xix).

The "thin veils of civilization," once torn, reveal the shadows within the garden of a late Victorian childhood in *To the Lighthouse*. Woolf's fictionalization of "father and mother and child in the garden" problematizes the Edenic features of that lush setting.[17] The agency of Virginia Woolf's complex narrative of indirection discloses the abuse at the heart of the Ramsays' family life. Through its narrative method, *To the Lighthouse* makes visible the denial of its characters, while the reader, in viewing the characters' denial, comes to understand what the characters cannot fully comprehend at the time of their experience. Able to verbalize repressed feelings that the characters cannot themselves acknowledge, like Lily Briscoe, the reader gains insight, knowledge that permits critical analysis of the family system. Never named as such, abuse of women and children within this family novel is clearly depicted. Hence, that which is denied by family members within the novel is seen and known by increasing numbers of readers of *To the Lighthouse*.

Notes

I want to express my thanks to Patricia Cramer, Professor of English and Women's Studies, University of Connecticut at Stamford, Cindy Cotner, Research Librarian, Ellis Library, University of Missouri/Columbia, and Marcia Deihl, Staff Assistant, Tozzer Library, Harvard University, for their generous help with research materials for this essay. References to *MOB* are to the 2nd edition (1985).

1. Richard McNally asserts that "[h]ow victims remember trauma is the most divisive issue facing psychology today" (1). His work presents a range of scholarly and research findings that question, once again, issues that have been contested since the concept of traumatic incursions into memory and cognition were first proposed in the nineteenth century (Herman, *Trauma* 15-17). Herman summarizes the consistent politicization of psychological treatment of trauma from the nineteenth through the twenty-first century: "The study of psychological trauma must contend with the tendency to discredit the victim and to render her invisible. Throughout the history of the field, dispute has raged over whether patients with post-traumatic conditions are entitled to care and respect or deserving of contempt, whether they are genuinely suffering or malingering, whether their histories are true or false, and if false, whether imagined or maliciously fabricated. In spite of a vast literature documenting the phenomena of psychological trauma, debate still centers on whether these phenomena are credible and real" (8). Here Herman implies that which Sandra Harding argues: science is not neutral; it arises out of and reinforces "androcentric epistemologies" (47). Scientific knowledge is imbricated in the institutions and states whose money and ideologies support it (Harding 19-50). McNally's research synthesis explores the malleability of memory, the construction of memory in traumatized and non-traumatized subjects, contests issues of traumatic amnesia, and attacks forms of therapeutic intervention that privilege the client rather than the putative abuser (18-22). McNally's claim that he has synthesized the essential work in the debates about repression, dissociation, and recalled memories is an interesting one, when one studies his ninety-six page bibliography. He does not include, for example, work directed to survivors or that based on their testimony, such as that of Janet Liebman Jacobs, *Victimized Daughters*; Anna Salter, *Transforming Trauma*; or Margo Rivera, *Fragment by Fragment*; nor the well-regarded work by psychologist Harvey L. Schwartz, *Dialogues*

with Forgotten Voices. Indeed, there are sections of McNally's book that directly attack the work of Bessel van der Kolk, considered by many to be the foremost specialist in treating psychological trauma today (177-185). To assertions such as those put forth by Richard McNally, Bessel van der Kolk and Andrew McFarlane answer thusly, "[t]he 'False Memory' issue illustrates that when discoveries of psychiatry come into conflict with society's cherished beliefs, psychiatry has traditionally been vulnerable to giving up the pursuit of science, and instead, to conforming to prevailing social attitudes" (*Traumatic* 568). Hence, evidence sustains the assertion that attacks on the psychological understanding of trauma may be motivated by concerns other than the desire to ascertain scientific accuracy. Thus it follows that "[t]he systematic study of psychological trauma therefore depends on the support of a political movement. Indeed, whether such study can be pursued or discussed in public is itself a political question" (Herman 9). Ironically, such debates touch on more than the biographical controversies about the effects of sexual abuse in Virginia Woolf's childhood; such debates are, in fact, aspects of the cultural context in which the writer Virginia Woolf herself lived. Whether women could speak the truth about the body first and then be heard and further believed, was an issue facing Woolf as a writer, as she asserted in the voice of the implied author of "Professions for Women": "telling the truth about my own experiences as a body, I do not think I solved" (*DM* 240).

    2. Emily Dalgarno is not alone in problematizing the work of Louise DeSalvo. Even some who agree with DeSalvo's interpretation and believe that Gerald Duckworth assaulted the little girl do so with a slight hesitation. For example, Toni McNaron feels compelled to note that "DeSalvo's work remains controversial, her critics insisting that she stretches the data or that she interprets too broadly . . ." (251). Even more insistent that DeSalvo has exaggerated the after-affects of Gerald's sexual violation, Hermione Lee terms the incident "sexual interference" (*Virginia* 124, 151) rather than incestuous assault, and summarizes the situation as "the distressing and contentious matter of Virginia Stephen's abuse as a child" (122). Her tone is all the more remarkable, for Hermione Lee refuses to reduce Virginia Woolf to her supposed mental illness (171) and insists throughout her biography on Woolf's intellectual and emotional strength. It would seem to buttress such an argument to acknowledge that Woolf's strength was also evident in her survival of childhood sexual abuse. Quentin Bell empathized with the young Virginia Stephen and was convinced that what he calls her madness is a possible result of her incest experiences (1: 43-44), a view that misunderstood mental instability and family systems theory, according to critiques by Roger Poole. For more discussion of this wide-ranging controversy, see Anne Olivier Bell, "Letter" 2, DeSalvo, "Letter" 3, and Olafson and Corwin 1-2. Although she disagrees with Louise DeSalvo as to the lasting harm arising from Gerald Duckworth's abuse of the six-year old Virginia Stephen, Hermione Lee agrees that "Virginia Woolf makes no written reference to this incident until 1939" (123). Virginia Woolf did discuss George Duckworth's incestuous advances with her tutor Janet Case (Bell 1: 43 n), and did confide in Violet Dickinson (Bell 1 82-84) and Vita Sackville-West (Lee 442), but exactly what, if anything, she recounted about Gerald Duckworth's attack is not clear in the remaining written records.

    3. Richard McNally and many of the scientists whose research he cites would question DeSalvo's claim that Woolf's recovered memory is an accurate rendering of past

experience, as I have noted in footnote 1 (McNally 177-185, 189-196, 208-9). That Virginia Woolf herself clearly believed that the mechanics of the unconscious could lead to repression of unbearable memory, Elizabeth Abel argues cogently in her rereading of James Ramsays' distorted but long-repressed memory of his father's verbal abuse of his mother (48-55).

4. Virginia Woolf notes in "A Sketch of the Past" that hers was a Victorian family: "Two different ages confronted each other in the drawing room at Hyde Park Gate: the Victorian Age; and the Edwardian age. We were not [Leslie Stephen's] children, but his grandchildren. . . . We were living say in 1920: they [Leslie and the Duckworth brothers] were living in 1860. . . . In 22 Hyde Park Gate round about 1900 there was to be found a complete model of Victorian society. If I had the power to live out a month of life as we lived it about 1900 I could extract a section of Victorian life, like one of those cases with glass covers in which one is shown ants or bees going about their affairs" (*MOB* 126-7. See also Lilienfeld, "Spear" 148-58).

5. Lee suggests that the insouciant tone in which Woolf couched the violations of the teenage sisters by their half-brothers undermines the truth-claims of the experience (153). As I have observed above, there was corroboration by her sister of the attacks at the time they happened and immediate medical intervention to halt them (Bell, 1: 95-6). The tone of the paragraph disclosing the incest in "22 Hyde Park Gate" might just as easily be interpreted as the use of rhetorical devices to distance pain and minimize shame, suggesting how difficult disclosing incest is, and how necessary for healing (Herman, *Trauma* 176-7).

6. Virginia Woolf was repeatedly dismissed as a charming liar and exaggerator by many of the male members of the Bloomsbury Group. See, for example, Clive Bell in "Old Bloomsbury" (98-9). Roger Poole brilliantly refutes the disparagement of Virginia Woolf as a liar first in *The Unknown Virginia Woolf* (21-32) and then even more forcefully in "'We All Put Up With You, Virginia'" (79, 83, 91-2).

7. The American psychiatrist Murray Bowen coined the term "family system theory" in 1966 (xvii). Through the therapeutic work with families, Bowen had observed certain persistent relational dynamics that, although unconscious, shaped personal emotional development that reinforced and intersected with "emotional processes in society" (Bowen xvi). Bowen himself was not a feminist, although what he observed in his practice, from the 1950s onward, usually demonstrated a male power hegemony within the middle-class white American family. Clinicians such as Monica McGoldrick and Deborah Luepnitz, who were influenced by Bowen, integrated his methods of analysis into their feminist therapeutic practice. What these feminist clinicians discovered, after working many hours with families seeking their help, were enmeshed and debilitating patterns of conscious and unconscious thought and behavior, patterns that sustained the placing of the needs of women and children below those of the male in familial importance. Over the course of her career as a novelist, in observing her own family of origin and others, Woolf recognized that gender, race, class, geographical and temporal situatedness interpenetrated and shaped the family's life, thereby reproducing individuals whose lives perpetuated cultural norms. *To the Lighthouse* is an earlier examination of such a system, which Woolf more fully represented in fiction in *The Years* and in theoretical analysis in *Three Guineas*.

8. Jane Marcus, Evelyn Haller, Beverly Ann Schlack, Kathy Phillips, and Janet Winston, along with many other North American critics, have demonstrated the feminist and political significance of the use of "symbol clusters" in Woolf's fiction, letters, diaries, and polemics.

9. There is extensive discussion in the critical literature of the connection between the Ramsays' home, the British Empire, and World War 1. See, for example, Phillips 94-115, Winston 42-7, 52-7, and S. Friedman 120-130. The same Imperial rights that Mr. Ramsay believes he should wield over home, family, and Empire, Mrs. Ramsay wields over women of lesser social standing (*TTL* 57) and working women, argues Mary Lou Emery, as I will note below. Recent work by Jane Marcus problematizes the question of race in Woolf's anti-imperialism (*Hearts* 8, 13, 18-20 24-58).

10. That Virginia Woolf is a painterly writer, rendering verbally the colors, shapes, textures, and patterns of the visible world, is a central tenet of much feminist criticism. Harvena Richter was among the first critics to insist that emotion took visual form in Woolf's narratives. Diane Gillespie's *The Sister's Arts* established Woolf's formidable sensitivity to the painterly aspects of experiential life, relating this to the complex relation to her sister Vanessa Bell and emphasizing the importance of the visual throughout Woolf's writings. Leslie Hankins' work on Woolf and cinema analyses Woolf's subtle and extensive discourse on gendered visual narratives. More recently, Maggie Humm's text extends Gillespie's and Hankins' arguments, focusing on the gendered familial and social contexts of Woolf's attention to the personal photograph.

11. Elizabeth Abel argues that the veil cloaks the maternal (53-4).

12. Lily Briscoe's feminist world-view is historically accurate, shared by some upper-middle-class and middle-class white women in Victorian and Edwardian England. See the work of Lucy Bland and Philippa Levine for the cultural context of Lily's political beliefs.

13. As Anne McClintock has observed, "[Victorian] maids were especially tasked with keeping their employers' shoes scrupulously clean" (171). Although Michael Tratner dissolves the binary opposition between Mrs. Ramsay, Mrs. McNab and Mrs. Bast (55-57), he delineates Woolf's ambivalence about working-class women (58) and believes that Woolf appropriated the voices of working women in *To the Lighthouse*. For a fuller discussion, see also Mary Lou Emery's analysis of the discourse of work and class in *To the Lighthouse*.

14. Ann-Marie Priest has pointed out that

> [t]he relationship between Mrs Ramsay and her husband in *To the Lighthouse* may well seem, as Harvena Richter notes (223), to have been lifted from the pages of *The Sacred Fount*—with its vampiric overtones intact. . . . It is as though we have come upon the . . . moment of transfer, the vampiric lover 'in the act of presenting his receptacle at the sacred fount' . . . Mr Ramsay drinks freely of the 'waters' of the other, feeding from his lover/mother like a vampire/baby until he is 'filled . . . like a child who drops off satisfied'. . . . His vicious 'beak of brass' . . . descending on its victim like a ravening bird. . . . Its victim . . . [is left] depleted: 'there was scarcely a shell of herself left for her to know herself by; all was so lavished and spent.'"

Professor Priest emphasizes the gendered nature of this passage in which "the 'vampire' is masculine by definition, and his 'fount' feminine."

Adrienne Rich in *Of Woman Born* notes that nursing a child is an erotic experience for many mothers (183). Indeed, Professor Priest's brilliant reading of the eroticized imagery depicting elite middle-class Victorian male characters as vampires, sexually ravishing their prey by sucking blood rather than by phallic penetration, has an historical context beyond that of the literary. Although the Washington State Library Catalogue does not contain the volume (Bauchart), Woolf need not have read Bram Stoker's *Dracula* as a source for this archetype. William T. Stead's arguments during the late-Victorian "social purity" campaign proposed that men of "'the vicious upper classes'" "openly defended access to working-class girls as a time-honored prerogative of gentlemen" (Walkowitz 250). Popular novels such as that of *Dr. Jekyll and Mr. Hyde* (published 1886) suggested, as did Stead's campaigning, that "civilized" Victorian elite males were half men/half beasts. Louise DeSalvo examines the hidden lives of Victorian gentlemen in her description of J. K. Stephen's pursuit of Virginia Woolf's sister Stella Duckworth (DeSalvo, *Impact* 51), noting that Stephen's lurid poetry was aimed not at London prostitutes, but at "women of his own class" (51). It is therefore not surprising that Woolf's novels, whose protagonists were born in mid-Victorian Britain, represent some men as beastly predators. Think, for example, of Mr. Dalloway's rapacious kiss of Rachel Vinrace in *The Voyage Out*, which leads to her nightmare of "a little deformed man who squatted on the floor gibbering, with long nails. His face was pitted and like the face of an animal" (77). Mr. Dalloway is ostensibly an elite gentleman, yet pictorially in Rachel's dreams he is similar to the "pock-marked" exhibitionist who makes a "mewing noise" at Rose Pargiter while chasing her home from her night-time ramble to Lamley's in *The Years* (28-9).

Woolf explicitly turned her familial molesters into beasts when she compared George Duckworth's eyes to those "of a pig," whose expression suggested that of a pig "grouting for truffles with his snout," adding that George "had the reputation of being the greediest young man in London ball-rooms" (*MOB* 168). Even more pointedly, Virginia Woolf connects Gerald Duckworth's molestation of her in the kitchen with a memory: "I dreamt that I was looking in a glass when a horrible face—the face of an animal—suddenly showed over my shoulder" (*MOB* 69). Thus the vampire imagery is imbricated in literary and familial history, one aspect of the "symbol clusters" linking male violence, blood lust, and sexual predation of women and indigenous peoples of the British Empire.

15. Cam Ramsay is neither so close to Mrs. Ramsay, nor so cherished by her. Her loyalty to her father and to her brother comes from different kinds of experiences in her childhood, not all of them so harsh. Elizabeth Abel describes Cam's emergence into consciousness as an abused teenager (58-67). See also DeSalvo, *Impact* 174-79 and 223-27.

16. For further discussion of the setting, see Virginia Blain's essay, "Dinner is served."

17. For further discussion of the allusions to John Milton's *Paradise Lost* in *To the Lighthouse*, see the work of Lisa Low, who has elucidated Woolf's complex interaction with Milton as icon and writer

THE WAVES AS ONTOLOGICAL TRAUMA NARRATIVE: THE ANXIETY OF A DEATH (UN)FORESEEN

Suzette Henke

In her diary entry for 14 March 1927, Virginia Woolf declared her intention of "starting [a] very serious, mystical poetical work" (*D3*: 131), *The Waves*, originally conceived as *The Moths* and laboriously brought forth over the next four years. In *The Waves*, Woolf would attempt to articulate the visionary and dissociative memories that continued to haunt her traumatized consciousness.[1] With *The Moths* hovering at the back of her brain, she tried to describe periodic moments of heightened perception: "Often down here I have entered into a sanctuary; a nunnery; had a religious retreat; of great agony once; and always some terror; so afraid one is of loneliness: of seeing to the bottom of the vessel. That is one of the experiences I have had here in some Augusts; and got then to a consciousness of what I call 'reality': a thing I see before me; something abstract; but residing in the downs or sky; beside which nothing matters; in which I shall rest & continue to exist" (*D3*: 196). A month later, Woolf alluded to similar premonitions: "Yes, but *The Moths*? That was to be an abstract mystical eyeless book: a playpoem. . . . I must come to terms with these mystical feelings" (*D3*: 203).

In a diary entry for 23 June 1929, Woolf connects these inchoate sensations with existential anxiety and associates the failure of meaning (the emptiness at the bottom of the vessel) with ontological depression at the total loss of self in a downward spiral into non-being: "I pitched into my great lake of melancholy. Lord how deep it is! What a born melancholiac I am! . . . I shall make myself face the fact that there is nothing—nothing for any of us. Work, reading, writing are all disguises; & relations with people. Yes, even having children would be useless" (*D3*: 235). Woolf described *The Waves* in its early stages as impersonal "Autobiography" (*D3*: 229)—a text that unfolds as a heavily disguised confessional narrative of post-traumatic stress and manic-depressive mood swings. In *Virginia Woolf: An Inner Life*, Julia Briggs situates the biographical impetus for the novel in Woolf's 1926 experience of "an intense depression that felt like a series of waves, rising and crashing down upon her" (240). And Daniel Ferrer points out that most of Woolf's "moments of being" in "A Sketch of the Past" are delineated as "profoundly traumatic" experiences, "one-off manifestations of an omnipresent antagonist," with "some of the most patently traumatic of these scenes return[ing], almost literally transcribed, in *The Waves*" (68).

As Kay Redfield Jamison argues in *Touched with Fire*, symptoms of melancholia might well reflect a realistic response to ontological anxiety and to an awareness of what Heidegger identifies as one's ownmost possible being-towards-death. Clinical depression, Jamison explains, "breaks down the barriers of denial and . . . looks onto the fleeting nature of life, its decaying core, the finality of death, and the finite role played by man in the history of the universe" (119). In tracing the trajectory of human consciousness from neonatal infancy (i.e. "without language") to the cessation of speech, from sunrise to waves lapping on a darkened shore, Woolf reminds her audience by solar analogy that "We are doomed, all of us" (*W* 152), yet find ourselves incapable of envisaging the trauma of a death (un)foreseen.[2]

At the heart of Woolf's modern psychological allegory in *The Waves* is the accidental death of Percival, a young Cambridge athlete sacrificed on the altar of British imperialism. Modeled on Woolf's brother, Thoby Stephen, who died prematurely of typhoid, Percival functions as the mythic center of Woolf's elegiac play-poem—a godlike hero or *eniautos daimon*, fascinating in his spectral inscrutability, but thoroughly opaque in his symbolic function as an absent presence throughout the novel. Behind the trauma of Percival's death, Woolf incorporates into *The Waves* subtle evocations of an original traumatic moment undefined and inexplicable—a Lacanian lack-in-being (*manque-à-être*) analogous to the Catholic doctrine of original sin, but all the more threatening in its utter uncanniness. Her aesthetic preoccupations shift in this experimental novel from the representation of trauma as a specific mental wound to more pervasive psychological anxieties precipitated by parturition and abjection, by neonatal separation from the maternal body, and by terrifying intimations of mortality. The shocking "event" of Percival's fatal accident serves primarily as a pre-text or cover story for Woolf's more expansive, thanatopic meditation on ontological trauma—the incipient shock precipitated by a perpetual, haunting awareness of the fragility of human life and the "rumour of death indefinitely extended" (Ferrer 74).[3]

Leonard Woolf articulates this sense of existential malaise when he confesses in the last volume of his memoir, *The Journey Not the Arrival*

Matters: "For me, 'death is the enemy,' the ultimate enemy, for it is death which will destroy, wipe out, annihilate me, my individuality, my 'I'" (19). He testifies to a morbid, almost pathological preoccupation with the topic of death "always very near the surface of Virginia's mind" (73). In *Death, Men, and Modernism*, Ariela Freedman argues that Virginia Woolf, like a number of other modernists, depicts "modernity as an endgame" dominated by Thanatos, a "fatalist and devolutionary death-plot . . . expressive of a twentieth-century crisis in meaning" (6). Along with Peter Brooks, Freedman identifies the death instinct as "Freud's masterplot" and reminds us that Freud, in *Beyond the Pleasure Principle*, claims "that repetition points to a universal trauma located not in a past event but in an event which is yet to come—the subject's own death. . . . [T]he movement of the subject is always a movement towards death: towards the trauma that has not yet occurred, but is still inscribed in the novel's anticipations and repetitions. Trauma becomes a foundational principle rather than an exceptional event" (Freedman 7).

In an inaugural draft of *The Waves*, Woolf sketched a surrealistic, almost mythic vision of oceanic parturition, of "waves endlessly sinking and falling, many mothers, & again many mothers, & behind them many more, . . . each held up as it raised its crest & flung itself on the shore, a child" (*WH* 1:63). Describing a congeries of vulnerable neonates cast ashore by a Darwinian life-force, Woolf remarks: "nothing could have been more ridiculous & base than the worm like, eel like, half conscious yet blindly impulsive & violent actions of these little bald animals" (*WH* 1: 62). The human subject-in-process appears to be an evolutionary enigma, bred of semiotic, wave-like undulations that crash on the shore of a hostile environment. The ubiquitous danger of corporeal annihilation heightens the pulsating sensations of instinctual life experienced by naked, helpless, abject creatures emerging from a sea of biological turbulence. For every species on earth, the shadow of death haunts the crest of a developmental process that yields to chthonic gravitational forces. The underside of the sea's whitecapped waves is projected metaphorically onto those blank spaces between the hours that measure the temporal span of individual consciousness and the finite experience of being-in-the-world.[4]

According to James Haule and Philip Smith, Woolf "was aware of the answers that science proposed to questions about the nature and origin of human life" and records in her diary (*D3*: 337) an allusion to the work of

Sir James Jeans, author of "*The Universe Around Us* and *The Mysterious Universe*, popularizations of the advances of quantum physics in the 1930's" (xxviii). Jeans "sees life as an 'accident' that occurred in the 'abyss' of space, 'an utterly unimportant by-product' of the stellar 'mechanism.' It is 'an utterly insignificant fraction of the total activity of the material universe'" (Haule and Smith 207). In response to scientific nihilism, Woolf posits an agnostic quest for meaning in an indifferent cosmos: "with this random flicker of light in us that we call brain and feeling, how can we do battle against this flood: what has permanence?" (*W* 227).

Woolf appears to instantiate in *The Waves* the resonance of post-traumatic stress disorder without offering a sufficient objective correlative to explain the kind of psychic fragmentation, intrusion, constriction, or incipient hysteria that haunts the narrative unconscious of her novel. She constructs a polyphonic chorus of six auto/biographical dramatic soliloquies that replicate a fluid stream of consciousness mediated by a voice that Daniel Ferrer attributes to an "interstitial" narrator, and that John Graham describes as a vatic perception by an "omnipercipient" translator "of the characters' inner experience" (106). Woolf notes in her diary that she intends to "invent a new kind of play," a new form for the lyrical novel not tied to historical facts: "free, yet concentrated; prose yet poetry; a novel & a play" (*D*3: 128). Sketching a plan for her experimental work, she wants to depict a "mind thinking" through free associations emanating from "two different currents"—one focusing on "moths flying along" and another on "a flower upright in the center; a perpetual crumbling and renewing of the plant. In its leaves she might see things happen. But who is she?" (*D*3: 229). As Christine Froula observes, Woolf "preserves her autobiographical subject's feminine origin but abstracts it from any particular mind" (*Virginia* 199). The phantasmal figure of *The Waves* invokes prosopopoeia, if not allegory (Ferrer 67), to narrate a "story of the world" in an indifferent cosmos where "no authority domesticates nature's violence or mitigates death's horror; no telos redeems human suffering" (Froula *Virginia*, 201-202; see also Katz). The lonely female mind of Woolf's inaugural drafts has been absorbed into the novel's lyrical interludes as a veiled phantom whose shadowy presence "evokes a pre-classical, matriarchal creator of light" (Sypher 195).[5]

Yet the six *dramatis personae* are initially introduced into an ambiance of radical lack haunted by the absence of maternal nurture. No parents inhabit the nursery environment that sets the stage for self-aware-ness, a stage on which "no mother or father, divine or human, walks" (Froula, *Virginia* 202). Abject separation from the body of the mother bears the weight of traumatic injury, even as these maturing subjects seek to construct through art and culture shared bulwarks against the trauma of a death (un)foreseen and the danger of personal despair. Hence the signif-icance of the fantasmatic world of Elvedon, with its lady writing and its gardeners sweeping—images that might suggest "a potent female artist located in an Eden where the female is now the namer" (Sypher 195), along with male gardeners who caricature a civil authority that keeps the world tidy and fends off chaos. The phantasmal shadow of death looms large in this prelapsarian paradise, where a man lies with his throat cut under an apple tree—an ironic allusion to the tree of the knowledge of good and evil that burgeoned in the Garden of Eden. In Woolf's lyrical exordia, nature red in tooth and claw continues a Darwinian struggle for survival, as savage birds disembowel the shells of vulnerable snails. "*Fear was in their song, and apprehension of pain*" (*W* 73).

Percival blossoms as an athletic youth who, like Thoby Stephen, will be cut down in his prime, to emerge emblematically as the novel's "absent centre" (Minow-Pinkney 176), the "questing knight, fertility god, and wounded fisher-king" (Froula, *Virginia* 206), whose life and career in the Indian civil service end abruptly (and absurdly) when his horse stum-bles during a race. The traumatic moment of Thoby/Percival's death gives shape to the specter of mortality and allows Woolf's novel to function as a protracted experiment in the therapeutic reformulation of bereavement evoked by the impotence of speaking subjects in an implicitly godless universe. As transient as the ocean waves, human beings naively trust Mother Nature to spawn their replacements in the cosmos. Yet each continues heroically to exert the enormous effort required to survive and take pleasure in a collective consciousness coalescing in rare moments of social integration. According to Gray Kochhar-Lindgren, "Woolf creates a composite self out of six separate voices, voices that speak . . . as a means of resisting the inevitability of death" (57). Each of the six *dramatis personae* in *The Waves* is involved in a search for meaning that will imbricate their lives in a shared, commu-nal discourse and perpetuate the Lacanian illusion (*méconaissance*) of coherent identity. As Lisa Marie Lucenti observes, although the "self" as psychological construct "may be nothing more than a rhetorical illusion, there is perhaps no other illusion so necessary for life" (76).

In *The Waves*, Woolf seeks to portray the luminous halo surrounding consciousness, in all its magical effulgence, through the unique prose style of an experimental play-poem. The novel might be compared to a musical symphony, whose theme is introduced in the lyrical interludes, then fully elaborated via the free indirect discourse of each persona's introspective soliloquies. Leitmotifs, reiterated with newly acquired resonance, resound in the reader's mind (Hite xlvi). Symbols gain cumulative force as they strike oft-repeated chords, until different motifs are brought together in a grand finale in the last chapter. It is for the perspicacious reader, saturated with the music of lyrical vision, to grasp the psychological import of Bernard's "summing up," a narrative directed not only to the unnamed auditor who listens to his speech, but to the novel's future audience, as well. Woolf claimed that she was writing *The Waves* "to a rhythm not to a plot" (*D*3: 316)—the literary equivalent of a musical form that Gerald Levin compares to Beethoven's fugues and to Schoenberg's "pantonal" experiments (165-170). "The sound of the waves," writes Molly Hite, "is like a continuous bass line underlying a piece of music: fundamental, repetitive, and suggesting eternity" (*xl*).

The opening chapter of *The Waves* takes place on a mythic stage, an Edenic garden always-already threatened with an inevitable fall from grace. From the moment Jinny kisses Louis, the creative forces of love and fatality begin to impinge on Woolf's lyrical drama. Bernard is a literary artist, a "maker of phrases" who resembles Woolf in vocation and psychological perspective. "He is shaded with innumerable perplexities" (*W* 49) and is, "in some ways, like Byron" (*W* 79), by virtue of amalgamating the "sensibility of a woman" with the "logical sobriety of a man" (*W* 76). Bernard's creative mind moves between two worlds, the seen and the unseen, in an effort to discover some mode of proportion that will connect the real world of dissociated perceptions with an aesthetic illusion of narrative coherence. As a child, Bernard sees a brass knob on a cupboard and the evanescent loop of light surrounding it; he observes a spider spinning gossamer webs from its entrails. His psychological refuge always lies in the salvific possibilities of aesthetic webs and social communion made possible by language: "'But when we sit together, close,' said Bernard, 'we melt into each other with phrases. . . . We make an unsubstantial territory'" (*W* 16) via "the power of words to distract and so subdue pain" (Sypher 202). Yet even his childish imagination is fraught with violence, as he conjures a dead elephant, shot through the eye, whose corpse is devoured by maggots and vultures.

Throughout his life, Bernard faces the spectral threat of "what is inescapable in our lot; death; the knowledge of limitations; how life is more obdurate than one had thought it" (*W* 269). When he hears the news of Percival's accident, he visits London's National Gallery and, in a welter of conflicting emotions, finds temporary solace in the beauty of paintings by Titian. These works of art serve the function of fetishistic objects that enable him tentatively to cope with overwhelming bereavement. Bernard forces himself to repress traumatic loss and to return to his domestic routine, despite "what death has done to [his] world" (*W* 153). The center is empty, the leader lost. "We have no ceremonies," he laments, "only private dirges and no conclusions" (*W* 157). Although he laments the dearth of a soothing elegiac lullaby in memory of his friend, the impact of traumatic shock is gradually "absorbed in growth" (*W* 257) and covered over by the calloused skin of quotidian habit.

When Bernard feels the stark vacuity of middle age, he cries in the dwindling afternoon, "I have lost my youth," then flees to Rome, the eternal city. Acutely aware of personal limitations, he reluctantly admits that he will never journey further than Rome, nor visit Tahiti, nor read the Vedas: "This drop falling is time tapering to a point" (*W* 184). "And I begin to ask, Are there stories?" (*W* 187). Unable to find consolation in traditional political or religious metanarratives, he situates himself in the chaotic flux of cultural production and takes refuge in a community of discourse: "Here am I shedding one of my life-skins. . . . I am moving too, am becoming involved in the general sequence" (*W* 188) of Tuesday following Monday. Bernard is the only character in *The Waves* who is able to achieve a tenuous emotional balance by reformulating painful experiences into a radically provisional narrative of communal solidarity. He confronts the incipient trauma of existential absurdity by self-consciously acknowledging the tragic imprisonment of each human being in a mortal frame bound by physiological contingency. Bernard knows, as Rhoda and Susan do not, that it is only through narrative constructs called "stories" that the human subject defines him/herself against the other who listens and validates the fragmented image of a Lacanian "body in pieces" in the form of a consoling, if illusory, persona. "To be myself," he admits, "I need the illumination of other people's eyes" (*W* 116).

Of Woolf's six characters, Rhoda is most clearly identifiable as a traumatized subject incapable of creating a life-world by ordering perceptual data. The enigmatic sources of her post-traumatic symptoms remain all the more foreboding in their perplexing inscrutability. As Makiko Minow-Pinkney remarks, in *The Waves* "even casual experiences . . . become major psychic traumas, involving violent images. . . . Falling into crevices or nothingness, being torn to morsels by others—such images closely parallel Rhoda's . . . fears" (170). "I have no face," Rhoda repeatedly insists, as she eschews the mirror image that would valorize the life-giving illusion, or Lacanian *méconaissance*, of coherent identity: "I hate looking-glasses which show me my real face" (*W* 44). Reflective surfaces like mirrors and puddles threaten to engulf her: "I came to the puddle. I could not cross it. Identity failed me . . . I returned very painfully, drawing myself back into my body over the grey, cadaverous space of the puddle" (*W* 64). The scene is almost identical to Woolf's description, in "A Sketch of the Past," of an uncanny moment of bewildering paralysis: "I was suspended; I could not step across the puddle; I tried to touch something . . . the whole world became unreal" (*MOB* 78).

Fearing the logical abstractions that so delight Neville, Rhoda interprets mathematical figures as threatening reminders of the abyss of non-being that circumscribes individual identity and beckons the body toward extinction. When attempting mathematical calculations, she panics and remains the mute victim of mounting anxiety. Her quotidian perceptions are clouded by a pervasive nihilism that precludes the construction of meaning. As a traumatized subject, Rhoda suffers perpetual dissociation and dysphoria, characterized by symptoms of "agitation, emptiness, and utter aloneness. . . . Depersonalization, derealization, and anesthesia" (Herman, *Trauma* 108-9). She finds herself incapable of composing a univocal subject position from the chaotic bombardment of fragmentary, atomized perceptions. Her *modus operandi* is entirely mimetic: unable to project significance onto her environment, she is forced to imitate the socially acceptable (and heterosexually normative) behavior of others.

At the same time, Rhoda cultivates a rich and vivid imaginary life whose limitless horizons compromise her grasp on reality. Frightened of being "blown for ever outside the loop of time" (*W* 22), she allows her mind symbolically to lodge in the utopian spaces represented by white circles between the hours, an *unheimlich* world that borders on chaos.

Louis, her future lover, envisions Rhoda in the guise of a small and help-less butterfly—a disembodied figure capable of enchanting metamorphosis, but doomed to ephemeralty. She is, for Bernard, a "nymph of the fountain always wet" (*W* 117), reminiscent of Arethusa, the nymph whom the goddess Artemis "turn[ed] into a fountain to escape the river god Alpheus" (Oxindine,"Rhoda" 212). As psyche or soul detached from the weight of physicality, Rhoda stumbles through life in a haze of anxiety, and her untamable "wildness" marks her as a "rebel-lious non-initiate into the heterosexual courtship ritual" (Oxindine, "Rhoda" 205). As a child lost in infant wonder and rocking her white petal-boats, Rhoda uncannily identifies with a drowning sailor seeking union with the Great Mother of oceanic bliss.[6]

Like Louis, Rhoda is a liminal figure whose first perceptions are auditory: "I hear a sound . . . cheep, chirp; going up and down" (*W* 9). Trapped within a solipsistic consciousness, she is unable to perceive the distinct colors and shapes of external objects. She lives in solitude, shut-ting her snail-colored eyes against the malevolent intrusion of visual stimuli. The only entrée into her world of white spaces is through the sense of hearing, as sounds register on a body cut off from other sensa-tions. When she contemplates mathematical figures on the classroom blackboard, Rhoda constructs startling and terrible metaphors of annihi-lation: "I begin to draw a figure and the world is looped in it, and I myself am outside the loop. . . . crying, 'Oh, save me, from being blown for ever outside the loop of time!'" (*W* 21-22). Rhoda recognizes that her flight from temporal reality is a dangerous symptom and takes refuge from a sea of troubles by clinging to material objects that prop up her body: "Alone, I often fall down into nothingness. . . . I have to bang my hand against some hard door to call myself back to the body" (*W* 44).

Rhoda's incipient hysteria becomes all the more acute as maturity demands active participation in a confusing, alienating, and heterosexu-ally normative culture. Attending a party, Rhoda acts like a trapped animal, an innocent beast hunted by aggressive savages. Timorously huddled in a corner, she resembles a shy guest at Clarissa Dalloway's party. With the entrance of each reveler into the ballroom, the "door opens; the tiger leaps" (*W* 105). Comparing herself to Saint Sebastian, Rhoda feels like a modern-day martyr to social opprobrium: "A million arrows pierce me. Scorn and ridicule pierce me" (*W* 105-6). As she hovers outside the circle of a body so foreign that she cannot relate to her own corporeal presence in the world, Rhoda experiences each physical sensation as a painful assault. She cannot grasp the proffered hand of a male dance partner. Nor can she connect separate instants of chronological time with the mechanical measurement of duration: "One moment does not lead to another . . . I cannot make one moment merge in the next. To me they are all . . . separate" (*W* 130). As Kochhar-Lindgren remarks, Rhoda's "metaphorical consciousness comes very close to a total disengagement from any referentiality or intersubjective purposefulness. . . . Without the anchoring points of discourse [Lacan's *points de capiton*], there is nothing to stabilize the narcissistically fixed ego, and the subject careens into fissures, the cadaverous space of death and dissolution of identity" (63,66). According to Garrett Stewart, Rhoda's panic is contingent on "a recognition of that death by severance underlying the analogy between time and language, a death whose gaping blank returns as soon as it is repressed" (430).

Only the white, sterile world of Rhoda's fantasy life seems to offer temporary palliation. She is seduced by pure abstraction and a "world immune from change" (*W* 107). Rhoda's sole refuge lies in her imagination, in pools envisaged "on the other side of the world reflecting marble columns" (*W* 105). She feels as evanescent as the "foam that sweeps and fills the uttermost rims of the rocks with whiteness" (*W* 107). Like foam on the ocean waves, Rhoda is continually dashed against the jagged rocks of ontological reality. Bobbing on the surface of the water, she is bruised and beaten by an ever-changing flux of painful stimuli and longs to escape this torrent of existential anxiety by plunging headlong into the sea. Like Phlebas the Phoenician in T. S. Eliot's *Waste Land*, she is destined to forget the cry of gulls and the deep sea swell and eventually to seek oblivion in a metaphorical death by water.

When Rhoda attends the farewell party for Percival at Hampton Court, she hopes to find a unitary symbol that will ground her disintegrating personality, "to light my fire at the general blaze of you who live wholly, indivisibly" (*W* 131). She attempts to anchor herself in an idealized image of Percival, the unselfconscious man of action who might prove a worthy consort in answer to Shelley's lyrical "Question" (Beer, *Virginia* 87). After Percival's death, Rhoda re-enacts the fallen hero's corporeal abjection by imagining herself "hung with other people like a joint of meat among other joints of meat" (*W* 162) and clustering like maggots on the body of a putrescent culture. Yet a musical program at the

Wigmore Hall reassures Rhoda, through images of architectural abstraction, of the symbolic value of human creativity as a triumph and a consolation. She romantically identifies Percival as her spiritual comrade: "We will gallop together over desert hills where the swallow dips her wings in dark pools and the pillars stand entire. Into the wave that dashes upon the shore . . . I throw my violets, my offering" (*W* 164).

Like the shellshocked Septimus Smith, Rhoda feels extreme revulsion toward her fellow human beings, whose callous insouciance torments her: "How you snatched from me the white spaces that lie between hour and hour and rolled them into dirty pellets and tossed them into the wastepaper basket with your greasy paws" (*W* 204). She "fears the presence of others," who "annihilate rather than cocreate her sense of her own subjectivity" (Kochhar-Lindgren 65). During the final reunion at Hampton Court, Rhoda predicts that she "shall fall alone through this thin sheet into the gulfs of fire" and mentally protests her friends' inadvertent brutality: "More cruel than the old torturers you will let me fall, and will tear me to pieces" (*W* 224). Just as Septimus hallucinates apocalyptic conflagration, a traumatized Rhoda envisions the scorching flames of a personal inferno. "For both [Septimus and Rhoda], the world is experienced as a place of incipient violence, unleashed ferocity, and personal insecurity" (Poole, *Unknown* 201). "Fatherless, husbandless, manless, childless, and 'wild'—Rhoda is a 'conspirator'" who shares her author's bisexual eroticism and life-long flirtation with suicide (Oxindine, "Rhoda" 219).

Rhoda pits herself against illimitable chaos in a frantic effort to stave off traumatic flashbacks and emotional constriction. She hopes that she and her comrades can momentarily take refuge in a vast bubble of social solidarity. Allowing herself the temporary elation evoked by this circle of compassion, "when the walls of the mind become transparent" (*W* 228), she realizes that such dreams of coherence are fleeting and evanescent. Whereas her friends will return to the realm of "musts," "the happy concatenation of one event following another" (*W* 234), Rhoda rejects social constructs that impose arbitrary meaning on quotidian experience. Ultimately, she trusts "only in solitude and the violence of death" (*W* 231). As a modern-day pilgrim ascending a Spanish mountain from which she hopes to see the dark continent of Africa, Rhoda has a premonition of death when, via daydream or nightmare, she imagines tumbling into the ocean waves: "I will suppose that this mule back is my bed and that I lie dying. . . . The sheets spotted with yellow holes let me fall through. . . . We launch out now over the precipice. . . . The sea will drum in my ears" (*W* 205-6). One might compare Rhoda's traumatic fantasy with Woolf's diary description, on 15 September 1926, of misery overwhelming her like a wave: "Oh its beginning its coming—the horror—physically like a painful wave about the heart—tossing me up. . . . Down—God, I wish I were dead. . . . Vanessa. Children. Failure. . . . Wave crashes. . . . I can't face this horror any more" (*D3*: 110). On 9 January 1924, she recalls "lying in bed, mad, & seeing the sunlight quivering like gold water, on the wall" and hearing other-worldly "voices of the dead" (*D2*: 283).

Roger Poole speculates that Woolf created the figure of Rhoda in order to "'exorcise' a certain view of herself" and aesthetically to reformulate her own experience of physicality as "open, exposed, threatened, surrounded, scrutinized, menaced" (*Unknown* 200)—an experience contingent on the "painful initiatiory moment of existential insecurity" precipitated by the trauma of childhood sexual abuse (202). "Rhoda's embodiment," Poole believes, and "the pain and embarrassment it brought with it, is exorcised in these passages of despair, of intense inwardness, of intense conviction" (200). The incipient trauma of personal extinction haunts Rhoda like a lover and seduces her toward a suicidal "leap" into oceanic engulfment. According to Garrett Stewart, she "leaves the novel as the most extravagant avatar of discontinuity in modern fiction," her death a "temporal blank" (452-53). Whether Rhoda leaps from a window or off a cliff, into air or into water, we do not know; the precise nature of her suicide is never revealed. The "doomed self in flight" vanishes "in a fatal crevice wedged open within time" (Stewart 454).[7]

In contrast to Rhoda as bisexual outsider, Susan represents a more extreme feminine/heterosexual adaptation to reality. She reacts with fierce, uncontrollable jealousy when, as a child, she spies Jinny kissing Louis. So intense is her passion to "possess one single thing" that she is swept up in a wave of exhilaration culminating in post-traumatic bereavement. Her outburst is that of a noble savage—a grieving maenad whose acute frustration erupts in emotional outrage. "I love . . . and I hate," she proclaims, echoing Catullus' "*Odi et amo*" (Hite 223) and acknowledging that Eros and Thanatos have both invaded the novel's Edenic garden. Impelled by primal libidinous urges that demand love and connection, Susan embraces images of death and decay that cast a shadow of gloom over infantile innocence: "I shall eat grass and die in a ditch in the brown water" (*W* 15). Love and death are defined as brutal antagonists in her emotional landscape, even before she witnesses a ferocious embrace between Ernest, "blind as a bull," and Florrie, swooning "in anguish." The scene presages a potentially traumatic confrontation with raw libidinal energy, an infernal landscape as baffling as it is menacing: "I see a crack in the earth and hot steam hisses up" (*W* 25).

Modeled, in part, on Woolf's sister Vanessa, Susan is depicted in the guise of a mysterious, larger than life earth-goddess who embodies the eternal feminine. Confident and reflective, she revels in the pleasures of country life and desires little more than reassuring love—first, from her father the clergyman; then from her husband and children. (Her mother, we learn, died of cancer.) A symbol of fertility, Susan counters the novel's pervasive mood of thanatopic depression by providing a stable psychological median between Jinny's animal spirits and Rhoda's desperate nihilism. In tune with the cycles of nature and the eternal rhythms of seasonal regeneration, she feels "glutted with natural happiness" (*W* 173). Yet her role as a modern-day Ceres exacts a heavy price. Susan sacrifices personal desire to the exigencies of motherhood, with its paradoxical amalgamation of primal emotions. She functions as a poetic presence linking vast expanses of cosmic and historical time, even though she realizes that nature's cycles of eternal recurrence eradicate the self-conscious subject in favor of racial perpetuation.

Jinny's passions, as opposed to Susan's enduring maternity, are manic—swift, intense, and meteoric, like the sharp colors of red and gold that imbue her childhood perceptions. Determined to eschew conjugal fidelity to a single partner, she carelessly flits like a moth or a butterfly from one amorous liaison to another, celebrating hedonistic pleasure. Unlike Susan's world of biological fruition, Jinny's ambiance exudes the marmoreal splendor of artificial flowers that never blossom or decay. She dances through life with the ecstatic fluidity of a Degas ballerina or Stravinsky's firebird, whose restless activity is dominated by vivacious but uncontrolled animal spirits. A protean and mercurial figure, Jinny resembles a frothy wave on the surface of the sea, tossed in perpetual motion.

Throughout her youth, Jinny's physical beauty and sexual allure offer temporary reprieve from direct confrontation with ontological trauma. But as an aging woman assailed by the ravages of bodily deterioration,

Jinny turns to the ideological state apparatus of British civilization for solace in the face of mortality. In a London Tube station, she gazes at her wizened body reflected in a mirror and exclaims: "How solitary, how shrunk, how aged!" (*W* 193). On the brink of senility, sucking in her flanks and trembling, she seeks comfort from the mystique of British imperialism and its "triumphant procession" of patriotic citizens exulting in global hegemony (*W* 194). Like a frightened animal caught in a moment of panic, Jinny feels terror-stricken at the sight of "upright bodies" descending into the bowels of the London Underground on "moving stairs like the pinioned and terrible descent of some army of the dead downwards" into a modern-day inferno (*W* 194). Seized with anxiety about aging and death, she casts her lot with Britain's "army of victory" sporting "banners and brass eagles"; with engineers of tunnels and scrawlers of graffiti; and with Englishmen who arrogantly claim racial superiority over "savages in loincloths" (*W* 194). Sharing modernity's xenophobic fear of contamination (Marcus, *Hearts* 64-65), Jinny feels enthralled by twentieth-century technology and by the dazzling products of an imperial culture whose commodity fetishism distracts its subjects with seductive material prizes. With childlike naiveté, she exonerates a hedonistic life-style by celebrating the splendor of its consummation: "we have sunk to ashes, leaving no relics, . . . no wisps of hair to be kept in lockets" (*W* 222). Unwittingly, she articulates a swan song both for herself as a vulnerable subject and for Britannia's crumbling empire.

Outwardly, Neville resembles Jinny in his sexual promiscuity. But unlike his female counterpart, he remains emotionally constant to Percival, the object of youthful fascination and adult elegiac bereavement. At the beginning of infantile awareness, Neville sees a globe "hanging down in a drop against the enormous flanks of some hill" (*W* 9)—the symbol of ordered experience and the key to self-integration. The harmony that he perceives in the outer world is the malignant unity of doom and destruction. He adopts an attitude of stoic cynicism that reflects a Faulknerian view of the great, indifferent Player who leads men and women in senseless games through life, only to defeat them at every turn. From early childhood, Neville's mind is filled with images of fatality. When he hears servants talking about a man lying under an apple tree with his throat cut, the figure comes to be associated with the "immitigable tree" at Cambridge—Neville's private symbol for death, mortality, abandonment, and psychological trauma similar to the iconic "apple tree" described by Woolf in "A Sketch of the Past."[8]

At school, Neville becomes a poet and a classical scholar, doomed to "run in and out of the skulls of Sophocles and Euripides like a maggot" (*W* 71). An atheist and a cynic, he scorns the "words of authority . . . corrupted by those who speak them" (*W* 35). Neville is attracted to Percival's unselfconscious sensuality and a purposive intensity focused on "one thing only." He sardonically protests when snubbed by the hero: "I could not live with him and suffer his stupidity. He will coarsen and snore" (*W* 48). Yet Neville cannot help worshipping the benighted athlete in the guise of an idealized pagan deity.

When Neville receives the news of Percival's fatal accident, his dire premonitions seem validated. His friend's death precipitates an ontological crisis that calls into question the meaning of human life—vitiated by threats of nihilism, on the one hand, and by a vindictive determinism on the other. The "immitigable reality" becomes a trope for the intrusions and flashbacks of post-traumatic stress: "He is dead. . . . The sails of the world have swung round and caught me on the head. . . . There stands the tree which I cannot pass" (*W* 151). In the wake of traumatic loss, the scholar retreats into an intellectual ivory tower and embraces melancholic isolation: "From this moment I am solitary. . . . Come, pain, feed on me. Bury your fangs in my flesh" (*W* 152). The only way to endure such agony, he concludes, is to shut one's eyes to the horror and deny the wound that shatters the psyche. In response to the "grinning," "sneering" subterfuge of fate, he vows: "I will not lift my foot to climb the stair" (*W* 152). Like Septimus Smith, he has lost the ability to feel and succumbs to symptoms of emotional constriction. Now, more than ever, he fears the inexorable progress of clock-time as a mechanical portent of doom, but heroically determines to oppose "this illimitable chaos, . . . this formless imbecility" (*W* 226).

Neville, like Jinny, seeks companionship through a succession of love affairs tainted by fear of rejection. Every emotional injury threatens to exacerbate the trauma of Percival's death. For Neville, traumatic repetition occludes the futility of erotic compulsion. He comes to define privacy as solitude with a younger man, always Percival's surrogate, in an effort to construct an emotional refuge from the assault of relentless post-traumatic flashbacks. Addressing one of his consorts, Neville confesses that he needs "to set this hubbub in order. . . . I love . . . the laughter and shouts of boys at play—naked cabin-boys squirting each other with hose-pipes. . . . You are you. That is what consoles me for . . . the depravity of the world, and the flight of youth and Percival's death" (*W* 180-81). He seeks to "abolish the ticking of time's clock with one blow" (*W* 181). The blow metaphorically delivered to the timepiece is, in effect, a symbolic reiteration of the psychic wound that obliterated time's progress after Percival's fateful end. Centered in the security of another male body, Neville takes comfort from (re)union with every Percival clone he seduces. Each love affair is haunted by the ghost of a mythic hero positioned at the apex of a triangle flanked by deceit and desire. As Neville fashions idealized renditions of the relationship he failed to achieve with Percival, he exults in the illusion of temporal suspension as a stay against traumatic injury: "Now this room seems to me central, something scooped out of the eternal night" (*W* 179).

Like Neville, Louis desires order and harmony; but unlike the Cambridge scholar, he attempts to impose on the outer world a false structure of mastery bred of a Nietzschean will to power. He feels compelled to forge a metaphorical ring of steel to heal traumatic "fractures" in his life (*W* 169) that make him "conscious of flux, of disorder; of annihilation and despair" (*W* 93). Though a successful businessman in charge of global commerce, he never attains the poetic illumination—or healing—fantasized in his solitary attic room, where he longs for "some gigantic amalgamation between the two discrepancies so hideously apparent" (*W* 53).

When, as a child, Louis hears waves crashing on the shore, he interprets the sound as the noise of a great beast stamping, an auditory image of a monstrous ontological presence. As Gerald Levin remarks, "[t]he 'something stamping' that he has feared from childhood is the threat of extinction, even the death of nature" (168). Despite his acute sense of racial and historical continuity, Louis will never feel at home in the heart of the British empire. As an Australian expatriate, his self-image is compromised by the stigma of subaltern status, and the gift of a Union Jack from atop a Christmas tree exacerbates his pathetic marginality. Using searing metaphors of torture that evoke the language of trauma, he deplores the "stigma burnt on [his] quivering flesh by a cowled man with a red-hot iron" (*W* 96). Mother England seems a cruel stepmother to this bullied schoolboy, who asserts mastery over others in compensation for a shameful conviction of colonial inferiority.

Louis tries to overcome the handicap of his Australian origins by pledging exaggerated allegiance to figures of authority and by emulating the great men of western civilization. Plagued by a "strange mixture of assurance and timidity," he projects a persona that is "acrid, suspicious, domineering, difficult," and "formidable" (*W* 119). Although Louis revels in mercantile accomplishment, he never succeeds in seeing life whole, or in feeling comfortable in his role as commercial magnate. "I am like some . . . insatiable mouth," he confesses. "I have tried to draw from the living flesh the stone lodged at the center" (*W* 201) in order to expel a traumatic nodule of shame and personal inadequacy, to expunge the stain of abjection and defilement. The structure he so tentatively fabricates, however, is held together by threads of an imperial hegemony soon to be challenged on a world-historical stage.[9]

At the farewell dinner for Percival, Louis has a fleeting vision of romantic triumph engendered by affection and social camaraderie. Percival emerges as the utopian symbol of a unitary presence, a self-identified hero who brings the friends together and distracts them from the ontological trauma of a death (un)foreseen by making them "aware that these attempts to say, 'I am this, I am that,' . . . are false" (*W* 137). Percival functions as the unifying center of the group's testimonial "witnessing" at a pagan eucharistic banquet. Through the sanctity of their ritual meal, the friends temporarily constitute "parts of one body and soul," an imaginary community that appears to defy mortality and to validate mutual aspiration. "Yes, we pray," says Louis, "holding in our hands this common feeling, 'Do not . . . let the swing-door cut to pieces the thing that we have made'" (*W* 145). Such radical solidarity proves exhilarating, but Louis sees in his impassioned comrades the manic enthusiasm of savages dancing round a camp fire, or of a Greek triumphal procession honoring soldiers with violets and laurel wreaths. "Death is woven in with the violets," Louis prophesies. "Death and again death" (*W* 141). "Look at us trooping after him, his faithful servants, to be shot like sheep" (*W* 37).

Louis, Woolf's logocentric businessman, is wracked by a frustrating dichotomy between public ambition and private creativity. Moving between office and bohemian attic, he cannot apply the success of his commercial ventures to secret romantic dreams. When he attempts to bring the hypersensitive Rhoda under his sway, he loses her companionship and turns for solace to a Cockney mistress. Toward the end of his life, he will still be searching for an elusive poetic ideal: "Let us suppose that I make reason of it all—one poem on a page, and then die" (*W* 202). Although Louis can add up figures and phrases, his skillfully devised sums will never be sufficient to palliate the trauma of solipsistic isolation and a pervasive awareness of mortality. When the six friends gather around Percival to celebrate their hero's departure for India, they are linked by what they call, "conveniently, love" (*W* 126). Their personalities intersect in passionate affection, and the community they create is symbolized by a seven-sided carnation reminiscent of the "flower upright in the center" earlier envisaged by Woolf (*D3*: 229). In a savage Dionysian ritual mimicking the death and rebirth of the Greek year-spirit or *eniautos daimon*, they cannibalistically feed on Percival's strength, "as if he were—what indeed he is—a God" (*W* 136). Years later, when they again meet at Hampton Court, the carnation will be six-sided and Percival will be dead. Bereavement transubstantiates their meal into a eucharistic feast predicated on mythic memory, "a ceremonial acknowledgment of the value and durability of the past" (Dick 38). As Bernard realizes, "the swelling and splendid moment created by us from Percival" binds the survivors in creative epiphany: "We too have made something that will join the innumerable congregations of past time" (*W* 146).

It is not, however, until the final chapter of *The Waves* that Bernard endeavors to construct an enabling myth of collective identity through powers of language and memory that allow him dramatically to re-enact and reformulate painful traumatic experiences. As an artist, he strives to configure the fragmentary shards of frozen imagery and sensation characteristic of post-traumatic stress into a meaningful and coherent narrative. His story's testimonial dimension proves crucial to emotional catharsis, insofar as it requires a sympathetic auditor to serve as witness to this "ritual of healing" (Herman, *Trauma* 181). Bernard's colloquy summons a stranger to hear his secular confession: "This, for the moment, seems to be my life. If it were possible, I would hand it to you entire. . . . I must tell you a story" (*W* 238).[10]

In his concluding monologue, Bernard compresses his own life story into the context of auto/biographical testimony. As Woolf notes in her diary on 22 December 1931: "It occurred to me last night while listening to a Beethoven quartet that I would merge all the interjected passages into Bernard's final speech and end with the words O solitude: thus making him absorb all those scenes and having no further break. This is also to show that the theme effort, effort, dominates: not the waves: and personality: and defiance" (*D*3: 339). Each of the monologues in *The Waves* reiterates Woolf's narrative preoccupation with the resurgence of human effort and the power of consciousness to process traumatic injury. In his final attempt to "sum up" a lifetime of haunting reminiscences, along with the lives of his friends, Bernard acknowledges the futility of static iterations balanced in aesthetic design. He abandons traditional literary form, as well as the rhetoric of mastery, in order to search for a lyrical discourse that might give utterance to human anguish: "some little language such as lovers use, broken words, inarticulate words" (*W* 238). He self-consciously seeks an experimental discourse to reflect "those moments of humiliation and triumph" that define Woolf's six *dramatis personae* (*W* 239). Narrative form simulates the wave-like movements of Eros and Thanatos, desire and death. Even in primitive Freudian terms, it is Eros, defined first as self-love or narcissism, then as anaclitic object love, that compels each human being to challenge thanatopic inertia through heroic efforts toward creative survival. Life proves to be a continuous battle against cosmic forces that thwart individual energies in an ongoing struggle to cope with trauma and shattering loss.

When Bernard asserts his identity as a speaking subject, he begins to emerge from a narcissistic state of infant omnipotence. He becomes aware of "the presence of those enemies who change, but are always there; the forces we fight against. To let oneself be carried on passively is unthinkable" (*W* 240). The decision to remain passive in the face of destiny and to accept, without murmur, an ineluctable trajectory toward the trauma of a death (un)foreseen, is simply unthinkable. One must fight, explore, and carve out personal agency in this vast, illimitable chaos: "We grew; we changed; for, of course, we are animals. . . . We exist not only separately but in undifferentiated blobs of matter" (*W* 245-6), bundles of tissue and electrical energy whose growth, dissolution, and death are contingent on physiological process.

As Bernard's reminiscences expand and develop, his narrative takes on the methodical rhythm of a wave. It appears stable, orderly, and purposeful until a defining moment, like Percival's death, breaks the rhythm of Tuesday following Monday and destroys emotional complacency. For the shattered psyche, pain is ineffable, defeat unspeakable. "But for pain words are lacking. There should be cries, cracks, fissures, . . . flesh being gashed and blood spurting" (*W* 263). At times such as these, the universal determination to go on living seems little more than a mindless, instinctual evolutionary drive toward self-preservation. Seized with a Lacanian conviction of radical lack, the speaking subject balances on a precipice of defeat. Yet Woolf insists that each human being is like an indomitable wave—temporarily quelled, but renewed by the energies of regenerative desire: "an impulse again runs through us; we rise, we toss back a mane of white spray; we pound on the shore; we are not to be confined" (*W* 267).

Interpreting his own mortality via the trope of an ephemeral wave, Bernard elucidates Woolf's fictional representation of trauma and reformulation through oceanic metaphors. His soliloquy is alternately joyous and despairing, nihilistic and sublime. We witness the reverberating cycles of Bernard's expanding consciousness, as he fluctuates with the waves of arduous growth and moves toward a healing vision of the world "seen without a self." After a visit to Susan, he perceives the recurrent cycles of nature as maliciously imposing ever smaller circles of constriction on his ego: "I thought then how we surrender, how we submit to the stupidity of nature. . . . [T]he gardeners sweeping, the lady writing—returned. . . . But I now made the contribution of maturity to childhood's intuitions—satiety and doom" (*W* 268-69).[11]

Against the impending trauma of personal annihilation, the six characters pit the "one thing" they have created in moments of communion. As they gather together, first for Percival's farewell dinner, then in bereavement at Hampton Court, they experience a healing conviction of solidarity that ushers in a sense of triumph and recovery. Time is held momentarily in stasis, as the social microcosm provides emotional sanctuary. Intimations of immortality reside in the collective consciousness that they, as a group, create. For an epiphanic moment, the walls of the ego grow porous and fuse with a larger empathic whole: "I am not one person; I am many people; I do not altogether know who I am—Jinny, Susan, Neville, Rhoda, or Louis: or how to distinguish my life from theirs" (*W* 276). As the boundaries of the self dissolve, the danger of annihilation looms large: "[W]e felt enlarge itself round us the huge blackness of what is outside us, of what we are not" (*W* 277). But a pugnacious subjectivity defies engulfment, and the moment is held in stasis, without dissolution: "We six, out of how many million millions, for one moment out of what measureless abundance of past time and time to come, burnt there triumphant. The moment was all; the moment was enough" (*W*

278). This utopian dream of community, pitted against the trauma of mortality, temporarily illumines the circumambient dark.[12]

Skeptically, Bernard wonders how long he will continue to beat his spoon on the table in defiance of extinction. Will he, too, succumb to despair? A simple haircut reminds him of a fragile corporeal integument that grows, decays, and dies. In his mirror reflection, he confronts a "pinioned" body wizened with age and unable to protect itself from hostile crowds passing in the streets. Bernard feels like a sheaf of wheat, metonymically identified with the locks of hair being sheared and falling to the ground: "So we are cut and laid in swathes. . . . We are cut, we are fallen" (*W* 280). He imagines the scissors of Atropos, a Roman fate, snipping the lock of his destiny and allowing him to fall, like a ripe stalk of wheat, into the general conflagration. The barber's chair reminds him of his impotence when, in a moment of Lacanian self-enunciation, he (mis)recognizes himself in a mirror as "the swathed figure in the hairdresser's shop taking up only so much space" (*W* 284). Like a thread of continuity through the fabric of life, the dream of community gives Bernard a symbol and an aspiration. It reminds him that he is larger than the reflection cast by his body, and that his creative gifts are buttressed by the strength and courage of the people he has loved: "For this is not one life; nor do I always know if I am man or woman, Bernard or Neville, Louis, Susan, Jinny or Rhoda—so strange is the contact of one with another" (*W* 281). In this shared reality of androgynous expansion into an unsubstantial territory created by social engagement, he finds the courage to wrestle with ontological trauma.

There comes a time when the rhythmic progression of Tuesday following Monday ceases to sustain the flagging spirit. The flowing stream of nonsense and poetry fails to support the vulnerable subject on tides of historical continuity: "For one day as I leant over a gate that led into a field, the rhythm stopped. . . . I regretted so much litter, so much unaccomplishment and separation. . . . I said life had been imperfect, an unfinished phrase" (*W* 283). As the rings of growth ossify into circles of constriction, Bernard gives way to psychic dissociation. Exploration is no longer possible. Accomplishment is defined and stratified, and ultimate coherence has eluded the storyteller. Imagining his life as a (melo)drama about to end, Bernard appraises his past as little more than a desiccated heap of orts, scraps, and fragments. He realizes that his auto/biography is a drama that refuses to yield Aristotelian anagnorisis. The phrasemaker cannot sum up the import of his phrases. Bernard the storyteller is unable to finish his crucial life-narrative.

Psychologically, Bernard's creative horizon is expanding with feverish exhilaration. He first proclaims the "everlasting nay" that rejects the framework of habitual activity. Like a snake shedding the skin it has recently outgrown, he divests himself of traditional values. (Hence the incongruous image of a dried adder's skin hanging from a nail). Bernard casts off the spurious roles of businessman and storyteller—roles that have technically defined his life. He discards a factitious past and brackets the ego constructed cumulatively, through world-making activities, as well as "that self who has been with me in many tremendous adventures; the faithful man who sits over the fire when everybody has gone to bed" (*W* 283). He temporarily suspends the Lacanian *moi*, the illusion of a totalizing self-presence that the mind constructs in its search for a stable identity. At this point in the novel, Bernard is accosted by the overwhelming doubt that precedes revelation. Even the illusory egoic center, the self that refuses dissolution, seems to fail: "the man who has collected himself in moments of emergency and banged his spoon on the table, saying 'I will not consent' . . . This self now . . . made me no answer. . . . I cried then with a sudden conviction of complete desertion, Now there is nothing. No fin breaks the waste of this immeasurable sea. Life has destroyed me" (*W* 284). The experience of mourning for an earlier, more vibrant self has reduced him to a morbid state of will-less passivity.

Bernard feels like a phantom beholding a colorless display of shadows reminiscent of the tableaux that lined the walls of Plato's cave in *The Republic*. He adopts the perspective of a shade from Hades, disillusioned by the discovery that his phrases have recorded little more than terrestrial mutability: "What a litter—what a confusion; with here birth, here death . . . and myself always running hither and thither. Now it was done with. I had no more appetites to glut" (*W* 285). Proclaiming the eradication of personal desire, the artist temporarily renounces the "effort and anguish" of purposive activity and seems to relinquish the struggle for vitality. Assaulted by the ontological trauma of a death (un)foreseen, he balances on the sharp edge of despair and treads a path of melancholic desolation. Bernard "discovers his mortality in a moment of eclipse when he loses the object of biographical narration" (Hite lvi). Only a weightless shadow-self continues to float, powerless and suspended, like a phantom over the illusory world of "musts."

When Bernard brackets the dust dance of habit, his undefended subject position collapses with dread in the face of nothingness. Gradually, however, the yawning gap of spiritual openness is filled by sensuous memory. Temporary nihilism ushers in vision, as the mind is released from psychological closure and contemplates the world in its absolute self-givenness. The everlasting nay gives way to prophetic affirmation—to a universe seen without a self and perceived with childlike astonishment. Light, replicating the wake of a solar eclipse, miraculously returns and bathes the terrain in kaleidoscopic brilliance: "I saw fields, . . . but now with this difference; I saw but was not seen. I walked unshadowed . . . alone in a new world" (*W* 286-7).[13]

Bernard experiences an ingenuous wonder at the mystery revealed: *that anything should be, rather than not*; that the environment should take on form and color before the beholding consciousness. The artist is "unable to speak save in a child's words of one syllable" (*W* 287). Overwhelmed by feelings of humility and wonder, he finds silence the only appropriate response: "But how describe the world seen without a self? There are no words" (*W* 287). Like all such moments of being in Woolf's fiction, the moment is all. The moment is enough. The veil has been lifted, reality disclosed. The fin rises in a waste of waters. Epiphany is ecstatic and healing, but evanescent. It fades and "undergoes a gradual transformation" (*W* 287). "But for a moment I had sat on the turf somewhere high above the flow of the sea. . . . The old nurse who turns the pages of the picture-book . . . had said, 'Look. This is the truth'" (*W* 287). At this point in the text, Bernard's expanding narrative merges with the impersonal voice of Woolf's lyrical *exordia*. The old nurse might be a symbol of fate, pointing like a seer to the horizon where "this little affair of 'being'" gives way to a discovery of universal cohesion (*W* 288). High above a raging sea, Bernard embraces the cosmic perspective of the novel's interludes and is able to confront the prospect of his own extinction as an individual, autonomous subject. Plato's cave of shadows has become a picture-book, illumined and symbolic.[14]

As the ego dissolves, Bernard feels a loss of identity and envisages, once again, a dream of community through psychological fusion with the other characters in the novel: "There is no division between me and them. . . . This difference we make so much of, this identity we so feverishly cherish, was overcome" (*W* 288-89). He sheds his spurious personae, casting off phantom images and half-articulate ghosts, along with the many "unborn selves" that crouch in the recesses of the unconscious. Finally, he exposes the evolutionary *id*, the primitive and savage dimension of the ego that squats at the heart of corporeal embodiment and, gibbering like a madman, turns a lascivious gaze toward objects of desire: "That man, the hairy, the ape-like, . . . has led me wild dances!" (*W* 290).

Renouncing this congeries of phantasms, Bernard exults in a moment of aesthetic revelation that bathes even "crumbled relics of bread" in beauty. In the far-off land of childhood, a juvenile artist had sculpted bread into "people pellets" that provided material for his stories. Now awestruck at the sight of "bare things . . . things in themselves" (*W* 295), he refuses to merge with the surrounding cosmos in quiet abandon. The mesmerized *regard* of his silent auditor reminds Bernard of his physical presence in the world. He feels humiliated at being reduced to the object of another's diminishing gaze: "I, who had been thinking myself so vast . . . am now nothing but what you see" (*W* 292). His mirror image is that of an elderly fatuous gentleman spouting prophecies in the midst of "disorder, sordidity and corruption." "Lord, how unutterably disgusting life is!" (*W* 292), he sardonically concludes.

The incredulous stare of his bewildered auditor finally returns Bernard to "the complexity and the reality and the struggle" (*W* 294), recalling him to the detestable "world of musts" to war with the most ancient of human antagonists, Death. Tossed by the ocean current, Bernard must once again rise and collect his forces to confront Thanatos, the primordial enemy of consciousness. "I have done with phrases," he proclaims (*W* 295) and, like Prospero, discards his book of magical metaphors. He will need a howl or a cry to give vent to visceral feelings. And yet, paradoxically, the break of day gives rise to a new dawn of the spirit, to the resuscitation of desire even in the weariest of travelers: "I, I, I, tired as I am, spent as I am, and almost worn out" (*W* 296). As Woolf declared in her diary, the narrative must "show that the theme effort, effort dominates: not the waves: and personality: and defiance" (*D*3: 339). True heroism lies, for Woolf, in human resilience—in the perpetual impulse toward heroic creation that draws each man and woman forward in a life-long struggle against the traumas of aging, impotence, loss, illness, death, and inevitable bereavement.[15]

Woolf everywhere celebrates the unacknowledged heroism of speaking beings who continue to project meaning onto quotidian experience, despite psychological trauma and corporeal pain. The ongoing quest for symbolic meaning and ethical value through memories sanctified by art and love is itself a testimony to the valor of the species. Like Samuel Beckett's beleaguered protagonists, Woolf's characters summon immense powers of perseverance to fight the concatenation of haunting traumatic flashbacks that assault individual consciousness—to face the dreariness of Tuesday following Monday; to put one foot in front of the other until they step into the grave. Wounded and grieving, they appear to succumb to pessimism and despair. Thanatos calls; silence and passivity beckon. Such troughs of nihilism, however, are balanced by healing moments that evoke a coherent vision of "something abstract; but residing in the downs or sky; beside which nothing matters; in which [they] shall rest and continue to exist" (*D*3: 196). In all Woolf's novels, the inexorable trauma of a death (un)foreseen, nature's ultimate victory over the vulnerable subject, makes spiritual endurance a mode of tragic heroism. Once the individual subject is able to confront the existential anxiety of personal contingency, each breath of life entails courageous persistence in the face of future oblivion.

At the end of *The Waves*, Bernard ritualistically girds himself for battle in the tradition of Don Quixote and, with Faustian bravado, dons the heroic mask of Percival to challenge his indomitable enemy. Woolf's fictional alter ego celebrates a tenuous victory of romantic aspiration, even as the last wave crashes on the shore: "It swells; it arches its back. I am aware once more of a new desire, something rising beneath me like the proud horse whose rider first spurs and then pulls him back. . . . Death is the enemy. . . . Against you I will fling myself, unvanquished and unyielding, O Death!" (*W* 297). Such militant defiance is shot through with indeterminacy. Bernard is simultaneously lauded as a valorous knight and skewered as a holy, quixotic fool. The monologue's ecstatic climax is lyrical and semiotic, but withholds from the reader traditional satisfactions of narrative closure and dramatic dénouement. The open-endedness of the text suggests that the reformulation of emotional trauma and metaphysical anxiety is a lifelong existential project that perpetually (re)constructs the elusive and illusory Lacanian phantasm of an enunciated ego; but that the self is never fully or finally identified, as essence or aesthetic object, until the ontological trauma of death. [16]

Woolf concludes her enigmatic play-poem with a puzzle or a rebus— a Gordian knot that cannot be untangled through the aegis of language. Each speaking subject confronts, in prospect but never in retrospect, the proleptic trauma of a death (un)foreseen—a final *coup de grâce* that defies iterability. The phenomenon of extinction haunts the psyche as a terrifying specter always-already repressed, rationalized, and denied in the medium of linguistic mastery. As Woolf implies in her diary analogy between Bernard's monologue and a Beethoven sonata, music and aural resonance transcend the boundaries of language and appeal to more primitive levels of autonomic response. Hearing is purportedly the last of the senses to expire, as speech deserts the dying brain. In a proclamation of aesthetic valor, Bernard employs language artistically to shore up the chaotic and deteriorating sensorium of individual perception. The atoms of sensation incessantly bombarding consciousness demand articulation in order to be comprehensible to the Lacanian subject, whose illusion of coherent identity is constructed on the rhetorical model of discourse and contingent on the reflective gaze of the other. As the sun sets, Bernard is dying. Yet he appeals to a performative speech act in a final assertion of his unique being-in-the-world, even as he confronts his own being-toward-death through the auspices of a language that defines the primacy of the speaking subject in its futile quest for ongoing self-affirmation.[17]

Woolf delineates the ultimate trauma of mortality in terms of a Faustian defiance of the wave of annihilation destined to overwhelm each autonomous subject. According to Haule and Smith, *The Waves* set in opposition to Sir James Jeans's popular theories of meaningless cosmic materiality "the miracle of human identity. Along with love and beauty, Woolf presented consciousness itself as the only thing to throw against the essential 'accident of life': the triumph of consciousness in an unconscious universe" (xxviii-xxix). In contrast to James Joyce, who depicts Anna Livia Plurabelle flowing "moananoaning" into her great feary Father in *Finnegans Wake*, Woolf identifies the primordial ocean waves as feminine and maternal, albeit terrible and threatening. For both authors, a traumatic awareness of death as the unimaginable annihilation of the speaking subject is represented metonymically as a return to the oceanic unconscious. Theories of Darwinian evolution that trace the origins of mammalian life to ancestral sea-creatures might well haunt the modernist imagination and find expression in fluid imagery associated with death by water in the writings of Virginia Woolf, James Joyce, D. H. Lawrence, and T. S. Eliot. At the end of *The Waves*, Woolf shares with her readers an uncanny premonition of her own future drowning in the River Ouse. Symbolically returning to a river-woman emblematic of the

Freudian unconscious, she would, in the end, plunge headlong into the dark embrace of Death, her most formidable—and unconquerable—enemy.

Notes

1. For a discussion of traumatic events that marked Virginia Stephen's childhood, adolescence, and early adult life, see the Introduction to this volume. My own interest in Woolf's "embodied texts" is longstanding and was inspired, in part, by Wilfred Stone's Bloomsbury seminar at Stanford and by work with Paul Ricoeur at the University of Paris. After researching the field of trauma studies in the 1990s for my book *Shattered Subjects*, I became convinced that feminist psychoanalytic criticism could profitably be amalgamated with phenomenological perspectives in the interpretation of Woolf's oeuvre. Charles Bernheimer was one of the first scholars to use the term "ontological trauma" in his essay, "A Shattered Globe," arguing that Woolf's "writing repeats and extends the traumatic constitution of her sexuality" (205-206). My own essay on *"The Waves* as Ontological Trauma," in the course of successive drafts, joined an ongoing conversation with other critics on the topic of ontology, subjectivity, and language in Woolf's fiction. For two recent contributions to the discussion, see essays by Lisa Marie Lucenti and Tamlyn Monson. This essay is dedicated to the memory of Lucio Ruotolo, whose moment was interrupted too soon.

2. The moment the human mind tries to conceptualize non-being, it represses proleptic trauma by positing the continuation of a perceiving consciousness that denies, even while attempting to imagine, the future death of the subject. As Heidegger points out, the human subject *knows*, intellectually, that s/he will eventually die; but his or her consciousness is so strongly defended against the specter of annihilation that its own being-toward-death is, at the level of emotional introjection, an inscrutable enigma, absorbed in the universal conundrum of the knowledge that *"one* dies." Death, as a personal experience of ontological trauma, remains both inevitable and unimaginable, i.e."(un)foreseen." Daniel Ferrer suggests that the palimpsestic text of *The Waves*, an enigmatic prose-poem self-consciously engaged in a "process of masking the void and denying madness and death, . . . is also, contradictorily, a reiteration of the void, a taking up of madness, a repetition of death" (94). For a discussion of Woolf's "spiritual quest," see Jane de Gay's chapter on *The Waves* (160-185). De Gay interprets Woolf's "moments of being" in the context of Wordsworth's "spots of time" and suggests that both "are formed in response to death" and "attempt to fend off death and dissolution" by capturing and freezing in memory fleeting moments of individual experience (167-68).

3. See Laird in this volume and Froula, *Virginia Woolf*. For a phenomenological analysis of Woolf's ontological anxieties, see Roger Poole, *The Unknown Virginia Woolf*. Gillian Beer identifies at the core of this "submarine book" a fascination with metaphysical issues of "human destiny and the meaning of life" (*Virginia* 75, 77). In *Hearts of Darkness*, Jane Marcus offers a counter-argument for interpreting *The Waves* as a postmodern novel that "undermines humanist faith in the coherent subject" and challenges the "English fetishization of selfhood and individualism as the struggle against death" (60, 63). Marcus identifies Percival as "a Siegfried, a superman, the strong silent bully who will by the end of the decade be a fascist idol," trusted to secure British imperial interests "by violent exertions of brute force" in the colonies (66). In contrast, Julia Briggs portrays him as a Christ figure and a replica of Jane Harrison's *eniautos daimon* or "year hero" that Woolf would have known from *Themis: A Study of the Social Origins of Greek Religion* (254, 471n.82). Patricia Cramer argues that "Woolf based her 'play-poem' on the woman-centered ritual drama described by Jane Harrison. . . . The Hogarth Press published *Reminiscences of a Student's Life* (1925), and Woolf owned *Epilegomena to the Study of Greek Religion* (1921), *Aspects, Aorists and the Classical Tripos* (1919), and *Ancient Art and Ritual* (1913)" ("Jane Harrison" 444). "According to Harrison, in pre-patriarchal communities, fertility rites centered on women and nature; in male-centered societies, art and ritual centered on the exploits and death of the male hero cut off from nature" (445). For Cramer, Percival is "akin to the heroic usurpers described by Harrison who masquerade violence and misogyny as idealism and high art" (448). In India, he uses force and "violent language" to impose western cultural practices on Britain's indigenous subalterns (*W* 136).

4. Briggs sees in this early holograph a "vision of life emerging from the sea, of individual lives endlessly begetting others, like waves, and of the endlessly repeated throes of childbirth . . . a vision of maternal genesis" (243). She cites a letter from Vanessa, written from the French seaside village of Cassis, describing an invasion of giant moths and imploring Virginia to write a book about the "maternal instinct" (Briggs 241). Gillian Beer finds in these holograph passages themes of "self-loss" and the "anonymity of childbirth and succession" (*Virginia* 83); whereas Makiko Minow-Pinkney identifies a "realm of inchoate motility" evocative of Julia Kristeva's semiotic *chora* (157). John Maze perceives not "pregnancy of meaning, . . . but the mere fleshly pregnancy that crowds the world with surplus millions," a "tone of disgust" and a "grim worldview" (121). Wave and oceanic analogies, associating anthropoid evolution with mammalian biological origins in ancestral sea creatures, seem to have been pervasive in the modernist imagination.

5. Gillian Beer reminds us that in the "first draft, an enigmatic figure, obscurely male or female, scrutinizes the scene from behind a veil" (*Virginia* 78) and seems to embody "The Lonely Mind" (*D3*: 251). In a critique of androgyny in *The Waves*, Elaine Sypher

traces the development of the novel from Woolf's initial representation of a female mind thinking about the "age of the earth" and the "death of humanity" in her 1927 diary entries and drafts, through various stages whereby this narrative voice gives way, in 1929, to Bernard as androgynous author. "What for two years was to have been a novel whose active or central narrative consciousness was female, then for six months a man or woman, becomes within a month a novel where the thinking mind has disappeared and a male central figure has emerged who is on the way to becoming self-consciously androgynous" (192-193). Sypher speculates that Woolf's authorial alter ego was originally to have been "a rather different Rhoda," initially described as a character who composes stories in an exercise book; claims omnipotence as "judge," "seer," and Hardy-esque "arranger"; and becomes a female savior and "avenger," "extremely valiant and adventurous" (193-194). Sypher skeptically dismisses the "myth" of Bernard's "androgyny as a strategy of evasion and suppression," whereby Woolf chose "a male center to repress her own voice"(210).

6. In her essay on "Autobiographical Ruptures," Alice D'Amore presents striking evidence from the original holograph drafts of *The Waves* to suggest that Woolf was initially "working from a single [female] character, which split into two opposing factions" in the personae of Rhoda and Jinny. The fatherless Rhoda, D'Amore contends, "springs not from the forehead of Zeus, but from the body of Jinny, the sensual self" (47). Woolf "appears to create Rhoda as an effort to separate her own traumatic past, one of sexual abuse and incest, from Jinny, a physical manifestation of survival" (46). D'Amore argues that although "Rhoda's trauma remains a mystery . . . locked forever in an inaccessible past," it clearly replicates Woolf's own autobiographical experience of incestuous abuse. For both character and author, "the failure to assume a complete self" is attributable to "the unsaid memory of abuse. . . . Rhoda emerges as an emotionally paralyzed being whose trauma surfaces, like Woolf's, through . . . scarred and dissociated refractions" (49). According to Annette Oxindine, earlier holograph drafts of *The Waves* supply evidence of Rhoda's "submerged" lesbian identity—a pleasurable and celebratory Sapphic proclivity which Woolf progressively censored in each successive draft. The published version of the novel suppresses Rhoda's lesbian fantasies and a "wondrous story" of homoerotic attraction to a female companion named Alice—a same-sex liaison "transferred in the published novel to Rhoda's feelings for Miss Lambert" (Oxindine, "Rhoda" 214-15).

7. Patricia Cramer makes a strong case for interpreting Rhoda's "lesbian desire as a countermagic against the seduction of patriarchal loyalties," evoking "feelings of life enhancement and transformation associated with fertility festivals" through a submerged and embedded "lesbian quest story with a utopian ending," a "Sapphic dream of a

women's intellectual community as the origin as well as the goal of Rhoda's flight" ("Jane Harrison" 451-53).

8. In "A Sketch of the Past," Woolf recounts her shock at hearing about a neighbor's suicide: "It seemed to me that the apple tree was connected with the horror of Mr Valpy's suicide. I could not pass it. . . . I seemed to be dragged down, hopelessly, into some pit of absolute despair from which I could not escape" (*MOB* 72). See also Jane de Gay's discussion of Neville's "moment of being" in relation to Wordsworth's "spots of time" (166-68).

9. Jane Marcus, like Doris Eder, Gillian Beer, and Molly Hite, associates Louis with T. S. Eliot: "As an ex-colonial subject, Louis is most afraid of the dissolution of the empire. He hears the great beast of revolution stamping on the shore" (82) and identifies with Chatham, Pitt, Burke, and Sir Robert Peel, "British politicians and lawmakers who were preoccupied with the Indian imperial enterprise" (Beer 88). Cramer points out that Louis and Percival are both associated with vegetation gods, and that Louis' "racial memories of the women by the Nile" link him "to the early corn goddess" (447). Like Percival, a "man at ease in the world of Empire" (Beer, *Virginia* 185), he seeks to assert "the omnipotent totalitarianism of the subject" (Monson 184).

10. For a discussion of the testimonial function of trauma narrative, see Henke, *Shattered Subjects*. According to Susan Dick, Bernard "undertakes this excursion into autobiography knowing that any design he imposes on his life is an illusion. Nevertheless, he cannot help being taken in by his own illusion" (42). Dick points out that Woolf's *Notebook* entries for the final chapter indicate that the "listener was not to be death, . . . but death was to 'come in as the antagonist' so that there could be an argument between them" (43). For a Bakhtinian interpretation of Bernard's monologic "attempt to 'rule' or 'read' *The Waves*," see Gabrielle McIntire, who postulates that his soliloquy "works as a constellated statement about the absurdity of efforts to contain the past within narrative" (34-35). For a provocative feminist reading of Bernard's monologue, see Andrea Harris, *Other Sexes*. Using linguistic theories gleaned from Cixous, Irigaray, Kristeva, and Butler, Harris concludes that, in his final soliloquy, Bernard appropriates Rhoda's female subject position and incorporates the fragmentary "little language" of women into a masculine, linear auto/biographical life-narrative to become a "differently gendered being, one in whom masculine and feminine coexist" (58-59). Patrick McGee argues that, in writing *The Waves*, Woolf "comes to herself in the place of the [Lacanian] Other" (229).

11. Joseph Allen Boone interprets the image of Elvedon as pivotal to Bernard's vision at the end of the novel. He identifies "the woman writing at the core of Bernard's mind" as a mother figure, an expanding phantasm that evokes "the *magna mater* of matriarchal creation myths" (634). Froula envisages the woman as Woolf's "phantasmal self-portrait," this "other nature's spectral author," who "persists in the forgetting of sexu-

al hierarchy" (*Virginia* 202). In contrast, Marcus interprets the "lady writing" as a trope for the upper middle-class white author inadvertently complicitous with the British class system and the elegiac perpetuation of Romanticism, patriotism, jingoism, and imperialism. The lady is Britannia herself, and Bernard offers "a parody of authorship" based on Woolf's antagonistic critic, Desmond MacCarthy (*Hearts* 61). The "sweeping classes and the writing classes" prove "eternal verities" of British culture (70),

12. On 27 October 1931, Woolf wrote to G. Lowes Dickinson about the dramatic personages in *The Waves*: "I did mean that in some vague way we are the same person, and not separate people. The six characters were supposed to be one" (*L4*: 397). James Naremore interprets the second meeting at Hampton Court as a reunion that effects a redemptive dissolution of egotism for the six individuals, ripened and battered by experiences over their lifetimes. Madeline Moore finds in *The Waves* a strong "social statement . . . embedded within a philosophical construct" (128) and sees as its focal point the characters' intense but futile yearning for a utopian dream of community. For Marcus, that dream is inescapably complicit with the "deadlock embrace of violence and poetry in the English male cultural script" (*Hearts* 78). Patrick McGee speculates that Woolf succeeds in capturing a "third voice," that "dimension of language that resists meaning and signification" (240).

13. A number of critics, including Susan Dick (47), compare Bernard's experience to Woolf's diary description of viewing a total eclipse of the sun on 29 June 1927. Woolf depicts the landscape becoming "darker & darker as at the beginning of a violent storm; the light sank & sank. . . . We had fallen. It was extinct. There was no colour. The earth was dead. . . . I had very strongly the feeling as the light went out of some vast obeisance; something kneeling down, & low & suddenly raised up, when the colours came. They came back astonishingly lightly & quickly & beautifully . . . with a miraculous glittering and aetheriality, . . . with a sense of great relief. It was like recovery" (*D3*: 143-44). In her 1928 essay "The Sun and the Fish," Woolf recalls: "The flesh and blood of the world was dead; only the skeleton was left" (*CDB* 215). For an "iconic" reading of Bernard's lyrical prose, see John Graham's transcription of Woolf's holograph, discussed by Edward L. Bishop in "The Alfa and the Avant-texte" (148).

14. According to Howard Harper, Bernard's final monologue "fulfills every author's dream. It represents the narrative's transcendence of its own story, the transformation of that story into a realm no longer threatened by interruption, distraction, or contradiction. And so the search for an authentic, satisfying mode of consciousness turns again, at last, to the same conclusion as the search in *To the Lighthouse*: That the essence of life can be discovered and expressed by the questing consciousness of the artist" (248). For Marcus, such dubious claims constitute the object of Woolf's postmodern, carnivalesque satire of Britannia's class consciousness, colonial apparatus, imperialist aggression, and pervasive

fear of savagery, contamination, and death. She reads *The Waves* as a "swan song of the white western male author. . . . Byronic man, the romantic artist-hero, sings his last aria against death" (*Hearts* 79).

15. On 11 October 1929 Woolf describes being "goaded on by what I call reality . . . & when I wake early I say to myself, Fight, fight. If I could catch the feeling, I would: the feeling of the singing of the real world, as one is driven by loneliness & silence from the habitable world; the sense that comes to me of being bound on an adventure" (*D3*: 260). Bernard experiences the ecstasy of what Heidegger describes as "an impassioned freedom towards death—a freedom which is factical, certain of itself, and anxious" (311). Susan Dick judges Bernard "more heroic than mock-heroic" (50), and Mitchell Leaska agrees that his "will to persist, his determination to confront death in solitude—despite the loneliness of old age and the ache of loss" endows him with "a kind of faded solemnity, even a faint nobility. For he is committed to life and to living; he is engaged in the struggle of life which daily renews itself—stripped of the meretricious veils of fame, fortune, and pleasure. His is the struggle which, in the existential sense, makes human destiny a human matter" (*Novels* 188). Marcus suggests that the interludes of the text invoke the Indian *Rig Veda*, as "Woolf's cousin Dorothea Stephen explained it in *Studies in Early Indian Thought*, to call up Indian philosophy and its emphasis on astronomy and the randomness of the universe, a major subject in *The Waves* as it incorporates relativity theory and the new physics into fiction" (*Hearts* 80). "Woolf surrounds the text of the decline and fall of the West (the transcendental self striving and struggling against death) with the text of the East, random natural recurrence" (80-81). For Marcus, the end of the novel celebrates Eastern mysticism and a "Hindu philosophy, which embraces death" (81).

16. Briggs draws an analogy with Virginia Woolf's near-death experience in summer 1930, when she fainted and "imagined herself dead and in the presence of God," but felt angrily resistant, shaking her fists in fury and defiance (257; *D3*: 315). Jean Guiguet aptly summarizes the metaphysical query posed by the novel's ending: "[W]ill death irrevocably swallow up all our losses, or will it be the ultimate recovery? The access to fusion, communion, unity to which we aspire[?]. The answer remains uncertain" (397). Does the last line of Bernard's monologue imply "nothingness sanctioning the victory of time and space, our enemies and our defeat, or does it mean eternity sanctioning our victory over their vain illusory opposition?" (397). James Naremore proposes an implicit balance: "Woolf sees death [equivocally] as a kind of victory and a kind of defeat," both a "loss of the self" and an "ecstatic embrace" (188). Howard Harper feels that Bernard's note of defiance is counterpointed by the book's ultimate acknowledgement of death: "Neither cancels the other; both remain in eternal suspension" (248). According to Briggs, "the wave rises like a horse beneath him, carrying him on a final ride against imminent dissolution. The theme of heroic struggle ends the novel, as imagination triumphs over the

irresistible advance of time and physical decay, in a gesture at once exultant and absurd" (262). For Tamar Katz, "Bernard's assertion of climactic victory, of an individual, triumphant ending, is ultimately undermined by the novel's final reassertion of death as a reabsorption of the waves into the sea, a reassertion of cyclical organization and transpersonal unity" (247-248). Jane de Gay associates Bernard's final ride against Death with the "shadowy, god-like figure on horseback" from the Apocalypse and with "Plato's image of the soul as a horse in *Phaedrus*" (181). On Woolf's prolific use of symbolic equine imagery, see Gillespie, "Godiva Still Rides."

17. Compare Poole's *The Unknown Virginia Woolf,* as well Kochhar-Lindgren's "The Voice of Narcissus" and Clifford Wulfman's essay in this volume. On finishing *The Waves*, Woolf recorded a sense of "triumph & relief" in her diary on 7 February 1931: "I have netted that fin in the waste of waters which appeared to me . . . at Rodmell" (*D4*: 10). Patrick McGee notes that, in netting her mythic/mystical fin, Woolf manages to "write the impossible as impossible, in the moment of its not reaching what no image can convey: a fin passing far out. . . . Bernard's discourse is the fin . . . [and] it is [*la*] *fin*—the end, the aim, the conclusion of this book of 'dramatic soliloquies.' . . . The effect is to foreground the materiality of language, that which symbolizes something beyond meaning—in Lacanian terms, *the discourse of the Other*" (242).

WOOLF AND THE DISCOURSE OF TRAUMA: THE LITTLE LANGUAGE OF *THE WAVES*

Clifford E. Wulfman

In "A Sketch of the Past," Virginia Woolf links shock to pattern recognition and places it at the heart of her literary ability. "Behind the cotton wool is hidden a pattern," she says, "[a]nd I see this when I have a shock" (*MOB* 72). The language of shock adheres to Woolf's writing more than to that of many other writers, not only because one of her finest creations, Septimus Smith, is often cited as a study of shell shock, but because her own life history is inextricably linked to trauma and mental illness.

Much has been said about the nature of Woolf's psychiatric condition, but the most perceptive commentary may belong to Hermione Lee, who suggests in her biography of Woolf the need to bracket clinical psychobiography by contextualizing the word *illness* as part of a specifically medical discourse, one that signifies a collection of subjective experiences and objective behaviors as *symptoms*. Lee allows different narratives to convey the story—past and present-day medical discourse, Leonard Woolf's recollections, as well as the recollections of others—and then lets Woolf's writing do the telling, thereby giving primacy to Woolf's own treatment of her condition:

> But the named illness is also "her" illness in that it took the material of her life as its subject-matter. It, and the treatment she received for it, affected her personality, her behaviour, her writing and her politics. And it is "her" illness in that much of what we know about it is derived from what she wrote about it. *Her illness has become her language* (172, emphasis mine).

The true psycho-physiological nature of Woolf's illness may never be known, but its clinical diagnosis is not important to the thesis I am advancing: namely, that insofar as Woolf derives a model of perception, recollection, and transmission from her experience of shock and dissociation, "her" illness, as Lee suggests, is divorced from her medical condition. If Woolf's illness has become her language, then we must think in Lacanian terms of her language as being structured like an illness. That is, Woolf's language is structured around the notion of shock, followed by transmission.

In "A Sketch of the Past," Woolf articulates both a model of mind and memory in which transmission is privileged over communication and a mode of fiction-making that aims at mimesis rather than at narration. This mimesis, says Perry Meisel, is the job of the modern writer: "not that of idealizing a lost life or nature that was never present to begin with, but to find a way to simulate it even as it accounts for its impossibility" (35). Meisel paraphrases "Modern Fiction," where in 1919 Woolf presents a science of fiction and consciousness, famously describing life as "a luminous halo, a semi-transparent envelope surrounding us from the beginning of consciousness to the end" (*CR*1 150). The matter of fiction, Woolf says, is "the incessant shower of innumerable atoms" that impresses upon the mind "a myriad impressions." The task of fiction, she continues, is to "record the atoms as they fall upon the mind in the order in which they fall," to "trace the pattern, however disconnected and incoherent in appearance, which each sight or incident scores upon the consciousness" (*CR*1 150).

Writing in 1939, however, Woolf recounts her own experience of those showers in more violent terms. In "A Sketch of the Past," she describes trackless stretches of childhood about which she has no memory—a condition she calls "non-being"—that are occasionally broken by moments of violent perception. She cites three of these moments: a fight with her brother Thoby; the perception of a plant in the earth; and the horrifying association of an apple tree with the suicide of a family acquaintance. Woolf confesses that these moments are difficult to describe, and she uses several metaphors to try to convey their effect. The blow from a sledge-hammer is one, a metaphor suggesting the intaglio of fiction-making she describes in the earlier essay. Here, however, the scoring is manifestly deep and violent: more than a delicate incision or a mere sketch of the past, this memory-making is the sudden, forceful gouging of an incident into mental stone. More interesting is Woolf's use of the metaphor of shock: "then, for no reason that I know about, there was a sudden violent shock; something happened so violently that I have remembered it all my life" (*MOB* 71). Most curiously, Woolf says, "I go on to suppose that the shock-receiving capacity is what makes me a writer" (*MOB* 72).

What, then, for Woolf, is the relationship between shock and the task of fiction? Juxtaposing these two essays, written twenty years apart, suggests some answers. In "Modern Fiction," Woolf is talking about perception; in "A Sketch of the Past," she is talking about memory. In both instances, the subject is the impression of stimuli on consciousness, but the stimuli she discusses and the writer's response to them are very different. In "Modern Fiction," stimuli are conceived as a steady, undifferentiated shower, much like the "cotton-wool" of "non-being" she describes in "A Sketch of the Past;" in the latter essay, they are abrupt, discontinuous, and highly differentiated. In the first essay, the writer's task, taken up abstractly and artistically, is to *reproduce* the impression-shower, to *transmit* the dynamics of perception by means of fiction; whereas in the second, the task of the writer—of Woolf, specifically—is to *tell* it, to *explain* it, "to make it real by putting it into words." Words do not create objects—rather, "putting into words" is the laying-down of circuits through which experience can be re-created: that is, by memory. "Making it real" means discovering the hidden pattern, making it whole, and thereby depriving it of its power to hurt.

The fundamental task of narrative is to say, even *in extremis*, "that's how it happened." But Woolf, like other modernist writers, is not content to describe how something happened. Instead, she wishes to come closer to the matter of perception and consciousness, to reproduce not only the pattern but the very act of tracing. The shortcoming of narrative in that view is that it is sequential, and sequentiality is inadequate for recreating the simultaneous, discontinuous, and incoherent shower of sense-impressions. To borrow from another discourse, Woolf's atom-showers are a *sjuzet* for which the story-line's *fabula* is an inadequate representational mode. As Woolf defines it, the task of fiction precedes the placing of these atom-showers into a coherent story. It is like the task of modern physics: to trace the track of atoms with the aid of human instruments and to discover the patterns of waves and ripples, secondarily interpreting the meaning of these tracks.[1]

In "Modern Fiction" and "A Sketch of the Past," Woolf employs an electromechanical metaphor for the primary activity of the mind and the secondary activity of fiction-making, as well as the romantic metaphor of the Aeolian harp, which figures the poet's mind as an instrument for recording the breath of nature and transmitting, transforming, and amplifying it into human language. Both metaphors figure the writer as a seismograph, or perhaps a phonograph: a passive relay of stimuli whose intensity varies from the gentleness of a shower to the sudden violence of a shock. This passive role is notable: it is her *capacity to receive* a "sudden violent shock" that makes Woolf a writer, not the ability to transmit, translate, record, or trace. In "Modern Fiction," it is a "shock" that comes while reading that allows her in her narrative about learning to be a novelist to part company with Joyce, admirable though his method may be, and to choose the path of life over death, the "fertile land" over "the dust and the desert." Like the shock she receives on perceiving the plant in the ground, the shock of opening English masterpieces and being "convinced that there are not only other aspects of life, but more important ones into the bargain" leads to action, to a struggle to break free of constraints (cotton-wool, the ill-fitting vestments of the traditional novel, the dark allure of Russian understanding) and "to contrive means of being free to set down what he chooses" (*CR*1 152). It is the shock of discovering life where it was least expected that recalls her to life, registers experience in memory, furnishes her with the grounds for fiction—the retracing of the atom-showers that ends in a state of satisfaction.

Woolf's "shock of recognition" is the shock of a knowledge that is both psychoanalytic and literary. The subject with such knowledge may recognize either the pattern itself, or only that a pattern exists. Recognizing specific patterns allows one to reconstruct, as though from a silhouette, the original form of a traumatic event. But the recognition may not be so specific; it may only be the recognition of form, or the recognition that a form exists and that therefore something beyond the reach of consciousness is warping what consciousness can perceive.

We must now draw more explicitly the parallel between Woolf's tropes for memory and experience and Freud's figures of trauma—not only in their direct parallel but in their inverse. Woolf's luminous halo resembles nothing so much as the psychic membrane Freud describes in *Beyond the Pleasure Principle*. In Freud's model, traumatic events do not protrude from a cotton-wool background. Rather, they linger, unperceived and unexperienced, beyond the reach of consciousness. But precisely because traumatic events are buried and unavailable, they motivate the relentless memory-search that one might call fiction. When applied to Freud's model, Woolf's task of fiction is to re-create trauma's stimulus upon the membrane of consciousness. There is a crucial difference, however: this attempt at re-creation is directed at a

consciousness—that of the reader—that has never experienced the original stimulus. The task of fiction is therefore fundamentally a traumatic
response: the repeated attempt to declaim an event that has been missed,
in an effort to transmit it to the reader.[2] Woolf pursues this task most
explicitly not in *Mrs. Dalloway*, where the theme of psychic trauma is
embodied in the character of Septimus Smith, but in *The Waves*, where
her formal experiments attempt to convey the dynamics of psychic trauma mimetically.

In attempting to articulate "that's how it happened" and in so doing,
to paraphrase Freud, artfully transform grief into ordinary unhappiness,
narrative embarks on the reclamation quest of romance. Maria DiBattista
calls *The Waves* a kind of romance (153), while also noting "the message
hidden in the beauty of words" that Septimus Smith discovers in *Mrs.
Dalloway*: "The secret signal which one generation passes, under
disguise, to the next is loathing, hatred, despair" (*MD* 134). The dark
message Septimus perceives inheres not in the meaning of the words but
in their beauty—in the quality with which and by which they impinge on
consciousness. Beneath whatever message is borne by content lies an
undecodable, traumatic secret carried by *form*: a secret about the unrep-
resentability of death and the ultimate failure of all mourning to reclaim,
restore, or relieve. For Woolf, as we have seen, the task of fiction is to
transcribe that transgenerational signal and to effect that scoring upon the
mind, a task which obeys trauma's impulse to make the unconscious
conscious. *The Waves*, then, is very far from romance. Its project is one
that rejects romance and recovery, both thematically and in narrative
technique, for the more primal purpose of transmission.

Woolf originally planned to call her thirteenth published work *The
Moths*, and at one point she explicitly likens the figures in the novel to
them: "Their eyes are like moth's wings moving so quickly that they do
not seem to move at all" (*W* 140). Moths are figures *par excellence* for
the death drive, and certainly repetition compulsion is one of this novel's
major themes. But in re-titling her work, Woolf seems to resist the relentless arabesque that Peter Brooks, in *Reading for the Plot,* identifies with
the drive of plotted narrative. Instead of sequential, if turbulent, linearity,
Woolf offers discontinuous juxtaposition as a new mode for accomplish-
ing the task of fiction.

The Waves is Woolf's most formally experimental novel, in two
different senses of the word "formal." In it Woolf makes her most radical

break with the form of traditional plotted narrative, but this break with form also constitutes a highly regular, distinctly patterned form of its own. *The Waves* is divided into nine unnumbered sequences of monologues, the juxtaposed voices of the six nominal characters whose intertwined yet disarticulated lives are the novel's manifest subject matter. Each sequence is preceded by italicized passages Woolf called interludes, which together describe a day's passage of the sun across the sky. Each interlude, in turn, is informally divided into five sub-sections, or movements, always in the same order: the movement of the sun; the waves; the garden; the birds; the light on a house.

The novel thus moves to two different rhythms and in two radically different sorts of time. The slow, sequential passage from dawn to dusk, from birth to death, throws down an ever-changing light on the mindless, rhythmic beating of the waves and the shifting juxtaposition of voices that are isolated, perceiving, and intensely self-aware. Woolf gives the frame-narrative technique a new dimension, for the frame of *The Waves* is not narrative at all, but the abstract concepts of time expressed in a vision of sea and sky. Story line has been abstracted away into a framework on the margins of the rhythmic motion of wavelike streams of consciousness. This double movement is the movement of waves, and of *The Waves*, and for Woolf a figure for the movement of consciousness and memory.

Woolf uses tropes of closure, breakdown, and entrapment throughout the novel to represent narrative as a frustrating sequential modality. Narrative and storytelling are linked to strings, sequences, threads, rising bubbles, and rings, and these linear tropes occur repeatedly in contexts of narrative frustration, where narrative is employed to some end and fails. Over and over again, *The Waves* reenacts a drama of narrative breakdown, representing and embodying the failure of narrative to establish a bond with others or with a luminous, unconstrained self. The repeated drama and its numerous leitmotifs illustrate that narrative fails because it is ultimately solipsistic.

Though *The Waves* is, at first glance, a novel without a narrator, one voice is given a prominent place: Bernard's. His is the voice that begins and ends the novel; it inaugurates all but two of the sections; and the final section belongs to Bernard's voice alone. One must therefore pay particular attention to Bernard's voice when examining the formal structure of the work. *Narrator* identifies Bernard's way of thinking and speaking; no other character in the novel—not even Neville, the poet—is so closely and consistently identified with a communicative mode. Bernard is the narrative leader: throughout the novel he tells stories which attempt to explain and to heal. To align Bernard with the role of narrator is not to say he plays this role in a conventional way, nor is it to say simply that Bernard's voice is in any way equivalent to Woolf's—that his is any sort of omniscient voice in the text.[3] Jean Guiguet, whom Maria DiBattista calls "one of the earliest and best of Woolf's French critics," comes closest when he argues that the six speakers in *The Waves* "are not six voices in search of characters, but a single being in search of voices" (285). The voice Bernard embodies, then, is the narrator's voice, or the voice of narrative: he is the spokesman for the novel form.

Throughout *The Waves*, Woolf places Bernard in scenes in which he both enacts and reflects upon the breakdown of narrative. In Woolf's pursuit of the task of fiction, this breakdown is a trauma of language, and as she deploys it in *The Waves*, it becomes a figure, a language of trauma, an illness of language transformed into a language of illness through which she attempts to articulate, to transmit, what narrative cannot.

One early passage in *The Waves* is paradigmatic for narrative and its breakdown. The scene is the boys' school; the children are lying in a ring in the grass after chapel. Neville speaks:

> "And now," said Neville, "let Bernard begin. Let him burble on, telling us stories, while we lie recumbent. Let him describe what we have all seen so that it becomes a sequence. Bernard says there is always a story. I am a story. Louis is a story. . . .
> "But Bernard goes on talking. Up they bubble—images. 'Like a camel,' . . . 'a vulture.' The camel is a vulture; the vulture a camel; for Bernard is a dangling wire, loose, but seductive. . . . And then we all feel Percival lying heavy among us. . . . Bernard at once perceives that we are bored. I detect a certain effort, an extravagance in his phrase, as if he said 'Look!' but Percival says 'No.' For he is always the first to detect insincerity; and is brutal in the extreme. The sentence tails off feebly. Yes, the appalling moment has come when Bernard's power fails him and there is no longer any sequence and he sags and twiddles a bit of string and falls silent. . . . Among the tortures and devastations of life is this then—our friends are not able to finish their stories." (*W* 37–39)

Bernard is the embodiment of, and chief spokesman for, the narrative mode, which for him articulates a sequentiality that is both ever-present and always necessary. With his storytelling, Bernard effects transformations, from visible to audible, from sight to story, from non-sequential to sequential. He is a filter that takes common experience and articulates it in a sequence. Bernard believes (as a child, at least) not only in the omnipresence of story and sequence, but in the ineluctable bond between story and person: stories are stories about persons, and persons are (nothing but) stories. At the meta-narrative level, of course, Bernard is right: Louis, Neville, and the rest are only stories contained within Woolf's novel. But this articulation of the difference between person and character is only one of the many indications within the novel of the characters' uncanny awareness of themselves as characters, as constructs of words.

Bernard burbles; *burble* (here functioning as a portmanteau combination of Bernard and bubble) is Neville's term for Bernard's technique of turning bubbling images into sequential phrases. Neville's tone throughout the passage, and throughout the novel, is dismissive of Bernard and his compulsion to name. To Neville, Bernard is a "dangling wire, loose, but seductive," like a trap: one can step in the loop and be caught, fixed, and named. Neville would like to fix his perceptions *as they are*, without explicit names: "If *that* blue could stay for ever; if *that* hole could remain for ever; if *this* moment could stay for ever—" (emphasis mine). For Neville, the clouds have no names; they are metonymic for the whole world's "flowing and curving." But Bernard's narrative seductively links narrative to nameless shapes and turns them into images: "Up they bubble—images. 'Like a camel,' . . . 'a vulture.'" Bernard's talking binds images to perceptions; as metaphors and similes do, it creates identifications. Neville's "images" are thus an interpreted, processed, signified form of "what we have all seen." Neville is critical of Bernard's nominal bindings, but he is caught by them, for it is he who turns Bernard's similes into tautological metaphors: "The camel is a vulture; the vulture a camel." His circular metaphors work like the disheveling breeze, returning the clouds to their indeterminate state. Neville resists Bernard's narrative traps by turning them, but he is seductively freed by them as well: "One floats, too, as if one were that bubble; one is freed; I have escaped, one feels" (*W* 38). The trope of escape turns when Percival disrupts Bernard's spell. Percival's "No" stops the seduction, prevents the capture. As *perce-voile*, the veil-piercer, Percival is at this moment a figure for psychic trauma in the Freudian sense—a rupture of the psychic membrane and the implantation of an external prohibition within the psychic apparatus in such a way that it cannot be abreacted.

Percival's prohibition comes, notably, at the moment when Bernard's burbling becomes "insincere," when Neville detects "a certain effort, an extravagance of phrase." Extra-vagance, in the sense of "wandering away," repeatedly derails Bernard's attempts at narrative seduction, whose failure becomes a thematic motif. In the novel's opening pages, for example, Bernard tries to comfort Susan, distraught at seeing Jinny kiss Louis, by focusing her attention on a beetle crawling in the dappled light beneath trees. Bernard encourages Susan to identify with the beetle: "You see the beetle *too* carrying off a leaf on its back" (*W* 15). The beetle is a link to the earlier scene of witnessed seduction, bearing on its back an element of the vegetal nature Louis had imagined himself becoming moments before. The rustling leaves are associated with Louis and Susan in the preceding pages, and the beetle scurrying back and forth with Jinny running back and forth in confusion, not knowing the source of the rustling.

Bernard's attempt to break Susan's single-minded desire "to possess one single thing" is subtle. Her desire, he suggests, will waver as its single cathexis splits, through metaphorical association, into leaf and beetle, Jinny and Louis. Once again, the ability to name, to identify, to pin down with words, is given power—in this case, the power to heal: "and then words, moving darkly, in the depths of your mind will break up this knot of hardness" (*W* 15). At the same time that he urges a healing dissolution of the single "knot of hardness" with *words*, Bernard also proffers a seductive merger by means of *phrases*. "We melt into each other with phrases," he tells her. "We make an unsubstantial territory." But his phrase-making leaves Susan behind:

> "I see the beetle," said Susan. "It is black, I see; it is green, I see; I am tied down with single words. But you wander off; you slip away; you rise up higher, with words and words in phrases." (*W* 16)

Bernard suggests that he and Susan make a territory, but they (or more precisely Bernard, because Susan cannot follow his flight of phrases) do not constitute the space so much as create it. Through Bernard's extravagant phrases, the unsubstantial territory becomes Elvedon, a secret and guarded place of (female) writing. Bernard turns the magical ring of writing into a narrative, a sort of boyish adventure story of gardener guards who will capture them. Their venture into this narrative space is a forbidden intrusion, but it is also, crucially, like the feelings and sense-impressions Bernard forever tries to nail down with phrases. By the end of the passage, Bernard has forgotten Susan completely, lost as he is in his attempt to pin down sense impressions:

> I hear nothing. That is only the murmur of the waves in the air. That is a wood-pigeon breaking cover in the tops of the beech trees. The pigeon . . . beats the air with wooden wings. (*W* 18)

Once again we can see Bernard's technique in action. As his phrases burble, *murmur* becomes *breaking* becomes *beats*; what starts as a matter-of-fact observation ("that is a wood-pigeon breaking cover") becomes a narrative figure ("the pigeon beats the air with wooden wings"). Susan, on the other hand, remains "tied down with single words." "I see the beetle," says Susan. "It is black, I see; it is green, I see." The beetle appears to change color because it is moving in and out of the wavering light, but Susan's speech is reminiscent of Benjy Compson's in Faulkner's *The Sound and the Fury* in its phenomenological lack of causal connectivity. Whereas Bernard is an agent of language, trying to pin things down with phrases, Susan seems to be language's victim, but her single words are much closer to an unmediated, impressionistic, phenomenological reporting of sense-impressions than are Bernard's figures.

Bernard fails because his extravagant language leaves Susan behind. Once again, phrases are associated with rising and tumescence. "Now you trail away," says Susan; "[N]ow you mount like an air-ball's string" (18). She, on the other hand, remains grounded in simple, concrete declarations: "Here is the garden. Here is the hedge." Later in the novel, Susan recalls this scene and again tries to articulate the contrast between words and phrases and the failure of narrative to heal or anneal, to be comprehensive or even comprehensible:

> The only sayings I understand are cries of love, hate, rage and pain. . . . I love with such ferocity that it kills me when the object of my love shows by a phrase that he can escape. He escapes, and I am left clutching at a string that slips in and out among the leaves on the tree-tops. I do not understand phrases. (*W* 131–132)

Phrasemaking signifies an ability to escape from the ferocious pre-linguistic world of primal cries. Susan's ferocious love is self-consuming, oroboros-like: it turns upon her and "kills" her when her love object escapes her line. Phrases are the string Susan uses to try to capture the beloved; they are also inherent in the love object. They can show, like the flip of a fish's tail or like a cat landing on its feet, that the love object is "slippery," agile, not to be caught or pinned down. But it is crucial for our understanding in this argument to note that this is the very technique of *The Waves*: to weave repeated phrases, incidents, and voices together in a fabric of association and recollection. *The Waves* is densely self-referential, to the point of solipsism, and it is to the argument that Bernard and his narrative are inherently and representatively solipsistic that I turn next.

Geoffrey Hartman suggests that "there is only one fully developed character in Mrs. Woolf's novels, and that is the completely expressive or androgynous mind" (38). We have seen how Bernard occupies a central place in *The Waves*; he is, to modify Hartman slightly, the completely expressive *narrative* mind, and in showing Bernard repeatedly tying himself in knots, Woolf seems to be suggesting that narrative breaks down when it becomes self-consciously self-referential, that the rupture thus produced in an ego constituted by narrative consciousness is a gap that narrative cannot explain. Once again, this gap is the gap of psychic trauma—a phenomenon that is beyond the explanatory reach of narrative but which nevertheless provokes an outpouring of verbal production that attempts to perform what narrative cannot.

Bernard's phrases and sequences constitute not only his stories, but Bernard himself:

> "Had I been born," said Bernard, "not knowing that one word follows another I might have been, who knows, perhaps anything. As it is, finding sequences everywhere, I cannot bear the pressure of solitude. When I cannot see words curling like rings of smoke round me I am in darkness—I am nothing." (*W* 132)

The trope of phrases as rings and strings occurs throughout *The Waves*, where rings are linked to sequences—sequences of words, but also, it appears, to sequence in the abstract, as here, where uterine ring-sequences of language constitute Bernard's self. One passage will serve as an example. At the beginning of section three, Bernard, while at college, finds he cannot express his "integrated" self with the many personae he affects. Bernard is aware that he deliberately constructs public personae, "that I have to effect different transitions; have to cover the entrances and exits of several different men who alternately act their parts as Bernard" (*W* 76). But he also believes in an essential self, detached from his fictional self-constructions and the social situations that produce them:

> But you understand, you, my self, who always comes at a call (that would be a harrowing experience to call and for no one to come; that would make the midnight hollow, and explains the expression of old men in clubs—they have given up calling for a self who does not come). (*W* 77)

To test this hypothesis, Bernard assumes the character of Byron, "that bold and deleterious figure, who, lightly throwing off his cloak, seizes his pen and at once flings off the following letter to the girl with whom he is passionately in love" (*W* 78). He cannot succeed in this project; despite taking "a sip of Byron" to refresh his impressions, "it falls flat. It peters out. I cannot get up steam enough to carry me over the transition. My true self breaks off from my assumed" (*W* 79). He tries again, this time imagining a story in which he is the Byronic hero visiting a country estate. All is well until he must imagine the squire's daughter speaking his name: "I can sketch the surroundings up to a point with extraordinary ease. But can I make it work? Can I hear her voice—the precise tone with which, when we are alone, she says 'Bernard'? And then what next?" (*W* 80).

Concluding that he needs the stimulus of other people to keep his stories going, Bernard contrasts himself with "the real novelist, the perfectly simple human being" who "could go on, indefinitely, imagining. He would not integrate, as I do. He would not have this devastating sense of grey ashes in a burnt-out grate." Bernard gives up for the evening, but not before revealing an uncanny awareness of himself as a literary construct: "which of these people am I? . . . When I say to myself, 'Bernard', who comes?" (*W* 81). Bernard begins the passage confident of his ability to "integrate," which for him seems to mean the ability to maintain, simultaneously, a projected fiction and a central, dispassionate self. But the capacity to integrate leaves open the possibility of disintegration, and the moments of labeling with words, which represent Bernard's entire narrative enterprise, open chasms of uncertainty. Bernard's narrative breakdowns come at moments of interpellation, of calling "Bernard" — solipsistic moments, as here, in which it becomes evident that the "essential self" is no more real than the personae he adopts. The magnitude of this error, of this self-destructive "infinite loop," is not yet evident to Bernard, who is still young and of his class; he can see the ashes of his failed attempt at imagination and still say, "Mrs. Moffat will come and sweep it all up" (*W* 81). The connection between "the real novelist, the perfectly simple human being," the maternal Mrs. Moffat, and Woolf herself is clear. Bernard, like the other characters, is simply a construct built of phrases, just as Bernard's put-on characters are. The narrative mind, be it the fictional mind of Bernard or his Byronic persona, or the narrative mind of Virginia Woolf, cannot construct a narrative that says "that's how it happened"; it must always and inevitably be solipsistically self-referential. And beneath Bernard's solipsistic unease is the darker fear of nihilism, the harrowing experience of giving up calling for a self who does not come. It is its inability to evoke the self to itself that links narrative, as a mode of discourse, to the traumatic in language.

Bernard's summation at the end of *The Waves* is therefore a kind of recapitulation of the narrative and of narrative—an apology of sorts. "Now to sum up," he begins; "now to explain to you the meaning of my life":

> The illusion is on me that something adheres for a moment, has roundness, weight, depth, is completed. This, for the moment, seems to be my life. If it were possible, I would hand it to you entire. I would break it off as one breaks off a bunch of grapes. I would say, 'Take it. This is my life.'(*W* 238)

This has always been Bernard's way: explication—explaining meaning—consists in arithmetic sequence, an addition of parts to make a completed whole which Bernard would now pass on entire. Bernard is in the midst of a self-reflexive mimetic illusion, one closely linked to the myth of Appelles, the Greek painter whose grapes were so realistic birds would peck at them: the illusion that explication, or narrative, has the power to transform his life into something beyond mere representation, something that is present and real and transmissible. This mimetic illusion is supported by the Eucharistic reference—"Take it. This is my life"—at this, the last supper of the book.[4] The reference to the Last Supper underscores the metaphoric (in terms of its etymology) nature of this encounter: it is a communion in which something is passed, transmitted, from one person to another. Deployed in a spoken simile ("as one breaks off a bunch of grapes"), the transmission is inescapably linguistic. As narrative's spokesman, Bernard articulates the desired function of narrative, and the function of narrative desire: to construct, through additive (that is to say, narrative) sequence, a mimetic representation of experience that, having been reified, may be assigned meaning and then be transmitted, or passed, or surrendered, to another.

But this scene shows Bernard with a difference. For the first time he is aware that the unified object of narrative desire is illusory and incommunicable:

> [I]n order to make you understand, to give you my life, I must tell you a story—and there are so many, and so many—stories of childhood, stories of school, love, marriage, death, and so on; and none of them are true. Yet like children we tell each other stories, and to decorate them we make up these ridiculous, flamboyant, beautiful phrases. How tired I am of stories, how tired I am of phrases that come down beautifully with all their feet on the ground! Also, how I distrust neat designs of life that are drawn upon half sheets of notepaper. I begin to long for some little language such as lovers use, broken words, inarticulate words, like the shuffling of feet on the pavement. I begin to seek some design more in accordance with those moments of humiliation and triumph that come now and then undeniably. (*W* 238)

Through the doubtful yearning of its aged spokesman, narrative itself seems to be aware of its own limitations and to call into question the authority of its foundational terms. In order for narrative to compel understanding, to transmit life to another, it must tell a comprehensive and comprehensible story, but the unifying story is unavoidably particulate and fragmentary, and each of the fragments is, in some sense of the word, untrue. Untruth does not here apply to the subject matter of story (life itself), but rather to the truth of story's application to life: narrative cannot be true to life, cannot stand in an isomorphic, mimetic relation to its object. Stories are not straight but always warped; they are not truth but trope, and trope, like narrative, seems ineluctable and limited. Tropes— here figured as phrases—are aesthetic objects that claim some groundedness, some attachment to truth, but they are at the same time both ridiculous and flamboyant decorations, like the naive pastework of a child, and neat formulas, collected and organized during a lifetime's observation, but now revealed to be untrustworthy.

We must pause over "truth" and "trust," for there appears to be a linkage between the neat designs of life that constitute the novelist's notebook and the sort of neatly designed life amenable to narrative description. The whole of life that Bernard would break off and transmit entire is a novelist's illusion of closure, and the sequence of life-stories—childhood, school, love, marriage, death—is, of course, the sequence of *The Waves* itself. Woolf's novel, standing behind Bernard in this final section, is revealed here either as an ironic artifact—it is, in some sense, "untrue"—or as a representative of an alternate modality to narrative. In its radical form, *The Waves* seems both to depict and to embody the new object of Bernard's longing: "some design more in accordance with those moments of humiliation and triumph that come now and then undeniably."

By the end of the final section, Bernard has literally thrown away the book; he has dropped his notebook of phrases kept over a lifetime onto the floor, presumably to be swept up, like his discarded Byronic phrases, by Mrs. Moffat. "I am done," Bernard says, "with phrases" (*W* 295). Like Prospero drowning his book, Bernard rejects the power of illusion—with its illusory power—that has sustained him. In short, Bernard seems to drop his own book and take up Woolf's; to abandon the solid ground of narrative and, in the novel's penultimate gesture, to charge, Faustlike, headlong into *The Waves*.

If *The Waves* is the instantiation of Bernard's desire, then its form constitutes a rejection of narrative itself. For the illusion of, and yearning for, closure is the plot of romance, and although the plot of narrative may be an arabesque, an arabesque is nevertheless a sequence. The task of fiction for Woolf is not to trace this arabesque but to re-create the perceptual patterns that created it. As we have seen, this compulsion to transmit rather than simply to communicate is not the death drive manifest in plotted narrative, but rather the relentless impulse of trauma, whose energies lie buried beyond the reach of narrative. To articulate the dynamics of trauma, *The Waves* seeks a new and paradoxical linguistic form, "a little language such as lovers use, broken words, inarticulate words" (*W* 238).

What, then, is this alternative linguistic form? In examining the four passages that explicitly mention the "little language" (*W* 143, 238, 263, and 295), it is clear that it is not lyric. In one passage, Bernard advocates the sufficiency of the little language over poetry: "Heaven be praised," he tells his wife, "we need not whip this prose into poetry. The little language is enough" (*W* 262). Here, the little language is aligned more closely with prose than with poetry, which Bernard deems excessive for the purpose at hand: as "the little language lovers use," this language seems to have been successfully put to the task of resolving a marital dispute. But as in all the other passages about the little language, this one seems to link it to the description of sense-impressions, such as the clear blue sky outside the window, and to suggest that it, unlike other linguistic forms, offers unmediated access to the phenomenal world.

In the other passages, Bernard links lyric to *phrase* and hence, in the associative web of *The Waves*, to the excessive and the extravagant:

> My book, stuffed with phrases, has dropped to the floor. . . . I need a little language such as lovers use, words of one syllable such as children speak. . . . I need a howl; a cry. When the storm crosses the marsh and sweeps over me where I lie in the ditch unregarded I need no words. Nothing neat. Nothing that comes down with all its feet on the floor. None of those resonances and lovely echoes that break and chime from nerve to nerve in our breasts, making wild music, false phrases. I have done with phrases. (*W* 294-295)

Phrase is a term from music as well as from poetry, and it contains within it connotations of duration, sequence, and closure. The little language, by contrast, is one of immediate sense perception and emotional expression—of communication with an immediacy beyond words.

It is important to notice the conditions under which Bernard feels the need for a new language. Here, and elsewhere, it is at a moment of encounter with turbulent nature. In Bernard's first mention of the little language, at the beginning of his final monologue, he also refers to the imagined experience of lying in a ditch "on a stormy day, when it has been raining":

> I begin to long for some little language such as lovers use, broken words, inarticulate words, like the shuffling of feet on the pavement. I begin to seek some design more in accordance with those moments of humiliation and triumph that come now and then undeniably. (*W* 238-239)

These conditions of "heavy weather" are precisely those celebrated and described in the poetry of the Romantic tradition, but Bernard finds lyricism to be inadequate to the task: lyric produces "resonances and lovely echoes" in a wave-like way, but they are ultimately "false phrases." Thus the need for the little language arises under conditions of the Romantic sublime, but lyric is inadequate for its expression.

To discover the little language of *The Waves*, one might begin with Bernard's invocation at the farewell party for Percival, at the very center of the novel:

> We are drawn into this communion by some deep, some common emotion. Shall we call it, conveniently, 'love'? . . . No, that is too small, too particular a name. We cannot attach the width and spread of our feelings to so small a mark. We have come together . . . to make one thing, not enduring—for what endures?—but seen by many eyes simultaneously. (*W* 126-127)

As always, Bernard is concerned with pinning a name or a phrase on something, this time on "some deep, some common emotion." But note particularly the way Bernard already rejects the phrases "love" and "love of Percival" as signifiers for the convoking emotion. These signifiers he designates "names" and "marks," and they are, he says, too small: too small, we must presume, to signify the emotion we must, self-consciously yet for convenience's sake, call "love." So Bernard, spokesman for narrative, rejects narrative signification and instead proposes action: a convocation for the making of a single transient thing. As Thierry de Duve notes, "at the intersection of magical action and scientific knowledge, artistic making attributes a symbolic power to the things it names, at times gathering together, at times dispersing, human communities" (5), and this idea of multi-perspectival seeing as an act of communal creation is the method, the purpose, of *The Waves* itself. Thus Woolf's little language, while clearly possessing elements of the narrative and the lyric, emphasizes, above all, the dimension of the dramatic.

As if by example, Bernard literally points to a flower on the table. Like Susan's language, this is a deictic language, a language of simple reference. The communal creation of the "whole flower" generates a seven-sided figure, seemingly one of seven different facets that are mirror faces of those seven characters whose perceptions create it. But the figure so generated is not simply an object in space. As Bernard says, it does not endure. It is thus an object of at least four dimensions, encompassing the temporal. And it is still more. For the language that generates the flower—"many-petalled, red, puce, purple-shaded, stiff with silver-tinted leaves"—evokes the phallus, which, in Lacanian language, symbolizes the desire of the Other, another way of naming the Unconscious. The Unconscious, Lacan famously says, is structured like a language, and that language of desire is precisely the little language Bernard and Woolf seek. If, as we proposed at the beginning, Woolf's language is structured like (her) illness, then in waves, and in *The Waves*, Woolf has attempted to fulfill the task of fiction with a language whose form is that of an illness, of trauma. It is a language that escapes the lovely phrases of hegemonic discourses (both medical and critical) by rejecting narrative and reproducing the atomic shock of experience on consciousness in a form outside language.

Like Susan's cries and sayings, like Stephen Dedalus's shout in the street, the little language aspires to be prelinguistic but to have the force of speech. The little language Bernard seeks in the end is oral/aural: the "broken words, inarticulate words, like the shuffling of feet on the pavement" (*W* 238). Bernard fears linguistic trauma—a severance of the paradigmatic from the syntagmatic axis—while also recognizing syntagmatic limits. He therefore proposes a different mapping of the paradigmatic axis: not onto a syntagmatic axis but onto something else. This something else is nothing less than *The Waves*, or, more explicitly, *waves as a form*.

The structure of the interludes offers clues about how to understand and read this new mapping. The movement of the sun is an ineluctable, cyclical synchronicity against which, or by means of which, a different pattern of telling is inscribed. That the movement of the waves is influenced by the moon suggests a gendered opposition of male, linear, solar writing to female, cyclical, lunar writing, but engenderment is only one perspective from which to see this opposition. The waves repeatedly reach up and leave marks on the shore, which they erase as the tide comes in. In this way, they are reminiscent of Bernard's reaching and failing: they enact a persistent attempt to inscribe, in sea-wrack, a mark on the shore. Within the sun pattern, which is a cycle, there is the wave pattern: a patterned repetition. The novel thus inscribes two kinds of repetition, moving in circles and moving in waves, and in the juxtaposition of these two repetitions it highlights the wave pattern: not that the same event (the sun rising, for example) keeps happening, but rather the same kind of sequence keeps happening, something that suggests an underlying binding pattern. Like ripples in a pool, the waves are the result of some perturbation that has occurred in the past. They are an inscription of the event, which is to say, they are history, in a Hegelian, Marxist, or even psychoanalytic sense: material events are nothing more than the instantiation of patterned energy as it moves through time.

This is precisely the linguistic phenomenon Derrida calls *différance*, the endless deferral of the signifier and its progression along the signifying chain. However, the signifying chain is not a chain at all, but a wave-pattern: a series of concentric circles moving out, influencing each other in specific, binary ways. The vibrations are detectable in the history of language (the way the language has been used over time), if one looks carefully enough. Strong perturbations create bigger and longer-lasting waves; the resulting patterned displacement is more abrupt, spreads further, and lasts longer.

Waves differ from facets. Facets (different points of view on the same object) are static and orthogonal; waves are influenced by the juxtaposition of one perspective with another: the sequence cannot be changed without destroying the wave. The energy is driven in one way, in one direction, with one period, one amplitude, and the structure of the energy determines the particle's (character's) behavior when infused with the wave. One is inspired when the wave passes through; it is an oracular moment, a moment of transmission and transfer, for the recipient of this energy is impelled to pass it on. Particles (six particles, for example) can be isolated (not connected) but may still oscillate in a pattern because of the wave-energy passing through them. Thus to read *The Waves*, to read at all, is to read the waves—to become a node in a life pattern that may be apprehended only in moments of shock.

Apprehension, though part of the symptomatology of trauma, seems curiously at odds with it—for, as Caruth points out in her introduction to *Trauma: Explorations in Memory*, it is in the nature of trauma that the traumatic event apprehends the victim: "to be traumatized is precisely to be possessed by an image or event" (4–5). And it is the failure to anticipate the blow that produces psychic trauma, the lack of knowledge or understanding that characterizes trauma's perturbation of memory. If, as Caruth says, trauma brings us to the limits of our understanding, then apprehension seems out of the question.

Apprehend is a paradoxical term, for it means both to understand, to grasp the meaning of (*apprehend* derives from the Latin *ad prehendere*, to grasp, take, or seize) and to anticipate, especially with anxiety, dread,

175

or fear. For the victim of trauma, to apprehend is precisely to fail to understand, to misplace the meaning of an occurrence, either in the present or in the future—or, in particular for us now, in the past. To borrow a term from Paul de Man, apprehension is like *Erkenntnis* (which, de Man says, implies recognition):

> Thought is proleptic: it projects the hypothesis of its possibility into a future, in the hyperbolic expectation that the process that made thought possible will eventually catch up with this projection. The hyperbolic I projects itself as thought in the hope of re-cognizing itself when it will have run its course. (99)

Apprehension is an attempt at recognition: an attempt to recognize in the manifest sign the signifier for an as yet inaccessible signified.

At the beginning of "Modern Fiction," Woolf says that fiction-making is not progressive but circular. The ancient voice of the English past that concludes that essay, the voice of the old woman at the Tube stop in *Mrs. Dalloway*, the shock of the plant growing out of the ground in "A Sketch of the Past," the little language of *The Waves*—all urge the crafting of a fiction that does not understand but simply repeats, simply reproduces, the tracing of life on consciousness—not so that it may be understood, but so that it may be passed on, transmitted, to another person's mind through the act of reading. Woolf's model for modern fiction is not based on the death drive and an abreaction of stimulation, but on the mimetic repetition of perception: her fiction traces the pattern the atom-showers make on the mind. Thus the *narrative,* the line, is not plot, but association—the trace of the reverberations an atom-impact creates in the mind of a character.

If the task of fiction is to trace these patterns, what is the task of reading? For both psychoanalysis and reading, the primary activity is both analytic and synthetic: it entails an archaeological decipherment of the traces fiction has reproduced. Literary knowledge is knowledge of form, and Woolf's fiction teaches a new way to read, demanding a reading not for the plot but for the impacts on the plot; that is, for the rain of impressions on the membrane of consciousness.

The little language of *The Waves*, like the voice from the ground in *Mrs. Dalloway*, then, is the sudden inscription or declamation of some past event heretofore unavailable to consciousness. The past event, unexperienced then, occurs and is registered for the first time now. The voice from the ground is the voice from *beneath* the plot, the sudden projection of a hidden pattern *onto* the plot. As such, the voice of Woolf's fiction creates the ground from which it erupts. Thus Woolf's language is structured like an illness; it traces the monotonous patter of cotton-wool-gathering atoms and also the sudden shocks, the abruptions that give pattern to the whole.

Notes

1. There have been several studies of the importance of the new physics in Woolf's work. For the relevance of quantum mechanics to the last three novels, see Friedman and Donley, and Killen; later papers have traced the influence of post-Newtonian physics to earlier work (see, for example, Clark, Hussey, Narey, Yom).

2. I have derived the rhetoric of claiming from the work of Cathy Caruth, whose *Unclaimed Experience: Trauma and the Possibility of History* is a starting-point for the present study. For a fuller exploration of the phenomenon of traumatic declaiming and its relation to modernist fiction, see my "Outraged Recapitulation and Artful Garrulousness."

3. Lucio Ruotolo is one critic who cautions against such an easy equation, while Jane Marcus makes Bernard the avatar of "the white male Western author" ("Britannia" 228). My reading treads close to Marcus's equation without, I hope, being quite so didactic.

4. This "last supper" is linked to the final supper for Percival in section four. Both scenes call attention to the modern quality of the setting: the door opening and closing, people passing in and out. In the first scene, Percival is the Christ figure, poised for a journey on which he will become an ironic sacrificial victim for the British Empire (though Bernard is, in this scene, the Bridegroom who presides over the communion and discovers his identity: "I am Bernard"). In the second scene Bernard has become the Christ figure, like Percival poised on the threshold of a journey to battle with death.

GUNPOWDER PLOTS: SEXUALITY AND CENSORSHIP IN WOOLF'S LATER WORKS
Patricia Moran

When Woolf first conceived of a sequel *to A Room of One's Own* in 1931, she imagined this new work would address "the sexual life of women" *(D3: 6)*, a subject that struck her as possessing incendiary potential: "I'm quivering and itching to write my-whats it to be called?—'Men are like that?'—no that's too patently feminist: the sequel then, for which I have collected enough powder to blow up St Pauls" *(D4: 77)*. Yet the various texts that arguably emerged from Woolf's engagement with "the sexual life of women"—"Professions for Women," *The Pargiters* (abandoned and published posthumously), *The Years,* and *Three Guineas*—play down or subordinate women's relationship to their corporeality. Instead, in these texts Woolf shifts her focus to the ways in which the middle-class woman's acculturation teaches her to censor her physicality, a censorship that typically results not only in female silence about physical experience, but in an atrophied or attenuated relationship to physicality altogether. These texts are also marked by increasingly negative assessments of maternity and female heterosexuality; and while Woolf at times condemns the cult of chastity in *The Years* and *Three Guineas,* she herself moves toward a valorization of the single or asexual woman—or the aged woman who Woolf imagines has outlived her sexuality—in her essays and fiction (e.g. Eleanor in *The Years* and Miss La Trobe and Lucy in *Between the Acts).* The revolutionary plots which were to blow up St. Pauls did not materialize.

What happened to the revolutionary fervor with which Woolf opened her last decade of writing? Why did Woolf never inscribe the "sexual life of women"? Or, perhaps more accurately, why did her inscriptions take such an attenuated and fragmentary bent? In tracing Woolf's revisions from *The Pargiters* to *The Years,* critics such as Charles G. Hoffman, Mitchell A. Leaska, and Grace Radin have suggested that Woolf's aesthetic principles influenced the removal or dilution of didactic and polemical passages on female sexuality. Such deletions would be consistent with Woolf's lifetime conviction that anger and didacticism damaged works of art and betrayed the personal grievances of the author; after all, she wrote a friend, "a novel is an impression not an argument" *(L5: 91)*. Still, another set of aesthetic principles might have governed the surviving traces of Woolf's original plan to examine "the sexual life of women," something we might call the aesthetics of sexual trauma. *The Years* and *Between the Acts* both feature a specific traumatic event which then reverberates throughout the text in question: in *The Years,* the six-year-old Rose encounters an exhibitionist on her forbidden trip to and from a toy store, an encounter which haunts her throughout the rest of her life; in *Between the Acts,* the thirty-nine-year old Isa reads in a newspaper about the gang rape of a young girl, and this shocking account intrudes upon her thoughts the rest of the novel's day. These scenes of trauma differ from those Woolf depicts in earlier novels: while not as debilitating as shell shock is to Septimus Smith in *Mrs. Dalloway,* for example, these sexual shocks are traumatic enough to alter irrevocably the characters to whom they occur.[1] The effect of traumatic sexual experience, moreover, reaches well beyond the individual woman: in *The Years* and other texts of this period, Woolf posits an evolutionary model of traumatic affect, whereby other female family members seem to "inherit" unconscious memory traces—and with those traces, a concomitant atrophy of sexuality and physicality.

Hence I propose that we read Woolf's "muting" of her critique in a somewhat different light than has hitherto been suggested: since the "sexual life" of English middle-class women meant for Woolf its abrogation and subsequent attenuation, her fictional methods needed to convey the process of repression that turned women's sexual desires into the shameful and guilty emotions she described as "subterranean instincts." As Grace Radin points out, Woolf's reading of Turgenev during her early work on *The Years* functions as a commentary on what Woolf herself was trying to do;[2] significantly, what Woolf admired in Turgenev was his habit of developing complex biographies for his characters, then eliminating most of the details, only allowing the essential aspects of the character to survive in the published version. This process of editing and elimination meant that "the writer states the essential and lets the reader do the rest," Woolf notes; the reader responds to what is "only a birds eye view of the pinnacle of an iceberg" *(D4: 173).* This conception of a submerged narrative foundation, invisible to the reader's eye but demanding the reader's active engagement with what is simultaneously essential and absent, seems particularly useful in considering Woolf's depictions of sexual trauma in her writing in the thirties; what becomes immediately obvious is that many of Woolf's female characters—not just the traumatized Rose or Isa—exhibit classic symptoms of shame when female sexual experience or desire is at issue. The tangled roots of shame and traumatic sexual experience, then, underpin Woolf's treatment of adult female characters; their invisible presence is key to understanding Woolf s revolutionary project of exploring "the sexual lives of women."

"What is the word for so dumb and mixed a feeling?"

The explicit connections between traumatic sexual experience and damaged female lives that Woolf drew in the thirties developed out of her intensive examination of her own sexuality, an examination spurred in large part by her new-found friendship in this decade with Ethel Smyth. Smyth's passionate response to and identification with the polemic of *A Room of One's Own* caused her to contact Woolf—together they delivered talks about the problems facing women artists.[3] It was in a letter to Smyth that Woolf first identified what she would later call the source of her artistic vision, her "shock-receiving capacity": "I have been thinking at a great rate—that is with profuse visibility," she told Smyth. "Do you find that is one of the effects of a shock—that pictures come up and up and up, without bidding or control?" *(L5: 334)*. And it was at the end of this decade—and during the writing of *Between the Acts*—that Woolf apparently recovered a specific memory of sexual abuse at the hands of her half-brother, a process of recognition and recovery that arguably emerged from her engagement with "the sexual life of women."[4] In the two brief discussions of this experience—one in a letter to Smyth, the other in the autobiographical sketch Woolf left unfinished before her suicide—Woolf connects sexual abuse to female speech and reticence in ways consistent with theoretical writing on trauma.[5] At the same time, she also questions the origins and meaning of the persistent and disabling sense of shame that pervades her memories of this event. In the first of these accounts, the letter to Smyth, Woolf writes,

> I'm interested that you can't write about masturbation. That I understand. What puzzles me is how this reticence co-habits with your ability to talk openly magnificently, freely about—say H.B. I couldn't do one or the other. But as so much of life is sexual—or so they say—it rather limits autobiography if this is blacked out. It must be, I suspect, for many generations, for women, for its like breaking the hymen—if thats the membrane's name—a painful operation, and I suppose connected with all sorts of subterranean instincts. I still shiver with shame at the memory of my half-brother, standing me on

> a ledge, aged about 6, and so exploring my private parts. Why should
> I have felt shame then? *(L6: 459-60)*

For Woolf, to speak about female sexual experience is analogous to the rupturing of the hymen and the loss of one's chastity, as I have shown elsewhere ("Flaw"). Here, I wish to focus on Woolf's enduring inability to account for the shame she (re)experiences in recalling this memory: "I still shiver with shame . . . Why should I have felt shame then?" she wonders. At the same time that this unaccountable shame from the past permeates her body, causing a corporeal reaction some fifty years after its originary cause, Woolf enacts the way in which censorship and repression converge at the site of her naming of female sexual experience: "as so much of life is sexual—or *so they say*—it rather limits autobiography if this is blacked out" (emphasis added). Even as Woolf comments on a constraint based upon repression/censorship, then, she replays it: an unnamed "they" say life is sexual, whereas Woolf apparently speaks from the assumed standpoint of an asexual woman whose experience has been blacked out.

Woolf was, of course, in the process of writing the autobiographical "A Sketch of the Past," wherein she first describes the scene of her abuse by her half-brother Gerald and her reaction to it in a passage dated April 1939:

> I remember how I hoped that he would stop; how I stiffened and wrig-
> gled as his hand approached my private parts. But it did not stop. His
> hand explored my private parts too. I remember resenting, disliking
> it—what is the word for so dumb and mixed a feeling? It must have
> been strong, since I still recall it. This seems to show that a feeling
> about certain parts of the body; how they must not be touched; how it
> is wrong to allow them to be touched; must be instinctive. *(MOB* 69)

Woolf tries to account for an emotion that evades description, a single "word" that somehow could contain so "dumb and mixed a feeling." Her explanation for this evasive feeling, moreover, turns the blame upon herself: it was wrong of her to allow herself to be touched, as if she had choice and control of the matter. And, even more interesting, she moves the question of shame away from a personal reaction to a broader, more generalized, evolutionary inheritance.

As in her letter to Smyth, Woolf puzzles over her mute reaction of shame, finally concluding that it derives from what she calls in that letter "subterranean instincts." Woolf links this "instinctive" reaction generally to female silence, as well as to her own life-long "looking-glass shame," in which the compulsive looking at her own image produced a deep sense of shame and guilt (*MOB* 68). She traces her dissociation from corporeal pleasure to these experiences: "this ["inherited dread"] did not prevent me from feeling ecstasies and raptures spontaneously and intensely and without any shame or the least sense of guilt, so long as they were disconnected with my own body" (*MOB* 68).

I do not intend to dwell upon the biographical aspects of trauma in Woolf's life, which have been much discussed (e.g. DeSalvo, McNaron). Instead, I wish to draw attention to how Woolf's descriptions correspond to theoretical models of traumatic memory and shame before proceeding to a discussion of how Woolf fashioned a narrative aesthetic in the nineteen-thirties that would accommodate sexually traumatic events and that would, simultaneously, extend the affect of traumatic sexual experience into an "inherited dread" and "subterranean instinct" reaching deep into the corporeal experiences of Woolf's fictional middle-class women. To begin with, Woolf's elimination of clear causal connections for her characters' traumatic reactions is consistent with what theorists know about how the mind reacts to traumatic events. Traumatic memory differs from what theorists label "narrative memory": the latter "consists of mental constructs, which people use to make sense out of experience" (van der Kolk and van der Hart 160); ordinary events can typically be integrated into subjective assessment almost automatically, without conscious awareness. Traumatic events, however, cannot:

> [F]rightening or novel experiences may not easily fit into existing cognitive schemes and either may be remembered with particular vividness or may totally resist integration.
>
> Under extreme conditions, existing meaning schemes may be entirely unable to accommodate frightening experiences, which causes the memories of these experiences to be stored differently and not be available under ordinary conditions: it becomes dissociated from conscious awareness and voluntary control. (van der Kolk and van der Hart 160)[6]

Traumatic events exist in a kind of time lag: they are not experienced fully by the victim at the time of the trauma, yet they recur with startling intensity, with a compulsive force over which the victim is powerless. These memories remain unnarratable: they "lack verbal narrative and context" and instead "are encoded in the form of vivid sensations and images" (Herman 31). Traumatic events *possess* their victims, moreover, forcing them to relive their terrorizing moments of self dispossession. Roberta Culbertson has written that, instead of normal memory, victims experience a series of "body memories" that accompany the threefold aspects of trauma—the numbness at the time of victimization, the absorption of the perpetrator's message, and the reduction to a survival mode of existence:

> These memories of the body's responses to events are primary, prior to any narrative, and they may well surpass the victim's narrative ability because they pass beyond his knowledge. Memories of these split bits of experience are for this reason intrusive and incomprehensible when they reappear: there is nothing to be done with them. They obey none of the standard rules of discourse: they are the self's discourse with itself and so occupy that channel between the conscious and the unconscious that speaks a body language. They appear at first when the chatter dies down, then more and more forcefully, as if they will come out, will be eliminated by the body. But they are fragments, not something told. (178)

Culbertson enacts the difference between the narrativization of trauma "something told"—and the fragmented intrusive remnants of actual traumatic memory by embedding within her essay several autobiographical passages about her own childhood sexual abuse. Most of these passages are logical accounts with clear beginnings, middles, and ends; Culbertson inserts these events in time and provides a retrospective meaning for them within the context of the essay and her present life. Several passages, however—jumbles of sensations, colors, emotions—illustrate the difference between *representations* of trauma and their actual felt and fragmentary "reality": traumatic memories do not make sense, can never make sense, for the very reason that they exist in a kind of limbo, the "channel between the conscious and the unconscious that speaks a body language." The victim in effect translates that body language into speech and story, reassembling the shards of memory into narrative—much as Freud first described the process in *Studies in Hysteria* in 1895. The story that results is just that, something that can be told to another.

In fact, writers on trauma such as Judith Herman, Suzette Henke, Dori Laub, and James Pennebaker stress the necessity for the victim's creating a narrative of the traumatic event, taking "fragmented components of frozen imagery and sensation" and reassembling them into "an organized, detailed, verbal account, oriented in time and historical content" (Herman, *Trauma* 177). In part, creating a narrative enables the victim to recover the emotional affect: "the patient must reconstruct not only what happened but also what she felt," Herman writes. "The description of emotional states must be as painstakingly detailed as the description of facts" (177). Here, Herman goes back to Freud, for in his Clark lectures on psychoanalysis in 1924 Freud stressed the same point: the hysteric cannot get rid of her symptom just by recounting the traumatic episode which underpinned it; the emotional affect must emerge in order for the symptom to subside and disappear. For Laub, creating a narrative is a way of counteracting the alterity of traumatic memories:

> The traumatic event, although real, took place outside the parameters of "normal" reality, such as causality, sequence, place and time. The trauma is thus an event that has no beginning, no ending, no before, no during and no after. This absence of categories that define it lends it a quality of "otherness," a salience, a timelessness and a ubiquity that puts it outside the range of associatively linked experiences, outside the range of comprehension, of recounting and of mastery. Trauma survivors live not with memories of the past, but with an event that could not and did not proceed through to its completion, has no ending, attained no closure, and therefore, as far as its survivors are concerned, continues into the present and is current in every respect. ("Truth" 69)

Hence Laub argues that the victim must "re-externalize" the event by articulating and transmitting the story to a listener and empathic witness, "and then take it back again, inside" (69). Crucial to Laub's argument is the listener: "The listener . . . is a party to the creation of knowledge . . . The testimony to the trauma thus includes its hearer, who is, so to speak, the blank screen on which the event comes to be inscribed for the first time" (57). According to Laub, then, the story does not exist and cannot be told in the absence of this empathic witness: "the absence of an *addressable other,* an other who can hear the anguish of one's memories and thus affirm and recognize their realness, annihilates the story" (68, emphasis in the original). Suzette Henke has extended this model of testimony to include writing, what she calls "scriptotherapy" (*Shattered* xii); the person who writes of trauma must address another, and indeed, writing may actually accentuate the benefits of disclosure in so far as that writing requires orientation in time, the ordering of events, and the creation of a narrative.

These models of the dialectical composition of testimony provide an important tool for distinguishing between Woolf's biographical accounts of sexual abuse and her portrayal of scenes of sexual trauma in *The Years* and *Between the Acts.* As I have shown elsewhere, Smyth does function as an empathic listener, an "addressable other," in exactly the manner Laub delineates; she was arguably Woolf's most important correspondent and sounding board in the thirties, someone with whom Woolf discussed, among other things, sexuality, mental illness, and suicide dreams. Woolf's letters to Smyth and her unfinished reminiscences demonstrate both the traumatic content of her memories—the fragmentary, intrusive, corporeal qualities identified by trauma theorists—and Woolf's ability and willingness to embed these memories in narrative, adding, for example, chronology and speculation about possible consequences (e.g. looking-glass shame and her inability to enjoy pleasures connected with the body). But the therapeutic narrative of trauma is not what Woolf creates in *The Years* and *Between the Acts.* Here Woolf focuses on "iconic" scenes of sexual trauma, particularized sets of images and bodily representations that crystallize the experience (Herman 38): these scenes intrude upon and rupture the narrative in a way that mimics traumatic experience and that refuses integration. Hence the reader bears witness in only the most limited way: instead of becoming a conduit for narrative coherence, as in Laub's or Henke's models, in reading about the traumatic event and its aftermath we are forced to experience the traumatic event as it functions for the character. We too encounter intrusive and recurring fragmentary memories that remain static, unexplained, incoherent. Given Woolf's customary anxiety about "the reader on the other side of the page," it seems important to consider what these intrusive, iconic memories accomplish in terms of Woolf's goal of inscribing "the sexual life of women."

In these last two novels, significantly, Woolf relegates traumatic experience to a modality of memory that contrasts with the models of memory she offers as "normative." Woolf develops two models of memory in *The Years*: the first model posits an "I" as a knot at the center of experience, a model Eleanor enacts in "drawing on the blotting-paper, digging little holes from which spokes radiated. Out and out they went; thing followed thing; scene obliterated scene" (*Y* 367). Here the model of memory is additive, broadening out from and glossing a primary sensory self or ego.[7] The second model does not foreground the "knot" but rather examines the interplay between the multiple strata of past memories and the present moment, a model that Woolf typically employs to depict inter-subjective relationships. When North meets Sarah and Maggie after many years, for example, he finds that "At first he scarcely remembered them. The surface sight was strange on top of his memory of them, as he had seen them years ago" (*Y* 346); later in the same episode, he wonders whether there was "always . . . something that came to the surface, inappropriately, unexpectedly, from the depths of people, and made ordinary actions, ordinary words, expressive of the whole being" (*Y* 349). The past lies beneath and glosses the present moment; significantly, the "something" that comes to the surface suggests that "knot" or "center" in the web of Eleanor's drawing, a coherent register of personality.

Rose's traumatic memories, by contrast, exist in the isolated medium of traumatic, "iconic" images that remain solely her own, recalling Culbertson's description of traumatic memory as the "self's discourse with itself" (178). After Rose first sees the exhibitionist, a sight that Woolf presents imagistically and in the more immediate format of free indirect discourse—"he sucked his lips in and out. He made a mewing noise. But he did not stretch his hands out at her; they were unbuttoning his clothes" (*Y* 29)—Rose experiences a traumatic nightmare, and then finds herself incapable of narrating the experience: "'I saw . . . ' Rose began. She made a great effort to tell her the truth; to tell [Eleanor] about the man at the pillar-box. 'I saw . . . ' she repeated. But here the door opened and Nurse came in" (*Y* 42). Many years later Rose again tries to narrate the trauma and again fails. A chance action recalls her past: suddenly "she saw Eleanor sitting with her account books; and she saw herself go up to her and say, 'Eleanor, I want to go to Lamley's.'"

> Her past seemed to be *rising above* her present. And for some reason she wanted to talk about her past; to tell them something about herself that she had never told anybody, something hidden. She paused, gazing at the flowers in the middle of the table without seeing them. There was a blue knot in the yellow glaze she noticed. (*Y* 166-67, emphasis added)

In contrast to North's encounter with Sarah and Maggie, when he feels the present float on top of the past, Rose's past "rises above" the present, dominates it, dominates the knot in the center, returning Rose to the perceptual, traumatic experience of her childhood. The knot Rose sees outside herself, furthermore, suggests the splitting and dissociation typi-

cal of traumatic memory: The traumatic event possesses her and dispos-
sesses the self, to use Laub's and Culbertson's language. No wonder,
then, in the same passage, when Martin comments "What awful lives
children live!" turning to his sister for affirmation—"Don't they,
Rose?"—she answers, "Yes . . . And they can't tell anybody" (*Y* 159).

Rose never does succeed in narrating her traumatic encounter to any
other character, a fact that gains significance from Eleanor's apprehension of the therapeutic model of narrative sharing: "sharing things lessens
things . . . Give pain, give pleasure an outer body, and by increasing the
surface diminish them," she thinks to herself late in the novel (*Y* 352).
The movement Woolf charts here is precisely that described by Herman,
Laub, Pennebaker, and others: the translation of inner experience to
narrative—with its concomitant requirements of chronology, empathic
witnessing, the reclamation of emotional affect—results in the attenuation and diminishing of painful memories at best, their management and
containment at least. Rose herself seems to understand the necessity of
narration: in the chapter in which she finds herself possessed by the traumatic return of the past, she protests to her cousins that "talk" is "the only
way we have of knowing each other" (*Y* 171). Yet Rose does not succeed
in giving pain a surface life, an outer body, and hence deep in the strata
of her memory she seems to retain vivid and fixed images of her traumatic experience. Indeed, Rose's inarticulate immersion in the traumatic
memory illustrates Dori Laub's sense of trauma's alterity, its "otherness,"
its "timelessness and ubiquity"; because such memory exists outside
normative narrative and chronological schemes, it "continues into the
present and is current in every respect" (69). By extension, her experience
remains unintegrated in the book: because she never "works through" the
experience, it remains an unchanging moment of stasis within the book's
shifting and mutable depictions of the multiple strata of the past. If indeed
talk "is the only way we have of knowing each other," Rose remains radically unknown.

"Why should i have felt shame then?"

I want to return to the question of shame that Woolf poses in conjunction with her own autobiographical account of sexual trauma. For the
opening section of *The Years* suggests that sexuality is both foreground-
ed and denied for the female characters in ways that embed sexual desire

and the female body in profound and inexplicable contexts of shame. Hence Rose's traumatic encounter with the exhibitionist—which she keeps to herself initially out of a sense of guilt and shame for defying her sister's instructions that she not go out alone—is only the most overt and explicit version of the shame affect that becomes associated with female sexuality.

Interest in shame has gathered momentum in recent decades, fueled by the work of Helen Block Lewis, Leon Wurmser, and Andrew P. Morrison, and by the revival and extension of the affect theorist Silvan Tomkins in the work of Donald L. Nathanson, Gershen Kaufman, and others, including Eve Sedgwick and Adam Frank, whose 1995 edition of *Shame and Its Sisters: A Silvan Tomkins Reader* notably brought shame into the mainstream of literary criticism. As Liz Constable notes in her excellent overview of shame theory, Helen Block Lewis's pathbreaking work clearly delineates two poles of the shame experience, one intrapsychic, the other intersubjective (although the terminology is that of recent relational psychoanalysis, particularly that of Jessica Benjamin).[8] Lewis writes,

> Because the self is the focus of awareness in shame, "identity" imagery is usually evoked. At the same time that this identity imagery is registering as one's own experiences, there is also vivid imagery of the self in the other's eyes. This creates a "doubleness of experience," which is characteristic of shame. Shame is the vicarious experience of the other's negative evaluation. In order for shame to occur, there must be a relationship between the self and the other in which the self cares about the other's evaluation. Fascination with the other and sensitivity to the other's treatment of the self render the self more vulnerable in shame. ("Shame" 107-8)

An actual witness or judge need not be present; Benjamin Kilbourne writes that, "Since shame is at bottom shame about the self, felt in interaction with an other, I am ashamed as I imagine I appear to you . . . shame deals not only with appearances (i.e., how I appear to you), but also with *imagined* appearances (i.e., how I *imagine* I appear to you), shame allows me to realize that I am that object that another is looking at and judging" (38). Similarly, the feminist philosopher Sandra Lee Bartky calls shame "the distressed apprehension of the self as inadequate or diminished: it requires if not an actual audience before whom my deficiencies are paraded, then an internalized audience with the capacity to judge me . . . shame requires the recognition that I *am,* in some important sense, as I am seen to be" (86). Wurmser, too, connects the experience of shame to an internal sense of contempt, that the self is exposed as "failing, weak, flawed, and dirty" ("Shame" 67). The experience of shame is, furthermore, soul-destroying, in part because the self feels radically cut off from the other or from society in general. Lewis calls shame "the 'sleeper' that fuels the irrational guilt whose malignant consequences Freud was the first to describe" ("Shame—the Sleeper" 1). She continues, "The metaphors for shame—'I could have died on the spot'; 'I wanted to sink through the floor' or 'crawl into a hole'—reflect our everyday understanding of shame's momentary lethal impact on the self" ("Shame—the Sleeper" 1). Elsewhere she remarks the diminution of self involved in the shaming experience: "The self feels not in control but overwhelmed and paralyzed. The self feels small, helpless, and childish" ("Shame" 111). Andrew P. Morrison, listing the types of shame-related phenomena—e.g. contempt, put-down, ridicule—adds "mortification": "its root indicates that shame 'kills'" ("The Eye Turned Inward" 287). He continues, " . . . this speaks eloquently to the importance of shame as a potentially overwhelming negative affect, the source . . . of some suicides of later adulthood that reflects the 'guiltless despair' of unrealized ambitions and goals" ("The Eye Turned Inward" 288). Silvan Tomkins eloquently describes the diminishment of and estrangement from self that is at the heart of the shame affect:

> shame is the affect of indignity, of defeat, of transgression, and of alienation. Though terror speaks to life and death and distress makes of the world a vale of tears, yet shame strikes deepest into the heart of man. Shame is felt as an inner torment, a sickness of the soul. It does not matter whether the humiliated one has been shamed by derisive laughter or whether he mocks himself. In either event he feels himself naked, defeated, alienated, lacking in dignity or worth. (*Reader* 133).

Tomkins, the originator of affect theory, links shame affect to curiosity and interest. He notes that shame is experienced more closely, more *as* self, than other affects; it is registered on the face and involves in particular emotional constellations linked to the perceptual register, to seeing and being seen: "Why is shame so close to the experienced self?" he asks. "It is because the self lives in the face, and within the face the self burns brightest in the eyes. Shame turns the attention of the self and others away from other objects to this most visible residence of self, increases its visibility, and thereby generates the torment of self-consciousness" (*Sedgwick and Frank* 136).

Similarly, Helen Block Lewis writes,

> Shame, which involves more self-consciousness and more self-imaging than guilt, is likely to involve a greater increase in feedback from all perceptual modalities. Shame thus has a special affinity for stirring autonomic reactions, including blushing, sweating, and increased heart rate. Shame usually involves more bodily awareness than guilt, as well as visual and verbal imaging of the self from the other's point of view. ("Shame" 108)

As many commentators note—and as many of us know from personal experience—the experience of blushing can lead to an exacerbation of the experience of shame. Tomkins observes, "when the face blushes, shame is compounded. And so it happens that one is as ashamed of being ashamed as of anything else" (137). Tomkins insists, however, that shame is profoundly ambivalent:

> In shame I wish to continue to look and to be looked at, but I also do not wish to do so. There is some serious impediment to communication which forces consciousness back to the face and the self. Because the self is not altogether willing to renounce the object, excitement may break through and displace shame at any moment, but while shame is dominant it is experienced as an enforced renunciation of the object. (*Sedgwick and Frank* 137-8)

He sums up this quandary thus: "Shame-humiliation involves an ambivalent turning of the eyes away from the object toward the face and the self" (*Sedgwick and Frank* 137). Indeed, shame often involves averting or covering the face, attempting to hide from the derision of the other. Otto Fenichel writes:

> "I feel ashamed" means "I do not want to be seen." Therefore, persons who feel ashamed hide themselves or at least avert their faces. However, they also close their eyes and refuse to look. This is a kind of magical gesture, arising from the magical belief that anyone who does not look cannot be looked at. (qtd. in Wurmser, "Shame: The Veiled Companion" 67)

Wurmser, like Tomkins, identifies the eyes and perception as the locus of shame: "the eye is the organ of shame par excellence," he writes ("Shame: The Veiled Companion" 67)

In her extensive work on shame, Helen Block Lewis found consistently that women suffered more from shame—often disguised as depression—than did men. To begin with, in her studies on field dependence, "a cognitive style that catches the self in relation not only to its physical surround but in relation to others," Lewis discovered that women were more field dependent than men ("Shame" 103). Lewis also proved a correlation between field dependence, shame, and later depression ("Shame" 104). Joseph Adamson and Hilary Clark summarize the connections between shame, humiliated fury, and depression thus:

> [S]hame has traditionally shaped the experience of women under patriarchy. Women and others who suffer from inequality in power are particularly prone to the humiliated rage that stems from unacknowledged shame, a rage turned on the self and transformed to guilt because one does not feel entitled to it. Again, as the passive experience of being devalued and disempowered, shame is linked with low self-esteem and depression; it has been established that roughly twice as many women as men suffer from depression. (*Scenes of Shame* 22)

Many women, furthermore, learn to associate shame with femininity and female flesh. As Susan Bordo notes in her extensive work on eating disorders, many women experience their appetites as excessive, as too much. So, too, do women experience their bodies as too much: too much flesh, too much blood, too many possibilities for embarrassment. Women learn that respectability means "not to make spectacles of oneself," not to draw untoward attention, not, in some sense, to be "seen."

Although trauma and shame seem linked in an intuitive way, theorists of trauma and theorists of shame have tended to work in parallel, non-intersecting paths.[9] Recently, however, both theorists of shame and literary critics have begun to turn their attention to the ways in which traumatic experience and shaming may be intertwined. Significantly, Lewis links "humiliated fury"—the rage generated by unacknowledged shame—to sexual and physical abuse. When a trusted other—a member of one's family or a well-known family friend—sexually abuses a child, the child experiences "the profound shame that this betrayal of trust always occasions" ("Shame" 100). The humiliated fury this shame generates is then turned upon the self: "Humiliated fury has very little place to go except back down on the self, when one has been seduced, to become a component of one's humiliation. It is for this reason that the violation of the incest barrier between the powerful adult and the relatively powerless youngster is so damaging" ("Shame" 100). William Martin distinguishes between trauma and shame thus: "Put simply, trauma theory focuses on the proto-experience of an individual and her need to have it conceptualized through language, while shame theory provides a framework explaining often pathological forms of behavior as symptoms of intense shame."[10] The similarities between the two experiences are more than causative, however. As Donald L. Nathanson points out, what made Lewis's 1971 study a landmark analysis of shame was "her meticulous demonstration that guilt is usually well-worded and easily accessible, whereas shame is silent, image dependent, and demanding of sympathetic confirmation before it can be approached in therapy" (Lewis, *Role* 184). In other words, both the traumatic experience and the shame experience are imagistic, bodily based, and speechless, and so painful as to require banishment from consciousness. Both kinds of experience can be processed only dialectically, in the presence of an empathic or sympathetic audience.

With these formulations in mind, let us turn back to *The Years* and its ur-text, *The Pargiters*. (In this respect, *The Pargiters* resembles the narratives Turgenev created for his characters and then eliminated.) Shame—specifically shame about female corporeality and sexual desire—is everywhere in these texts. Woolf is particularly astute at grasping the ways in which shame requires a sense of another, a witness, before whom the person so affected feels "caught" in a light beamed upon the person's shortcomings. "Don't be caught looking," Eleanor warns her younger sisters when they peer through the window at an eligible young man: they are in the impossible position of needing to find husbands yet forbidden to exhibit sexual desire or even sexual curiosity (*Y* 19, *P* 18). Eleanor, the maternal surrogate, here functions as the voice of "enforced renunciation" of interest and enjoyment, to use Tomkins' phrasing. In *The Pargiters,* Woolf elaborates upon the sisters' experience of shame:

> Both Delia and Milly blushed with a peculiar shame, when Eleanor said, "Don't be caught looking"—they wanted to look at the young man; they knew it was wrong to look; they were caught looking; they disliked being caught: they were ashamed, indignant, confused—all in one—& the feeling, since it was never exposed, save by a blush or a giggle; wriggled deep down into their minds & sometimes woke them in the middle of the night with curious sensations, unpleasant dreams that seemed to come from one fact—that Abercorn Terrace was besieged on all sides by what may be called street love. (*P* 38)

193

Sexual desire—curious sensations that immediately transmute into unpleasant dreams—gets entangled in shame affect and "wriggles deep into their minds," a phrasing that suggests Eve's sexual fall as the result of the serpent's temptation. After all, wanting to know what one is explicitly forbidden to know is the basis of Western culture's most enduring myths of female perfidy—Pandora and her box, Eve and the forbidden fruit, Bluebeard's wife and the bloody chamber, Psyche and her mysterious lover Eros. What Woolf suggests, moreover, is that sexual curiosity and desire are literally driven underground, significant in light of Woolf's pervasive linking of sexual interest and desire with the word and location of the "subterranean." Similarly, when Rose encounters the exhibitionist, she is worried that her father will be angry at her for having seen what she shouldn't have seen. Her shame and guilt render her speechless:

> The grey face that hung on a string in front of her eyes somehow suggested to her a range of emotion in herself of which she was instinctively afraid; as if, *without being told a word about it, she knew that she was able to feel what it was wrong to feel* . . . what she could not say to her sister, even, was that she had seen a sight that puzzled her, and shocked her, and suggested that there were things brooding round her, unspoken of, which roused *curiosity* and physical fear. (*P* 50, emphasis added).

Female sexual curiosity/experience becomes linked to furtive, shameful emotions; throughout these descriptions Woolf's emphasis is on forbidden sight and curiosity, followed by and shrouded in subsequent shame and silence. To use Tomkins' formulations, shame is inextricably linked to the ambivalent desire to look, "an auxiliary to the affect interest-excitement and enjoyment-joy" (Nathanson, *Many Faces* 20). Shame thus functions as a means of modulating interest in or excitement about an object. As Nathanson observes, "the universal caution 'curiosity killed the cat' seems to indicate a general cultural awareness that the affect interest needs a modulator" (*Many Faces* 20). That Woolf herself linked her ambivalent "looking-glass shame"—the compulsive and yet shameful specular encounter with her own image—to her experience of sexual molestation further supports the link between forbidden sights and experiences and subsequent shame and silence.

In her third essay in *The Pargiters,* Woolf explicitly links Rose's experience of seeing something that interested her but that she somehow knew was wrong for her to see to Eleanor's caution to Delia and Milly against looking. Considering the constrictions which surrounded these young women in order to protect them (silently) from "street love," Woolf writes, "not only did it restrict their lives, and to some extent poison their minds—lies of all sorts undoubtedly have a crippling and distorting effect, and none the less if the liar feels that his lie is justified—but it also helped to bolster up, to harden, and substantiate a conception of the utmost importance about conduct, not only in the minds of the Pargiter sisters, but in the minds of their brothers" (*P* 52). This "hardening" introduces into the passage an indictment of phallicism, and of patriarchal law which restricts women because men are unrestrained. Woolf continues: "And yet they were all completely uncertain as to what conduct was right; and yet they all had dangling before them, as they grew older, the conviction that some convention was absolutely necessary for them, and not for their brothers. The question of chastity was therefore complicated in the extreme" (*P* 53). Significantly, the word "dangling" will recur in Woolf's final revision of Rose's traumatic nightmare of the exhibitionist, the man at the pillar box:

> Something had swum up on top of the blackness. An oval white shape hung in front of her—dangling, as if it hung from a string. She half opened her eyes and looked at it. It bubbled with grey spots that went in and out. She woke completely. A face was hanging close to her as if it dangled on a bit of string. She shut her eyes; but the face was still there, bubbling in and out, grey, white, purplish and pock-marked. (*Y* 41)

Woolf's layering of sexual imagery is quite dense: she limns not only the face of a man masturbating and reaching climax, but the physical description—the mottled coloring and the rhythmic movement, the enlarging and deflating of the "dangling," elongated oval—evokes a grotesque image of male genitalia. In light of Woolf's own experiences with her half-brothers, it is perhaps not surprising that in the draft version of Rose's trauma the experience results in her mistrust of her brother. "After the adventure in the street," Woolf writes, "Rose changed slightly but decidedly in her feeling for Bobby. Again it is difficult to say how far this change was the result of the shock; how far she felt some fear or dislike for her brother because of his sex" (*P* 54). Woolf's refusal to pin down the exact nature of Rose's "adventure" is consistent with her final version, in which the event affects Rose throughout her life in ways Woolf refuses to narrate.

Woolf's persistent use of the word "subterranean" to describe women's so-called "instincts" must also be contextualized within the forbidden, in particular the taboos placed upon female curiosity and interest in the sexual aspects of self or other. Woolf develops this aspect of shame most fully in her narrative about the Pargiters' cousin Kitty, whose full name—Katharine Persephone Malone (*P* 69)—hints at the abrogation and burial of her sexuality. Even if Kitty had felt attraction for someone, Woolf writes, "she was so much restrained by the conventions of the society in which she lived that her response . . . would have been instantly checked by the knowledge she must conceal it" (*P* 109). Woolf details the "very strict moral code" that Kitty has learned since she was a little girl, from kicking up her legs to standing at her window at night in her nightgown, "from saying or doing anything which could suggest even remotely that she felt physically or ideally attracted" by men (*P* 109). Hence her kissing the farm boy behind the haystack, although pleasurable, rouses considerable guilt: "she knew that she was committing an appalling crime" (*P* 109). The end result is the atrophying of her sexual desire and interest:

> she felt much less, physically, than [young men her age] did—for the physical side of love had been so repressed not only in her, but in her mothers and grandmothers, that it was much weaker, even in a girl of perfect physique like Kitty, than in a young man like Tony Ashton who was physically less perfect, but sexually much better developed, since no restrictions had been placed either on him or on his fathers or grandfathers that were comparable in severity with those that had surrounded Kitty almost since birth. (*P* 109)

Here Woolf introduces the evolutionary concept of sexual restraint, developed after generations of restrictions on middle-class women's sexuality. She reiterates: "Kitty . . . therefore inherited the effects of an education which, if we attribute any importance to education, was bound not merely to teach her a certain code of behaviour, but also to modify the passion itself" (*P* 110).

Hence in the Victorian age "the young girl . . . has hardly any passion left":

> Either it has been extinguished by the process of education, or as happened with Kitty, passion still existed but was so much restricted that it was a furtive, ill-grown, secret, subterranean vice, to be concealed in shame, until by some fortunate chance, a man gave the

girl a chance, by putting a wedding ring on her finger, to canalise all
her passion, for the rest of their lives, solely upon him. (*P* 110)

Woolf links here the wedding ring to the "canalising" of women's
passion, a linkage that suggests patriarchal ownership of the hymen and
the vagina. The word "subterranean" suggests that by the time passion
does become legitimated in marriage, it is too late: passion no longer
exists, except in a furtive and somehow shame-filled form. Consider, too,
Woolf's use of subterranean passages in *The Voyage Out*, where the traumatic shock of Richard Dalloway's kiss provokes the following
nightmare of Rachel's "walking down a long tunnel," that opens into a
vault where she finds herself "trapped" in the company of "a deformed
man who squatted on the floor gibbering, with long nails. His face was
pitted and like the face of an animal" (*VO* 77). This passage anticipates
Woolf's memory of sexual assault in "A Sketch of the Past," where Woolf
links the assault to her "looking-glass shame" and a dream of seeing "the
face of an animal" in a mirror (*MOB* 69). Yet the bestial, deformed man's
appearance in a nightmarish and constrictive female terrain suggests that
femaleness is a deformed and lunatic manifestation of maleness. After all,
Woolf characterizes herself at fifteen as "a nervous, gibbering, little
monkey . . . mopping and mowing, and leaping into dark corners" (*MOB*
116). As she tells Smyth in a letter, moreover, her recurrent "suicide
dream" is one of finding herself alone in a drainpipe: "suddenly, I
approach madness and that end of a drainpipe with a gibbering old man"
(*L4*: 298).

Subterranean Instincts

"But as so much of life—is sexual—or so they say—it rather limits
autobiography if this is blacked out. It must be, I suspect, for many generations, for women, for its like breaking the hymen—if thats the
membrane's name—a painful operation, and I suppose connected with all
sorts of subterranean instincts" (*L6*: 460).

Woolf's strong belief in a kind of Darwinian process of atrophy in
middle-class women's sexuality is striking; she insists again and again on
the ways in which generations of acculturation have made women unwittingly connive in their own sexual frigidity and deformation. Given what
we now know about the ways in which the children of trauma survivors
are themselves affected by the parents' experience, it is necessary to

consider Woolf's portrayals of women's "subterranean instincts" as yet another ramification of female sexual disinheritance through forms of sexual assault. Woolf s sense of the "inherited dread" and "subterranean instincts" clustered around female corporeal experience anticipates the current theoretical interest in understanding the way in which trauma extends beyond the individual into the community. In particular, her writing resonates with that of the psychoanalytic theorists Abraham and Torok, whose work focuses on trauma experiences that pass intergenerationally through inherited unconscious "phantoms."

For Abraham and Torok, the basis of psychic life is the principle of "introjection," the way in which we "open and fashion and enrich ourselves, transcend trauma, adjust to internal or external upheaval and change, create forms of coherence in the face of emotional panic and chaos" (14). Introjection is a three-fold process:

> 1. Something—good or bad—occurs to someone.
>
> 2. The person "appropriates" the experience through play, creativity, fantasy, or any number of activities.
>
> 3. The person becomes aware of the occurrence and understands "why and how the scope of self has been modified and expanded" (14). The event, in other words, is given a place in the person's emotional existence.

Trouble occurs when something interferes with the process of introjection. Abraham and Torok, like the early Freud and like their countryman Sandor Ferenczi, returned to the early problems in psychoanalysis, "the effects of forgotten painful memories, the nature of traumas, and their role in the development of neurosis" (16). Abraham and Torok examine the "mental landscapes of submerged family secrets" and "the preservation of a shut-up or excluded reality" (18). In particular they analyze the psychological weight of "unwanted, shameful, or untoward reality" and the process by which such reality becomes psychically isolated, split off from "the free circulation of our ideas, emotions, imaginations, creations, responses, initiatives, and contact with other people." This process of confining unbearable experiences to an inaccessible region of the mind is what Torok terms "incorporation" or "preservative repression": "Preservative repression seals off access to part of one's own life in order to shelter from view the traumatic moment of an obliterated event" (18). Abraham and Torok go on to develop a model of the psychic "secret," by which they mean a trauma "whose very occurrence and devastating emotional consequences are entombed and therefore consigned to internal silence, albeit unwittingly, by the sufferers themselves" (99-100). These "secrets," in turn, can become "phantoms," mechanisms by which a family's secrets are transmitted unconsciously and intergenerationally. One family member's unconscious fear or conflict can thus become a legacy, warping and distorting the lives of his or her descendants.

Abraham and Torok's belief in the unconscious transmission of traumatic conflict resonates with Woolf's conviction that forms of "inherited dread" distorted the sexual lives of middle-class women, a conviction she develops most fully in *The Years* and *Between the Acts*. As noted above, Rose's encounter with the exhibitionist remains unintegrated and inarticulate in *The Years*. Yet aspects of that repressed memory do seem to affect, even to enter the subconscious mind, of another member of her family. At the family reunion that closes the novel, Rose's niece Peggy suddenly glimpses "a state of being, in which there was real laughter and happiness, and this fractured world was whole; whole, vast, and free" (*Y* 390). Her problem becomes one of articulation: "But how could she say it?" (*Y* 390). Her attempt to articulate this sudden vision of coherence, of a moment when "this fractured world was whole" fails miserably. In spite of herself, Peggy's felicitous vision suddenly evokes a vicious personal attack on her brother. Peggy herself recognizes that something has gone horribly awry: "She had got it wrong. She had meant to say something impersonal, but she was being personal" (*Y* 390). In fact, Peggy's fragmented effort echoes Woolf's description of Rose's traumatic vision of a "face . . . hanging close to her as if it dangled on a bit of string":

> There was the vision still, but she had not grasped it. She had broken off only a little fragment of what she meant to say . . . Yet there it hung before her, the thing she had seen, the thing she had not said. But as she fell back with a jerk against the wall, she felt relieved of some oppression . . . She had not said it, but she had tried to say it. (*Y* 391)

Peggy tries to protect herself from a counterattack by dissociating herself from the present, by going back to a happy memory of a summer evening when she and her brother North are adolescents with a shared secret. She is afraid of ridicule, ashamed of herself. But all sit in silence until Kitty Lasswade arrives: "They all got up. Peggy got up. Yes, it was over, it was destroyed, she felt. Directly something got together, it broke. She had a feeling of desolation. And then to have to pick up the pieces, and make something new, something different, she thought, and crossed the room" (*Y 392*).

Why does Peggy's attempt to articulate an impersonal vision of wholeness veer off into an attack on her brother? Why do all sit in silence instead of responding? And why does Peggy feel "relieved of some oppression" because she has attempted, however unsuccessfully, to describe an unnamed and inarticulate "it"? At some level, it seems that Rose's repressed memory has intruded into the novel's "present day." For Peggy's attack on her brother recalls the passage in *The Pargiters* wherein Woolf states that the encounter with the exhibitionist changes Rose's relationship to her brother (there named Bobby, not Martin). As Woolf makes clear, Peggy's memories of her brother are of harmony and a united front towards their parents, making her compulsive attack on him even more illogical. That no one responds—Eleanor, the original intended recipient of Rose's experience is, significantly, one of those present—suggests that Peggy's attempt to say what cannot be said is *itself* important, as if all instinctively understand Eleanor's apprehension that "sharing things lessens things. . . . Give pain, give pleasure an outer body, and by increasing the surface diminish them" (*Y 352*).

Peggy's sense of fragmentation, of a rupture of wholeness, reverberates with other such scenes in Woolf's fiction, most notably Mrs. Ramsay's pause on the threshold of the dinner party before bringing it to an end, as well as Lily Briscoe's later memory of Mrs. Ramsay, Charles Tansley, and herself on the beach. "Making of the moment something permanent" (*TTL* 161) is the very essence of Woolf s aesthetic, as she makes clear in her development of the concept of "moments of being" in "A Sketch of the Past." What is distinct about this scene in *The Years* is that the moment expresses disharmony and anger against the brother and that the family witnesses this anger in some kind of silent recognition.

In *The Years,* Woolf succeeds in inscribing the "sexual life of women," not by describing and enumerating the kind of factual material she initially envisioned, but by using her considerable skills in writing novels about silence and the things people don't say—in other words, by capturing the more elusive and more fragmentary corporeal shock of sexual trauma and the kinds of experiences that evade language. Instead of trying to explain women's sexual lives, Woolf represents the traumatic events that dispossess women and that curtail female sexual expression. She thereby succeeds in finding words that can describe "so dumb and mixed a feeling." Significantly, when Woolf returned to the subject of sexual trauma in *Between the Acts,* her use of the myth of the rape of Philomela as a paradigmatic and originary account of female story-telling situates rape as the foundational moment of women's sexual/textual experience. That account is unspoken yet hauntingly present, pervading *Between the Acts* much as Rose's sight of the exhibitionist haunts other characters' psyches in *The Years.* Thus when Isa attempts to come to her husband's aid by expanding a Shakespeare passage he is reciting, the "first words that came into her head" are not Shakespeare, but a line from Keats's "Ode to a Nightingale": "'Fade far away and quite forget what thou amongst the leaves has never known,'" Isa quotes *(BA* 54). What Woolf demonstrates is that "what we would forget" is never forgotten; the spectral traces of the traumatic past linger on, haunting us all.

Notes

1. Marlene Briggs, Karen DeMeester, and Toni McNaron have also discussed Woolf's work in relation to trauma theory; Briggs and DeMeester focus on war trauma in *Mrs. Dalloway.* McNaron studies more generally the effect of Woolf's traumatic experiences upon her narrative aesthetic.

2. Radin draws this connection in her work on *The Years* (xii); here I wish to extend her argument to the specific issue of female sexuality.

3. For a typescript of Woolf's speech to the London/National Society for Women's Service on January 21 1931 see *The Pargiters,* xxvii-xliv. Woolf's speech apparently followed Smyth's; for a contemporaneous review of it see Vera Brittain's column in the *Nation* of January 31 (p. 571). Woolf would eventually revise her speech into "Professions for Women."

4. I refer not to Woolf's experiences with George, which she discussed much earlier, but to the experience with Gerald, which she does not discuss until 1939.

5. That language is inadequate in conveying the nature of traumatic experience is a hallmark of trauma literature. Many theorists of trauma discuss this aspect at length (e.g. Felman and Laub, Herman, Tal, van der Kolk and van der Hart).

6. Contemporary cognitive science offers a number of complex models that explain how certain types of memories may undergo a form of amnesia and then become available for retrieval at a later date. See, for example, Joseph LeDoux, *The Emotional Brain,* especially 138-225; and Daniel Schacter, *Searching for Memory.* Schacter's account is especially useful in that he juxtaposes his understanding of memory loss and retrieval with

a balanced overview of the contemporary "memory wars" over what has come to be called "Recovered Memory Syndrome." The latter refers to the wave of recovered memories of sexual abuse that arose in the eighties and nineties. Such memories typically arose in a therapeutic setting and/or with the help of self-help manuals, contexts which may have encouraged the development of false memories. For some analyses of "Recovered Memory Syndrome," see, in addition to Schacter, Janice Haaken, *Pillar of Salt* and Marita Sturken, "Narratives of Recovery: Repressed Memory as Cultural Memory," in *Acts of Memory*, eds. Bal, Crewe, and Spitzer. A discussion of the differences between Woolf's memories and those of contemporary women who fit the "Recovered Memory Syndrome" paradigm is outside the scope of this essay, although I do discuss this issue in *Virginia Woolf, Jean Rhys, and the Aesthetics of Trauma* (NY: Palgrave Macmillan, 2006).

7. Woolf's model strongly resembles the cognitive model of memory and identity that Antonio Damasio develops in *The Feeling of What Happens*. Damasio posits a "core consciousness," a self aware of the here and now, and an "extended consciousness," which provides the person with "an elaborate sense of self" (16). These two kinds of consciousness correspond to two versions of selfhood:

> The sense of self which emerges in core consciousness is the *core self*, a transient entity, ceaselessly re-created for each and every object with which the brain interacts. Our traditional notion of self, however, is linked to the idea of identity and corresponds to a nontransient collection of unique facts and ways of being which characterize a person.
>
> My term for that entity is the *autobiographical self*. The autobiographical self depends on systematized memories of situations in which core consciousness was involved in the knowing of the most invariant characteristics of an organism's life . . . I use the term *autobiographical memory* to denote the organized record of the main aspects of an organism's biography (17-18).

Damasio's model provides a means for understanding why members of a family, who share some invariant characteristics (common homes, parents, relatives, and so forth), may nonetheless develop different autobiographical narratives which seemingly contradict one another, as in fact occurs in the Pargiter family.

For an overview of contemporary cognitive science and models of memory and the emotions, see Suzanne Nalbantian, *Memory in Literature*, esp. 135-52. Nalbantian also provides an overview of turn-of-the-century models of memory and assesses a number of Woolf's texts in relation to these models; Nalbantian concludes that Woolf's method is one of associative memory. I believe, however, that Woolf provides different models of memory throughout her work. It is telling that Nalbantian limits her discussion to *Mrs. Dalloway, To the Lighthouse,* and "A Sketch of the Past," but says very little about *The Waves, The Years,* or *Between the Acts*, which all develop concepts of collective memory and different kinds of personal memory. See Nalbantian, 77-85.

8. See "Introduction: States of Shame," in *L 'Esprit Créateur*.

9. An important exception is J. Brooks Bouson' s recent analysis of the intersections of shame, trauma, and race in Toni Morrison's work in *Quiet As It's Kept*.

10. I take this passage from Martin's 10 January 2001 call for MLA papers for a panel "Theorizing Shame Affect and Trauma Interdependency."

FACE TO FACE: TRAUMA AND AUDIENCE IN *BETWEEN THE ACTS*

David Eberly

*B*etween the Acts records Virginia Woolf's struggle to explore the meaning of relationship, inherent in the communication between self and other, and between author and audience. Employing the concept of "the face of the other" developed by the philosopher Emmanuel Levinas, this essay will show how the multifaceted personal and social exchanges portrayed in *Between the Acts* can be understood as dialogues of trauma in which the novel's characters search for relief in the responsive face-to-face encounter of an attentive and listening other. It is in the circumstance of the audience of the other that Woolf seeks in her novel to discover a community that will alleviate the anxiety of the traumatized self and offer respite, if not recovery, from the repercussions of trauma.

Woolf made her own search for this community during the early years of World War II in the midst of a global conflagration that damaged her London home, ruined her beloved city, and threatened her and her husband with death, should Hitler's army successfully invade England. Isolated in Rodmell with "no room of my own," as she suggestively wrote in her diary, where "for 11 days I've been contracting in the glare of different faces," Woolf sought a reading audience that she feared was vanishing in the flames of war, together with the centuries-long tradition that had sustained her work. "All the walls," she wrote, "the protecting & reflecting walls, wear so terribly thin. . . . There's no standard to write for: no public to echo back" (*D*5: 303-304). In *Between the Acts*, Woolf would attempt to imagine a public assembled to applaud the village pageant she imagined, rooted in the British cultural tradition that it records.

The Idea of the Face

Writing in *The Juridical Unconscious*, Shoshana Felman specifically links Emmanuel Levinas' idea of the face to "those whom violence has deprived of expression. . . . to those whom violence has paralyzed, effaced, or deadened, to those whom violence has treated in their lives as though they were *already dead*"—in other words, those who have been traumatized.[1] Levinas, "the avatar of the traumatized degradation of the self" (Moyn 21), makes an extraordinary and challenging claim for the idea of the face.[2] "In my philosophical essays," he states, "I have spoken a great deal about the face of the other man as being the original locus of the meaningful," where "the essential nature of being is put into question" (*Entre Nous* 145). It is in the encounter with the face, he argues, that we discover the uniqueness of "the 'I' called and elected to responsibility for others." Commenting elsewhere about the nature of the self, Levinas writes that "the human 'I' is not a self-enclosed unit like the unit of the atom; it is an opening, the opening of responsibility that is the true beginning of the human and of spirituality" (*History* 130), a characterization of the self that resonates with Woolf's conceptualization of the porous nature of human subjects in relationship with each other. Arguably the most familiar concept of his philosophy, the "face" is where Levinas situated his complex challenge to Western philosophy, which he accused as having been unable to prevent the violence of war and to have been complicit in the genocide of the Jews. Thus rooted in a "fear for all the violence and murder that [our] existing—despite its intentional and conscious innocence—can bring about," the face, according to Levinas, represents "extreme exposure, defenselessness, vulnerability itself" (*Entre Nous* 144-145).

The face, as defined by Levinas, is not a physical countenance, "not at all what has been seen." "Face," Levinas writes, is "nakedness, helplessness, perhaps an exposure to death" (*Righteous* 145), those overwhelming states that are so often reported by victims of violence and abuse. The relation to the face, Levinas argues, "is a relation to the absolutely weak, to what is absolutely exposed, naked, and destitute" (*Righteous* 166).[3] As such, it is the proximity of the face of the other that demands the response that lies at the heart of humanness. "This facing of the face in its expression," Levinas writes, "summons me, demands me, claims me. . . . It is precisely in this call to my responsibility by the face . . . that the other is my neighbor" (*Entre Nous* 145-146). Extending his discussion of the idea of the face, Levinas explores elsewhere the relationship between the face of the other and speech: "Face and discourse are tied. The face speaks. It speaks, it is in this that it renders possible and begins all discourse" (*Ethics* 89). We cannot simply contemplate the face; we must greet and respond to it: "It is difficult to be silent in someone's presence," Levinas reminds us. "It is necessary to speak of something, of rain and fine weather, no matter what, but to speak" (88). The characters of Woolf's novel search persistently for the greeting that Levinas will claim in his philosophy to be the response to the other, even as they come together to attend the pageant at Pointz Hall, contemplate the view surrounding them, and discuss the threat of rain.

The opening pages of *Between the Acts* contain a multiplicity of direct and indirect face-to-face encounters. Almost immediately, in a physical description that resembles some of the most disturbing to be found in her diaries, Woolf introduces "Mrs. Haines, the wife of the gentleman farmer, a goosefaced woman with eyes protruding as if they saw something to gobble in the gutter," who remembers how "as a small child in a perambulator, a great cart-horse had brushed within an inch of her face" (*BA* 3). Glaring from her "goose-like eyes," she will upon her departure demand from Isa Oliver "the kindness to recognize my existence," as Levinasian an invitation as might be imagined. In response to this implicit appeal, Isa finds herself "forced" to comply (*BA* 6). Earlier, when entering into the drawing room discussion, Isa had inclined her head toward Mrs. Haines's husband Rupert, in whose "ravaged face [Isa] always felt mystery" (*BA* 5). "On going up the principal staircase," the reader is told, "there was a portrait," yet another face.[4] Interrupting the daydreaming Mrs. Swithin when she brings breakfast, Grace, the maid, looks at her and thinks, "Batty . . . as she felt on her face the divided glance that was half meant for a beast in the swamp, half for a maid in a print frock and white apron." Immediately following the departure of Grace, Mrs. Swithin remembers her mother "in that very room rebuking her. 'Don't stand gaping, Lucy, or the wind'll change'" (*BA* 9), an interdiction to the gaze to which the book's characters will subject one another throughout the novel. As if to underscore the number of facial encounters that occur at the beginning of the text, Woolf situates Isa before a "three-folded" bedroom mirror, "so that she could see three separate versions of her rather heavy, yet handsome, face" (*BA* 13-14).

Woolf creates a more ominous face-to-face encounter in the morning meeting of Bartholomew Oliver and his grandson, George. Distorting his face with a mask improvised from the morning's newspaper—daily purveyor of politics, violence, and war—Bartholomew turns himself into "a terrible peaked eyeless monster moving on legs, brandishing arms." Confronted by this terrifying apparition, "George stood gaping. George stood gazing." Bewildering to the young child, the specter morphs into a more familiar form when "Mr. Oliver crumpled the paper which he had cocked into a snout and appeared in person. A very old man, with gleaming eyes, wrinkled cheeks, and a head with no hair on it" (*BA* 11-12). Isa will later pick up this same paper dropped by her father-in-law, "the old brute," and read: "The troopers told her the horse had a green tail; but she found it was just an ordinary horse. And they dragged her up to the barrack room where she was thrown upon a bed. Then one of the troopers removed part of her clothing, and she screamed and hit him about the face . . . That was real" (*BA* 20). The graphic rape of the young girl by Royal Guardsmen, based on a well-known contemporary episode, is a curiously doubled description, evocative of the two episodes of sexual trauma Woolf reported in her memoir. In the victim's incredulity, we might glimpse the numbed disbelief felt by Virginia as she endured the genital abuse by Gerald; in her violent response, the suppressed terror she may have felt in her bed beneath the weight of George. Like the incident of indecent exposure that so troubles the life of Rose in *The Years*, the rape reported here remains embedded in the tissue of the text like a shard.[5]

Woolf stains what might seem an otherwise ordinary prank foisted on a startled child by a looming adult by introducing a disconcerting suggestion of intrusive male sexuality. In calling our attention to the phallic imagery of "an obliging thrush hopping across the lawn," "a coil of pinkish rubber twisted in its beak" (*BA* 9), Woolf foreshadows the implicit sexual advance on George by his grandfather Bartholomew, whose voice "boomed at him from a beak of paper" (*BA* 12). George's outburst seems to be provoked by a subtle association of Bartholomew's Afghan hound to the penis: "The hairy flanks were sucked in and out; there was a blob of foam on its nostrils. He burst out crying" (*BA* 13). Woolf's description of the hound disconcertingly echoes that of the exhibitionist who terrified Rose: "[H]e sucked his lips in and out. . . . But he did not stretch his hands out at her; they were unbuttoning his clothes" (*Y* 29). Moreover, by earlier introducing the sighting of the pinkish coil with Mrs. Swithin's exclamation "How those birds sing," Woolf indirectly links the incident not only to the most notorious symptom of her own breakdowns —hearing birds singing in Greek—but also to the post-traumatic stress of the shell-shocked Septimus Smith, another victim of male violence.

By the late 1930s, Woolf had begun to explore the effects of her sexual abuse perpetrated by her half-brothers with increasing urgency and specificity in both her fiction and her memoirs. In doing so, she returned to the subject of her personal trauma with none of the problematic comedy that characterized her first attempt to describe it in "22 Hyde Park Gate," or that she routinely employed in her letters when speaking about it. Her levity was startlingly at odds with the response of Janet Case, a confidant who saw past Woolf's performance and was "sickened" by the situation Woolf disclosed (Lee, *Virginia* 153-154).[6] Woolf's emotional vulnerability as she surveyed her past from a more mature perspective was exacerbated by her forced relocation to Rodmell during the war. Feeling trapped in Sussex, and isolated from friends who provided psychological relief from the anxiety of intimate relationship common among incest survivors, Woolf struggled to cope with the emotions that her exploration aroused. She compares this process of what she implies is a sexual autobiography to the painful breaking of the hymen. In her often-cited letter of January 12, 1941, to Ethel Smyth, Woolf explicitly describes a memory of her molestation by Gerald Duckworth, who stood her on a ledge at the age of six and explored her "private parts" (*L6*: 460). "But why should I be writing these sexual speculations now?" she asks. "Every other second I take my eyes off the page to look at the elms outside," she adds, as if to alleviate the distress of facing her past by breaking her attention to view the pastoral countryside surrounding her. In *Between the Acts* her characters employ a similar strategy to ease the tension rising among them by detaching themselves from the group to gaze on the landscape surrounding Pointz Hall. Uncomfortable, they frequently turn their faces away from one another. "They stared at the view, as if something might happen in one of those fields to relieve them of the intolerable burden of sitting silent, doing nothing, in company" (*BA* 65).

The Boundary of Skin

For Levinas, the face is neither a physical entity nor a countenance. Yet, while arguing that "the face is not at all what has been seen" and that it should not be confused with "a way of looking, a way of knowing, for example, what color your eyes are," (*Righteous* 144), Levinas never abandons physical specificity when philosophizing the face of the other. The face is first encountered in its plasticity, its musculature, and above all in its most superficial and vulnerable guise, the skin. "A face approached, a contact with a skin—a face weighted down with skin, and a skin in which, even in obscenity, the altered face breathes—are already absent from themselves. . . . The skin caressed is not the protection of an organism, simply the surface of an entity" (*Being* 89). A rhetoric of vulnerability often accompanies Levinas' discussion of the meaning of the face. "The face of the neighbor," he claims, "escapes representation . . . because in a sense it is too weak. . . . [I]t is poverty, skin with wrinkles." This vulnerability, Levinas writes elsewhere, "is more (or less) than passivity receiving form or shock. It is the aptitude—that any being in its 'natural pride' would be ashamed to admit—for 'being beaten,' for 'getting slapped.'"[7] Paradoxically, it is in this vulnerability associated with "the nakedness of the skin" that Levinas situates "the relation to the other" (*Humanism* 63-64).

One of the most important effects of trauma is the victim's loss of the protective sense of boundary upon which a sense of selfhood, safety, and trust depends. Without the secure boundary of selfhood, founded on the inviolability of the body, an individual lives in a heightened state of fear and defensiveness, which can have an impact on the development of intimate and social relationships. As Barry Cohen and Anne Mills note in their study, "Skin/Paper/Bark," "Skin is our largest organ. . . . It is our largest physical boundary, distinguishing the *me* from the *not-me*, and contains auto-immune defenses. Its hues, textures and smells have social value and can show membership in the group" (206). Mrs. Manresa— florid, powdered, made up—displays an easy and, to Isa, an enviable participation in the group, comfortably taking her place among the luncheon guests and the pageant's larger audience. Uninvited, she enjoys "her own capacity to surmount, without turning a hair, this minor social crisis, this laying of two more places. For had she not complete faith in flesh and blood? and aren't we all flesh and blood? and how silly to make bones and trifles when we are all flesh and blood under the skin" (*BA* 39). Comfortable in her skin, and cognizant of her sexuality, she displays the *self*-satisfaction denied the trauma survivor.

"Skin," Cohen and Mills continue, "senses both inwardly and outwardly, participating in both subjective and objective reality. . . . Skin can even speak—by blushing (shame) and exhibiting gooseflesh (fear)." Holding the physical contents of our body in its container, it also "houses all manner of psychic data." Thus the skin ego, they argue, confers both a bodily and an emotional sense of boundary and individuality. "When poked"—and here one might be reminded of the genital poking by her half-brother Gerald which Woolf reported—the skin ego "registers a mark—whether from a broken epidermis, a broken heart or a broken boundary" (Cohen 207). These markings, they add, can create a map of the person's post-traumatic lifestyle and can be externalized in art.

Woolf was famously thin-skinned; any social interaction had the potential to shame her. Woolf's diaries are replete with incidents of what she perceived as social humiliation at the hands of servants, shopkeepers, and dressmakers who, after all, are employed to fashion us yet another skin. One of the most perilous of these interactions for Woolf was with her reading audience. The esteem of her colleagues and the approval of her readers were crucial to maintaining the fragile sense of self-regard that allowed her to continue writing, an activity that for Woolf was tantamount to living. The seemingly insurmountable threat to her writing posed by her increasing mental instability was one of the primary reasons she gave in her suicide notes for taking her life. Quentin Bell observed that for Woolf, "A favorable notice was a kind of certificate of sanity." "The point," Bell wrote when considering her extreme sensitivity to criticism, which he believed could be considered "morbid," was that "it arose from a diseased condition." The pokes and thrusts of critics, which "more robust" authors might successfully resist, reopened in Woolf's case "wounds that had never quite healed and had never ceased to be acutely tender" (Bell 2: 29). "A skin-deep nervousness," Woolf herself named it, when waiting to read E. M. Forster's opinion of her biography of Roger Fry (D5: 305). "Many nights," she observed in her diary several years earlier, "I wake in shudder thinking of some atrocity of mine," giving voice to the overwhelming self-consciousness and shame that torments the victims of sexual trauma. "I bring home pinpricks which magnify in the middle of the night into gaping wounds" (D3: 95).

The Search for Audience

Skin, the body's first and most fragile protection against the penetration of another, is only the most superficial of the body's boundaries to fail when one experiences trauma. As Judith Herman has written, "When neither resistance nor escape is possible, the human system of self-defense becomes overwhelmed and disorganized" (Trauma 34). Once a victim's defenses are breached, traumatic events shatter not only her secure sense of selfhood, but any possibility of a trusting relationship between herself and others. The damage to a victim's belief in community is "particularly severe when the traumatic events themselves involve the betrayal of important relationships" (Herman, *Trauma* 55). Noting this passage in her memoir of rape and near-murder, the philosopher Susan Brison argues that without this belief, "one can no longer *be oneself* even to oneself, since the self exists fundamentally in relation to others" (40). Given this damage to a victim's sense of community, one might further speculate that the relationship between a writer who has suffered abuse and her audience might be a disordered one as consequence of the trauma. Certainly, the inability to relate securely to her audience had dire consequences for Woolf. If a stray comment about her hat by Clive Bell—her first critic—could make Woolf "as unhappy as I have been these ten years" (*D3*: 91), the failure of an author to connect with her audience might risk far more, as Woolf suggests in the character of the pageant's creator Miss La Trobe. When confronted with a sudden lapse in the audibility of her actors and the threatened unintelligibility of her drama, Miss La Trobe, who only a moment before "glowed with glory," collapses: she "leant against the tree, paralyzed. Her power had left her. Beads of perspiration broke on her forehead. Illusion had failed. 'This is death,'" she murmured, 'death'" (*BA* 140).

"All encounter begins with a benediction, contained in the word 'hello,'" Levinas has written. "This greeting addressed to the other man is an invocation. I therefore insist on the primacy of the well-intentioned relation toward the other" (*Alterity* 98). His claim will be tested throughout *Between the Acts*, as its characters search for the greeting, the welcoming audience, that each might be for the other. While the most obvious and sustained of these attempts is the staging of Miss La Trobe's pageant on which she feels that she has staked her life, the novel is replete with social introduction and the attendant anxiety in meeting other people. Throughout the novel, characters introduce themselves in a variety of circumstances, shielding or revealing their humanness in their attempts to welcome or to avoid meaningful contact. Each is, in fact, as much an audience member as an actor. "Our part," as Bartholomew says, "is to be the audience. And a very important part too." "Also," his sister notes, "we provide the tea" (*BA* 58). This comic aside not only deflates the male pretension to the universal, it also indirectly marks a shared need among the play's spectators to alleviate the anxiety evoked by the responsibility of being present and listening, of attending to the story of another. "'Shan't we go and help?' said Mrs. Manresa. 'Cut up bread and butter?' 'No, no, said Mr. Oliver. 'We are the audience'" (*BA* 59).

Woolf quickly makes clear the importance of the concept of audience and the threat that participating in the pageant implies by explicitly repeating the statement when Isa thinks to herself, "'We remain seated—we are the audience.' Words this afternoon ceased to lie flat in the sentence. They rose, became menacing and shook their fists at you" (*BA* 59). All of the characters initially resist becoming a part of the audience. Isa feels imprisoned and escapes into fantasy, a "sleep haze" that obscures the bars of her jail, conjuring a cooling glass of water. Mrs. Swithin and Dodge sit and survey the fields "with detachment." Mrs. Manresa longs "to relax and curl in a corner with a cushion, a picture paper, and a bag of sweets." Yet none of these strategies succeeds. "The flat fields glared green yellow, blue yellow, red yellow, then blue again. The repetition was senseless, hideous, stupefying" (*BA* 66-67).

But Giles embodies the angriest resistance to the invitation to join the audience and to take his place in the inclusive humanness of it, "manacled to a rock he was, and forced passively to behold indescribable horror." Isa sees the anger in her husband's face and "not knowing what to say" knocks over a coffee cup, which is caught by Dodge, who gives himself away as a homosexual when his expression registers a fleeting cognizance of its value. In doing so, he gives Giles "another peg on which to hang his rage as one hangs a coat on a peg, conveniently. A toady; a lickspittle; not a downright plain man of his senses, but a teaser and twitcher" (*BA* 60). Giles's homophobic rant has been discussed at length by other critics.[8] What is important to note here is not so much his hatred of Dodge but his refusal to greet the (homosexual) other and to take his place among the audience of humanity. The ultimate consequence of Giles's rejection can be seen when he later crushes the "monstrous inversion" of the snake he discovers choked with a toad in its mouth:

> It was birth the wrong way round—a monstrous inversion. So, raising his foot, he stamped on them. The mass crushed and slithered. The white canvas on his tennis shoes was blood stained and sticky. But it was action. Action relieved him. He strode to the barn with blood on his shoes. (*BA* 99).

In refusing to speak even the name of the other and thus give it an existence, no matter how pejorative or marginalized, Giles refuses to engage in the dialogic encounter on which the human community is built and instead exposes the underlying violence that traumatizes those seen as other-than-ourselves.

In contrast to Giles's refusal of the Levinasian invitation to greet the other, speaking or narrating creates the opportunity to reestablish the relationship between self and other which has been dissolved as a result of the trauma. The act of narrating, as Brison describes it, "is a social interaction—actual or imagined or anticipated or remembered—in which what gets told is shaped by the (perceived) interests of the listeners, by what the listeners want to know and also by what they cannot or will not hear" (102). Trauma, in other words, must necessarily seek an audience if it is to be resolved, or at least successfully endured. As a result, the audience has become a contested site in which the expectation of the victim to speak and be heard "in that rectitude from me to you" (*Alterity* 93), as Levinas has described it, is challenged by those who refuse the face-to-face engagement of meaningful exchange. Judith Herman has emphasized the crucial role that the healing relationship, most often exemplified in the client-therapist dyad, plays in the recovery of the survivor (*Trauma* 134-135). Responding to the impact of the "false memory syndrome" movement which has questioned the reliability of the testimony of sexual trauma survivors, Sue Campbell argues that, in seeking to discredit female victims as suggestible to the implantation of false memory by their (usually) female therapists, the movement is invalidating the therapeutic site of personal and social healing (149-150). As a result of the impact of the false memory syndrome movement on the public perception of the truthfulness of survivor testimony, the audience for trauma narrative has again become a contested site. Campbell implicates "the role of the audience to testimony in its possible success, stressing the relationality of our engagements over memory narrative" (66). Woolf recognized this relationality and its potential for harm when, in reading her early autobiography "22 Hyde Park Gate" to the Memoir Club, she glimpsed the discomfort and denial of her male friends in response to her revelations of adolescent abuse. "It started with loud laughter; this was soon quelched; & then I couldn't help fighting a kind of uncomfortable boredom on the part of the males; to whose genial sense my revelations were at once mawkish and distasteful" (*D2*: 260). Woolf will give the same life-and-death need to find and claim a validating audience to Miss La Trobe and William Dodge, whose homosexuality would have led to isolation and victimization.

In *Between the Acts,* Dodge is forced repeatedly to introduce himself to his hosts and their guests in an attempt to shed his invisibility and to be greeted as a person of dignity. Woolf shows how difficult such a greeting can prove to be when she brings Dodge, Isa, and Giles together with Mrs. Parker for tea during one of the play's intervals. She can only assimilate Dodge among them by excluding the village idiot, deploring his visibility in the pageant. "But surely," she says to Giles, "we're more civilized?" "*'We?'* said Giles. *'We?'* He looked, once, at William. He knew not his name. . . . It was a bit of luck—that he could despise him, not himself" (*BA* 111). Once more Giles refuses an invitation, even one as ambivalent as the one offered by Mrs. Parker, to extend to Dodge that greeting that Levinas would argue should be his by right. "Surely," Mrs. Parker presses. "Surely we are?" (*BA* 111). Giles again shuts his lips, not speaking, as he had done earlier, and Isa, reacting, looks not at his face but at his bloodstained boots. No one in this social exchange enters into what Levinas has described as "this call to my responsibility by the face that summons me, that demands me, that claims me," where "the other is my neighbor" (*Entre Nous* 146).

Similarly, an earlier attempt by Dodge and Mrs. Swithin to meet as listening "others" had also ended in confusion, silence, and failure. Despite her desire "to overcome her tiredness out of charity towards a stranger, a guest," Mrs. Swithin forgets Dodge's name. He, too, remains silent. "Standing by the cupboard in the corner he saw her reflected in the glass. Cut off from their bodies, their eyes smiled, their bodiless eyes, at their eyes in the glass" (*BA* 71). Their attempted meeting is *reflected* face to *reflected* face, and thus unreal. Later, when Mrs. Swithin touches "her bony forehead upon which a blue vein wriggled like a blue worm" (*BA* 73), simultaneously evoking not only the traumatic phallic memory embedded in her earlier sight of the bird on the lawn but also the specific physical detail that Levinas gives to the idea of the face, Dodge remains silent about the details of his trauma:

> "At school they held me under a bucket of dirty water, Mrs. Swithin; when I looked up the world was dirty, Mrs. Swithin; so I married; but the child's not my child, Mrs. Swithin. I am a half-man, Mrs. Swithin; a flickering, mind-divided little snake in the grass, Mrs. Swithin; as Giles saw; but you've healed me. . . ." So he wished to say; but said nothing (*BA* 73).

As if to emphasize the missed opportunity to meet and provide a healing audience to one another despite their intentions, both Dodge and Mrs. Swithin engage in the characteristic gesture of disengagement observed

earlier. "Once more he looked and she looked down on the yellow grav-
el that made a crescent around the door" (*BA* 73).

Isa, however, motivated as much by revenge for her husband's infi-
delity as by generosity towards her guest, breaks from the group at tea
and suddenly invites Dodge to visit the greenhouse, where they meet in
the only authentic face-to-face human encounter in the novel. For it to
happen, however, Dodge's homosexuality, and thus his sexual neutrality
and safety, must be established: "and you—married?" Isa asks. "From her
tone he knew she guessed, as women always guessed, everything. They
knew at once they had nothing to fear, nothing to hope" (*BA* 113). Only
then does the pair introduce themselves by their first names and talk.
"They talked as if they had known each other all their lives; which was
odd," Isa thinks, "considering she'd known him perhaps an hour. Weren't
they, though, seekers after hidden faces?" (*BA* 114). How could they
speak so openly to each other when they have never met and might never
meet again? "The doom of sudden death hanging over us" (*BA* 114)
William answers. In this central interaction between William and Isa, we
can glimpse the promise of ethical dialogue admitting and accepting the
humanness of the other in which, as Levinas proposes, our "being-
toward-death . . . is interrupted in the presence of the face of the other"
(*Entre Nous* 147).

The Mirrored Face

No image holds more of Woolf's traumatic memory than that of the
mirror. In "A Sketch of the Past" she describes the looking glass in the
hall of Talland House and her shame at catching her reflection in it. She
recalls being perched as a small child on the mantel slab outside the
dining room door by her half-brother Gerald Duckworth, who explores
her private parts. Following this memory she recounts a dream which
"may refer to the incident of the looking glass," in which she dreamt "I
was looking in a glass when a horrible face—the face of an animal—
suddenly showed over my shoulder." Unsure of its reality, Woolf has
"always remembered the other face in the glass, whether it was a dream
or a fact, and that it frightens me" (*MOB* 68-69). The mirror in her story
"The Lady in the Looking-Glass" empties its heroine of all life. "Isabella
was perfectly empty. She had no thoughts. She had no friends. She cared
for nobody" (*CSF* 225). The trauma survivor's face-to-face relationship
of the self to itself is as deeply disturbed as any other. Caught in the

bedroom mirror's thrall, Dodge and Mrs. Swithin cannot but fail in their attempt to meet.

From this perspective, the pageant's conclusion seems as much an exorcism of the trauma of the mirror as it is a metaphor for the momentary union of its audience. In the massed "hand glasses, tin cans, scraps of scullery glasses, harness room glass, and heavily embossed silver mirrors" the audience sees themselves "not whole by any means, but at any rate sitting still" (*BA* 185). Can it really be "Ourselves! Ourselves!" found amid the fragments of self-reflection? Initially it would seem not. The audience is discomfited. "All shifted, preened, minced; hands were raised, legs shifted. Even Bart, even Lucy turned away" (*BA* 186). Only Mrs. Manresa, a monster of congratulatory self-regard, looks at her reflection without flinching, straightening her hair. Yet in this confusion of reflected images and sound, we can also glimpse the emergence of an audience that suggests a new kind of communal listening. "If we are socially constructed, Susan Brison argues, "in large part through our group-based narratives, the self is not a single, unified, coherent entity. Its structure is more chaotic, with harmonious and contradictory aspects, like the particles of an atom, attracting and repelling one another, hanging together in a whirling ever changing dance that any attempt at observation—or narration—alters" (95). *"Look at ourselves, ladies and gentlemen!"* the pageant's disembodied voice urges. *"Then at the wall, which we call, perhaps miscall civilization, to be built by* (here the mirrors flicked and flashed) *orts, scraps, and fragments like ourselves?"* (*BA* 188).

Woolf provides one answer to how this new civilization might be built on the fragmentary foundation of the face-to-face encounter seen in the conclusion of the pageant in the response of the Reverend G. W. Streatfield. Mocked as "a piece of traditional church furniture; a corner cupboard; or the top beam of a gate, fashioned by generations of village carpenters after some lost-in-the-mists-of antiquity model" (*BA* 190), Streatfield must assume the role of (male) expert, interpreting the meaning of the play to the others. That he succeeds in temporarily uniting the pageant's audience is the result of his refusal finally to take the role he might have claimed in his privileged position. "'I am not here to explain. That role has not been assigned to me. I speak only as one of the audience, one of ourselves. I caught myself too reflected, as it happened in my own mirror . . .' (Laughter)" (*BA* 192). He can in the moment extend the recognition of human otherness to the idiot excluded earlier from the "*we*" of civilization. "He too, Mr. Streatfield appeared to be saying, is a part of ourselves. But not a part we like to recognize, Mrs. Springett added silently, dropping her sixpence" (*BA* 194).

At the same time, Woolf presents to the reader a counter lesson to the potential valorization of the human community in the figure of the lesbian director Miss La Trobe, an outcast who is snubbed by the village women. "Nature had somehow set her apart from her kind. Yet she had scribbled in the margin of her manuscript: 'I am a slave of my audience'" (*BA* 211). Although she is the play's author, La Trobe excludes herself from the audience at its conclusion, and so cannot partake in its communal release. Instead, "she had suffered triumph, humiliation, ecstasy, despair—for nothing. Her heels had ground a hole in the grass" (*BA* 210). La Trobe is terrified of being alone and excluded from the human community. Entering the pub, she is greeted by silence as the villagers, who had been gossiping about her, stop talking, denying her what Levinas calls "the marvel of the social relation" and "the directness of the face-to-face, a 'between us' [*entre nous*], already conversation" (*Alterity* 93). Telling herself that her ostracism doesn't matter, La Trobe sits by herself and drinks.

> And listened. Words of one syllable sank down into the mud. She drowsed; she nodded. The mud became fertile. Words rose above the intolerably laden dumb oxen plodding through the mud. Words without meaning—wonderful words. (*BA* 212)

Despite Woolf's ostensible valorization of these words, La Trobe's creativity arises from the trauma of isolation, indeed retribution, for being other, and thus resembles that of the incest victim, similarly isolated and frequently assailed as an unreliable, if not mendacious, witness. Sue Campbell, in her discussion of how the testimony of women incest survivors is framed, notes the crucial role the audience plays in determining the success of the testimony. When "denied a community of experience with other women and the recognition of group harm," the incest victim "must bear the vulnerabilities of memory narrative alone, in an atmosphere of social distrust and public cross-examination, and without the possibility of a reciprocal challenge" (66). Shunned by the villagers, La Trobe is left to speak her words to herself, to be her own audience.

If Miss La Trobe cannot benefit from the potential for audience that is contained in her play's production, other of the novel's characters do. Immediately before she greets Dodge in the barn and recognizes his humanity in their encounter, Isa remarks on the power that the pageant has had on her, which seems to precipitate her ability to speak: "I wish the play didn't run in my head,' she said." (*BA* 113) "Still the play," Dodge asks her shortly after, reinforcing Isa's thought not as a distraction to their meeting, but as a motivator. Woolf concludes her novel with the same trope of the play. By implying that marriage is a performance, Woolf suggests not only that each spouse is an actor but also that each is an audience to the other. Written at the end of a life shadowed by the suicide that would follow its completion, *Between the Acts* is nevertheless hopeful. Incorporating the details of her own sexual abuse and its aftermath in the thoughts and actions of her characters, and reflecting the fear of violence and the failure of relationship that the trauma survivors may experience in their quest for a receptive and compassionate audience, Woolf nonetheless proffers in her novel's conclusion the possibility of interpersonal communication. "Left alone together for the first time that day" (*BA* 219), Isa and Giles are initially silent. Later, we are told, they will fight and embrace. But in the darkening house, as the curtain rises on the intimate marital play that readers are invited to imagine, Woolf gives to the fictional couple what may be her greatest benediction: "They spoke."

Notes

1. "The court," Felman claims, "gives stage to 'the tradition of the oppressed,' in helping the 'expressionless' of that tradition (the silence of the persecuted, the unspeakability of the trauma of oppression) to come into expression" (13). In doing so, she suggests an interesting perspective on Levinas' distrust of the "art of the theater" and Woolf's embrace of it in her novel.

2. Introducing his collection of essays on Levinas, Thomas Trezise suggests that "Levinas would not have achieved his current status and influence were it not that the ethical relation to 'the other' . . . continues to raise more questions than it answers" (1). Judith Butler has noted that the "Levinasian notion of the 'face' has caused critical consternation for a long time" and that "the imperative it delivers is not immediately translatable into a prescription that might be linguistically formulated and followed" (Butler *Life* 131). Indeed, one of Levinas' most recent translators has discussed the diffi-

culties of translating the key concept of the *visage*, the paradox of which is "neither presented nor represented and yet unique and individual, that bears above and beyond, that is, beneath all features the expression of the human condition, that opens being to the ethical dimension beyond being, this visage that is not a face" (*Humanism* xlv). Colin Davis has observed that "even such a sensitive and intelligent reviewer as Philippe Nemo gets rapped on the knuckles" by Levinas for missing the point, when trying to make the philosopher's thought more accessible to a popular audience, he continues to talk of faces as if they were real objects. "The temptation," Davis observes, "never quite goes away" (33).

3. In quoting from the later work and interviews of Levinas to describe the concept of the face, I am following the practice of Judith Butler who, in *Precarious Life*, also chose quotations from his later work because she believed that "they give a more mature and incisive formulation of the face" (159).

4. "'What is there in the face?'" Levinas asks. "In my analysis, the face is definitely not a plastic form like a portrait. The relation to the face is a relation to the absolutely weak. . . . It is a relation with destitution and consequently with what is alone and can undergo the supreme isolation called death" (*Righteous* 166). Understood in this context, the portrait in Pointz Hall signifies a prosperity at odds with the destitution that Levinas posits as an attribute of the concept of the face, even as it paradoxically reminds the viewer of the mortality that he claims as a principal characteristic. Woolf seems to share Levinas' distinction between the living face and the silencing (deadening) portrait. Sitting among the luncheon guests of Pointz Hall, William Dodge is caught off guard by a question interrupting his thoughts. "But he sat staring. 'I beg your pardon, sir?' he said. They all looked at him. 'I was looking at the pictures.' The picture looked at nobody. The picture drew them down the paths of silence" (*BA* 45). The portrait, Woolf implies, interdicts the speech that Levinas believes to be the response to the "invitation" of the face of the other.

5. In her essay included in this volume, Claire Kahane offers a more detailed reading of the rape, based on a true crime reported in the *Times* and known to Woolf.

6. In her recounting of this episode, Hermione Lee seems to take Woolf's jocular style at face value. I would argue instead that Janet Case's response is an indicator of the seriousness of the abuse that Woolf was reporting and which Woolf, like so many incest survivors, minimized. In the two instances of disclosure outside the family circle that we know of, both Case and Woolf's family physician, George Savage, reacted with shock and alarm. Savage, often mocked by Woolf, directly intervened and confronted her half-brother. For a more detailed analysis of Woolf's complex and seemingly contradictory report

of her abuse by her half-brothers see Pat Cramer's essay, "Trauma and Lesbian Returns," in this volume.

7. Woolf anticipates Levinas' "passivity receiving form or shock" in "Sketch of the Past." There, in a now-familiar passage, she describes "a sudden violent shock" that disrupted weeks of what she describes as "non-being." Fighting with her brother Thoby, as she is about to raise her fist, Woolf thinks, "[W]hy hurt another person?," after which she "dropped [her] hand instantly and let him beat [her]" (*MOB* 71). While Woolf reports feelings of "hopeless sadness," "powerlessness," and depression, she nonetheless argues that these sudden shocks are "particularly valuable." "And so I go on to suppose," she continues, "that the shock-receiving capacity is what makes me a writer" (72).

8. For an early discussion of this passage, which explicitly links Giles's outburst to the period's prevailing homophobia that refused to "name" its victim, see Eberly's "Talking It All Out".

9. Levinas suggests that "[p]erhaps the names of persons whose *saying* signifies a face—proper names, in the middle of all these common names and commonplaces—can resist the dissolution of meaning and help us to speak" (*Proper* 4). In eradicating—for "knew not" implies a rejection redolent of a biblical injunction—Dodge's proper name from memory, Giles refuses any recognition of the other facing him, and thus forecloses communication. Yet it is Giles whom Woolf describes as silenced in this social encounter: "Giles again shut his lips, not speaking" (*BA* 111).

OF SNAKES, TOADS, AND DUCKWEED: TRAUMATIC ACTS AND HISTORICAL ACTIONS IN *BETWEEN THE ACTS*

Claire Kahane

I

History, as a number of critics have noted, can be thought of as the record of traumatic events.[1] According to this logic, we recognize historical change and movement through the disruption of the ordinary flow of time, through the inherent violence of the extra-ordinary act, which ruptures sheer being. Otherwise, it seems, nothing happens.[2] The ambiguous title of Virginia Woolf's posthumous novel *Between the Acts* refers to the time between such events, both public and private, collective and individual. Set in England in June, 1939, on the brink of World War II, the novel's interactions take place literally between the two big acts of the twentieth century, the world wars, but also between the Spanish civil war—itself seen as a prelude—and the larger conflagration it foreshadowed. Indeed, written in the years 1939-40, the novel in its mood literally reflects the public mood of that time between Great Britain's declaration of war on Germany, which followed the collapse of Poland, and the actual fighting, which began almost a year later, a period of lull that was dubbed the *"Sitzkrieg."* [3] Although traumatic acts such as war and rape as well as the more domestic traumas of childhood enter the text, because this novel focuses on what happens between the acts, for the most part they enter it aslant, and remain in the background—an echo, a flash of vision, a memory—evoking a context of anxiety. Meanwhile, in the foreground, the flow of ordinary life with its social exchanges and private thoughts goes on in an unmarked stream.

It is in the midst of such an ordinary evening that the novel opens: a small group of people are sitting around having a desultory conversation on a midsummer's night at Pointz Hall, the country estate that is the novel's setting. As they emerge from their anonymity in the opening pages, we meet Bart Oliver, the gruff host, retired from the Indian Civil Service and nostalgic for the empire of his youth; his dreamy sister Lucy Swithin, an elderly woman who clings to religious visions of an essential unity of Being; his daughter-in-law Isa, who passively drifts through the novel composing poetic lines for no one's ears; and a neighboring gentleman farmer and his wife, Mr. and Mrs. Rupert Haines, who disappear from the novel after this prelude. The next day, we move through the points of view of the principal characters as they engage in family relations, ruminate about past and present, and prepare for the annual pageant to be performed at Pointz Hall. Some visitors—the flirtatious Mrs. Manresa and her gay male companion William Dodge—drop by; Giles, Isa's stockbroker husband, arrives from London. Local villagers appear and take their places as actors or as audience, and the pageant is performed, with intervals between the acts. Periodically, from off stage, the mooing of cows, the whirring of airplanes, and other contingent background sounds threaten to disrupt the illusion demanded by the playwright, Miss La Trobe, the figure of the artist in the novel, who hovers anxiously over her production. At the pageant's conclusion, a clergyman attempts to articulate its meaning and the audience disperses—the playwright to the pub, and Isa and Giles, the conjugal couple, to their bedroom.

So much for the novel's action—or rather inaction. If history is the record of traumatic events that mark historical moments, in this novel, the characters seem to be in stasis, like England itself, passing the time, waiting for the action to begin. Yet this summary is itself misleading, for in the foreground of this novel are "acts"—not the real traumas of history, but the play-acts of the pageant. This year's pageant is a kind of dramatized outline of English cultural history from its infantile primitive origins to the present moment, representing precisely that developmental English identity to be defended in the coming war.[4] Each period is performed as a separate act in a literary-historical procession—Elizabethan, Restoration, Victorian—that ends with "present time"—the time of the novel; and each act mimes the literary style of its period, as if to convey historical shifts as rhetorical style rather than substance. Between these acts, the characters of the frame-novel inter-act in innocuous social exchanges that suggest they too are in effect playing a role, each living in an islanded imagination. What connects them all, of course, is the attenuated Woolfian narrative voice that weaves a network of language through these stranded subjectivities, a voice itself precariously located "between" characters, a voice that keeps the "real" acts of history—the immanence of war and the possibility of invasion—distanced yet present, on the edge of the narrative frame and consciousness.

Moreover, this history pageant is acted by local villagers, that stratum of society traditionally most silent and least active in recorded history.[5] Absent from the historical record as significant personae, like the tobacconist Eliza Clark, who plays Queen Elizabeth, they enact and embody a kind of cultural devolution—a downward spiral from the heroic figures of the Renaissance to the licentious aristocracy of Restoration comedy to the prim and proper Victorian bourgeoisie and beyond—to the undefined "scraps, orts and fragments" of modern times, as Woolf phrases it, herself quoting from *Troilus and Cressida*, Shakespeare's ironic play about acts of sexuality, corruption, and betrayal played against a backdrop of war.[6]

As I mean to suggest by this brief summary, the word *act* itself becomes pivotal; like Freud's primal words, it is an ironic and ambiguous signifier of the real and the unreal, of history and fiction, its meaning antithetical and unstable.[7] Similarly, as in an alternating field-ground representation, the novel's central characters shift between being the audience to the acted "pageant," (which to some extent mirrors the emotional dynamics of their lives, though in different idioms) and acting as the primary protagonists of a modern domestic drama of inaction.[8] Isa is imprisoned in her own psyche, unable to speak the poetic words that flow through her mind; her husband Giles, like a diminished Prometheus chained to a rock, strains toward some heroic manly action but feels trapped in the liminality of the *status quo*; the elderly Bart Oliver no longer dances, but limps, yet dreams of himself as a young soldier in India, and acts the bullying brute, terrifying his young grandson as he tries to instill in him the martial virtue of bravery. His sister, Lucy Swithin, recollecting herself as a young girl forced by her brother to remove a bloody fishhook—an image that suggests a traumatic wounding—dreams of an imaginary past in which all creation was once a unified whole. In short, wrapped in illusion and nostalgia, the principal characters in the frame narrative speak hollow words that convey little more than the distance between their own desire and their alienated places in the social script of the present time. Thus the dialogue between them often seems more performance than performative, their speech acts serving as a cover-up of what cannot be said, at times even to the self.

II

Woolf's fiction has always engaged the question of a cover-up, depicting the subtle strategies people use to avoid traumatic confrontation. In *To the Lighthouse*, for example, Mrs. Ramsay, experiencing herself as a wedge of darkness, finds herself drifting toward the comforts of religion. But whereas Mrs. Ramsay quickly shakes herself out of her momentary lapse, Mrs. Swithin in *Between the Acts* prefers to remain swaddled in a religious vision of harmony, and recurrently fingering her cross, refuses history. Art too can function as a cover-up, offering like religion the illusion of connection—what Gilbert Rose calls "the illusion of responsive presence" that allows us to live with and recuperate from history's woundings.[9] Woolf's text implicitly interrogates this function of art through La Trobe's anxious desire to sustain the aesthetic illusion for her audience and keep them in her net of language. Similarly, the structure and literary conventions of the pageant itself, segmented into defined historical periods, each with its own literary style, offers its audience (including the reader) the related pleasure of recognizable form and ordered sequence. Its very divisions—each of which has a plot familiar to an English audience—are meant to function as aesthetic containers of the chaos of sheer being. But its last act, "Present Time: Ourselves," gives the lie to such conventional containment; the all-too-familiar comedic plot of misrecognition, loss, and regeneration no longer works. Instead, presenting the audience with mirror fragments of themselves, without language or exposition, La Trobe reaches for a new modern form, a form we might call traumatic, which fractures the performative space of illusion. In this way, she attempts to represent, and awaken in her audience, a disturbing awareness of the tenuousness of modern subjectivity. "Dispersed are we," the gramophone insistently repeats, and this paradoxically becomes the unifying theme.

Like La Trobe's pageant, Woolf's novel also radically attempts to represent and thus contain the fractured state of modern subjectivity and its magnified reflection in the coming theatre of war. Unlike her previous work, however, *Between the Acts* focuses on the anticipation of an actual catastrophe which it attempts to transmit to readers through novelistic form.[10] For example, *Between the Acts* begins *in medias res*, without clarifying exposition, and proceeds to present the reader with an almost seamless surface, without boundaries, without formal breaks into chapters or sections—in other words, without those conventional narrative devices that mark the passing of time. Reading this novel requires an act of rupture, a disorienting penetration into an ambiguous situation that mimes the novel's thematic apprehensions. Moreover, once inside the novel's opening pages, although the reader is soon offered a familiar romantic plot—Isa, entering the drawing room, finds herself attracted to the gentleman farmer Rupert Haines—this plot goes nowhere, or rather remains fixed as an undeveloped fantasy-fragment in Isa's imagination. Indeed, after this initial prelude, the silent Rupert Haines drops out of sight, glimpsed only once from afar later in the novel. As Isa herself remarks—and here Woolf makes a point that Melanie Klein had developed into a theory—"Did the plot matter? . . . The plot was only there to beget emotion. There were only two emotions, love; and hate. Don't bother about the plot. The plot's nothing" (90-91). Without the plot and its structuration of desire around an action, the conventional means by which we can literally locate our position in relation to characters are opaque; we must look elsewhere for the generation of meaning. That elsewhere, I would suggest, is in the medium itself; as with poetry or music, it is the affective resonance of Woolf's semiosis that becomes the ambiguous site of the novel's murky truths.

III

Whereas there is little real action in the present time of *Between the Acts*, the sense of incipient trauma is pervasive. This anticipatory effect is achieved in great part through Woolf's *rhetorical* manipulations: using anaphoric linguistic patterns and textual disjunctions, playing with the semiotics of the word, its sound as well as its sense, scattering literary and historical allusions that function as troubling memory-associations, Woolf conveys to the reader that something awful has happened or will happen that cannot be directly spoken.[11] Indeed, Woolf induces an anxiety of reading in this novel that from the very beginning resonates with the more extensive historical anxiety of its context: the imminent breach of national boundaries by the invading barbarian hordes and its foreshadowing of an even greater meta-trauma—the potential devastation of Western civilization through a terrifying liberation of its discontents. Even the opening delineation of the English countryside—a literal overview from the perspective of an airplane—points toward the material manifestations of historical trauma; from a distance we see "the scars" left on the landscape by history: "by the Britons; by the Romans; by the Elizabethan manor house; and by the plough, when they ploughed the hill to grow wheat in the Napoleonic wars" (4). This virtual archeology of England's past will, in the course of the novel, be linked to a present time seemingly fated to repeat a traumatic moment.

Appropriately, the novel opens with a series of jarring disjunctions. It is a midsummer night, conventionally signifying a romantic time-space, but the conversation into which the reader is thrown is about a cesspool that needs repair. Immediately, we are confronted with the apparatus that evacuates the detritus of civilization—the abject functions of the body that we would cover up in order to sustain the ideal. To underscore this de-idealization, the phonemes of the text sound a harsh and brutal opening theme. Mrs. Haines, wife of the gentleman farmer Rupert Haines (the object of Isa's romantic fantasies), is described as a "goosefaced woman with eyes protruding as if they saw something to gobble in the gutter" (3). This repetitive succession of hard "g's" recurs, as in the subsequent reference to her "goose-like eyes, gobbling"—a description that anaphorically recalls the German "goosestep" marching through and also "gobbling" up Europe, thus linking Mrs. Haines with a devouring force being loosed upon Europe. This proliferation of assaultive gutturals is matched by a proliferation of devouring images on the opening page. The song of a bird heard through the window is not the conventional nightingale's, we are told, but the sound of daylight birds "chuckling over the substance and succulence of the day, over worms, snails, grit, even in sleep"(3). Of course, the nightingale itself has a mythic association to trauma—the rape of Philomela by her brother-in-law, who then has her tongue cut out to keep hidden his incestuous assault. This initial allusion is repeated later, in Bart's recurrent imaginary address to Lucy as "sister swallow"—an invocation that evokes Procne, the sister of the raped Philomela.[12]

Indeed, rape as a traumatic event with reverberations in both literary and historical memory enters the text quickly and is linked, as I will argue, to Woolf's own personal history through these literary allusions. When, for example, Isa, fantasizing a romance between herself and the silent gentleman farmer Mr. Haines, hears her father-in-law quoting Byron, the words materialize as "two rings, perfect rings, that floated them, herself and Haines, like two swans down stream" (5). The simile, which recalls Spenser's "Prothalamion"—a celebration of marriage embodied in the "two perfect rings"—is turned inside out as the swans, images of purity in Spenser, are now sullied: "his snow-white breast was circled with a tangle of dirty duckweed; and she too, in her webbed feet was entangled, by her husband" (5). But it is not only the manifest content of the image—the tangle of dirty duckweed—that conveys affective meaning here; for those familiar with Woolf's autobiography, the very sound of the metaphor resonates with allusions to transgressive family relations, for it echoes the family name of Woolf's childhood seducers, her half-brothers, Gerald and George Duckworth.[13] Duckworth/duck-weed: Woolf's text plays variations on a linguistic differential that also sounds a personal counterpoint to the apprehensions that trouble her final fiction.[14]

IV

It is perhaps no accident that while Woolf was writing *Between the Acts* and its theatrical sketches of English history, she was also engaged in a more personal sketch of the past, a fragmentary account of her life and art that was informed by a consciousness of trauma and its relationship to writing. "The shock receiving capacity is what makes me a writer," Woolf remarks in "A Sketch of the Past," also written in 1939-1940. In this brief but extraordinary memoir-essay, Woolf meditates on the link between a disruptive traumatic event—a shock—and the process of writing, through which she can restore the order of things. As she implies in commenting on "the strongest pleasure known to me," her "great delight to put the severed parts together," the writer engaged in composing a work re-asserts an efficacy that is a powerful counterforce to experiences of disintegration that characterize trauma. In finding metaphors and metonymies for traumatic experience, the writer can put together through language a simulacrum of trauma in an act that restores her sense of subjective agency. But while the writer can thus "re-present" the process of trauma in a way that is psychologically satisfying, the reader who experiences the trauma vicariously in representation can be unsettled through the very act of reading. As when Isa unexpectedly comes upon the newspaper description of the rape, readerly identifications can strike a disturbing chord. What seems to save both reader and writer is the containing form of language, of literary composition as an aesthetic object that links both writer and reader in an experience of rapport and integration.[15]

The shock to the reader in "A Sketch" is Woolf's revelation of her own sexual violation in childhood. Finally opening a door she had kept closed to the public, Woolf reveals in one brief, tantalizing and climactic passage—its placement at the end of a paragraph a dramatic punctuation—that she was sexually molested by the intrusive fingerings of her half-brother, Gerald Duckworth. In this context, might one hear in her homely metaphor of trauma—the "enemy hidden behind the cotton wool of daily life"—a suggestion of a literal bodily, indeed phallic, threat "hidden" in the ordinary cotton wool fabric of domestic appurtenances? In any case, it seems germane that while in her letters and in reported conversations, she frequently referred to the forced sexual attentions she had endured as an adolescent from her half-brother George, whose fondlings became a subject of sardonic humor for her, until this late memoir, she herself had kept hidden and unverbalized Gerald's much earlier violation of her body when she was a child.[16]

Significantly, at the very time she was probing her memories of familial violations in "A Sketch," she and Leonard were in despair about Germany's imminent invasion of Britain, as indeed was all of Britain. How seriously they viewed the situation is captured by the fact that both Leonard and Virginia had discussed suicide as a possible response should Hitler successfully invade. When war was finally declared, Woolf wrote in her diary: "this is the worst of all my life's experiences" (*D5*: 234). Given the traumatic public events through which Woolf was living in 1939-1940, it is likely that this anxious political moment evoked more personal memories of past traumatic intrusions not fully assimilated. Certainly, it seems more than coincidental that she both names a remembered early violation of her body in the memoir and makes rape a key trope of the present time in the novel, while anticipating a national violation on the real historical horizon: a future rape writ large.

With this overarching metaphor that encompasses both a personal and a political act of boundary violation, Woolf's writing trajectory seems to have come full circle. In *Three Guineas* (1938), she had explicitly blamed the patriarchal structure of social relations for the destructive policies and rapaciousness of the present time. Yet, in her first novel, *The Voyage Out* (1915), she had introduced the theme of suspect and intrusive fathers and had implicitly criticized the domestic Oedipal politics of the patriarchal family. Take, for example, her description at the beginning of that first novel of the uncomfortable physical proximity between Rachel and her widower father: "he drew his arm round Rachel's shoulder, thus making them come uncomfortably close . . ." (21). Not only does Woolf insinuate a paternal violation of the boundaries of familial intimacy, but she also compounds that insinuation by her allusive intra-textual use of *The Rape of Lucrece*, which Ridley Ambrose, another paternal figure, loudly declaims in a penetrating voice to anyone in ear range. These textual hints of paternal transgression in *The Voyage Out* come to a climax in Richard Dalloway's traumatic embrace of Rachel in a scene that recalls Woolf's descriptions of George Duckworth's behavior. It also evokes the domestic drama of corrupt fathers abusing naïve daughters that Freud described in his case history of Dora: "Fragment of an Analysis of a Case of Hysteria."[17] *Between the Acts* returns to this theme of sexual and political trauma at the heart of the home and the homeland but is more severe in its critical assessment of corrupt patriarchal structures.

Given this dark shadow on the whitewashed representations of domestic intimacy and public virtue, how ironic sounds the repetition of "Home Sweet Home," the familiar bourgeois refrain in *Between the Acts* that closes La Trobe's playlet about the eminent Victorians. Foregrounding the voice of the totemic policeman, who smugly asserts the values of the Victorian age, La Trobe, the lesbian artist, criticizes the Victorian patriarchy for its authoritarianism, its materialism, its spiritual and sexual hypocrisy—a critique Woolf had made in her own voice in *Three Guineas*. But she does this by filling the policeman's dialogue with abjected body images that contrast middle-class purity with the pollution of the working class, confirming the need to keep them oppressed and exploited, but most of all separate, in their own class space.

> Purity our watchword; prosperity and respectability. If not, why let 'em fester in . . . Cripplegate; St. Giles's; Whitechapel; the Minories. Let 'em sweat at the mines; cough at the looms; rightly endure their lot. That's the price of Empire; that's the white man's burden. (*BA* 163)

Yet in spite of her critique of the Victorians, Woolf simultaneously recognizes a powerful longing in her audience for the Victorian dream-family, for "Papa's beard," and "Mama's knitting" (173). No one really wants to strip away the Emperor's clothes; no one wants to see what's really happening in the obscure corners of the home sweet home. Nevertheless, there is a suspicious trace of "something": when the actors depart from the stage, we hear someone in the audience retrospectively wonder whether there was "something . . . 'unhygienic' about the home? Like a bit of meat gone sour, with whiskers?" (174). If this is a timid interrogation, the repugnant tenor of the image of spoiled meat—a very literal metaphor of carnal corruption—gives it a very material reality that is linked specifically to corrupt Victorian fathers through the word "whiskers," Woolf's recurrent metonymy for the Victorian patriarch.

Between the Acts subverts the idea that the home is a safe space, repeatedly implying it may hide the threat of potentially traumatizing acts; in contrast, "A Sketch of the Past," which gives us a vision of the containing and renewing function of art, is, as I have suggested, less bleak. If traumatic acts fragment the subject through an assault on its integrity, Woolf suggests in the memoir, as she does in such novels as *To the Lighthouse* and *The Waves*, that they can also spark a creative reaction by tapping into the binding force of Eros, a primary function of aesthetic form. Indeed, not just the pleasure of *composition* but the validation of life itself, Woolf suggests, can paradoxically emerge from trauma; its break-up of ordinary experience can remove the blinders of convention and lead to a moment of "revelation," a transient apprehension of emotional meaning.

This I take to be the connection between Woolf's revelation of the traumatic autobiographical moment in "A Sketch of the Past" and her simultaneous elaboration of the concept so crucial to her writing, "moments of being"— the sudden experience of full being in the midst of daily life. Although, to some extent, Woolf's "moments" are similar to the Joycean epiphany, there is a significant difference that speaks to the traumatic basis of Woolf's concept: each of the exemplary experiences Woolf uses to illustrate a moment of being is a moment of horror, a revelation of death in the midst of life, of the abyss underlying daily life. "Week after week passed . . . and nothing made any dint upon me. Then, for no reason that I know about, there was a sudden violent shock" (*MOB* 71) Paradoxically, while consciousness of being, like history itself, emerges through the effect of a trauma, it is at the same time shadowed by a violence that turns the subject, already split, into scraps, orts and fragments that have again to be re-formed and composed. In "A Sketch," Woolf gives us a personal version of the Freudian dialectics of life and death, of Eros and Thanatos, that informs her fiction and impels her to write.

Certainly one can see her attempt to insert that dualism into *Between the Acts*: in the final act of La Trobe's pageant, "Present Time: Ourselves," after the anonymous voice of the artist has compelled the audience to see themselves as abject scraps of a ruined civilization, that voice insists—with a kind of faith that, like Lucy Swithin's, is itself suspect—on an affirmation through aesthetic compositions, in this case, music, the purest of the arts. Someone puts a record on the gramophone— Bach? Beethoven? No matter, the reader is assured:

> Like quicksilver sliding, filings magnetized, the distracted united. The tune began; the first note meant a second; the second a third. Then down beneath a force was born in opposition; then another. On different levels ourselves went forward; flower gathering some on the surface; others descending to wrestle with the meaning; but all comprehending; all enlisted. (189)

Yet as the somewhat ridiculous figure of Lucy Swithin suggests, this "all" remains a fragile wish: in 1939, the dialectical struggle between Life and Death was an uneven one, and neither synthesis nor progressive historical movement seemed likely. Rather, music itself becomes a figure of cosmic disjunction: "What a cackle, what a cacophony!" (187). Thus, while nothing much happens in the novel, as Maria DiBattista remarked so cogently, "*Between the Acts* is a war book of the most compelling and searching kind, a novel that makes history its subject matter in order to question the validity of art, the limits of the book, and the powers of illusion in a world absorbed in the work of destruction" (195). It does so, however, by invoking the continuing effects of the most personal traumas of childhood.

V

Woolf introduces the specific theme of childhood trauma on the opening pages of the novel when Mrs. Haines, remarking on the inappropriateness of their conversation about cesspools on a midsummer's night, recalls a traumatic experience from her past: "As a small child in a perambulator, a great carthorse had brushed within an inch of her face"(3). This reference may well be an intentional allusion on Woolf's part to Freud's major case history of little Hans, "Analysis of a Phobia in a Five-Year-Old Boy" (1909), his clinical ground for theorizing the Oedipal complex and the significance of incestuous desire in psychic development.

Whether intentional or not, Freud's interpretation of the child's horse phobia seems strikingly relevant to Woolf's text. In Freud's interpretation, the child's Oedipal desire evokes a retaliatory anxiety—fear of the phallic father, fear of the devouring mother, of precisely those parental figures of infantile love and hate upon whom one depends for survival. Little Hans assuages these fears by displacing the parental threats and his own unconscious aggression onto the horse, or more accurately, onto its monstrous and exposed parts, experiencing a danger from the horse that is both oral and phallic. Woolf's spin reverses the gender—Mrs. Haines has the horse phobia —suggesting a feminine fear of oral and phallic aggression that will emerge in the novel as a central thematic, even though the character to which it is initially attached disappears.[18]

After Mrs. Haines's reference to her childhood horse phobia—its oral anxieties intensified by the description of daylight birds chuckling over their feed—in the very next scene, Woolf presents her own version of a childhood trauma that could result in an animal phobia: little George's traumatic brush with a giant hairy animal, Bart's Afghan hound, and its monstrous master, who is subsequently revealed to be his grandfather. Moreover, in identifying Bart's dog as an Afghan, Woolf hints at another historical trauma: imperial Britain's three disastrous military incursions into Afghanistan in deployments which devastated the British troops when they imprudently tried to conquer Afghan territory.[19]

The childhood scene begins innocently enough, with little George's exploration of the parts of a flower, described through a multi-sensory discourse that evokes both his primitive immersion in sensuous being, and that epistemological "drive to know" that Melanie Klein theorized:

> The little boy had lagged and was grouting in the grass. . . . George grubbed. The flower blazed between the angles of the roots. Membrane after membrane was torn. It blazed a soft yellow, a lambent light under a film of velvet; it filled the caverns behind the eyes with light. All that inner darkness became a hall, leaf smelling, earth smelling, of yellow light. And the tree was beyond the flower; the grass, the flower, and the tree were entire. Down on his knees grubbing he held the flower complete. Then there was a roar and a hot breath and a stream of coarse grey hair rushed between him and the flower. Up he leapt, toppling in his fright, and saw coming towards him a terrible peaked eyeless monster moving on legs, brandishing arms. "Good morning sir," a hollow voice boomed at him from a beak of paper. (11-12)

Significantly, the scene is presented through the perception of the trauma-tized child so that the reader is, like the child, confounded about the roar and the stream of coarse grey hair that is the Afghan hound; we too are initially ignorant of the eyeless monster's true identity—his grandfather, who, playacting, has jumped out from the bushes with a newspaper rolled around his nose. This is a scene of misrecognition that neither party is likely to forget. But what is particularly meaningful in Woolf's presenta-tion of this scene is that it first invokes the child's active curiosity—his pleasurable grubbing, so that "membrane after membrane was torn, . . he held the flower complete"—and then, by means of a sudden shift of narrative perspective, dislocates the reader's secure relation to the text, so that we too do not know that what has come between George and his flower is his grandfather—insensitively playing, and not bearing down to commit some fearsome act.

George's tearing of "membrane after membrane" to possess the flower, however, also rhetorically foreshadows another description of an implicitly torn membrane, one hidden in the newspaper wrapped around his grandfather's nose, an account of a gang rape at Whitehall contained in that same paper which Isa reads in the very next scene. If it is the little boy who tears the membrane of the flower, it is the big boys, the guards at Whitehall, seat of the military, who deflower a young girl, in a scene of rape that is subsequently placed at the center of Isa's consciousness. Not only does the rape scene at Whitehall continue to reverberate in Isa's consciousness as a real act in the present time that she tries to assimilate, but so does its political extrapolation as a metaphor of current history: the rape of Europe by the Nazi bull.

In this context of personal and political transgression, is it too much of a stretch to suggest that Woolf, in naming her little Oedipus George, had in mind her half brother George Duckworth, that incestuous groper in the very heart of the Stephen family? Whether or not Woolf intended that association, in moving from a childhood trauma to an adult woman's reading about trauma, the novel's sequence makes a connection between childhood trauma and its later representations and deferred effects; it also raises some key questions about the transmission of trauma as a second-ary traumatic experience through representation—what I will call the traumatic imaginary. Does the traumatic effect of representation depend on a real prior experience that is evoked? If trauma is unrepresentable, can one transfer trauma from the real to the symbolic? Can one experience trauma through an act of empathic reading? Moreover, do the particular traumatic acts of the novel suggest a gendering of trauma? Certainly, in the novel's thinking about the relation between trauma and representation, the literal and metaphoric meanings of rape assume a gendered particularity crucial to the novel.

The scene of reading which literally depicts the rape of a young girl, actually begins with a prelude on reading and its effects: Bart, having read his newspaper, sinks into sleep and dreams of himself as a young military man in India. Did Bart read the rape story before he fell asleep? Has it provoked his dreaming of himself as a virile young soldier? Certainly, this sequence itself offers an implicit critique of phallic desire and militaristic power. In a passage echoing T.S. Eliot's vision of contemporary life, Woolf creates the old man's imperialist dreamscape as a nightmare consequence of the wars of empire: "a wasteland, . . . no water . . . and in the sand a hoop of ribs; a bullock maggot-eaten in the sun; and in the shadow of the rock, savages; and in his hand a gun. . ." (*BA* 17). Isa, entering the library, awakens Bart from this vision and, attacked by him for rearing a cowardly son, looks first at the books in the library for distraction, but sees nothing to answer her need. Instead, what catches her eye is the newspaper and the words: "A horse with a green tail", a phrase which seduces her into the act of reading. Given the prior allusions to horses, this is a resonant moment in the text.[20] Showing us the process of seduction by a text and its psychic consequences once its meaning is digested, Woolf depicts Isa, in a mimicry of developmental stages, falling into an identification with the victimized girl: first, like a child, seduced by the fantastic "horse with a green tail;" then, like an adolescent, seduced by the romantic image evoked by the phrase, "the guard at Whitehall"; but ultimately, "building word upon word" and arriving at the whole story, horrified by the revelation of its meaning:

> The troopers told her the horse had a green tail; but she found it was just an ordinary horse. And they dragged her up to the barrack room where she was thrown upon a bed. Then one of the troopers removed part of her clothing, and she screamed and hit him about the face . . . (*BA* 20).

Significantly, the climax of the rape is covered over in the text by an ellipsis, a conventional sign of repression. But what is missing from the scene, the representation of the actual bodily violation, can be discovered in displaced form in the prior scene when little George, grubbing in the earth, discovers the flower and pulls it from the earth, tearing its membrane. Reading backward, one can infer a core displacement of the traumatic scene of rape, from the newspaper story that Isa reads, to the more innocent tearing of the flower and its membrane in the scene that precedes it.

There is, however, a significant difference in these two scenes: in the garden we see George's *active* infantile curiosity interrupted, as he himself is traumatized by the sudden appearance of threatening figures; in contrast, Isa's act of reading produces an empathic *identification* with the trauma of *being* violated. Indeed, Woolf seems to insinuate a conventional gendering of trauma that depends on an imagined subject or object position in a primal scene and its cultural ramifications. George's apprenticeship to the patriarchy seems exemplified in his act of appropriation—possessing the flower—even though it is followed by a threat to his well-being; Isa's place as mother and wife seems, in contrast, to stifle her poetic acts, for even though she transforms her desires and dissatisfactions into a flow of poetic lines, they remain unspoken, even aborted.

Nevertheless, reading about the rape seems to shock Isa into a moment of being, the trauma reverberating in her consciousness for the next several pages: "That was real; so real that on the mahogany door panels she saw the Arch in Whitehall; through the Arch the barrack room; in the barrack room the bed, and on the bed the girl was screaming and hitting him about the face, when the door (for in fact it was a door) opened and in came Mrs. Swithin carrying a hammer" (*BA* 20). Having imaginatively zoomed toward the secret center of a traumatic event, Isa's imaginary reconstruction of the rape scene is interrupted, its conclusion foreclosed, this time not through an ellipsis (repression) but through an abrupt impingement of the external world: Mrs. Swithin enters through an actual door, carrying a hammer. Immediately, however, Mrs. Swithin's hammer—both a tool and a weapon—is incorporated into Isa's traumatic imaginary as a kind of defensive screen memory covering over the gap. The next time the rape scene returns to her mind, the hammer fills in the ellipsis:

> Every summer, for seven summers now, Isa had heard the same words; about the hammer and the nails; the pageant and the weather. Every year they said, would it be wet or fine; and every year it was – one or the other. The same chime followed the same chime, only this

> year beneath the chime she heard: "The girl screamed and hit him
> about the face with a hammer." (*BA* 22)

Beneath the music and the chime of repetition is the traumatic event, inaccessible. But now the hammer is strategically placed over the blank space, producing an image of a defensive hitting about the face *that blots out* the act of violation with a vengeance. Although through this revision of the scene, which moves the event from the real to the symbolic, Isa moves to recover some agency, still, the traumatic core, what happens to the girl, remains unrepresented.

VI

To recapitulate: from the opening scene, which functions in the novel as a prelude, in which Woolf first lays down through the associative resonance of language the theme of childhood sexual trauma, to the scene in the garden between little George and his grandfather, to the library scene where rape is literalized as a fact in the daily news, Woolf develops a theme on which she plays variations throughout the text: the breaking through into consciousness of a violent act, whether public or private, that reveals a brutish world threatened by regressive primal forces that may overwhelm or cause a deadly breach in the protective barrier of civilization. Breakthrough; rupture of the ego's protective barrier; this was literally Freud's definition of trauma, and it is also, by definition, analogous to the apprehension of rape that is both literal and metaphoric in *Between the Acts*. If Woolf's contemporary autobiographical "Sketch" comments on her taking pleasure in putting the severed parts together, her last novel presents a more traumatic vision of ontological dis-integration, an urge to return to a previous state of things, to use Freud's description of the death drive, an urge that is given aesthetic form at the novel's conclusion, in a violent primal meta-scene of origins.[21]

Of course, all of Woolf's fictions on some level give us a glimpse of an underlying violence that seems to be inherent in the human condition; but in other fictions, Woolf contained that violence in a particular character or in a thematic metaphor. In *Mrs. Dalloway*, for example, traumatic violence remains confined primarily within the consciousness of Septimus Smith; his memories of war and his flight into suicidal oblivion allow Clarissa Dalloway to acknowledge the death drive through her projective identification with Septimus, but also to contain it through this split, and thus to be able to commit herself to life. But in *Between the Acts*, language, like history itself, is on the verge of a breakdown, beset by primitive drives which threaten imminent fragmentation and catastrophe, not just to individual characters, but to the entire fabric of Western civilization.[22] Those figures who think they can escape, like Mrs. Swithin, called "Batty" by the servants, or like La Trobe, who hopes that art can provide coherence, are chasing rainbows. Clearly, the library has given way to the newspaper; in the present time, trauma is not remembered and recuperated through enduring literary compositions that make it whole, but instead repeated in daily reports of violent fragments of history that are impossible to assimilate into a narrative of identity and wholeness. Instead, the newspaper is the source of a daily assault on readers that creates black holes of consciousness, dissociations and denials and a numbing paralysis that attempt to block or ward off a traumatic identification with the victims of daily life, or with the real itself.

There is, however, one directly represented action in the frame narrative that, occurring during one of the intervals between the acts of the pageant, breaks through the stasis. In a surprising and sudden act of violence—an act that in a sense provides a climax, or perhaps more appropriately, an *ejaculatio praecox*, to the traumatic undercurrents I have been tracing here—Giles kills a snake that has become engorged with a toad. Unable to swallow the toad or to disgorge it, this reptile, carrying also the burden of its own discursive history as a figure of evil, is now caught literally between the acts in a paralysis that will kill it.

> There, crouched in the grass, curled in an olive green ring, was a snake. Dead? No, choked with a toad in its mouth. The snake was unable to swallow; the toad was unable to die. A spasm made the ribs contract; blood oozed. It was birth the wrong way round—a monstrous inversion. So, raising his foot, he stamped on them. The mass crushed and slithered. The white canvas on his tennis shoes was bloodstained and sticky. But it was action. Action relieved him. He strode to the Barn, with blood on his shoes. (99)

Here, in an Aesopian metaphor, the snake and the toad, both predator and prey, are stuck in a perpetual coupling that means not life, but death for both. Impulsively stomping on this "monstrous inversion"—the word itself is loaded with Giles's phobic revulsion at homosexuality—Giles acts to obliterate both victim and victimizer in a frenzy of aggressive rage at the *status quo*.

We might call this the bloody primal scene of the mid twentieth century, which haunts *Between the Acts*: a scene of paralysis provoking reactive rage and destruction.

If paralysis and enforced passivity is unbearable, the bloodstained and sticky white tennis shoes provide a vivid image of the lethal consequences of action; the image recurs explicitly as a metaphor of La Trobe's despair when the play fails to sustain the audience in aesthetic illusion: "Panic seized her. Blood flowed from her shoes. This is death, death, death, she noted in the margin of her mind; when illusion fails" (*BA* 180). In both instances, the text marks a sudden and devastating confrontation with an unsupportable reality. La Trobe, the artist, deals with her traumatic recognition by once again sinking into the *"fertile mud"* of her imagination, and again conceiving an image, apprehending "words without meaning, wonderful words" (212, italics mine): a new play. Giles, however, unable to tolerate the stasis in his own life, and at an impasse in his marriage, using extramarital affairs (we get hints of his affairs in his flirtation with Mrs. Manresa) to sustain the illusion of potency, lashes out in a brutal stomping of the helpless snake-in-the-grass, a projection of his own intolerable condition. While that destructive act may relieve his impotent rage, it also links him to the militant forces of a death-worshipping fascism that Britain will be called upon to fight.

VII

I have been tracing the effects of an anticipated trauma, an apprehension about a future event that reaches backward into the past for confirmation: something terrible that happened is fated to happen again, and one is helpless to ward it off. Writing during the *"Sitzkrieg"* and seemingly captured by the mood of political paralysis and apprehension that pervaded England, Woolf herself captured that public mood in the novel and linked it to the traumatic psychohistory of the individual subject. In this context, we can read *Between the Acts* as a trauma pageant in three acts. First act: the (male) infantile fear of castration, represented by George's terrifying perception of a disapproving grandfather who will punish him. Second act: the (female) infantile fear of bodily violation— the torn membrane—an apprehension manifest in Isa's response to the newspaper account of the gang rape of a young girl, a fear too readily *actualized* during wartime. Third act: a stark representation of the unrepresented bloody act, the blood itself that is missing in the first two scenes here gushing forth to testify to the reality of the traumatic wound, imaged in a devastating primal scene of mutual destruction.

But the three-part drama that runs through the novel's surface does not move forward: love, hate, impasse. Impasse and repetition is the overt theme of this plotless novel; without a plot, there is no climax, no resolution, not even a dialectics of progress; only the repetitive struggle between oppositional forces. Through Isa's consciousness, however, Woolf turns the impasse into a kind of resolution, evoking peace. "Love. Hate. Peace," Isa thinks, is "the ply of human life" (*BA* 111). And indeed, who would reject peace after the struggle between warring affects? But Isa's peace is not a synthesis; it is rather the peace of Freud's death drive, the urge to move out of the fray into homeostatic stillness. While it is Isa who gives voice to this urge, her lines a continual repetition of the burden of unfulfilled desire and its consequence, a desire to fade out of existence—"Oh, that the waters should cover me"—one cannot help hearing a prophetic echo of Woolf's own urgent last act. In the novel, such peace, like all-out war, is deferred; in her diary, which became in its fragmented prose style more and more similar to her novel, Woolf records her mood of waiting for what seemed the end: "Will the 9 o'clock bulletin end it all?—our lives, oh yes, & everything for the next 50 years?" (*D5*: 231).

In the last act of the novel, even as the seeds of La Trobe's new play are beginning to burgeon, Isa and Giles retire to the bedroom, which expands and metamorphoses from a domestic space into a giant cave, while they, losing their particular identity, become male and female engaged in a recurrent act of brutish coupling far removed from Mrs. Swithin's dreamy musings about the origins of being. In a rhetoric that becomes allegorical, Woolf moves us from the social to the mythic, to a trans-historical scene of creation now imagined as a violent encounter beyond the pleasure principle.

> Alone, enmity was bared; also love. Before they slept, they must fight; after they had fought, they would embrace. From that embrace another life might be born. But first they must fight, as the dog fox fights with the vixen, in the heart of darkness, in the fields of night. (*BA* 219)

While this conclusion seems to assimilate Thanatos to Eros—new life perpetually being reborn—the closing metaphor of "the heart of darkness" suggests otherwise. Raising aggression to a universal principle, the last lines of the novel allude to a text that is a major pre-text for Woolf's novel: Conrad's *Heart of Darkness*, with its own mythic representation of the death drive, and its own flirtation with the dissolution of boundaries.[23]

Conrad represented Marlow's journey into the heart of Africa as a symbolic journey back into prehistoric time, before the rule of law and reason, but also into the depths of the human psyche. "We penetrated deeper and deeper into the heart of darkness. . . . We were wanderers on a prehistoric earth. . . . we were traveling in the night of first ages, of those ages that are gone, leaving hardly a sigh—and no memories" (63). The phrase "no memories" suggests the absence of representations of the past and therefore a deracination from history. Marlow, however, haunted by the voice that has enunciated "the horror" at the heart of European history, is compelled to pass on his story to a circle of listeners; Conrad, after his own traumatic witnessing of the unspeakable human abuses of European empires in Africa, writes *Heart of Darkness*. Similarly, haunted by the imminence of invasion and the specter of fascism, Woolf writes *Between the Acts*, a text that moves inexorably closer to her precursor's apprehension of a primitive heart of darkness engulfing Europe. Indeed, one can hear echoes of Conrad's allusions to prehistory in Woolf's concluding passage:

> The great hooded chairs had become enormous. And Giles too. And Isa too against the window. The window was all sky without colour. The house had lost its shelter. It was night before roads were made, or houses. It was the night that dwellers in caves had watched from some high place among rocks. (*BA* 219)

But there is one more sentence that is strictly Woolf, not Conrad: "Then the curtain rose. They spoke" (*BA* 219). Words, and with words a limit, a possible break in the infinity of night, but also a performance, an act on which the curtain rises repeatedly: a speech-act that itself is unrepresented in this text, and perhaps ultimately unrepresentable. But one can sense Woolf reaching for it, reaching through the rhythms and rhymes, the assonances and dissonances of her language, for the word that can recuperate the thing itself.

VIII

If history is symptomatic of trauma, is literature an attempt at cure? This question around which I have been circling might have been asked by Woolf herself as she set herself the task of writing a new kind of novel that would incorporate both the anxious state of England in 1939-40 and the state of her own mind under the threat of invasion. In a diary entry, Woolf had proposed her idea for such a novel: "I rejected; we substituted; we composed of many different things; all life all art, all waifs and strays—a rambling capricious but somehow unified whole—the present state of my mind'?"(*D5*: 135). "The present state of my mind" is what she gives us in *Between the Acts*, but the "we-ness" remains elusive. Writing while Britain was being threatened with a barbarism that would recall its own savage origins, menaced from without by the Nazi juggernaut that was already goose-stepping its way across the European continent, and from within by a sense that her inner demons were about to break out, Woolf found it impossible to sustain a vision of the "somehow unified whole." "Who will be killed tonight?' (*D5*: 330) she asks and the question—uncannily similar to one that occurs in her first novel—now reverberates more menacingly as an undercurrent in her last.[24]

In sum, *Between the Acts* is not sanguine about the possibility of recuperation through literature; it does not give art the victory over trauma; history cannot be overridden by an aesthetic illusion of coherence. If Eros is the force of uniting and binding [Freud, *SE* 19:45], in 1940, it is not the binding force of Eros, but the unraveling force of Thanatos that is now loosed upon the world, and the consequences—"scraps orts and fragments"—are the waste products of an entropic civilization too much bent under the violent blows of a brutal reality to be knit together. "Reality too strong," (*BA* 180) La Trobe acknowledges, recognizing in despair that her pageant has failed. Apparently Woolf also felt her completed draft of *Between the Acts* insufficient to her reach; she did not send it out for publication before she herself exited.

But Woolf's text was more prescient than she perhaps recognized, as applicable to the politics of our time as to hers. The image of the snake engorged with the toad is a powerful metaphor of the fate of Germany, snake attempting to swallow England as toad, but biting off more than it could chew. A half-century later, that metaphor is even more uncanny as an image of our American psycho-political reality today. Whetted by our own imperial appetites, we too have been caught by and in an action that is unspeakable, paralyzed by what we have attempted to swallow.

Notes

1. See for example, Dominick LaCapra's *Writing History, Writing Trauma*, as well as numerous articles in *History and Memory*, vol.9, no.1-2 (1997). In contrast, Paul Ricoeur suggests that history depends upon the repression of trauma (*Memory, History, Forgetting*). More recently, Robert Darnton has reviewed the ways in which the historical landscape has undergone a curious change: he points to the emergence of a new genre of history writing that analyzes catastrophes and follows their repercussions through the social order (60).

2. The relation of the act to history and the possibility of transformation is explored in a recent Lacanian seminar, "Psychoanalysis, Politics, and the Event" taught by Alain Badiou, Joan Copjec, Slavoj Zizek, Alenka Zupancic, Summer Seminar in Experimental Critical Theory, University of California Humanities Research Institute, August, 2004. To quote from the course description:

> The concept of *the act* that Lacan develops, in opposition to the repetitive symptomatic behavior that Freud called "acting out," is tied to the idea of trauma, and comes to stand for the possibility of transforming the political field of the subject, and allowing a new modality of social and discursive structure to arise. In Alain Badiou's terms, this is the possibility of the *event*, the break that shifts the paradigm and syntagm in which a particular situation of political, scientific, aesthetic, and amorous life unfolds.

3. As has been reported, after the Polish campaign, everyone in Britain expected heavy combat, as in the summer of 1914. "The British Expeditionary Force landed in France; British children were sent to Canada or the countryside; and neutral Belgium and Holland braced for invasion, but for a time nothing happened. Instead, the warring nations settled into a lull in fighting. The British press dubbed it the '*Sitzkrieg*'—the expected terror of Total War had not yet emerged." This period became known as the time of the phony war. (www.worldwar2database.com).

4. Elizabeth Abel, in a finely nuanced juxtaposition of Freud's "Moses and Monotheism" and *Between The Acts*, notes Freud's characterization of present time as "a relapse into almost prehistoric barbarism" (54). As Abel convincingly argues, Freud's influence on Woolf's vision of prehistoric consciousness in *Between the Acts* is striking. Woolf had visited Freud when he moved to Hampstead, and had conversed with him about Hitler. See Quentin Bell, 2: 209.

5. Woolf had been asked to write a play for the local villagers of Rodmell to act; she never did it, but through the persona of the writer, La Trobe, creates fragments of the play she didn't write.

6. In *Troilus and Cressida*, the actual words "scraps, orts and fragments" occur not in a single phrase, but in separate though linked phrases. The specific reference is to the fate of love, which devolves from an ideal bond to an abjected one based on appetite: "The bonds of heaven are slipp'd, dissolved, and loosed; / And with another knot, five-finger tied,/ The fractions of her faith, orts of her love,/ The fragments, scraps, the bits and greasy relics/ Of her o'er eaten faith, are bound to Diomed" (Act 5, scene 2, ll.153-57). Appetite

is Shakespeare's recurrent metaphor for personal and political relations in his version of the Trojan war: "Then everything includes itself in power/ Power into will; will appetite/ And appetite, that universal wolf/ So seconded by will and power/ Must make perforce a universal prey/ And last eat up itself" (Act I, iii, ll. 119-24).

7. See Freud, "The Antithetical Meaning of Primal Words" (1910).

8. The word "pageant," when used as a verb, can mean "mimic"; the pageant does mimic the history of England as well as the emotional dynamics of the audience.

9. Compare this with Christopher Bollas's discussion of the transformational object, a form of D.W. Winnicott's transitional object which provides the aesthetic experience of self-integration (*The Shadow of the Object*, 1987).

10. Catastrophic consciousness, which was a popular concept in the 1930's, is fundamental to the narrative voice of this novel, and not surprisingly, since the novel was being written during the Dunkirk evacuation in May 1940, the Battle of Britain and the London Blitz.

11. For an elaborated discussion of Woolf's skillful manipulation of the musical semiotics of language, see Patricia Ondek Laurence, *The Reading of Silence: Virginia Woolf in the English Tradition* (1991).

12. Bart intones lines from Swinburne's poem "Itylus" in which Philomela, nightingale sister to Procne, bemoans her sister's forgetting of the memory of her slain first-born. Here the theme of rape is entwined with that of slain children, and calls to mind the recent death of Woolf's young nephew Julian in the Spanish civil war.

13. Louise DeSalvo locates a similar punning on the dangers of duckweed in an early autobiographical piece of reportage written by Woolf, in which describing the dangerous capsizing of a boat in a duckpond, she imagined herself drowned and shrouded in duckweed (257-58).

14. The verse from "Prothalamion" alludes not only to the purity of the swans, but to Jove's transformation into a blameless swan when he appeared to Leda, founding a presumptive narrative of British history that begins with a mythical rape and continues with the abduction/rape of Helen that initiates the Trojan war.

15. Cathy Caruth suggests such a paradigm in *Unclaimed Experience*, as does Suzette Henke in her discussion of "scriptotherapy" in *Shattered Subjects*. As Henke notes, "the very process of articulating painful experiences especially in written form has been seen as a way of healing traumatic wounds"(xi).

16. See Hermione Lee's biography, *Virginia Woolf* (124-27).

17. For a fuller discussion of the similarities between Rachel and Dora, see my reading of *The Voyage Out*, "The Great Refusal," in *Passions of the Voice*. For a description of Woolf's own experience with George Duckworth, see Lee's discussion, (154-57).

18. Woolf herself may have had a horse phobia; Louise DeSalvo notes that Woolf recorded horse accidents she noticed on her trips around London, and that these "have been described as figments of her imagination" (*Impact* 216).

19. Suzette Henke alerted me to this allusion. In one instance, as she pointed out, 14,000 British troops were lost, with only one survivor to tell the tale.

20. For details of the actual case on which this scene was based, see also Stuart Clarke's essay, "The Horse with a Green Tail," in *Virginia Woolf Miscellany* (Spring, 1990) 34:3-4.

21. See "Beyond the Pleasure Principle" (1920) for Freud's discussion of the death drive as the inherent impulsion in life-forms from the beginning toward a return to the inorganic state from which they emerged

22. The publisher of the English translation of Freud's *Standard Edition*, Woolf certainly had some familiarity with Freud's work before his arrival in England. But, as Hermione Lee notes, Woolf began reading Freud more seriously after the outbreak of war, and specifically referred to "Moses and Monotheism," "Civilization and its Discontents," and "Group Psychology and the Analysis of the Ego." According to Lee, Woolf found Freud "upsetting." "If we're all instinct, the unconscious, what's all this about civilization, the whole man, freedom &?" (*Virginia*, 722-23). See also Bell's and Abel's account of Woolf's relation to Freud, Klein, and the British Psychoanalytic Society.

23. *Heart of Darkness* is not the only literary referent in this passage; the "fields of night" can also be read as an allusion to Ovid's "Elegy XI," in which Corinna, in a familiar Woolfian metaphor, is about to venture into dangerous seas and is warned of the dangers she will face on "the treacherous main":

> Not on the open sea wilt thou discover dainty shells and pebbles many-hued; they are the pastime of the sandy shore; leave on the sands, my sweet ones, the imprint of your lovely feet; there doth safety lie; beyond, who knows what perils lurk?

Although the passage refers to the dangers of this voyage out (was this elegy a pre-text for Woolf's first novel?), especially to women, the speaker assumes Corinna's safe return, imagines his delight in welcoming her back, and anticipates her tall travel tales, which he will understand as a defensive denial of anxiety. "They may be travellers' tales, yet I'll believe them, every one. Wherefore should I not smile on what I long for most? Oh, may the Morning Star, that has no rival in *the fields of night*, spur on his steed and bring with speed that happy day" (italics mine). Narrative here implicitly masks traumatic apprehension, turning anxiety into comedy with happy endings.

24. Rachel, below deck in an early scene in *The Voyage Out*, hears a man's voice saying "'On a dark night one could fall down these stairs head foremost' to which a woman's voice added, 'And be killed'" (*VO* 14). Such traumatic apprehensions recur throughout Woolf's first novel.

READING "VIRGINIA'S DEATH": A (POST)TRAUMATIC NARRATIVE OF SUICIDE

Holly Laird

Those 319 days of headlong and yet slow-moving catastrophe were the most terrible and agonizing days of my life. The world of my private life and of English history and of the bricks and mortar of London disintegrated. To drag the memory of them out of one's memory, as I must do now if I am to continue publicly to remember, is difficult and painful. The reluctant recollection of protracted pain is peculiarly painful. The excitement in the moment of catastrophe, the day-to-day, hour-to-hour, minute-to-minute stimulus of having to act, produce an infallible anodyne for misery. I am always astonished to find that one instantly becomes oblivious of the most acute pain if one has to concentrate on anything else, even on a triviality. . . . But there are no distractions or alleviation in one's recollection of misery. (Leonard Woolf 44)

The thrust of this essay is quite deliberately not another reading of the multiple, elusive causalities of Virginia Woolf's suicide; rather, I wish here to redirect attention to the lengthy eighty-seven-page opening chapter—"Virginia's Death"—of the final volume in Leonard Woolf's autobiography, *The Journey Not the Arrival Matters*.[1] Although this autobiographical volume was published in 1969, twenty-eight years after Virginia Woolf's suicide, "Virginia's Death" stands out as a separate, framed narrative that explicitly emphasizes "catastrophe" following upon endlessly dreary waiting rather than either a journey or an arrival (9-10). Although critics have emphasized Leonard's consciously detached, even "cold" attitude in this narrative (Meyerowitz 197), his chapter in fact admits—as in the passage cited in the epigraph—the nearly intolerable pain of recollecting past trauma as well as of recollected endless waiting for a catastrophic future (44).

Autobiography has long been recognized as a peculiarly "literary" form of writing, one especially suitable for critical analysis; and yet no one, so far as I can ascertain, has provided a close textual analysis of the structure, breaks, and contradictions of this paradoxical text.[2] The narrative of "Virginia's Death" is a tightly controlled, yet occasionally ruptured, intentionally rational, yet anti-rationally achronological, carefully teleological, yet frequently digressive, hugely influential record of the end of Virginia Woolf's life, by a husband who saw himself as largely dedicated to her achievements and her survival. As Leonard Woolf says during a "moment [of] digress[ing] about autobiographical digressions," "For the autobiographer to force his life and his memories of it into a strictly chronological straight line is to distort its shape and fake and falsify his memories. If one is to try to record one's life truthfully, one must aim at getting into the record of it something of the disorderly discontinuity which makes it so absurd, unpredictable, bearable" (68-69). But Leonard Woolf succeeded beyond his conscious aims or "deliberate" indulgence in digression (69) to permit a level of logical "absurdity" that may make painful memories temporarily "bearable" for him, but leaves undigested a multi-leveled traumatic past, "to concentrate on anything else, even on a triviality" (44). Directly following the passage in my epigraph, for instance, he spends no more than three pages on material related to Virginia's state of mind, then postpones that story for another twenty-two pages to tell, instead, a series of unrelated anecdotes, several of which are about the war, at times with seemingly inconsequential details. "In 1940," he writes, "the descendants of the Scottish serf and the ghetto Jew, on payment of 2s. 6d. each, visited the banqueting hall" at Penshurst (58). This is not a text, then, that one should interpret sheerly as a transparent vessel of fact, although it has usually been dealt with as if it were—a text one may comb for unequivocal evidence for (or against) the final cause of Virginia's suicide. Constituted by complexity, amounting to contradiction, of logic and affect, the chapter is a partly self-absolving, partly self-indicting record of Leonard Woolf's own traumatic past; and it continually diverts attention from "Virginia's death" to Leonard's observations about the circumstances of their lives during her last months at Rodmell.

Most scholars now consider Virginia Woolf one of the greatest modernist writers, and her suicide is the most famous literary suicide of that period. For many more scholars and readers, she herself is "Shakespeare's sister," whom she wished for, but imagined committing suicide and being buried in ignominy at a crossroads. The narrative rendering of the survivor who lived closest to Woolf should command special interest in any general account of her life and death, but particularly so in an account focused (as mine is) on how the notoriously enigmatic phenomenon of suicide was read by modernists and by modernists' rereaders. In the larger work in progress of which this essay is a part, I reconsider "modernist suicide" among both suicidal and nonsuicidal authors from 1880 to the 1940s as a problem of how we read suicide, then and now, as identity construct and terminally defining event. Thus I redirect attention from the effort to explain or make sense of famous suicides in themselves to analyzing the often unanalyzed narratives by the suicides' contemporaries and by subsequent critical and scholarly readers. I propose in the present essay to consider the question of how—in the midst of claims to authoritative diagnosis and prescriptions for "care"—the trauma produced by the suicidal event may be partially reproduced in survivor discourse.[3] What can we learn about Leonard's own (narrative) relationship to the traumatic event of suicide? From close scrutiny of a nonfictional narrative of so intimate a survivor as Leonard, what can we learn about the ways Virginia Woolf, Woolf's suicide, and the trauma of her suicide have been constructed after the fact? Even when the only direct citation of his narrative appears in a bibliography at the end of a book, Leonard Woolf's account looms as the largest (though sometimes almost entirely concealed) pillar in subsequent readings of Virginia Woolf's suicide, from Quentin Bell to the present.

The story of "Virginia's Death" might be read as a three-stranded narrative of trauma: Virginia's, Leonard's, and the world's during World War II. Of the three, Virginia's sense of personal, professional, conjugal, and global trauma, whether past or present, is the thinnest, most marginal strand. This text is—like the previous volumes of this work—pronouncedly Leonard's autobiography, not Virginia's biography. Yet even when she occupies center stage as the subject of the narrative, Leonard relates nothing about the violent moments of Virginia Woolf's traumatic past and almost nothing about her terrible moments in the narrative's present—almost nothing, then, of the detail that a psychoanalytically minded critic would scrutinize for layers of explanation in Virginia's death. In fact, even as Leonard describes the world war taking place above their heads, he portrays a peculiarly peaceful Virginia in its midst. So sparse are his own memories of "signs" of her impending suicide that he scours her diaries for details about her state of mind, thence substituting for his own narrated recollections the few possibly indicative passages he finds. He spends far more time portraying the backdrop of "Virginia's Death" as a traumatic crisis of civilization; its wounding effects are presented more often as global than as personally felt by him. As much as Leonard cares about and foregrounds the horrors of these world- and life-changing events, the passage cited in my epigraph stands almost alone in recording any personal "agony;" on the contrary, he presents himself as harboring no deep ills or recurrent nightmares and, until the last week of his wife's life, does not feel "alarmed" (90). Leonard appears ever calm in the midst of the looming, breaking storms both of the war and within his wife's psyche. Why then should this narrative be read, nonetheless, in terms of trauma?

A close interrogation of Leonard's chapter discloses not only the profound correlation doctors and scholars have repeatedly found between world war and trauma, but also, more personally for Leonard, precisely the kinds of narrative breaks or dissociation, scattered memories, psychic numbing, and repetitive displacement of terrified affect to alternative objects that one finds in post-traumatic cases. Moreover, in the process, one uncovers a record of the re-traumatizing effects of Leonard's reading habits for Virginia in her last months—hence also for any reader of Leonard's narrative who found herself identifying with Virginia's story. As Judith Lewis Herman argues, "The dialectic of trauma [whereby the subject may "alternate between feeling numb and reliving the event"] gives rise to complicated, sometimes uncanny alterations of consciousness, which George Orwell, one of the committed truth-tellers of our century, called 'doublethink,' and which mental health professionals, searching for a calm, precise language, call 'dissociation'" (*Trauma* 1). Such "double think" is, as I will show, precisely the form of thought that Leonard unwittingly develops in "Virginia's Death."

"Trauma" and the "post-traumatic" are contested terms for certain experiences and their effects on memory; in essence, "trauma" is—like suicide itself (often partially motivated by trauma)—always already a matter of interpretation. Kirby Farrell notes that "Despite its ambiguities . . . [the post-traumatic] is the most serviceable term I can find for trauma understood as an interpretive process. I don't expect readers to be able to make absolute distinctions between post-traumatic and traumatic symptoms: much of the time clinicians cannot either" (12). No term other than trauma better captures that sense of memorably disruptive "violent" experience or of horror so "acute" as to disrupt other more continuous memory processes, while nonetheless leaving lasting memory traces, which patients, doctors, and scholars alike have characterized as at the heart of trauma (Farrell 14, 5). As Herman observes, "Traumatic events generally involve threats to life or bodily integrity, or a close personal encounter with violence and death. They confront human beings with the extremities of helplessness and terror, and evoke the responses of catastrophe" (*Trauma* 33). Nonetheless, no term or condition has also proven more slippery to define than "trauma," and it remains intractably an issue of reading. Like suicide,[4] an "original" traumatic event becomes lost in the past as soon as it is completed, only to be re-membered in bits and pieces by survivors and reconstructed by the scattered and scattering effects of wounded memories. Thus, whereas the "event" of suicide is certain once it has been accomplished and its "causes" (including trauma) remain radically uncertain, the event of trauma remains uncertain, even while its apparently traumatizing and traumatized effects and symptoms appear undeniable. As Cathy Caruth remarks, "trauma is not locatable in the simple violent or original event in an individual's past, but rather in the way that its very unassimilated nature—the way it was precisely *not known* in the first instance—returns to haunt the survivor later on" (*Unclaimed* 4).

For these reasons, in addition to Farrell's, it makes sense to employ the term "post-traumatic" rather than "traumatic" for a reading of trauma in general, not merely for Leonard Woolf's temporally distant, self-distancing retrospective rereading of Woolf's death and World War II. To this rationale, I would add the resonances of "post" in "post-traumatic" that resemble those acquired through usage in other contemporary terminology, like "postmodernity" and "postcoloniality": at the time of writing his autobiography, Leonard occupies a period in his life when he sees himself as having passed beyond the traumatic events of the past, yet is still living within their long, painfully remembered wake. Moreover, just as early postmodern artists included "modernist" elements in their work specifically to signal the ways in which postmodernists were "anti-modernist," Leonard Woolf attempts, though at a cost, to stand utterly outside of the kinds of destruction, death, and horror represented by both the war and Virginia's suicide. Nonetheless, I would also qualify this term "post," placing it in parentheses, because the effect of "trauma" persists in the writing of the narrative, even as it is assiduously denied by its narrator, Leonard Woolf; in denial, trauma's affect is readmitted in displaced terms that reproduce this violence as an effect of narrative.

I wish to begin, however, not directly with Leonard Woolf's narrative, but argumentatively and analogically with the place of Leonard

Woolf's writing in one scholar's critical rereading of Virginia Woolf's suicidal writings. This rereading appears in one of two full-length books written thus far on twentieth-century "literary suicide"—it is a book thus with considerable opportunity to influence future explanation of modernist suicide.[5] Jeffrey Berman's 1999 *Surviving Literary Suicide* is explicitly a teaching text, designed to be accessible as a "self-help" book to anyone in the literate public. It addresses the questions of how a teacher-scholar should deal with the topic of suicide in major, widely taught twentieth-century novels and novelists, from a writer who did not actually kill herself, Kate Chopin, through two major modernists who did, Virginia Woolf and Ernest Hemingway, to two equally famous contemporary suicides, Sylvia Plath and Anne Sexton, concluding with a survivor's memoir by William Styron.[6] Berman's study is unabashedly polemical in its call to work for survival and never to minimize the trauma of suicide, even in fiction. In tone and dictum, Berman's work is characteristic of popular contemporary self-help books on suicide; more than polemical, the assumption that suicide is as great a disaster for the survivor as for the suicidal person is the governing assumption.[7] But therein too reside some problems, and these are not only logical and historical, important though those are (since at various times, places, and circumstances, people have found ample reason for differing in their views of suicide); the highly medicalized form of "urgent" care-giving proffered by these books, with their fierce anti-death stances, can be a problem for those who wrestle with or have ever wrestled with such a choice—a problem for survivors and suicide-attempters alike. The intensely didactic message inadvertently echoes and evokes the traumatic effects of suicide, closing down the sense of independent agency and complex apperception on the part of their readers.

In his chapter on Woolf, Berman sets up good and bad sides in what is by now a very old battle among critics assessing the Woolfs' marriage as pivotal to an understanding of Virginia's suicide.[8] Rallying statistics from Kay Redfield Jamison's self-help studies in his favor (statistical analysis remains something most literary critics like Berman are untrained to do), he settles quickly upon "manic depressiveness" as the culprit in Woolf's suicide and takes "social constructionism" to task for minimizing Woolf's "genetic" make up (71)[9]—even though social constructionist literary critics have not yet concerned themselves with the construct of the suicidal person (as I am doing here) but rather with the various forms identity takes during people's lives (female, white, upper-middle class in Woolf's case).[10] He castigates such critics, and Woolf herself, both when they celebrate any heroic or defiant element in Woolf's suicide or in her occasional fictional depictions of it, and when they assign blame to Leonard Woolf or to the doctors who worked with the Woolfs. Berman labels such arguments "conspiracy theories" (71) and marvels at the unanimity of "affirmation" of the suicide in *Mrs. Dalloway* from the 60s to the 90s across all sorts of theoretical approaches (86). While acknowledging the patriarchal character of medicine at that time, Berman nonetheless omits mention of the woman doctor Woolf actually worked with at the time of her suicide, Octavia Wilberforce, and he praises the practices of the state asylums, which the Woolfs both sought to avoid: "Despite the primitive state of psychiatry a century ago, Victorian physicians were remarkably successful in preventing men and women from killing themselves in state-run asylums and private homes. To accomplish this, physicians employed vigilant surveillance of their patients and, before it became outlawed, mechanical restraints" (88-89). One is left with a sense that Woolf in her own day and contemporary critics in ours should simply have deferred to the single verdict of science, not raising questions about its authority. In opposition to the contemporary Woolf critic and to Woolf herself, Berman sets Leonard, Virginia's doctors,[11] and the author's own diaries and letters—viewing Woolf on the one hand as against suicide when she is writing "rational," nonfictional work and on the other as erroneously in favor of suicide in her visionary fiction, especially in *Mrs. Dalloway*. Ironically, Berman is like a number of Virginia Woolf's biographers and critics who dichotomize the Woolfs—that is, in seeing Leonard Woolf as a rationalist and a nonfiction writer, and Virginia Woolf as irrational and visionary, thus excelling in her fiction rather than in nonfiction—a set of oppositions inaugurated, in part, by her husband.

When one turns to the opening of Leonard Woolf's text, however, one finds Leonard profoundly concerned first, not with Virginia Woolf's state of mind, as one would expect from reading Berman, but with world war.[12] "Virginia's Death" might accurately have been titled instead "World War II: Personal Survival or Suicide." Her death forms the intensely personal climax and conclusion of a chapter consisting mostly of description and criticism of a world on the brink, then gradually invaded by wartime "madness." This text thereby joins the many twentieth-century suicidology studies, first catalyzed by World War I, and more recent turn-of-the-twenty-first century trauma studies, which not only disclose profound connections between trauma, suicide, and war, but view world war as a globally traumatic and suicidal event defining the "crisis" of modern civilization (see, especially, Menninger; Farrell; and Kleber, Figley, and Gersons). Leonard Woolf does review the role of the medical profession in the closing months of Virginia Woolf's life and explains in some detail the decisions he made regarding what medicine might do for her. While medicine is far from framing this story, it becomes a final "player" in Leonard Woolf's thoughts and actions prior to the suicide; but it does so in a semi-feminist guise rather than in the entirely patriarchal form which Berman examines and Woolf critiques in *Mrs. Dalloway*.[13] In addition, two important further contexts play major roles in Leonard Woolf's discussion: the first, of course, the Woolfs' relationship to each other, and the second, their larger social and professional lives—two inescapable sets of factors that are inextricably intertwined.

To start, then, where, with his first words, Leonard Woolf begins, "the second of the great world wars through which I have lived" (9), Woolf instantly characterizes this war as distinct from World War I in not being "historically and psychologically, a bolt from the blue" (9). Jane Lilienfeld argues (recalling Herman's definition of trauma), "For many, traumatic events are at first interpreted as accidents—unforeseen and inexplicable—a random chain of circumstances which seem to make no rational sense. Violence and abuse may be perceived as accidental because these assaults shatter the human desire for security and justice—hence the survivor's inadvertent denial of the human causes of violence and abuse" ("Accident" 153; see also Caruth, *Unclaimed* 6). While accidentalism remains an important characteristic of Leonard's wartime recollections, the advent of World War II contrasts with World War I in being a horror all too familiar, so familiar that he must use redundancy to convey its intolerable boredom and, in trauma discourse, its psychic numbing: "endlessly waiting in a dirty, grey railway station waiting-room . . .with nothing to do but wait endlessly for the next catastrophe" (10); his "chief recollection of war is its intolerable boredom" (64). One is reminded in this description of Julien Green's observation, which Farrell cites, of ennui as "quite simply . . . one of the faces of death" (Farrell 8). War's "horror" and "barbarity" start for Leonard even before England's declaration of war, its trauma originating in no single moment but in a more indefinite, recent past.

War is defined, moreover, as much by its ever more insane or "imbecile" brutality as by its dull monotony, which made "the last years of peace before war broke upon us in 1939 . . . the most horrible period of my life" (10); "one gradually realized that power to determine history and the fate of Europe and all Europeans had slipped into the hands of a sadistic madman" (10-11). Leonard himself was Jewish: after recollecting his own political courage in speaking out as early as 1939 against communism, on the one hand, and against the ills of western civilization that contributed to begetting the brutal events of the Nazis in World War II (including the program against Jews in Germany), on the other hand, he now indicts Hitler's genocide. In cool, formal language, he makes explicit the previously implicit links between the death and madness of the larger political scene and the personal disaster he endured: "these horrible events and their effect upon personal and communal psychology in the world in which I have had to spend my life seem to me of profound importance" (17). Since most of what Leonard knew about the Nazis developed after the fact—between Virginia's death and his writing of this narrative—this particular (post)traumatic effect took its most acute form for him, as for the many Jews living outside Europe, in its delayed aftershocks.

War plays such a large role in this narrative as to make death—ultimately, "Virginia's death"—appear inevitable: the necessary personal correlative to the impersonal global event. Bombs dot this chapter, from generalizations about the hundreds of missiles Leonard saw falling from the skies from 1940 to 1945 (32) through deployment as a metaphor for history-making catastrophes—whether in earlier times when "history had fallen about the ears of the Sidneys and the Leicesters" or in the present moment of "history . . . falling about the ears of us all" (58)—to the foreshadowing event of the literal bombardment of the River Ouse (34), where Virginia Woolf eventually drowned herself. The bombs in Leonard's narrative reenact what Lilienfeld observes in Woolf's writing about the "'ordinary mind'. . . assaulted by sensual and visual onslaughts," which feel not only like "unsought trauma memory" but like "the daily details of life from the vantage point of having survived trauma" (154). The paradoxically ordinary accidentalism of the bombings in

Leonard's narrative forecasts, moreover, the accidental way in which Virginia Woolf's anticipated death occurs at the end of his chapter.

Even before England entered the war, however, the Woolfs and other couples in their circle had begun to make death their own by planning joint suicides in the event of a German occupation of England, as in the following account of "five ordinary intelligent people in England":

> Adrian told us that he would commit suicide rather than fall into German hands, and that he had provided himself with means of doing so; he offered to Virginia and me, who would certainly have been among the proscribed, a portion of this protective poison. I gather from Harold Nicolson's memoirs that he and Vita provided themselves with a similar "bare bodkin," so that they might make their quietus in order to avoid the fate which would be theirs if they fell into German hands. Here again is terrible evidence of the difference in savagery between the Europe of 1939 and 1914. For here in 1939 were five ordinary intelligent people in England, coolly and prudently supplying themselves with means for committing suicide in order to avoid the tortures which almost certainly awaited them if the Germans ever got hold of them. (15)

As the war developed and the bombs grew ever nearer, more insistent, and "sinister" (39), as Leonard Woolf terms it—destroying the Woolfs' house in London (38, 62-63) and landing outside her window in Rodmell (72)—he and his wife, along with friends like Rose Macaulay and Kingsley Martin, continued to discuss their plans for suicide (45, 46, 54). The thought of joint suicide itself became as "routine" as "cook[ing] and eat[ing] one's eggs and bacon for breakfast" (46-47).

These suicide plans, too, are left unmentioned by Berman; indeed, Leonard himself does not recall them once he has turned his attention to the final narrative of Virginia's death. But in the first half of his chapter, Leonard clearly perceives suicide as a preferable kind of death not only to proscription by the Germans but to death in a crowded underground shelter (38, 59). Rather than sounding courageously defiant when he marks this preference, Leonard sounds as if he had introjected the Hitleresque mood of the times: "I hated the stuffiness and smell of human beings, and, if a bomb was going to get me, I preferred to die a solitary death above ground and in the open air" (59). "Survival" for Leonard Woolf, then, is not a purpose to be clung to in the face of any death or other horror. Far from constituting the most abhorred manner of passing,

there are at least two forms of "life" over which Leonard Woolf obviously prefers suicide.

In the last third of this chapter, Leonard turns his attention, in fits and
starts, to the saga of Virginia Woolf's glide toward suicide, until it gradually takes over his narrative. At the beginning of this final third, Leonard
associates her approaching death both metaphorically with natural disas-
ters (a cyclone, tornado, and hurricane [69]) and literally with the bombs:
thus he rediscovers his wife, through the words of her diary, recording a
bomb fallen just under her window and contemplating death, "which"—
in Leonard's words—"might at any moment come falling with a great
bang out of the sky—and annihilate us." Though she writes, "I don't want
to die yet," she goes on to imagine in detail what it would feel like to be
killed by a bomb (72-73). Leonard Woolf treats the war in this closing
section, to some extent, in the manner of a nineteenth-century novel's
storm clouds, as a premonitory event, background scene, or mirroring
enlargement—much as in the final imagery of the chapter, where he
recounts one of the two great elms in the Woolfs' backyard, which they
had named Leonard and Virginia, destroyed by a storm (96). Yet Leonard
simultaneously insists that, at the time, he could read none of the "signs":

> I thought at the time and still think that her mind was calmer and more
> stable, her spirits happier and more serene, than was usual with her. If
> one is in the exact centre of a cyclone or tornado, one finds oneself in
> a deathly calm while all round one is the turmoil of roaring wind and
> waves. It seemed as if in Rodmell in those last months of 1940 we had
> suddenly entered into the silent, motionless centre of the hurricane of
> war. It was a pause, only a pause, as we waited for the next catastro-
> phe. (69)

Later too, in words this time echoing his description of the "accident" of
World War I, he writes, "this time there were no warning symptoms . . .
The depression struck her like a sudden blow" (79).

Regardless of their function as unread warning signs in this narrative,
the bombs also are, unlike the more natural storms, an intrinsic, anti-
magical, causal, and traumatic dimension of the context in which Virginia
Woolf took her life. Thus at the climactic juncture, Leonard deliberately
dissociates himself from conscious thought of the war, but nonetheless
vividly recalls it for the reader. Speaking to Dr. Octavia Wilberforce after
her consultation with Virginia, Leonard writes: "suddenly . . . a German
bomber flew, almost as it were just above our heads . . . it roared away

towards the sea and almost immediately there was a crash of exploding bombs. We were so overwhelmed by our problem and so deep in thought and conversation that the sight and sound were not at the moment even consciously registered" (92). If he is unconscious of these bombs, he is also unconscious of the imminence of his wife's suicide: "It seemed possible that Octavia's talk had had some effect upon Virginia and it was left that she would come and see Virginia again in Rodmell in a day or two" (92). Within the same paragraph, he discloses Virginia's farewell letter: "I found the following letter on the sitting-room mantelpiece: 'Dearest, I feel certain that I am going mad again. I feel we can't go through another of those terrible times.'" (93). Amid Leonard's gaps of consciousness and memory, the war and Virginia's death almost slip away.

From the opening section of this narrative, Leonard Woolf situates the lonely autobiographical "I" poised in battle with death or, rather, in a situation of perpetual evasive maneuvering, as he wards off, as best he can, the looming deaths of war and Woolf's suicide. In terms that arise, as well, in declarations of anti-suicide self-help books, Leonard Woolf writes: "For me 'death is the enemy,' the ultimate enemy, for it is death which will destroy, wipe out, annihilate me, my individuality, my 'I'" (19).[14] But he seems in this narrative not unlike the "lone wolf" of a German plane that he notices apparently trying to avoid involvement, as it veers away from the squadrons targeting London, yet nonetheless remains a recurrent participant in the raids until finally (so Leonard and others suspect) it falls victim to his fellow fighting planes and returns no more over the Channel (39). This passive posture of evasive maneuvering turns out to be just another recipe for suicidal death.

The "I" that Leonard seeks to preserve is not only the egotistical "I" of his solitary selfhood, but the empathetic "I" of victimized others, for "all other human beings, . . . even the chicken, . . . each and all have a precisely similar 'I'" (19). In these early pages, Leonard Woolf resonates with feminist, anti-racist perspectives in representing this particular war and universal death in larger philosophical as well as personal terms, not as a conflict of nations but as the "cruelty" (a term and its metaphysical connotations that he derives from Montaigne) of a tyrant or tyrannical institutions against helpless others and their vulnerable subjectivities (17-20). Using animals not merely as metaphor but as "other" beings to illustrate the growth of his personal philosophy, he takes a maliciously drowned blind puppy as his baseline for protest against all cruelties, among which he mentions slavery, anti-Semitism, the Armenian genocide, and Captain Dreyfus. His declaration of war against death on behalf of "all other human beings"— "even the chicken, the pig, and the dew bedabled hare" (19)—winds up producing an explanatory context as well for the incipient feminism that emerges in this narrative. This feminism first appears implicitly in these same early pages, when Leonard acknowledges the profound influence on his beliefs of a headmistress who, on the occasion of Gladstone's protest movement against the Turkish destruction of the Armenians, threw herself into promoting the cause. Later, Leonard Woolf refers explicitly to the woman question at a surprising juncture, when after pages of suspense in which, among other topics, he dwells on Woolf's lifelong preoccupation with death, suddenly he shifts to arguing that the problem of women not being on the London Library Committee is not "trivial." "The struggle to end the subjection of women has been bitter and prolonged; it was not by any means over in 1940," he argues, and goes on to explain and defend Virginia Woolf's refusal when finally asked to become the first, but token, woman member of that committee (75-76).

So too his introduction of Woolf's doctor at this time interrupts his narrative of the war and of Woolf's deepening depression. After pages of discussion of Virginia's "unbalanced" state of mind, he devotes a small section of his narrative to two "great women's" biographies: of the Woolfs' friend and doctor, Octavia Wilberforce, and another friend of the Woolfs, the feminist actress and writer Elizabeth Robins. These two women rank alongside Leonard's headmistress of the narrative's opening pages as authentic lone-wolf heroes of their times. Is he thus anticipating criticism for not supporting Virginia Woolf fully enough, or is he betraying a tendency, as at least one Woolf critic has argued, to contrast his wife with other, more resilient women (Coates 364)? These passages interrupt the narrative of Woolf's death even as they create a context in which Virginia Woolf may be placed in a company of great women and so operate ambiguously for Leonard as both self-vindicating and self-betraying.

The medical profession, meanwhile, thereby enters not in the shape— as in Berman's discussion—of authoritative male doctors, worthy representatives of long lineages of scientists of the mind, but rather in the shape of two maverick women friends of the family, one of them not a doctor but a fellow writer, who has eluded the war by traveling to Canada.

Further, Leonard Woolf presents himself as having learned his lesson from past mistakes in his choice of doctors: "Haunted" by memories of his interview with Dr. Head and Virginia's attempted suicide immediately afterwards in 1913 (91-92), he "once more" was "faced" with a "terrifying decision." It seemed "essential for her to resign herself to illness and the drastic regime which alone could stave off insanity," but he had to "urge her" to accept "the verge of disaster" as "the only method" to avoid it, and "a wrong word, a mere hint of pressure . . . might be enough to drive her over the verge into suicide" (91). (As in the "agony" briefly registered earlier in this narrative, this clearly emotional "haunting" and "terror" that necessitate "drastic steps" are not the terms of a thoroughly numbed, let alone cool, objective discourse.) Quite unlike Dr. Head, Octavia Wilberforce approaches Woolf (in Leonard's narrative) through friendship and conversation, not dictation, and, as he further notes, with parental attempts to ensure that despite wartime rations, Virginia has enough milk: "drastic steps meant going to bed, complete rest, plenty of food and milk. . . . Food in any case was a problem owing to rationing and shortages" (86-87).

But if the enemy for Leonard Woolf is "death," then the enemy is also inside Virginia, and the structure of war is necessarily reproduced in the structure of the Woolfs' relationship,[15] with Leonard seeking to preserve one Virginia against another Virginia. Even as Leonard aligns himself sympathetically with the lonely, the victimized, the other—whether a woman, a chicken, or a German renegade—he betrays antipathies that disrupt and militate against such sympathies. As indicated in several passages above, Leonard Woolf is not only a self-declared "enemy" of "death," but a man for whom death-dealing and insanity are one and the same. Hitler is that "madman"; the war is that "madness." Moreover, Leonard appears completely unable to identify within himself any impulses toward death or madness. Herein lies perhaps the most jagged of fault lines in his relationship with Virginia, for whom, as he explains, shortly after launching the narrative of her final depression:

> Death . . . was always very near the surface of Virginia's mind, the
> contemplation of death. It was part of the deep imbalance of her mind.
> She was "half in love with easeful Death." I can understand this, but
> only intellectually; emotionally it is completely alien to me. Until I
> began to grow old, I hardly ever even thought of death. (73)

Possibly the oddest narrative digression pivots around his horrified dis-identification from insanity. Just after having recollected a social call from G. E. Moore and Desmond MacCarthy and the "cocoon of friendship and nostalgic memories" which enveloped him during their brief visit (49), he abruptly shifts to a seemingly unrelated anecdote illustrating the "passionate devotion of mothers to imbecile children" (51)—the case of a neighbor who "adored" and "devoted her life to looking after" her "completely 'retarded'" youngest son (49-50). Near the end of this anecdote, pronouncing this "kind of tragedy" "terrible, but in detail often grotesque and even ridiculous," though "not uncommon in village life" (51), he finally reveals to the close reader the deeply ambivalent personal relevance this anecdote holds for him. "I can see," Leonard Woolf says, "and sympathize with the appeal of helplessness and vulnerability in a very young living creature . . . there is the appeal of physical beauty. . . . But there is something horrible and repulsive in the slobbering imbecility of a human being" (51-52). His ability to imagine an "I" in minoritized others stops short of the "horror" and "repulsiveness" of mental illness or mental disability.

Recollecting this incident as itself an interruption in "the restless foreboding of those days" (49), he nonetheless ultimately casts this experience as a fateful fulfillment precisely of that "restless foreboding." Becoming involved, albeit reluctantly, when the eldest son asked him to talk his mother into placing the child in an asylum, Leonard and the son saw her as "ruining her life by immuring herself with the child" (50). Though he succeeded in persuading the woman, "Mrs. X" subsequently became distressed about the boy "being starved and ill-treated" and "getting very ill" in the hospital, whereupon she demanded his return home (50) and made the "wildest accusations" against the hospital (51). "Obviously ill," the boy returned home (51). Seven to ten days later, the sick boy died. But for Leonard, the fact of the boy's physical illness appears to validate neither the mother's "wild" concern for her son nor her abrupt action in bringing him home. Leonard Woolf views this "strange and even disturbing phenomenon" as instead "sardonically . . . fit[ting] into the pattern of a private and public world threatened with destruction" (51). Indeed, he holds up for some of his sharpest criticism in this chapter the "exaggerated devotion of the mother to this child, which nearly always seems to be far greater than her devotion to her normal, attractive children"—criticism he caps off with pseudo-psychoanalytic self-distancing when he says, it is "partly determined by an unconscious sense of guilt and desire to vindicate herself and her child" (52). What is "threaten[ing]" the "private and public world . . . with destruction," in this case, is the mother's own unconfessed (and implicitly mad) guilt coupled with her child's madness. Yet is not Leonard in a comparable position by his own account, though similarly unconfessed at this moment, of "exaggerated devotion" to Virginia, and is this not "partly determined by an unconscious sense of guilt and desire to vindicate" himself? Having chosen long ago not to have children with Virginia, Leonard had made her his only object of care.

Just as his "regular routine" of those days is "broken" by this incident, so this incident breaks into his narrative of "those days"—tempting a close reader to observe Leonard Woolf's "horror" and "repulsion" as "unconsciously" symptomatic not only of post-traumatic, recollected pain, but also of continued self-distancing from those identified as "insane." Here again, though less obviously than in his discussions of Hitler and of Virginia, insanity is intimately linked to and leads to death. Read in this way, the further narrative shift back to the Woolfs' "regular routine" immediately following this anecdote (though with the Moore and MacCarthy visit now left behind) is not so abrupt, after all. Virginia Woolf is "within sight of the end" of writing *Between the Acts* (52) and thus also, as the by-now well-informed reader knows, of her final descent into "madness" and death. In this context, Leonard Woolf's occasional characterizations of war as an "an ominous and threatening unreality, a feeling that one was living in a bad dream and that one was on the point of waking up from this horrible unreality into a still more horrible reality" (53), express not only a literal, oft-reported experience of what war is like, but a specifically personal denial of "the other."[16] Leonard aligns reality, sanity, and life in absolute opposition to unreality, insanity, and death.

These oppositions define the Woolfs' differences from each other, as Leonard details them, not merely in the personal realm of Virginia's attraction to death and her haunting by madness, but in the professional realm as well; for in this chapter evidence of Leonard's criticism of Woolf's nonfictional writing also appears. As scholars have often noted, several strongly worded passages of Leonard's chapter are devoted to persuading the reader that he was right in his criticism of his wife's work on *The Years* and *Roger Fry* (74) —decades after the fact. Leonard presents himself, in opposition to Virginia, as master of the factual: by self-report, he possesses a down-to-earth, sane, and practical hold on "reality" in his writing, whereas Virginia possesses the "genius" of "vision" and thus courts failure when she writes nonfiction. For her to write biography or family history is to "repress" her "genius," to "write against the grain, to resist her own genius, added to the mental and physical strain of writing a book, the exhaustion and depression which nearly always overwhelmed her when the umbilical cord was severed and the MS sent to the printer" (43). The larger picture of this autobiography emerges of a husband who exerted control over the practicalities of their lives, so that his opinion on such matters carried disproportionate weight.

When he declared to his wife that she should not write something (*Roger Fry*) that she had promised a friend to write, he reminded her of the differences between the two of them, "cruelly" setting them at odds with each other. While we need not see this incident necessarily as the smoking gun behind Woolf's death, Leonard positions it as a possible trigger for what ensued, admitting some complicity: "I tried—no doubt too emphatically—to explain to her what I felt about it. . . . The umbilical cord which had bound *Roger Fry: A Biography* to Virginia's brain was, as I said, finally cut when she returned the proofs to the printers on May 13, 1940; 319 days later on March 28, 1941, she committed suicide" (41, 44). Moreover, this episode gives us a glimpse into that place in their relationship where they polarized each other, becoming intimate "enemies" in life and subsequently, almost thirty years after her suicide, across the border of death. In what can only be read in the context of this chapter as charged phrasing, Leonard insists this book was "slightly broken-backed and never came alive as a whole;" indeed, that it was conceived "slightly dead even at the moment of birth" (42)—a stillbirth something like that "grotesque and ridiculous" spectacle of the imbecile child with its devoted mother. This episode becomes, like Woolf's madness and her eventual suicide, yet another occasion on which Leonard tried, and failed, to save her from herself. What it would have felt like to a highly sensitive person immersed in her writing and struggling to meet a deadline for a friend who had specifically requested and supported one's work, to have the person who lived closest to her trying "emphatically" to stop her work on the project—basing this argument on a judgment about the character of her mind and "vision"—is poignant to imagine. Just a few pages into the chapter's final third, Leonard's narrative momentarily becomes a clear record of Virginia's mixed marital-and-professional trauma.

When critics assign "blame" to Leonard Woolf, however, they take sides in this marital situation in a manner that cannot do justice to the intricate ways in which the two participants in a couple affect each other until they form a semi-autonomous constellation of their relational habits. Thus one should recall that, paralleling Leonard's views of "imbeciles," Woolf herself wrote that mentally retarded people "should certainly be killed" (*D1*: 13). While the Woolfs' relationship was more fraught than what couples experience when unaffected by exacerbating traumatic histories such as Virginia's childhood sexual abuse, Leonard's representation of Woolf participates in a common couple's dynamic where intimacy leads to a hyper-awareness of differences and neglect of affinities to the point that the two partners become polarized. As Natania Rosenfeld argues, Woolf herself "metaphorized" "the difficult intersection of opposing (and sometimes overlapping) principles and ideologies" as "'marriage' or conjugation" (10).[17] Leonard's narrative presents merely one side of this process: his contributions to polarizing her or to imagining their polarization of each other. Thus the picture is one-sided by definition, unaccompanied by a correlative "chapter" of response by Virginia; the very different, if equally single-authored, generic forms of her farewell letters and sparse diary entries, cited by Leonard, are not comparable to his autobiographical memoir. Still, Leonard also provides evidence that counters his portrait of their differences. At times he does this in order to exonerate himself, at times to exonerate his wife (that part of her not "insane"), at times inadvertently—complicating the either-or aspects of his war with her melancholia, mental wildness, and visionary unreality.

Thus, for example, he mentions that, while he himself disliked *Roger Fry*, Fry's sister, who had commissioned it, liked the book, as did "Vanessa, and [Roger's] friends and relations" (42). Can a biography constitute a failure, a half-dead thing, if the people who are most personally invested in it approve and admire it? In addition, Leonard records his belief that Woolf actually possessed a "strong, logical, down to earth brain" (42). How, then, could she fail entirely to possess such a brain when it came to writing? Meanwhile, Leonard takes great pains to show how often Virginia was "sane," especially in the last days of her life, when she was so serene that he failed to recognize the warning signs. The process of identifying strict differences where there are also affinities—moreover, frequent agreement about the differences—placed the Woolfs at weirdly ambiguous cross-purposes; if, in her closing months, Virginia is so sane that, for consistency's sake, her madness must become a mysterious, invisible demonic other self in Leonard's view, Virginia seems, in her suicide notes, to attribute her choice of suicide to her desire to avoid madness (especially in her haunting by other "voices") and to include deliberate statements vindicating Leonard: "If anybody could have saved me it would have been you. Everything has gone from me but the certainty of your goodness. I can't go on spoiling your life any longer. I don't think two people could have been happier than we have been" (94).

Although Leonard does take the tone of a factual observer throughout most of the narrative, "Virginia's Death" is an emotionally inflected autobiographical text that reveals not only Virginia's affinities with Leonard's valued traits, but Leonard's affinities with those that he himself devalued. Much of what he deplores in others recurs in Leonard, including, of course, a "mother's" "adoration" of and "devotion" to his "imbecile" wife and that mother's extreme reluctance to place the dependent child in a mental institution. Perhaps most astonishing is the passage cited above, in which Leonard records his complete lack of identification with Virginia's preoccupation with death. It is something of a shock to realize the extent of his denial: these words, "I can understand [her tendency to contemplate death], but only intellectually; emotionally it is completely alien to me. Until I began to grow old, I hardly ever even thought of death" (73), directly contradict his continual references to the couple's collaborative plans for suicide, and his own emotional preference for death even in the open street rather than taking cover in a crowded shelter. He "hardly ever even thought of death"? The autobiography's detailed exposition of Leonard's responses to World War II utterly belies this moment of selective memory.

Somewhat like an individual, an intimate couple can rapidly develop its own subjectivity, which increasingly may become a dense mesh of similarities and differences, mutual likes and dislikes, unmutual likes and dislikes, affiliations across differences and severances in the heart of identifications; then, too, disaffection with the most continuous and continuity-making of shared habits and routine, and sudden merging when routine disagreements shift—abrupt refusal to insist any longer upon disagreement. It is perhaps more difficult to sustain the contradictions at the heart of coupling than to sustain the multiplicities of one's own subjectivity, but the processes are analogous and, indeed, intertwined. What I have dwelled on in this essay is, of course, a single-authored auto-biography written many years after the fact—the survivor's narrative—as opposed, say, to the partially co-authored story produced in John Stuart Mill's autobiography. Nonetheless, one may apply habits of reading learned from examining coauthorships to the single-authored work with the purpose of reconsidering Leonard's narrative of Virginia's suicide as a representation, in part, of what we might term the Woolfs' "co-subjec-tivities." In doing this, we must remain mindful of the ways in which still other intermeshing factors are marginalized, or neglected entirely in this autobiography, including Virginia's traumatic and post-traumatic memo-ries: from Virginia's relationships to her sister Vanessa (from whom Virginia was somewhat alienated at this time) and her family (with its history of difficult deaths and of Virginia's sexual abuse) through her former lover Vita, to the servants in the Woolfs' house and the larger village, the city of London, and social groups with which they sometimes awkwardly mixed. But while a "whole" representation of this relationship is not available, a fascinating corner emerges as long as we remember that "Virginia's Death" is itself a narrative to be read and reread—in this case, a particular type of narrative, that of a suicide survivor.[18]

If "Virginia's Death" proved to be a therapeutic act of life-writing for Leonard Woolf, where—shortly before his own "natural" death in 1969—the traumas of living during World War II with Virginia and then with her death were revisited and made bearable, it also inscribed a version of events that perpetuates a vision of himself (contradictory as this must be) at odds with Woolf, with death, with madness, and with unreality: in a battle no one could win.[19] No matter how empathic Leonard might have thought himself toward marginalized others (indirectly claiming empathy for himself as a Jew), empathy failed at the traumatic sites of Hitleresque "madness," of devoted mothers of "imbecile" children, of world war's "unreality," and of suicidal "contemplation of death." But despite every effort to replace empathy—when it failed—with sharply bounded self-identification as rational, sane, realistic, and non-suicidal, Leonard, in fact, also leaned toward his designated opposites. He could no more rid himself of such "others" than his wife could resist the appeals of death. As Leonard Woolf's own political biographer Duncan Wilson writes, Leonard revered "close logical argument" with its "shocking simplicities" and "systems (too often closed systems) of thought," and "the difficulties experienced by the good rationalist in achieving quick results seemed often to plunge Woolf into the depths of a cosmic despair" (243, 244).[20] What has often been viewed as the lonely, exilic modernist "I" led, in Leonard Woolf's case, to a simplistically rational system of polarized binaries, not only between "I" and the "other," but between the rational and the irrational, and the real and the unreal, hence betraying Leonard into a false "othering" of Virginia. When biographers or critics ground identification and evaluation of Virginia Woolf (and suicidal people like her) in this kind of narrative, they cannot begin to do justice either to the complex circumstances within which she managed to live a relatively long and extraordinarily productive life or to the nuanced representations of and diversified struggles with suicide in her writing. If, moreover, readers cloak analysis in the guise of modern medical rationalism, they may well reproduce a sense of the confounding impasse that trauma always involves: in Leonard Woolf's case, the confusingly contradictory "bolt from the blue" of Virginia Woolf's long-awaited death; and, in the case of critics like Berman, the equally confusing, urgent demand that, to survive the trauma of suicide and to enable our students to survive, we must extirpate any tendency to admire Woolf in her fictional renderings of suicide or in her self-inflicted death.

Notes

1. For an excellent analysis of many cultural factors informing Woolf's suicide, see Gough: although Gough begins with the aim of establishing Woolf's suicide as "a rational choice" (183), she ultimately details a "suicide culture" too "complex" to determine one cause or logical rationale for Woolf's act. For a more general history of suicide in the Victorian and Edwardian periods, see Anderson. One could certainly also further examine Woolf's frequent writings about suicide, about her suicide attempts, and her suicidal feelings and thoughts—expanding upon previous readings of the fascinatingly complex ways she herself "read" suicide —but a great deal has already been written about all these writings (see especially Kenney's groundbreaking study of Woolf's suicide in relation to *Between the Acts*). I begin instead with Leonard Woolf's reading as well as other lesser known writers and texts, in order to work against the grain of "identification" of suicide only with authors who killed themselves (like Virginia Woolf) or lived self-destructive lives (like Dylan Thomas) during a period in which many authors and thinkers were grappling with this issue. See Alvarez's classic study of literary suicide, *The Savage God,*

which treats the twentieth century as the most suicidal century in all of western history for writers, including Woolf in his list of famous suicides or self-destructive lives (258).

2. In 1970, Gervais published a review of all volumes of the autobiography that offered an extended analysis of Woolf's ideas, emphasizing Leonard's urbane manner in this work. More recently, for a brief summary of the ideas in the chapter on Virginia's death, see Meyerowitz 190-95.

3. For a persuasive reading of the way in which Virginia Woolf herself responded self-therapeutically to trauma, particularly in the suicidal Septimus Smith of *Mrs. Dalloway*, see Henke's "Virginia Woolf."

4. For a useful introduction to suicidology (now a vast academic field) and suicide's challenge to any final definition, see Shneidman, 200 and *passim*. Among the more compelling recent discussions of literary suicide (especially by European women authors) and suicide's enigmas is a series of articles by Higonnet, for example, "Frames of Female Suicide" and "Speaking Silences: Women's Suicide."

5. The second book, *Final Drafts: Suicides of World-Famous Authors*, by novelist Mark Seinfelt, presents a series of short biographical profiles of twentieth-century writers, lively summaries of prior published work on these writers' lives and deaths; though Berman's target of attack is Woolf critics and scholars, Seinfelt's treatment of Woolf presents exactly the sort of romanticization of Woolf's suicide that Berman deplores.

6. Berman presents no evidence that Chopin and Woolf's novels have contributed to the suicide of any students; nor does he speculate about why and how such novels have proved to be harmless.

7. What follows should be viewed, however, not as broad condemnation of the entire self-help genre; much of Jamison's work and other parts of Berman's (for example, his presentations of his students' journal entries) are moving and give an uncensored, complex portrait of affect related to suicide. Indeed, my own essay's position can be partly traced to the influence of Harriet Goldhor Lerner's work on intimacy twenty years ago.

8. See Hussey *Virginia Woolf A to Z* for references to critics on both sides of this battle line as well as somewhere in between (371-72).

9. Berman sees Thomas Caramagno's diagnosis of Woolf's illness as "manic depressive illness," "bipolar affective disorder" with a hereditary component (70), as the only valid way to understand her suicide. Here Berman ignores Caramagno's own more subtle views and his warning to us to "relinquish the demand for an answer [to 'Why did Woolf die?'] that satisfies *our* need for narrative unity" (61).

10. Although as an identity construct, "suicide" has received little attention from critics thus far, it is routinely treated as an identity and constitutes one of the chief features

of Woolf's retrospectively constructed identity, but feminists often also include it in lists that stress non-identity features (or even Woolf's own politically conscious interests): see, for example, Lee's list—"Bloomsbury gossip. Madness. Lesbianism. Suicide. It is not difficult to see why the more uncommon aspects of Woolf's life have lured readers to her diaries and letters" ("Essays" 110)—or Silver's—"Does she preside [in *Sammie and Rosie Get Laid*] as modernist, as feminist, as pacifist, as highbrow, as sapphist, as suicide, as failed liberal anti-imperialist?" (164).

11. Unlike Berman, one of Virginia Woolf's earliest doctors, George Savage, writes of suicide's medical causes in a far more nuanced manner: while classifying suicide, conventionally at that time, as among "the general symptoms of melancholia," he "object[s]" against "classify[ing] cases purely from the existence of one symptom" and argues that suicide "deserves consideration rather more in detail than many other special symptoms" of melancholia; he proceeds: "We have seen that ideas of self-destruction may arise from various feelings bodily and mental, and I know no special class characteristics which would enable me to say there is a special suicidal insanity" (188).

12. Despite extensive analysis of Virginia Woolf's portrayal of war veteran Septimus Smith as a double for her protagonist Clarissa Dalloway and for Woolf herself, Berman never mentions the influence of war in Woolf's suicide (82-94). In the heat of the moment, Leonard Woolf saw multiple reasons for Woolf's death, including the war, as his letters testify: "She has been really very ill these last weeks & was terrified that she was going mad again. It was, I suppose, the strain of the war & finishing her book & she could not rest or eat. Today she went for a walk leaving behind a letter saying that she was committing suicide" (Spotts 250).

13. Berman's larger argument is also semi-feminist; his critique of feminist readings of Woolf and of Woolf's feminist criticism of male doctors appears in juxtaposition with some feminist arguments, most importantly a feminist defense of Dorothy Parker against Ernest Hemingway's sexism (119-33).

14. Biographers and critics like to quote Woolf herself "against death," but do so by drawing upon the doubled-edged sword of her closing words to one of her novels, *The Waves*—as, for example, Nicolson does to end his own book, "'Against you I will fling myself unvanquished and unyielding, O Death'" (191).

15. Hussey's analysis of the early fiction of the Woolfs discloses an especially troubling set of associations in Leonard's semi-autobiographical *The Wise Virgins* between heterosexual love and death ("Refractions" 131).

16. That Leonard differed "fundamental[ly]" also from Virginia in his political views of the war is demonstrated by Gottlieb, though she sees the Woolfs as never to "have openly acknowledged their political differences" on this particular issue (250).

17. Though she does not look closely at the narrative of "Virginia's Death," Rosenfeld focuses on the "intersubjective principle" in both Woolfs' writings, especially Virginia's, and emphasizes that, while marriage "all too easily becomes a battleground, even a burial ground," she nonetheless "read[s]" the Woolfs' actual marriage as "a remarkably successful negotiation of tension and breakdown" (3, 10).

18. The terms of this paragraph derive primarily from my *Women Coauthors* (which includes a chapter on Mill and Harriet Taylor); for a discussion of such collaboration specifically between the Woolfs, see Chapman and Manson who argue, against Gottlieb, "That they eventually became antagonists (see Gottlieb) is a contestable thesis that fails to appreciate the full extent of Virginia Woolf's involvement in Leonard Woolf's activities, indeed in her own" (61). For further feminist discussions of collaboration, see especially Peck and Mink; and for various discussions of literary and academic collaboration, see Hutcheon and the series of articles under "Theories and Methodologies" in the March, May, and October 2001 issues of *PMLA*.

19. For contrasts to this autobiography, see the discussions of post-traumatic therapeutic life-writing in Henke's *Shattered Subjects*.

20. Unfortunately, Wilson leaves Woolf's political views almost entirely out of this biography, referring to her primarily in relation to her introductions of her husband to political figures whom she knew; his struggle with their marriage; and the impact of her illness on his career.

AFTERWORD
Suzette Henke

If one peruses Virginia Woolf's manuscripts in the British Library in London, it is a poignant experience to handle the single epistolary folder that contains her three suicide notes.[1] Two of the letters were left by Virginia in the sitting-room at Monk's House on 28 March, 1941, the morning of her suicide. One is addressed to Leonard, the other to Vanessa. Appended to the library folder is Leonard's handwritten annotation attesting to their provenance. But what about the third, undated letter, which Nicolson and Trautmann assign to 28 March? Leonard is careful to explain that he discovered this anomalous document, also addressed to him, later that afternoon, on Virginia's desk in her writing lodge at the back of Monk's House garden (a renovated shed separate from the cottage). On 11 May, 1941, like a scientist dating an object from an archeological dig, Leonard wrote on the back of the third note: "This letter was not the one left for me by V. I found it later in the writing block on which she was writing when I went out to see her in the Lodge about 11 in the morning of March 28" (*L6*: 486n3). He assumes that Virginia composed the two suicide notes left on the mantel for him and Vanessa "in the house immediately afterwards" (*L6*: 486n3). In their edition of Woolf's *Letters*, Nigel Nicolson and Joanne Trautmann speculate "that her suicide was premeditated by ten days" and that the Tuesday letter to Leonard was written on 18 March, the Sunday letter to Vanessa on 23 March, and the shorter note to Leonard on 28 March. The letter which Quentin Bell, along with Leonard, "considers to be the last of the three," they "deduce to be the first" (*L6*: 489). Another biographer, James King, also believes that the note to Leonard left in the sitting room and dated "Tuesday" was composed by Virginia on 18 March, prior to a purported suicide attempt that failed. Hermione Lee accepts this speculative dating in her recent biography of Woolf. Only Panthea Reid, in *Art and Affection* (1996), challenges the premises of Nicolson and Trautmann by proposing a "Redating of Virginia Woolf's Suicide Letters" in an Appendix (471-77). She contends that the Tuesday letter to Leonard should be dated 25 March (rather than 18 March) and that the shorter, undated note might possibly have been a draft.

In the face of such enigmatic archival evidence, I would like to suggest that Woolf's composition of two different versions of her last communication to Leonard attests both to the obsessive-compulsive nature of her suicidal ideation and to her unflagging commitment to the craft of writing. In the letter dated "Tuesday," Virginia repeatedly attempts to vindicate and reassure her husband: "You have given me the greatest possible happiness. You have been in every way all that anyone could be. I don't think two people could have been happier till this terrible disease came. . . . I owe all the happiness of my life to you. . . . If anybody could have saved me it would have been you. . . . I don't think two people could have been happier than we have been." She explains: "I begin to hear voices, and can't concentrate. So I am doing what seems the best thing to do" (*L6*: 481). The shorter version of the letter is more emotionally intense and exhibits clear psychological distress over what Virginia perceives to be the degeneration of her writing: "But I know that I shall never get over this: and I am wasting your life. It is this madness. Nothing anyone says can persuade me. You can work, and you will be much better without me. You see I can't write this even, which shows I am right" (*L6*: 487). Virginia protests that she is ruining Leonard's life and that, without her, he could be happier and more productive. Her death would liberate him to work more efficiently and free him from onerous duties of spousal care. Virginia clearly dreaded the possibility of being forced to endure yet another "rest cure," the remedy that her physician Octavia Wilberforce had recommended the day before Woolf's suicide. At the end of her shorter note to Leonard, Virginia asks in a postscript: "Will you destroy all my papers [?]" (*L6*: 487). The implicit interrogation mark leaves open the possibility that he will, or will not, do so.

Was the Tuesday letter composed, as King and Lee believe, on 18 March and provocatively left on the mantel, later to be scooped up by Virginia before anyone had a chance to notice it? Or could the shorter communication have been authored as yet another version of Virginia's epistolary farewell to her husband, with a somewhat different purpose? Addressing her Tuesday letter to Leonard, but anticipating that it might be read by a larger audience, Woolf proffers a strong exoneration of her spouse: "You have been entirely patient with me and incredibly good. I want to say that—everybody knows it" (*L6*: 481). And should "everybody" not know it, Virginia is informing the public and clearing Leonard of the slightest suspicion of blame for her death. But for Leonard himself, she perhaps left behind a more private communication meant for his eyes only (not for the police; or for the coroner Edward Hoare; or for a public audience). She must have realized that Leonard would be asked to relinquish her suicide notes to investigating authorities.

Later, when her husband went to the writing lodge, he would discover another epistolary farewell, written in the secret language of conjugal sentiment, "some little language such as lovers use, broken words, inarticulate words" (*W* 238): "I want to tell you that you have given me complete happiness" (*L6*: 486), she reassures her spouse. Virginia may have intended for the shorter note to be shared with one person only, then destroyed. Whatever the dating of this more laconic and distraught text, which might have constituted a "draft," or which might represent the last words Virginia ever penned, Woolf's duplication of suicide letters proves that she was, without question, a writer to the end. In this context, it makes perfect sense that she would have written a penultimate version of her suicide letter, one of the most significant documents she would ever compose. Woolf's long career as a serious author, passionately devoted to the craft of word-shaping, would have demanded that she create more than one version of her final communication to the man whose loyalty she cherished and who, in the role of her first and best reader, would forever mourn her passing.

Like Panthea Reid, Roger Poole interprets the shorter, undated version of Woolf's suicide note as a "preliminary draft" of her "last message to Leonard," whereby she explains "in terms which make sense to him, that she cannot endure any more" (*Unknown* 256). At the same time, in composing the Tuesday letter, Virginia "wanted to give him an absolutely clean record, so far as her death was concerned. . . . Preparing to die, she writes the most generous letter of which she is capable. Her prime concern is to make sure that he will never reproach himself for her death" (257).

As Claire Kahane points out in her essay on "Snakes, Toads, and Duckweed," at the time Woolf was "probing her memories of familial violations" and incest abuse in "A Sketch of the Past," both she and Leonard "were in despair about Germany's imminent invasion of Britain"—an invasion that got as far as the Channel Islands. The couple made a suicide pact and kept a supply of gasoline in the garage, with plans to asphyxiate themselves through carbon monoxide poisoning should Hitler's storm-troopers reach the British mainland. Kahane notes a striking conflation of the personal and the political in the late work of Virginia Woolf, insofar as Woolf "both names a remembered early violation of her body in the memoir and makes rape a key trope of the present time in the novel [*Between the Acts*], while anticipating a national violation on the real historical horizon: a future rape writ large" (230).

On 28 March, 1941, Woolf relinquished her battle with hallucinatory voices by plunging, two months after her 59th birthday, into a river torrent that would obliterate the lifelong resonance of trauma and spare her the continuing threat of Nazi domination. One should, however, resist the temptation to romanticize Virginia's death. I would take exception to Michael Cunningham's nostalgic evocation of the author's lyrical extinction in *The Hours*, as well as to Roger Poole's suggestion that death by water "had no terrors for Virginia. In a sense she regarded it as a happy release, a going home" (*Unknown* 273).[2] The reality of her drowning must have been otherwise. The water of the River Ouse would have been frigidly cold in March; the sludge of the riverbank viscous and muddy; the stones, desperately gathered, solid anchors to oblivion. Surely Virginia's helpless body instinctively struggled against fluid suffocation and her lungs gasped for air, as she fought the engulfing current. "She could swim, but she allowed herself to be drowned" (Lee, *Virginia* 748).

For Virginia Woolf, as for Bernard in *The Waves*, all the rest was silence. And yet, before the silence overwhelmed her, Woolf functioned successfully, into her 60th year, as a creative and productive writer who incorporated her experiences as a trauma survivor into an extraordinary modernist oeuvre. As she declares in "A Sketch of the Past," the "whole world is a work of art. . . . But . . . certainly and emphatically there is no God; we are the words; we are the music; we are the thing itself" (*MOB* 72).

Notes

1. Edward L. (Ted) Bishop describes the *frisson* of discovering Virginia Woolf's suicide notes in the British Library when he celebrates the "Archival Jolt" in his memoir, *Riding with Rilke*. He attributes such serendipitous moments of scholarly discovery to the Egyptian goddess Seshat and explains that seeing Woolf's "suicide note added nothing to my textual knowledge, but it added enormously to my corporeal knowledge, a knowledge difficult to quantify or describe" (34-36, 112).

2. For further discussion of Woolf and Cunningham, see Henke, "Bloomsbury Blues."

WORKS CITED

Abel, Elizabeth. *Virginia Woolf and the Fictions of Psychoanalysis.* Chicago: U of Chicago P, 1989.

Abraham, Nicolas, and Maria Torok. *The Shell and the Kernel: Renewals of Psychoanalysis, Volume One.* Trans., ed., and with an Introduction by Nicholas T. Rand. Chicago: U of Chicago P, 1994.

Adamson, Joseph, and Hilary Clark, eds. *Scenes of Shame: Psychoanalysis, Shame, and Writing.* Albany, NY: State U of New York P, 1999.

Alvarez, A. *The Savage God: A Study of Suicide.* New York: Norton, 1971.

Anderson, Olive. *Suicide in Victorian and Edwardian England.* Oxford, UK: Clarendon, 1987.

Ardis, Ann and Bonnie Kime Scott, eds. *Virginia Woolf: Turning the Centuries. Selected Papers from the Ninth Annual Conference on Virginia Woolf.* New York: Pace UP, 2000.

Armstrong, Louise. *Rocking the Cradle: What Happened When Women Said Incest.* Reading, MA: Addison-Wesley, 1994.

Bal, Mieke, Jonathan Crewe, and Leo Spitzer, eds. *Acts of Memory: Cultural Recall in the Present.* Hanover, NH: UP of New England, 1999.

Barker, Pat. *The Ghost Road.* New York: Plume, 1996.

——. *Regeneration.* New York: Plume, 1993.

Barrett, Eileen. Introduction. Barrett and Cramer, *Lesbian Readings* 3-9.

——. "Unmasking Lesbian Passion: The Inverted World of *Mrs. Dalloway.*" Barrett and Cramer, *Lesbian Readings* 146-64.

——, and Patricia Cramer, eds. *Re: Reading, Re: Writing, Re: Teaching Virginia Woolf: Selected Papers from the Fourth Annual Conference on Virginia Woolf.* New York: Pace UP, 1995.

——, and Patricia Cramer, eds. *Virginia Woolf: Lesbian Readings.* New York: NYU Press, 1997.

Bartky, Sandra Lee. *Femininity and Domination: Studies in the Phenomenology of Oppression.* New York: Routledge, 1990.

Bass, Ellen, and Laura Davis. *The Courage to Heal: A Guide for Women Survivors of Child Sexual Abuse.* New York: Harper & Row, 1988.

Bauchart, Hélène. E-mail to Jane Lilienfeld. 17 May 2006.

Bazin, Nancy Topping, and Jane Hamovit Lauter. "Virginia Woolf's Keen Sensitivity to War." Hussey, *War* 143-39.

Bean, Margaret. "Denial and the Psychological Consequences of Alcoholism." *Dynamic Approaches to the Understanding and Treatment of Alcoholism.* Ed. Norman Zinberg and Margaret Bean. New York: Free Press-Simon & Schuster, 1981. 55-97.

Beer, Gillian. *Virginia Woolf: The Common Ground.* Ann Arbor: U of Michigan P, 1996.

——. *Wave, Atom, Dinosaur: Woolf's Science.* London: Virginia Woolf Society of Great Britain, 2000.

Bell, Anne Olivier. Letter. *Virginia Woolf Miscellany* 38 (1992): 1-2.

Bell, Clive. *Civilization and Old Friends, Two Volumes in One.* Chicago: U of Chicago P, 1973.

Bell, Quentin. *Virginia Woolf: A Biography.* New York: Harcourt, 1972.

Berman, Jeffrey. *Surviving Literary Suicide.* Amherst, MA: U of Massachusetts P, 1999.

Bernheimer, Charles. "A Shattered Globe: Narcissism and Masochism in Woolf's Life-Writing." *Psychoanalysis and . . .* Ed. Richard Feldstein and Henry Sussman. New York: Routledge, 1990. 187-206.

Bersani, Leo. *The Culture of Redemption.* Cambridge, MA: Harvard UP, 1990.

——. *The Freudian Body: Psychoanalysis and Art.* New York: Columbia UP, 1986.

Bishop, Edward L. "The Alfa and the *Avant-texte*: Transcribing Virginia Woolf's Manuscripts." *Editing Virginia Woolf: Interpreting the Modernist Text.* Ed. James M. Haule and J. H. Stape. New York: Palgrave, 2002. 139-157.

Bishop, Ted. *Riding with Rilke: Reflections on Motorcycles and Books.* Toronto: Viking Penguin, 2005.

Black, Naomi. *Virginia Woolf as Feminist.* Ithaca: Cornell UP, 2004.

Blain, Virginia. "'Dinner is Served': The Hogarth Press, Sexual Abuse, and the Ritual of the Dining Room." *Virginia Woolf Miscellany* 42 (1994): 5.

Bland, Lucy. "Marriage Laid Bare: Middle Class Women and Marital Sex c. 1880-1914." *Labour and Love: Women's Experience of Home and Family, 1850-1940.* Ed. Jane Lewis. New York: Blackwell, 1996. 123-48.

Bollas, Christopher. *The Shadow of the Object.* New York: Columbia UP, 1987.

Boone, Joseph Allen. "The Meaning of Elvedon in *The Waves*: A Key to Bernard's Experience and Woolf's Vision." *Modern Fiction Studies* 27.4 (1981-2): 629-37.

Bordo, Susan. "Anorexia Nervosa: Psychopathology as the Crystallization of Culture." *Unbearable Weight.* 2nd ed. Berkeley: U of California P, 2004. 139-163.

Bouson, J. Brooks. *Quiet As It's Kept: Shame, Trauma, and Race in the Novels of Toni Morrison.* Albany, NY: State U of New York P, 2000.

Bowen, Murray. *Family Therapy in Clinical Practice.* Northvale, NJ: Jason Aronson, 1985.

Briggs, Julia. *Virginia Woolf: An Inner Life.* New York: Harcourt, 2005.

Briggs, Marlene. "Veterans and Civilians: Traumatic Knowledge and Cultural Appropriation in *Mrs. Dalloway*." McVicker and Davis 43-50.

Brison, Susan. *Aftermath: Violence and the Remaking of a Self.* Princeton: Princeton UP, 2002.

———. "Trauma Narratives and the Remaking of the Self." Bal, Crewe and Spitzer 39-54.

Broe, Mary Lynn, ed. *Silence and Power: A Reevaluation of Djuna Barnes.* Carbondale: Southern Illinois UP, 1991.

Brooks, Peter. *Reading for the Plot: Design and Intention in Narrative.* New York: Knopf, 1984.

Browning, Diane, and Bonny Boatman. "Incest: Children at Risk." *American Journal of Psychiatry* 134.1 (1977): 69-72.

Butler, Judith. *Precarious Life: The Powers of Mourning and Violence.* London: Verso, 2004.

Butler, Sandra. *Conspiracy of Silence: The Trauma of Incest.* San Francisco: Volcano, 1978.

———. *Conspiracy of Silence: The Trauma of Incest.* San Francisco: Bantam, 1979.

Cameron, Marcia. *Broken Child.* New York: Kensington, 1995.

Cameron, Norman. "The Experimental Analysis of Schizophrenic Thinking." *Language and Thought in Schizophrenia*. 1944. Ed. J. S. Kasanin. New York: Norton, 1964. 50-64.

Campbell, Sue. *Relational Remembering: Rethinking the Memory Wars*. Lanham, MD: Rowman & Littlefield, 2003.

Caramagno, Thomas. *The Flight of the Mind: Virginia Woolf's Art and Manic-Depressive Illness*. Berkeley: U of California P, 1992.

Caruth, Cathy. ed. *Trauma: Explorations in Memory*. Baltimore: Johns Hopkins UP, 1995.

——. *Unclaimed Experience: Trauma, Narrative, and History*. Baltimore: Johns Hopkins UP, 1996.

Chapman, Wayne K., and Janet M. Manson. "Carte and Tierce: Leonard, Virginia Woolf, and War for Peace." Hussey, *War* 58-78.

Clark, Miriam Marty. "Consciousness, Stream and Quanta in *To the Lighthouse*." *Studies in the Novel* 21.4 (1989): 413–423.

Coates, Irene. *Who's Afraid of Leonard Woolf? A Case for the Sanity of Virginia Woolf*. New York: Soho, 1998.

Cohen, Barry and Anne Mills. "Skin/Paper/Bark: Body Image, Trauma and the Diagnostic Drawing Series." *Images of the Body in Trauma*. Ed. Jean M. Goodwin and Reina Attias. New York: Basic, 1999.

Conrad, Joseph. *Heart of Darkness*. 1902. New York: Penguin, 1999.

Constable, Liz, ed. Introduction. "States of Shame." Spec. issue of *L'Esprit Créateur* 39.4 (1999): 3-12.

Courtois, Christine. *Healing the Incest World: Adult Survivors in Therapy*. New York: Norton, 1988.

Cramer, Patricia. Introduction. Barrett and Cramer, *Lesbian Readings* 117-27.

——. "Jane Harrison and Lesbian Plots: The Absent Lover in Virginia Woolf's *The Waves*." *Studies in the Novel* 37.4 (2005): 443-63.

——. "Notes from Underground: Lesbian Ritual in Virginia Woolf." *Virginia Woolf Miscellanies: Proceedings of the First Annual Conference on Virginia Woolf*. Ed. Mark Hussey and Vara Neverow-Turk. New York: Pace UP, 1992. 177-88.

——. "'Pearls and the Porpoise:' *The Years*—A Lesbian Memoir." Barrett and Cramer, *Lesbian Readings* 222-40.

——. "*Vita Nuova*: Courtly Love and Lesbian Romance in *The Years*." *Woolf Studies Annual* 10 (2004): 173-202.

Crossley, Michele L. "Narrative Psychology, Trauma and the Study of Self/Identity." *Theory and Psychology* 10. 4 (2000): 528-46.

Culbertson, Roberta. "Embodied Memory, Transcendence, and Telling: Recounting Trauma, Re-establishing the Self." *New Literary History* 26 (1995): 169-95.

Cunningham, Michael. *The Hours.* New York: Farrar, Straus, & Giroux, 1998.

Daly, Brenda. *Authoring a Life: A Woman's Survival in and through Literary Studies.* Albany, NY: State U of New York P, 1998.

Dalgarno, Emily. *Virginia Woolf and the Visible World.* Cambridge, UK: Cambridge UP, 2001.

Dalsimer, Katherine. *Virginia Woolf: Becoming a Writer.* New Haven: Yale UP, 2001.

Damasio, Antonio. *The Feeling of What Happens: Body and Emotion in the Making of Consciousness.* San Diego: Harcourt, 1999.

D'Amore, Alice. "Autobiographical Ruptures: Rhoda's Traumatic Displacement." Southworth and Sparks 44-49.

Danica, Elly. *Don't, a Woman's Word: A Personal Chronicle of Childhood Incest and Adult Recovery.* Pittsburgh: Cleis, 1988.

David and Sara. "The Pillar of the Community and the Pillar of Strength." *Kiss Daddy Goodnight: Ten Years Later.* Ed. Louise Armstrong. New York: Pocket, 1987. 204-29.

Darnton, Robert. "It Happened One Night." *New York Review of Books.* 51.11 (24 June, 2004).

Davies, Jody Messler. "Dissociation, Repression, and Reality Testing in the Countertransference." *Memories of Sexual Betrayal: Truth, Fantasy, Repression, and Dissociation.* Ed. Richard B. Gartner. Northdale, NJ: Jason Aronson, 1997. 45-93.

Davis, Colin. *Levinas: An Introduction.* Notre Dame, IN: U of Notre Dame P, 1996.

de Duve, Thierry. *Kant after Duchamp.* Cambridge, MA: MIT P, 1996.

DeFazio, Victor J. "Dynamic Perspectives on the Nature and Effect of Combat Stress." *Stress Disorders Among Vietnam Veterans: Theory, Research and Treatment.* Ed. Charles R. Figley. New York: Brunner, 1978. 23-42.

Del Vecchio, John. *Carry Me Home.* New York: Bantam, 1995.

De Gay, Jane. *Virginia Woolf's Novels and the Literary Past.* Edinburgh: Edinburgh UP, 2006.

de Man, Paul. "Sign and Symbol in Hegel's *Aesthetics." Aesthetic Ideology.* Ed. Andrzej Warminski. Minneapolis: U of Minnesota P, 1996.

DeMeester, Karen. "Trauma and Recovery in Virginia Woolf's *Mrs. Dalloway.*" *Modern Fiction Studies* 44.3 (1998): 649-73.

DeSalvo, Louise. *Conceived with Malice.* New York: Dutton, 1994.

———. Letter. *Virginia Woolf Miscellany* 38 (1992): 3.

———. "'To Make her Mutton at Sixteen': Rape, Incest, and Child Abuse in *The Antiphon.*" Broe 300-315.

———. *Virginia Woolf: The Impact of Childhood Sexual Abuse on Her Life and Work.* Boston: Beacon, 1989.

———. *Virginia Woolf's First Voyage: A Novel in the Making.* Totowa, NJ: Rowman & Littlefield, 1980.

———. "Virginia, Virginius, Virginity." *Faith of a (Woman) Writer.* Ed. Alice Kessler-Harris and William McBrien. New York: Greenwood, 1988. 179-89.

———. *Writing as a Way of Healing: How Telling Our Stories Transforms Our Lives.* New York: Harper Collins, 1999.

DiBattista, Maria. *Virginia Woolf's Major Novels: The Fables of Anon.* New Haven: Yale UP, 1980.

Dick, Susan. "I Remembered, I Forgotten: Bernard's Final Soliloquy in *The Waves.*" *Modern Language Studies* 13.3 (1983): 38-52.

Dobash, Emerson, and Russell P. Dobash. *Women, Violence and Social Change.* New York: Routledge, 1992.

DSM-IV. Diagnostic and Statistical Manual of Mental Disorders. 4th ed. Arlington, VA: American Psychiatric Publishing, 2000.

Dumézil, Georges. *The Destiny of the Warrior.* Trans. Alf Hiltebeitel. Chicago: U of Chicago P, 1970.

Eberly, David. "Incest, Erasure, and *The Years.*" Hussey and Neverow 147-50.

———. "Safety Pins and Semicolons." Ardis and Scott 134-39.

———. "Talking It All Out: Homosexual Disclosure in Virginia Woolf." Neverow-Turk and Hussey 128-34.

Eder, Doris. "Louis Unmasked: T. S. Eliot in *The Waves.*" *Virginia Woolf Quarterly* 2 (1975): 13-27.

Ehrenberg, Darlene Bergman. "Abuse and Desire: A Case of Father-Daughter Incest." *Contemporary Psychoanalysis* 23.4 (1987): 593-604.

Emery, Mary Lou. "'Robbed of Meaning': The Work at the Center of *To the Lighthouse*." *Modern Fiction Studies* 38.1 (1992): 217-34.

Ensler, Eve. Introduction. *Central Park* 22 (Spring 1993): 7-12.

Farrell, Kirby. *Post-traumatic Culture: Injury and Interpretation in the Nineties*. Baltimore: Johns Hopkins UP, 1998.

Felman, Shoshana. *The Juridical Unconscious: Trials and Traumas in the Twentieth Century*. Cambridge, MA: Harvard UP, 2002.

Felman, Shoshana, and Dori Laub, eds. *Testimony: Crises of Witnessing in Literature, Psychoanalysis, and History*. New York: Routledge, 1991.

Ferenczi, Sandor. "Confusion of Tongues Between Adults and the Child." 1933. *Contemporary Psychoanalysis* 24 (1988): 196-206.

Ferrer, Daniel. *Virginia Woolf and the Madness of Language*. Trans. Geoffrey Bennington and Rachel Bowlby. London: Routledge, 1990.

Fisher-Taylor, Gail. "In the Presence of Ghosts: Transforming Realities." Rivera 91-105.

Fleishman, Avrom. "'To Return to St. Ives:' Woolf's Autobiographical Writings." *English Language Notes* 48.3 (1981): 606-18.

——. *Betrayal of Innocence: Incest and its Devastation*. Los Angeles: Tarcher, 1978.

Forward, Susan and Craig Buck. *Betrayal of Innocence: Incest and Its Devastation*. Rev. ed. New York: Penguin, 1988.

Frank, Joseph. *The Idea of Spatial Form*. New Brunswick: Rutgers UP, 1991.

Frankl, Viktor E. *Man's Search for Meaning*. Rev. ed. New York: Pocket, 1984.

Fraser, Sylvia. *My Father's House: A Memoir of Incest and of Healing*. New York: Ticknor & Fields, 1988.

Freedman, Ariela. *Death, Men, and Modernism: Trauma and Narrative in British Fiction from Hardy to Woolf*. New York: Routledge, 2003.

Freud, Sigmund. *The Standard Edition of the Complete Psychological Works of Sigmund Freud*. 24 vols. Trans. and ed. James Strachey et al. London: Hogarth Press and the Institute of Psychoanalysis, 1924-1953. Cited as *SE*.

——. *Beyond the Pleasure Principle*. Trans. James Strachey. London: Hogarth, 1920.

Freyd, Jennifer. *Betrayal Trauma: The Logic of Forgetting Childhood Abuse*. Cambridge, MA: Harvard UP, 1996.

Friedman, Alan J. and Carol C. Donley. *Einstein as Myth and Muse*. Cambridge, UK: Cambridge UP, 1985.

Friedman, Norman. "Point of View in Fiction: The Development of a Critical Concept." *PMLA* 70.5 (1955): 1160-84.

Friedman, Susan Stanford. *Mappings: Feminisms and the Cultural Geography of Encounter*. Princeton: Princeton UP, 1998.

Froula, Christine. "*Mrs. Dalloway*'s Postwar Elegy: Women, War, and the Art of Mourning." *Modernism/Modernity* 9.1 (2002): 125-63.

———. "Out of the Chrysalis: Female Initiation and Female Authority in Virginia Woolf's *The Voyage Out*." *Tulsa Studies in Women's Literature* 5.1 (1986): 63-90.

———. *Virginia Woolf and the Bloomsbury Avant-Garde: War, Civilization, Modernity*. New York: Columbia UP, 2005.

Fuss, Diana. "Reading Like a Feminist." *The Essential Difference*. Ed. Naomi Schor and Elizabeth Weed. Bloomington: Indiana UP, 1994. 98-115.

Gartner, Richard B. *Memories of Sexual Betrayal: Truth, Fantasy, Repression, and Dissociation*. Northvale, NJ: Jason Aronson, 1997.

Gervais, David. "Leonard Woolf's Autobiography." Rev. of *Sowing; Growing; Beginning Again; Downhill All the Way; The Journey not the Arrival Matters. Cambridge Quarterly* 5.1 (1970): 82-98.

Gillespie, Diane F. "Godiva Still Rides: Virginia Woolf, Divestiture, and *Three Guineas*." Southworth and Sparks 2-27.

———. *The Sisters' Arts: The Writing and Painting of Virginia Woolf and Vanessa Bell*. Syracuse: Syracuse UP, 1998.

Gilligan, James. *Violence: Reflections on a National Epidemic*. New York: Vintage, 1996.

Gilmartin, Pat. *Rape, Incest, and Child Sexual Abuse: Consequences and Recovery*. New York: Garland, 1994.

Gilmore, Leigh. *Autobiographics: A Feminist Theory of Women's Self-Representation*. Ithaca: Cornell UP, 1994.

Ginsberg, Elaine and Laura Gottlieb, eds. *Virginia Woolf: Centennial Essays*. Troy, NY: Whitston, 1983.

Glendinning, Victoria. *Vita: The Life of Vita Sackville-West*. New York: Knopf, 1983.

Goleman, Daniel. *Vital Lies, Simple Truths: The Psychology of Self-Deception and Shared Illusions.* New York: Simon & Schuster, 1985.

Gottlieb, Laura Moss. "The War Between the Woolfs." *Virginia Woolf and Bloomsbury.* Ed. Jane Marcus. Bloomington: Indiana UP, 1987. 242-52.

Gough, Val. "'A Responsible Person Like Her': Woolf's Suicide Culture." Ardis and Scott 183-91.

Graham, Dee L. R. *Loving to Survive: Sexual Terror, Men's Violence, and Women's Lives.* New York: New York UP, 1994.

Graham, John. "Point of View in *The Waves*: Some Services of the Style." *University of Toronto Quarterly* 39 (1970): 193-211.

Guiguet, Jean. *Virginia Woolf and Her Works.* London: Hogarth, 1965.

Guth, Deborah. "'What a Lark! What a Plunge!': Fiction as Self-Evasion in *Mrs. Dalloway.*" *Modern Language Review* 84 (1989): 18-25.

Haaken, Janice. *Pillar of Salt: Gender, Memory, and the Perils of Looking Back.* New Brunswick: Rutgers UP, 1998.

Haller, Evelyn. "The Anti-Madonna in the Work and Thought of Virginia Woolf." Ginsberg and Gottlieb 93-109.

Hankins, Leslie. "HyperWoolf: HyperMedia or HyperHypes? Thoughts on New Technologies for Adaptations of Literature." Tenth Annual Conference on Virginia Woolf. University of Maryland, Baltimore County. 10 June 2000.

——. "Woolf's 'The Cinema' and Film Forums of the Twenties." *The Multiple Muses of Virginia Woolf.* Ed. Diane F. Gillespie. Columbia, MO: U of Missouri P, 1993. 148-79.

Harding, Sandra. *Whose Science? Whose Knowledge? Thinking from Women's Lives.* Ithaca: Cornell UP, 1991.

Harper, Howard. *Between Language and Silence.* Baton Rouge: Louisiana State UP, 1982.

Harris, Andrea. *Other Sexes: Rewriting Difference from Woolf to Winterson.* Albany, NY: State U of New York P, 2000.

Hartman, Geoffrey. "Virginia's Web." *Chicago Review* 14 (Spring, 1961): 20–32. Rpt. in Homans 35–45.

Haule, James M., and Philip H. Smith, Jr., eds. *The Waves.* By Virginia Woolf. Oxford: Blackwell, 1993.

Heidegger, Martin. *Being and Time.* Trans. John Macquarrie and Edward Robinson. New York: Harper & Row, 1962.

Henke, Suzette. "Bloomsbury Blues: Virginia Woolf's Moments and Michael Cunningham's *Hours*." *From Camera Lens to Critical Lens: A Collection of Best Essays on Film Adaptation*. Ed. Rebecca Housel. Newcastle: Cambridge Scholars Press, 2006. 9-20

——. "De/Colonizing the Subject in Virginia Woolf's *Voyage Out*: Rachel Vinrace as *La Mystérique*." Hussey and Neverow 103-07.

——. "*Mrs. Dalloway*: The Communion of Saints." Marcus, *New Feminist Essays* 125-47.

——. *Shattered Subjects: Trauma and Testimony in Women's Life-Writing*. Rev. ed. New York: St. Martin's, 2000.

——. "Virginia Woolf's *Prime Minister*: A Key to *Mrs. Dalloway*." Ginsberg and Gottlieb 127-41.

——. "Modernism, Trauma, and Narrative Reformulation." *Gender in Modernism: New Geographies, Complex Intersections*. Ed. Bonnie Kime Scott. Urbana: U of Illinois P, 2007. 555-63.

——. "Virginia Woolf and Post-Traumatic Subjectivity." Ardis and Scott 147-52.

Herman, Judith. *Trauma and Recovery: The Aftermath of Violence—From Domestic Abuse to Political Terror*. New York: Basic, 1992.

Herman, Judith Lewis, with Lisa Hirschman. *Father-Daughter Incest*. 1981. Cambridge MA: Harvard UP, 2000.

Higonnet, Margaret. "Frames of Female Suicide." *Studies in the Novel* 32.2 (2000): 229-42.

——. "Speaking Silences: Women's Suicide." *The Female Body in Western Culture*. Ed. Susan Rubin Suleiman. Cambridge, MA: Harvard UP, 1985. 68-83.

Hite, Molly. Introduction. *The Waves*. By Virginia Woolf. San Diego: Harcourt, 2006.

Homans, Margaret, ed. *Virginia Woolf: A Collection of Critical Essays*. Englewood Cliffs, NJ: Prentice Hall, 1993.

Horowitz, Mardi J., ed. *Essential Papers on Posttraumatic Stress Disorder*. New York: New York UP, 1999.

Humm, Maggie. *Modernist Women and Visual Cultures: Virginia Woolf, Vanessa Bell, Photography and Cinema*. New Brunswick: Rutgers UP, 2003.

Humphrey, Robert. *Stream of Consciousness in the Modern Novel.* Berkeley: U of California P, 1954.

Hussey, Mark. "Refractions of Desire: The Early Fiction of Virginia and Leonard Woolf." *Modern Fiction Studies* 38.1 (1992): 127-46.

———. "*To the Lighthouse* and Physics: The Cosmology of David Bohm and Virginia Woolf." *New Essays on Virginia Woolf.* Ed. Helen Wussow. Dallas: Contemporary Research, 1995. 79–97.

———. and Ariel Orr Jordan. "A Violent Hunger for Lost Feelings." *Central Park* 22 (Spring 1993): 69-91.

———, ed. *Virginia Woolf and War: Fiction, Reality and Myth.* Syracuse: Syracuse UP, 1991.

———. and Vara Neverow, eds. *Virginia Woolf: Emerging Perspectives. Selected Papers from the Third Annual Conference on Virginia Woolf.* New York: Pace UP, 1994.

———. *Virginia Woolf A to Z.* New York: Facts on File, 1995.

Hutcheon, Linda. Presidential Address 2000, "She Do the President in Different Voices." *PMLA* 116.3 (2001): 518-30.

Hynes, Samuel. *The Auden Generation: Literature and Politics in England in the 1930s.* New York: Viking, 1977.

Jacobs, Janet Liebman. *Victimized Daughters: Incest and the Development of the Female Self.* New York: Routledge, 1994.

Jamison, Kay Redfield. *Touched with Fire: Manic-Depressive Illness and the Artistic Temperament.* New York: Simon & Schuster, 1993.

Janoff-Bulman, Ronnie. *Shattered Assumptions: Towards a New Psychology of Trauma.* New York: Free Press, 1992.

Johnston, Mona. *Spectral Evidence: The Ramona Case: Incest, Memory and Truth on Trial in Napa Valley.* Boston: Houghton Mifflin, 1997.

Kacandes, Irene. "Narrative Witnessing as Memory Work: Reading Gertrud Kolmar's *A Jewish Mother.*" Bal, Crewe, and Spitzer 55-71.

Kahane, Claire. *Passions of the Voice: Hysteria, Narrative, and the Figure of the Speaking Woman, 1850-1915.* Baltimore: Johns Hopkins UP, 1995.

Katz, Tamar. "Modernism, Subjectivity, and Narrative Form: Abstraction in *The Waves.*" *Narrative* 3.3 (1995): 232-51.

Kaufman, Gershen. *The Psychology of Shame: Theory and Treatment of Shame-Based Syndromes.* New York: Springer, 1989.

Kenney, Susan. "Two Endings: Virginia Woolf's Suicide and *Between the Acts*." *University of Toronto Quarterly* 44.4 (1975): 265-89.

Kilborne, Benjamin. "The Disappearing Who: Kierkegaard, Shame, and the Self." Adamson and Clark 35-51.

Killen, Judith. "Virginia Woolf in the Light of Modern Physics." Diss. U of Louisville 1985.

King, James. *Virginia Woolf.* New York: Norton, 1994.

Kleber, Rolf J., Charles R. Figley, and Berthold P. R. Gersons, eds. *Beyond Trauma: Cultural and Societal Dynamics.* New York: Plenum, 1995.

Knox-Shaw, Peter. "The Otherness of Septimus Warren Smith." *Durham University Journal* 87.1 (1995): 99-110.

Kochhar-Lindgren, Gray. *Narcissus Transformed: The Textual Subject in Psychoanalysis and Literature.* University Park: Pennsylvania State UP, 1993.

LaCapra, Dominick. *Writing History, Writing Trauma.* Baltimore: Johns Hopkins UP, 2001.

Laird, Holly. *Women Coauthors.* Urbana: U of Illinois P, 2000.

Lanser, Susan Sniader. *Fictions of Authority: Women Writers and Narrative Voice.* Ithaca: Cornell UP, 1992.

Lantz, Jim. "Using Frankl's Concepts with PTSD Clients." *Journal of Traumatic Stress* 5 (1992): 485-90.

Laub, Dori. "Truth and Testimony: The Process and the Struggle." Caruth, *Trauma* 61-75.

——, and Nanette C. Auerhahn. "Knowing and Not Knowing Massive Psychic Trauma: Forms of Traumatic Memory." *International Journal of Psycho-analysis* 74 (1993): 287-302.

Laurence, Patricia O. *The Reading of Silence: Virginia Woolf in the English Tradition.* Palo Alto: Stanford UP, 1991.

Leaska, Mitchell. *Granite and Rainbow: The Hidden Life of Virginia Woolf.* New York: Farrar, Straus, & Giroux, 1998.

——. *The Novels of Virginia Woolf from Beginning to End.* New York: John Jay, 1977.

LeDoux, Joseph. *The Emotional Brain: The Mysterious Underpinnings of Emotional Life.* New York: Simon & Schuster, 1996.

Lee, Hermione. "Virginia Woolf's Essays." *The Cambridge Companion to Virginia Woolf.* Ed. Sue Roe and Susan Sellers. Cambridge, UK: Cambridge UP, 2000. 91-108.

——. *Virginia Woolf.* New York: Knopf, 1997.

Lee, Judith. "'This Hideous Shaping and Moulding': War and *The Waves.*" Hussey, *War* 180-202.

Lee, So Hee. "Madness, Marginalization, and Power in *Mrs. Dalloway.*" *Journal of English Language and Literature* 36.4 (1990): 691-712.

Leed, Eric J. *No Man's Land: Combat and Identity in World War I.* Cambridge, UK: Cambridge UP, 1979.

Lerner, Harriet. *The Dance of Anger.* New York: Harper Collins, 1985.

Levenback, Karen L. *Virginia Woolf and the Great War.* Syracuse: Syracuse UP, 1999.

——. "Woolf's 'War in the Village' and 'The War from the Street': An Illusion of Immunity." Hussey, *War* 40-57.

Levin, Gerald. "The Musical Style of *The Waves.*" *Journal of Narrative Technique* 13.3 (1983): 164-71.

Levine, Philippa. *Feminist Lives in Victorian England: Private Roles and Public Commitment.* Oxford, UK: Oxford UP, 1990.

Levinas, Emmanuel. *Alterity and Transcendence.* Trans. Michael B. Smith. New York: Columbia UP, 1999.

——. *Entre Nous: On Thinking-of-the-Other.* Trans. Michael B. Smith and Barbara Harshav. New York: Columbia UP, 1998.

——. *Humanism and the Other.* Trans. Nidra Poller. Urbana: U of Illinois P, 2003.

——. *Is It Righteous to Be? Interviews with Emmanuel Levinas.* Ed. Jill Robbins. Stanford: Stanford UP, 2001.

——. *Otherwise than Being or Beyond Essence.* Trans. Alphonso Lingis. Pittsburgh: Duquesne UP, 1998.

——. "Peace and Proximity." *Basic Philosophical Writings.* Ed. Adriaan T. Peperzak, et al. Bloomington: Indiana UP, 1996.

——. *Proper Names.* Trans. Michael B. Smith. Stanford: Stanford UP, 1996.

——. *Totality and Infinity: An Essay on Exteriority.* Trans. Alphonso Lingis. Pittsburgh: Duquesne UP, 1969.

——. *Unforeseen History.* Trans. Nidra Poller. Urbana: U of Illinois P, 2004.

Lewis, Helen Block, ed. *The Role of Shame in Symptom Formation.* Hillsdale, NJ: Erlbaum, 1987.

——. *Shame and Guilt in Neurosis.* New York: International UP, 1971.

——. "Shame and the Narcissistic Personality." Nathanson, *Many Faces* 93-132.

Lilienfeld, Jane. "Accident, Incident, and Meaning: Traces of Trauma in Virginia Woolf's Narrativity." Ardis and Scott 153-58.

——. "'[The Critic] Can't Say That, Can She?': Naming Co-dependence and Family Dysfunction in *To the Lighthouse*." Hussey and Neverow 151-63.

——. "'The Deceptiveness of Beauty': Mother Love and Mother Hate in *To the Lighthouse*." *Twentieth Century Literature* 23.3 (1977): 345-76.

——. *Reading Alcoholisms: Theorizing Character and Narrative in Selected Novels by Thomas Hardy, James Joyce, and Virginia Woolf.* New York: St. Martin's, 1999.

——. "'Where the Spear Plants Grew': The Ramsays' Marriage in *To the Lighthouse*." Marcus, *New Feminist Essays* 148-169.

Low, Lisa. "Feminist Elegy/Feminist Prophecy: *Lycidas*, *The Waves*, Kristeva, Cixous." *Virginia Woolf & Literary History: Part 1.* Ed. Jane Lilienfeld, Jeffrey Oxford, and Lisa Low. *Woolf Studies Annual* 9 (2003): 221-42.

Lucenti, Lisa Marie. "Virginia Woolf's *The Waves*: To Defer That 'Appalling Moment.'" *Criticism* 40.1 (1998): 75-98.

Luepnitz, Deborah Anna. *The Family Interpreted: Feminist Theory in Clinical Practice.* New York: Basic, 1988.

Marcus, Jane. "Britannia Rules *The Waves*." *Decolonizing Tradition: New Views of Twentieth-Century "British" Literary Canons.* Ed. Karen R. Lawrence. Urbana: U of Illinois P, 1992. 136–62. Rpt. Homans 227-48.

——. *Hearts of Darkness: White Women Write Race.* New Brunswick: Rutgers UP, 2004.

——, ed. *New Feminist Essays on Virginia Woolf.* Lincoln: U of Nebraska P, 1981.

——. *Virginia Woolf and The Languages of Patriarchy.* Bloomington: Indiana UP, 1987.

——. "Wrapped in the Stars and Stripes: Virginia Woolf in the USA." *South Carolina Review* 29.1 (1996): 17-23.

Masson, Jeffrey Moussaieff. *The Assault on Truth: Freud's Suppression of the Seduction Theory.* New York: Farrar, Straus, & Giroux, 1984.

Maze, John R. *Virginia Woolf: Feminism, Creativity, and the Unconscious.* Westport, CT: Greenwood, 1997.

McClintock, Anne. *Imperial Leather: Race, Gender and Sexuality in the Colonial Contest.* New York: Routledge, 1995.

McGee, Patrick. "Woolf's Other: The University in Her Eye." *Novel* 23 (1990): 229-46.

McGoldrick, Monica, Carol M. Anderson, and Froma Walsh, eds. *Women in Families: A Framework for Family Therapy.* New York: Norton, 1991.

McIntire, Gabrielle. "Heteroglossia, Monologism, and Fascism: Bernard Reads *The Waves.*" *Narrative* 13.1 (2005): 29-35.

McNally, Richard. *Remembering Trauma.* Cambridge, MA: Harvard UP, 2003.

McNaron, Toni. "The Uneasy Solace of Art: The Effect of Sexual Abuse on Virginia Woolf's Aesthetic." *Women's Studies: An International Forum.* 15.2 (1992): 251-66.

———. and Yarrow Morgan, eds. *Voices in the Night: Women Speaking about Incest.* Pittsburgh: Cleis, 1985.

McVicker, Jeanette, and Laura Davis, eds. *Virginia Woolf and Communities: Selected Papers from the Eighth Annual Virginia Woolf Conference.* New York: Pace UP, 1999.

Meares, Russell. "Episodic Memory, Trauma, and the Narrative of Self." *Contemporary Psychoanalysis* 31. 4 (1995): 541-56.

Meisel, Perry. *The Myth of the Modern: A Study in British Literature and Criticism After 1850.* New Haven: Yale UP, 1987.

Menninger, Karl. *Man Against Himself.* New York: Harcourt, 1938.

Meyerowitz, Selma S. *Leonard Woolf.* Boston: Twayne, 1982.

Mezei, Kathy. "Who is Speaking Here? Free Indirect Discourse, Gender and Authority in *Emma, Howards End* and *Mrs. Dalloway.*" *Ambiguous Discourse: Feminist Narratology and British Women Writers.* Ed. Kathy Mezei. Chapel Hill: U of North Carolina P, 1996. 66-92.

Miller, Alice K. *Banished Knowledge. Facing Childhood Injuries.* New York: Doubleday, 1985.

———. *For Your Own Good: Hidden Cruelty in Child-Rearing and the Roots of Violence.* New York: Farrar, Straus, & Giroux, 1983.

———. *Thou Shalt Not Be Aware: Society's Betrayal of the Child.* New York: Farrar, Straus, & Giroux, 1984.

———. *The Untouched Key: Tracing Childhood Trauma in Creativity and Destructiveness*. New York: Doubleday, 1990.

Miller, J. Hillis. "Mr. Carmichael and Lily Briscoe: The Rhythm of Creativity in *To the Lighthouse*." *Modernism Reconsidered*. Ed. Robert Kiely. Cambridge, MA: Harvard UP, 1983. 167-89.

Minow-Pinkney, Makiko. *Virginia Woolf and the Problem of the Subject*. New Brunswick: Rutgers UP, 1987.

Mollon, Phil. *Multiple Selves, Multiple Voices: Working with Trauma, Violation and Dissociation*. Chichester, UK: Wiley, 1996.

Monson, Tamlyn. "'A Trick of the Mind': Alterity, Ontology, and Representation in Virginia Woolf's *The Waves*." *Modern Fiction Studies* 50.1 (2004): 173-196.

Moore, Madeline. *The Short Season Between Two Silences*. Boston: Allen and Unwin, 1984.

Moran, Patricia. "'The Flaw in the Centre': Writing as Hymenal Rupture in Virginia Woolf's Work." *Tulsa Studies in Women's Literature* 17.1 (1998): 101-121.

———. *Virginia Woolf, Jean Rhys, and the Aesthetics of Trauma*. New York: Palgrave, 2007.

Morrison, Andrew P. *The Culture of Shame*. New York: Ballantine, 1996.

———. "The Eye Turned Inward: Shame and the Self." Nathanson, *Many Faces* 271-91.

———. "Shame, Ideal Self, and Narcissism." *Contemporary Psychoanalysis* 19.2 (1983): 295-318.

———. *Shame: The Underside of Narcissism*. Hillsdale, NJ: Analytic, 1989.

Moyn, Samuel. *Origins of the Other: Emmanuel Levinas between Revelation and Ethics*. Ithaca: Cornell UP, 2005.

Nachmani, Gilead. "Discussion: Reconstructing the Methods of Victimization." *Memories of Sexual Betrayal: Truth, Fantasy, Repression, and Dissociation*. 189-208.

———. "Trauma and Ignorance." *Contemporary Psychoanalysis* 31 (1995): 423-50.

Nalbantian, Suzanne. *Memory in Literature: From Rousseau to Neuroscience*. New York: Palgrave Macmillan, 2003.

Naremore, James. *The World Without a Self: Virginia Woolf and the Novel*. New Haven: Yale UP, 1973.

Narey, Wayne. "Virginia Woolf's 'The Mark on the Wall': An Einsteinian View of Art." *Studies in Short Fiction* 29.1 (1992): 35–42.

Nathanson, Donald L., ed. *The Many Faces of Shame.* New York: Guilford Press, 1987.

——. *Shame and Pride: Affect, Sex, and the Birth of the Self.* New York: Norton, 1992.

Neverow-Turk, Vara, and Mark Hussey, eds. *Virginia Woolf: Themes and Variations. Selected Papers from the Second Annual Conference on Virginia Woolf.* New York: Pace UP, 1993.

Nicolson, Nigel. *Virginia Woolf.* New York: Penguin, 2000.

Nussbaum, Martha. "The Window: Knowledge of Other Minds in Virginia Woolf's *To the Lighthouse.*" *Ordinary Language Criticism: Literary Thinking after Cavell after Wittgenstein.* Ed. Kenneth Dauber and Walter Jost. Evanston, IL: Northwestern UP, 2003. 55-76.

Olafson, Ema and David Corwin. "The Sexual Abuse of Children." *Virginia Woolf Miscellany* 34 (1990): 2-3.

Oldfield, Sybil. *Afterwords: Letters on the Death of Virginia Woolf.* New Brunswick: Rutgers UP, 2005.

Oxindine, Annette. "Rhoda Submerged: Lesbian Suicide in *The Waves.*" Barrett and Cramer, *Lesbian Readings* 203-221.

——. "Sexing the Epiphany in 'Moments of Being,' Woolf's Nice Little Story about Sapphism." *Journal of the Short Story in English* 31 (1998): 51-61.

Ovid. *The Elegies of Ovid.* Translation by Christopher Marlowe. Text by C. F. Tucker Brooke. Swinford: Fantasy, 1954.

Peck, Elizabeth G., and Joanna Stephens Mink, eds. *Common Ground: Feminist Collaboration in the Academy.* Albany, NY: State U of New York P, 1998.

Pennebaker, James W. *Opening Up: The Healing Powers of Confiding in Others.* New York: Morrow, 1990.

Phillips, Kathy. *Virginia Woolf Against Empire.* Knoxville: U of Tennessee P, 1994.

Pittman, Roger K. et al. "Legal Issues in Posttraumatic Stress Disorder." Van der Kolk, McFarlane, and Weisaeth 378-97.

Poole, Roger. *The Unknown Virginia Woolf.* 1978. 4th ed. Cambridge, UK: Cambridge UP, 1995.

——. "'We All Put Up with You, Virginia': Irreceivable Wisdom About War." Hussey, *War* 79-100.

Priest, Ann-Marie. "Re: Dracula." E-mail to Jane Lilienfeld. 18 May 2006.

Prince, Gerald. *A Dictionary of Narratology*. Lincoln: U of Nebraska P, 1987.

Putnum, Frank W. "Pierre Janet and Modern Views of Dissociation." Horowitz 116-35.

Radin, Grace. *Virginia Woolf's "The Years": The Evolution of a Novel*. Knoxville: U of Tennessee P, 1981.

Raine, Nancy Venable. *After Silence: Rape and My Journey Back*. New York: Crown, 1998.

Raitt, Suzanne. "The Voyage Back." Back To Bloomsbury: 14th Annual Conference on Virginia Woolf. 23-26 June 2004. Conference Program: 11.

Rashkin, Esther. *Family Secrets and the Psychoanalysis of Narrative*. Princeton: Princeton UP, 1992.

Reid, Panthea. *Art and Affection: A Life of Virginia Woolf*. New York: Oxford UP, 1996.

Restuccia, Frances L. "'Untying the Mother Tongue': Female Difference in Virginia Woolf's *A Room of One's Own*." *Tulsa Studies in Women's Literature* 4.2 (1985): 253-64.

Rich, Adrienne. *Of Woman Born: Motherhood as Experience and Institution*. New York: Norton, 1976.

Richter, Harvena. *Virginia Woolf: The Inward Voyage*. Princeton: Princeton UP, 1970.

Ricoeur, Paul. *Memory, History, Forgetting*. Chicago: U of Chicago P, 2004.

Rimmon-Kenan, Shlomith. *Narrative Fiction*. London: RKP, 1983.

Risolo, Donna. "Outing Mrs. Ramsay: Reading the Lesbian Subtext in Virginia Woolf's *To the Lighthouse*." Neverow-Turk and Hussey 238-48.

Rivera, Margo, ed. *Fragment by Fragment: Feminist Perspectives on Memory and Child Sexual Abuse*. Charlottetown, Canada: Gynergy, 1999.

Rose, Gilbert. Qtd. in "Art and Trauma." *International Journal of Psychoanalysis* 76.5 (1995).

Rosenfeld, Natania. *Outsiders Together: Virginia and Leonard Woolf.* Princeton: Princeton UP, 2000.

Rothschild, Babette. *The Body Remembers. The Psychophysiology of Trauma and Trauma Treatment.* New York: Norton, 1957.

Ruotolo, Lucio P. *The Interrupted Moment: A View of Virginia Woolf's Novels.* Palo Alto: Stanford UP, 1986.

Rush, Florence. *The Best Kept Secret: Sexual Abuse of Children.* New York: McGraw-Hill, 1980.

Russell, Diana. *The Secret Trauma: Incest in the Lives of Girls and Women.* New York: Basic, 1986.

Sackville-West, Vita. *The Letters of Vita Sackville-West to Virginia Woolf.* Ed. Louise DeSalvo and Mitchell A. Leaska. New York: Morrow, 1985.

Salter, Anna. *Transforming Trauma: A Guide to Understanding and Treating Adult Survivors of Child Sexual Abuse.* Thousand Oaks, CA: Sage, 1995.

——. "Truth, Lies, and Sex Offenders." Videotape No. 81492 of *Listening to Sex Offenders.* Thousand Oaks, CA: Sage, 1997.

Sartre, Jean-Paul. "Situation of the Writer in 1947." *"What is Literature?" and Other Essays.* Cambridge, MA: Harvard UP, 1988. 141-238.

Savage, George H. *Insanity and Allied Neuroses: Practical and Clinical.* Philadelphia: Lea's, 1884.

Schacter, Daniel. *Searching for Memory: The Brain, The Mind, and The Past.* New York: Basic, 1996.

Schechter, Susan. *Women and Male Violence: The Vision and Struggles of the Battered Women's Movement.* Boston: South End, 1982.

Schetky, Diane H., M.D. "A Review of the Literature of the Long-Term Effects of Childhood Sexual Abuse." *Incest-Related Syndromes of Adult Psychopatholgy.* Ed. Richard P. Kluft, M.D. Arlington, VA: American Psychiatric Publishing, 1990.

Schlack, Beverly Ann. *Continuing Presences: Virginia Woolf's Use of Literary Allusion.* University Park: Penn State UP, 1979.

Schwartz, Harvey L. *Dialogues with Forgotten Voices: Relational Perspectives on Child Abuse, Trauma, and Treatment of Dissociative Disorders.* New York: Basic, 2000.

Sedgwick, Eve Kosofsky, and Adam Frank, eds. *Shame and Its Sisters: A Silvan Tomkins Reader.* Durham: Duke UP, 1995.

Seinfelt, Mark. *Final Drafts: Suicides of World-Famous Authors.* New York: Prometheus, 1999.

Shakespeare, William. *Troilus and Cressida.* New York: New American Library, 1963.

Shay, Jonathan. *Achilles in Vietnam: Combat Trauma and the Undoing of Character.* New York: Touchstone, 1994.

———. *Odysseus in America: Combat Trauma and the Trials of Homecoming.* New York: Scribner, 2002.

Shelton, Jen. "'Don't Say Such Foolish Things, Dear': Speaking Incest in *The Voyage Out.*" *Incest and the Literary Imagination.* Ed. Elizabeth L. Barnes. Gainesville: UP of Florida, 2002. 224-48.

Shengold, Leonard. *Soul Murder: The Effects of Childhood Abuse and Deprivation.* New York: Yale UP, 1989.

Sherry, Vincent. *The Great War and the Language of Modernism.* New York: Oxford UP, 2003.

Shneidman, Edwin S. *Comprehending Suicide: Landmarks in 20th-Century Suicidology.* Washington, D.C.: American Psychological Association, 2001.

Showalter, Elaine. *The Female Malady: Women, Madness, and English Culture 1830-1980.* 1985; rpt. New York: Viking Penguin, 1987.

Siegel, Daniel J. "An Interpersonal Neurobiology of Psychotherapy: The Developing Mind and the Resolution of Trauma." Solomon and Siegel 1-56.

Silver, Brenda R. *Virginia Woolf Icon.* Chicago: U of Chicago P, 1999.

Smith, Patricia Juliana. *Lesbian Panic: Homoeroticism in Modern British Women's Fiction.* New York: Columbia UP, 1997.

———. "'The Things People Don't Say': Lesbian Panic in *The Voyage Out.*" Barrett and Cramer, *Lesbian Readings* 128-46.

Solomon, Marian F. "Connection, Disruption, Repair: Treating the Effects of Attachment Trauma on Intimate Relationships." Solomon and Siegel 322-45.

———, and Daniel J. Siegel, eds. *Healing Trauma: Attachment, Mind, Body and Brain.* New York: Norton, 2003.

Southworth, Helen and Elisa Kay Sparks, eds. *Woolf and the Art of Exploration: Selected Papers from the Fifteenth International Conference on Virginia Woolf.* Clemson, SC: Clemson U Digital Press, 2006.

Spilka, Mark. *Virginia Woolf's Quarrel with Grieving*. Lincoln: U of Nebraska P, 1980.

Spenser, Edmund. "Prothalamion." *Spenser's Selected Shorter Poems*. London: Longman, 1995.

Spiegel, David, Thurman Hunt, and Harvey E. Dondershine. "Dissociation and Hypnotizability in Posttraumatic Stress Disorder." Horowitz 243-52.

Spotts, Frederic, ed. *Letters of Leonard Woolf*. San Diego: Harcourt Brace Jovanovich, 1989.

Squier, Susan. "Mirroring and Mothering: Reflections on the Mirror Encounter Metaphor in Virginia Woolf's Works." *Twentieth Century Literature* 27.3 (1981): 272-88.

Stewart, Garrett. "Catching the Stylistic D/Rift: Sound Defects in Woolf's *The Waves*." *ELH* 54 (1987): 421-61.

Sturken, Marita. "Narratives of Recovery: Repressed Memory as Cultural Memory." Bal, Crewe, and Spitzer 231-48.

Sutcliffe, Rebecca. "*Really* Writing: Feminist Biography and the Languages of Pain in Louise DeSalvo's *Virginia Woolf: The Impact of Childhood Sexual Abuse on Her Life and Work*." Hussey and Neverow 156-63.

Swanson, Diana L. "'My Boldness Terrifies Me': Sexual Abuse and Female Subjectivity in *The Voyage Out*." *Twentieth Century Literature* 41.4 (1995): 284-309.

Swinburne, Algernon Charles. "Itylus." *The Oxford Book of English Verse, 1250–1900*. Ed. A. T. Quiller-Couch. Oxford, UK: Clarendon, 1919.

Sypher, Eileen B. "*The Waves*: A Utopia of Androgyny?" Ginsberg and Gottlieb 187-213.

Tal, Kali. "Speaking the Language of Pain: Vietnam War Literature in the Context of a Literature of Trauma." *Fourteen Landing Zones: Approaches to Vietnam War Literature*. Ed. Philip K. Jason. Iowa City: U of Iowa P, 1991. 217-50.

——. *Worlds of Hurt: Reading the Literatures of Trauma*. Cambridge, UK: Cambridge UP, 1996.

Terr, Lenore C. "Childhood Traumas: An Outline and Overview." Horowitz 61-81.

——. *Unchained Memories: True Stories of Traumatic Memories Lost and Found*. New York: Basic, 1994.

Thomas, Sue. "Virginia Woolf's Septimus Smith and Contemporary Perceptions of Shell Shock." *English Language Notes* 25.2 (1987): 49-57.

Tomkins, Silvan. "Shame." Nathanson, *Many Faces* 133-61.

——. "Shame-Humiliation and Contempt-Disgust." Sedgwick and Frank 133-178.

Tratner, Michael. *Modernism and Mass Politics: Joyce, Woolf, Eliot, Yeats.* Palo Alto: Stanford UP, 1995.

Trezise, Thomas, ed. Editor's Preface. *Yale French Studies* 104 (2003): 1-3.

Trombley, Stephen. *'All That Summer She Was Mad': Virginia Woolf and Her Doctors.* London: Junction, 1981.

Tyler, Lisa. "'Nameless Atrocities' and the Name of the Father: Literary Allusion and Incest in Virginia Woolf's *The Voyage Out.*" *Woolf Studies Annual* 1 (1995): 26-46.

——. "Mother-Daughter Passion and Rapture: The Demeter Myth in the Fiction of Virginia Woolf and Doris Lessing." *Woolf and Lessing: Breaking the Mold.* Ed. Ruth Saxton and Jean Tobin. New York: St. Martin's, 1994. 73-91.

Valentine, Kylie. *Psychoanalysis, Psychiatry, and Modernist Literature.* New York: Palgrave, 2003.

Van Alphen, Ernst. "Symptoms of Discursivity: Experience, Memory, and Trauma." Bal, Crewe, and Spitzer 24-38.

Van der Kolk, Bessel A. "The Black Hole of Trauma." Van der Kolk et. al. *Traumatic Stress* 3-23.

——. "The Body Keeps Score: Approaches to the Psychobiology of Posttraumatic Stress Disorder." Van der Kolk et. al., *Traumatic Stress* 214-41.

——. "The Compulsion to Repeat the Trauma: Re-enactment, Revictimization, and Masochism." *Psychiatric Clinics of North America* 12.2 (1989): 389-411.

——. "Posttraumatic Stress Disorder and the Nature of Trauma." Solomon and Siegel 168-95.

——. "The Psychological Consequences of Overwhelming Life Experiences." *Psychological Trauma.* Ed. Bessel A. Van der Kolk. Arlington, VA.: American Psychiatric Publishing, 1987. 1-30.

——. "Trauma and Memory." Van der Kolk et. al., *Traumatic Stress* 279-302.

——, et al. "History of Trauma in Psychiatry." Van der Kolk et. al., *Traumatic Stress* 47-74.

——, and van der Hart, Onno. "The Intrusive Past: The Flexibility of Memory and the Engraving of Trauma." Caruth, *Trauma* 158-182.

——, Onno van der Hart, and Charles R. Marmar. "Dissociation and Information Processing in Posttraumatic Stress Disorder." Van der Kolk et. al., *Traumatic Stress* 303-27.

——, Alexander C. McFarlane, and Lars Weisaeth, eds. *Traumatic Stress: The Effects of Overwhelming Experience on Mind, Body, and Society.* New York: Guilford, 1996.

Veldhuis, Cindy B., and Jennifer J. Freyd. "Groomed for Silence, Groomed for Betrayal." Rivera 253-81.

Walkowitz, Judith R. *Prostitution and Victorian Society: Women, Class, and the State.* Cambridge, UK: Cambridge UP, 1980.

Wang, Ban. "'I' on the Run: Crisis of Identity in *Mrs. Dalloway.*" *Modern Fiction Studies* 38 (1992): 177-91.

Webb, Caroline. "Life After Death: The Allegorical Progress of *Mrs. Dalloway.*" *Modern Fiction Studies* 40 (1994): 279-98.

Westerlund, Elaine. *Women's Sexuality after Childhood Incest.* New York: Norton, 1992.

Whitfield, Charles L. *Memory and Abuse: Remembering and Healing the Effects of Trauma.* Deerfield Beach, FL: Health Communications, 1995.

Wiesel, Elie. "Why I Write." *Confronting the Holocaust: The Impact of Elie Wiesel.* Ed. Alvin Rosenfeld. Bloomington: Indiana UP, 1978.

Williams, Linda Meyer. "Recall of Childhood Trauma: A Prospective Study of Women's Memories of Child Sexual Abuse." *Journal of Consulting and Clinical Psychology* 62.6 (1994): 1167-76.

——. "Recovered Memories of Abuse in Women with Documented Child Sexual Victimization Histories." *Journal of Traumatic Stress* 8.4 (1995): 649-73.

Wiley, Chris. "'When a Woman Speaks the Truth about her Body': Ethel Smyth, Virginia Woolf and the Challenges of Lesbian Auto/biography." *Virginia Woolf Bulletin* 9 (2002): 19-28.

Wilson, Duncan. *Leonard Woolf: A Political Biography.* London: Hogarth, 1978.

Wilson, Melba. *Crossing the Boundary: Black Women Survive Incest.* Seattle: Seal, 1993.

Winkler, Cathy. "Rape as Social Murder." *Anthropology Today.* 7.3 (1991): 12-14.

Winston, Janet. "'Something Out of Harmony': *To the Lighthouse* and the Subjects of Empire." *Woolf Studies Annual* 2 (1996): 39-70.

Wolfe, Susan, and Julia Penelope. *Sexual Practice, Textual Theory: Lesbian Cultural Criticism.* Cambridge, UK: Blackwell, 1993.

Wolman, Benjamin B., ed. *The Encyclopedia of Psychiatry, Psychology, and Psycho-Analysis.* New York: Henry Holt, 1996.

Woolf, Leonard. *The Journey Not the Arrival Matters: An Autobiography of the Years 1939 to 1969.* New York: Harcourt, 1969.

Woolf, Virginia. *Between the Acts.* 1941. San Diego: Harcourt, 1969.

——. *The Captain's Death Bed and Other Essays.* New York: Harcourt, 1950.

——. *Collected Essays.* 4 vols. New York: Harcourt, 1967.

——. *The Complete Shorter Fiction of Virginia Woolf.* Ed. Susan Dick. 2nd ed. San Diego: Harcourt, 1989.

——. *The Death of the Moth and Other Essays.* 1942. New York: Harcourt, 1970.

——. *The Diary of Virginia Woolf.* 5 vols. Ed. Anne Oliver Bell. Assisted by Andrew McNeillie. New York: Harcourt, 1977-1984.

——. *Granite and Rainbow.* New York, Harcourt, 1958.

——. *Jacob's Room.* 1922. San Diego: Harcourt, 1978.

——. *The Letters of Virginia Woolf.* Ed. Nigel Nicolson and Joanne Trautmann. 6 vols. New York: Harcourt, 1975-1980.

——. *The Moment and Other Essays.* New York: Hogarth Press, 1964.

——. *Moments of Being: Unpublished Autobiographical Writings of Virginia Woolf.* Ed. Jeanne Schulkind. NY: Harcourt Brace, 1976.

——. *Moments of Being: Unpublished Autobiographical Writings of Virginia Woolf.* Ed. Jeanne Schulkind. 2nd ed. San Diego: Harcourt, 1985.

——. *The Common Reader.* 1925. New York: Harcourt, 1966.

——. *Mrs. Dalloway.* 1925. San Diego: Harcourt, 1990.

——. *The Pargiters. The Novel-Essay Portion of* The Years. Ed. Mitchell A. Leaska. San Diego: Harcourt, 1978.

——. *A Passionate Apprentice: The Early Journals 1897-1909.* Ed. Mitchell A. Leaska. San Diego: Harcourt, 1990.

——. *A Room of One's Own.* 1929. San Diego: Harcourt, 1981.

——. *Three Guineas.* 1938. New York: Harcourt, 1966.

——. *To the Lighthouse.* 1927. New York: Harcourt, 1981.

——. *The Years* Holograph. Microfilm. "[The Years] *The Pargiters*; a novel-essay based upon a paper read to the London, National Society for women's service. Holograph, unsigned, dated 11 Oct. 1932-15 Nov. 1934. 8 vols." *The Virginia Woolf Manuscripts from the Henry W. and Albert A. Berg Collection at the New York Public Library.* Woodbridge, CT: Research Publications International, 1993.

——. *The Voyage Out.* 1920. New York: Harcourt, 1968.

——. *The Waves.* 1931. New York: Harcourt, 1978.

——. *The Waves: The Two Holograph Drafts.* Ed. J. W. Graham. Toronto: U of Toronto P, 1976.

——. *A Writer's Diary.* Ed. Leonard Woolf. New York: Harcourt, 1954.

——. *The Years.* 1937. San Diego: Harcourt, 1969.

Wulfman, Clifford E. "Outraged Recapitulation and Artful Garrulousness." *Méconnaissances: Misrecognition, Race, and the Real in Faulkner's Fiction.* Ed. Michael Zeitlin, André Bleikasten, and Nicole Moulinoux. *Études Faulknériennes* 4. Rennes: Presses Universitaires de Rennes, 2004. 89–100.

Wurmser, Leon. *The Mask of Shame.* Baltimore: Johns Hopkins UP, 1981.

——. *The Power of the Inner Judge: Psychodynamic Treatment of the Severe Neuroses.* Northvale, NJ: Jason Aronson, 2000.

——. "Shame: The Veiled Companion of Narcissism." Nathanson, *Many Faces* 64-92.

Yom, Sue Sun. "Virginia Woolf and Science." *Virginia Woolf: Texts and Contexts. Selected Papers from the Fifth Annual Conference on Virginia Woolf.* Ed. Beth Rigel Daugherty and Eileen Barrett. New York: Pace UP, 1996. 145–50.

NOTES ON CONTRIBUTORS

Patricia Morgne Cramer is Associate Professor of English at the University of Connecticut at Stamford. She is co-editor of *Virginia Woolf: Lesbian Readings* and *Re: Reading, Re: Writing, Re: Teaching Virginia Woolf. Selected Papers from the Fourth Annual Conference on Virginia Woolf.* In addition to articles on Woolf, her work includes essays on William Blake, Chaucer, and feminist teaching. She is currently working on a book entitled *Virginia Woolf: The Lesbian Years.*

Karen DeMeester is currently an Assistant in Research and Project Management at the Learning Systems Institute at Florida State University, where she has also taught writing and literature. DeMeester completed her Ph.D. in English at Florida State University, specializing in trauma psychology as a context for reading modern war fiction. Her work on Virginia Woolf focused primarily in Woolf's talent for representing the trauma survivor's psychological injuries and journey to recovery. A licensed CPA with a B. A. in Accounting and Finance, DeMeester has worked as a financial auditor and consultant, specializing in nonprofit and governmental clients, and as a policy analyst for Florida's Office of Program Policy and Government Accountability.

David Eberly is an independent scholar. His work includes papers on the subject of Virginia Woolf and trauma, as well as essays and reviews on Walt Whitman, Frank O'Hara, Frank Bidart, and other gay male poets. A past member of the editorial board of the *International Journal of Sexuality and Gender Studies*, he has published essays and articles on homophobia and the impact of censorship in the arts. David Eberly is also the author of *What Has Been Lost*, a collection of poetry. He has worked in the nonprofit sector for over twenty-five years, and is currently Director of Prospect Development at Children's Hospital Trust Boston.

Suzette Henke joined the University of Louisville in 1991 as Thruston B. Morton, Sr. Professor of Literary Studies. She is author of *Joyce's Moraculous Sindbook: A Study of "Ulysses"* and of *James Joyce and the Politics of Desire*; and, with Elaine Unkeless, co-editor of *Women in Joyce*. Her publications in the field of 20th-century literature include essays on Virginia Woolf, Dorothy Richardson, H. D., Samuel Beckett, and Doris Lessing, as well as postcolonial authors Sally Morgan, Keri Hulme, and Janet Frame. Her most recent book is *Shattered Subjects: Trauma And Testimony in Women's Life-Writing* (St. Martin's, 2000), and she is currently working on a study of trauma narrative in modern literature.

Claire Kahane, Professor Emerita of English at SUNY-Buffalo, is currently a Visiting Scholar in the Department of English at UC Berkeley, and a postgraduate member of the San Francisco Psychoanalytic Institute. A psychoanalytic and feminist critic, she has written extensively on feminism, hysteria and modern narrative and is author of *Passions of the Voice: Hysteria, Narrative, and the Figure of the Speaking Woman, 1850-1915*. Her more recent publications have focused on literary representations of mourning and trauma, with particular emphasis on holocaust trauma. She is currently writing on anticipations of catastrophe in Ian McEwan's fiction.

Holly Laird, Professor of English at the University of Tulsa, is executive editor of *Tulsa Studies in Women's Literature* and author of *Women Coauthors* (University of Illinois Press, 2000), on late-nineteenth century to contemporary women literary collaborators, as well as numerous articles on Victorian and modern writers. The chapter in this book is part of a work in progress, provisionally entitled *Modernist Suicide*.

Jane Lilienfeld is Professor of English at Lincoln University, an historically Black college in Jefferson City, Missouri, where she hosted the 1993 International Virginia Woolf Conference. Lilienfeld is the author of *Reading Alcoholisms*, a CHOICE award winner in 2000, and her essays on *To the Lighthouse* are widely cited in the field of Woolf studies. Her comparative essay on the narrative techniques of Toni Morrison and Virginia Woolf appeared in *Modern Fiction Studies* in Spring, 2006. Jane Lilienfeld's recent work includes essays on Lydia Minatoya (in *Tulsa Studies in Women's Literature*, Spring, 2004) and Lalithambika Antherjanam, in progress.

Toni McNaron is Distinguished Teaching Professor Emerita in English at the University of Minnesota, Minneapolis. Her research has focused on Renaissance literature, feminist writing, and GLBT literature and culture. Publications include *I Dwell in Possibility: A Memoir*; *Voices* *in the Night: Women Speaking About Incest; The Sister Bond: A Feminist View of a Timeless Connection; Poisoned Ivy: Lesbian and Gay Academics Confront Homophobia;* and *New Lesbian Studies: Into the 21st Century.* From 1990-1999, she coordinated a university-wide faculty development program focusing on excellence and diversity in teaching. While at the University of Minnesota, she began and chaired the Women's Studies Program, the Center for Advanced Feminist Studies, and the GLBT Studies Program. Currently, she directs the College in the Schools Literature program through the College of Continuing Education at the University of Minnesota.

Patricia Moran is Professor of English at the University of California, Davis. She is the author of *Word of Mouth: Body/Language in Katherine Mansfield and Virginia Woolf* (University of Virginia, 1996) and *Virginia Woolf, Jean Rhys, and the Aesthetics of Trauma* (Palgrave Macmillan, 2006); and coeditor, with Tamar Heller, of *Scenes of the Apple: Food and the Female Body in Nineteenth and Twentieth Century Women's Writing* (SUNY, 2003).

Clifford E. Wulfman received his PhD from Yale University in 2000. He has written extensively about Virginia Woolf, William Faulkner, and psychoanalysis. His essays have appeared in such scholarly venues as *The Faulkner Journal, Études Faulknériennes,* and *Studies in American Fiction.* His most recent work concerns digital humanities, digital libraries, and new media. He is affiliated with Brown University, where he is project manager and technical director of the Modernist Journals Project, and with the Rhode Island School of Design, where he teaches digital new media.

INDEX

CPSIA information can be obtained at www.ICGtesting.com
Printed in the USA
BVOW08s2247200114

342531BV00001B/57/A